# Dunst

## and Distr

# at War

## FROM EYEWITNESS ACCOUNTS

Compiled by

# Jean Yates & Sue King

*above* LOCAL ATC with a Kirby Kite Glider built in 1939 *(JY)*

*previous page* 'SALUTE THE SOLDIER' – Parade and Fundraising Event 16 May 1944 *(DG) (LMS)*

First published November 2006 by
The Book Castle
12 Church Street
Dunstable
Bedfordshire LU5 4RU

ISBN  1 903747 79 1
ISBN  978 1 903747 79 7

Designed and typeset by Caroline and Roger Hillier
The Old Chapel Graphic Design  www.theoldchapelivinghoe.com

Printed in Great Britain by TJ International Ltd, Padstow, Cornwall

# Contents

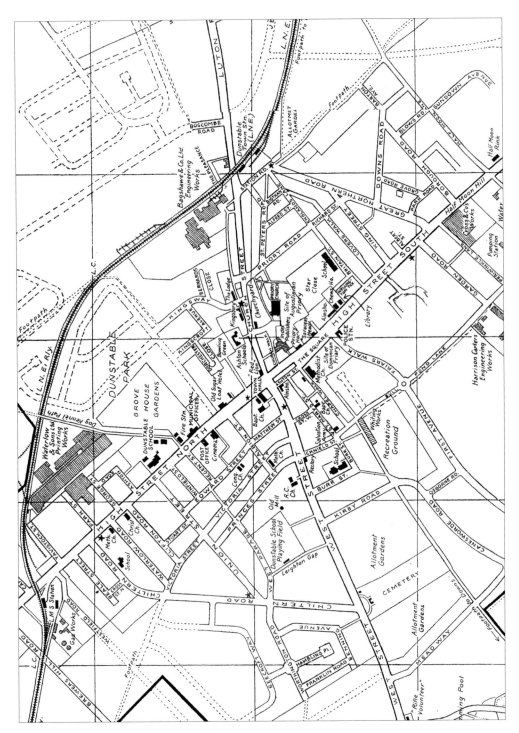

MAP OF DUNSTABLE circa 1941 *(DDLHS)*

# Introduction

When we began, we intended this book to be a comprehensive study of Dunstable during World War II. It very soon became obvious that this would not be achieved within the time restrictions that we had been set.

Various groups in the town took on WWII projects – our Local History Society, Manshead Archaeologists, the Grammar School Old Boys Association and many individuals, all of whom have made huge contributions to the book. As we progressed with our research we uncovered more stories and interesting facts about our town than we had ever anticipated.

Dunstable at War is mainly a collection of stories and reminiscences, individual and personal views of people who lived here or who called Dunstable home during the Second World War. Memories change and fade over sixty years and where possible we have cross-referenced verbal reports from more than one source. We apologise in advance for omissions and inaccuracies.

There is still a band of secrecy concerning World War II and therefore some stories will never be told, others are still waiting to be found. Bedfordshire was at the heart of the Secret War and Dunstable was very much a part of it. This book therefore tries to give a feel for where Dunstable sat in the wider picture; the relationships it had and the part it played in conjunction with Bletchley Park, Black Propaganda, SOE and our Allies. We have also included a section for those of our Allies who sought refuge in Dunstable after the war.

As a background we need to remember that Dunstable in 1939 had a population of approximately 16,000, less than half of that today, and was a small market town. The cattle and open-air markets were well supported by the local community, and the town and surrounding villages had a much more agricultural feel than we have today.

There were two railway stations, a police station and a fire station. The London Gliding Club was already at the bottom of the Downs, having opened in 1930. The A5 was a busy road before the building of the M1 and provided the bombers with a path to the Midlands as well as a route to the coast for locally made tanks and troop embarkation.

Our volunteer story-gatherers have done a wonderful job. They have

MARGUERITE PATTEN at Priory Church (JY)

collected more than a hundred stories, most of which are produced here. None of us were sure of what we were taking on when the project started in 2004 but having recruited our story-gatherers we put them through the British Library Sound Archive Oral History training course. This ensured that we asked our story-givers the right questions and knew how to deal with some long-hidden emotions that surfaced with the storytelling.

Enclosed with this book is an audio disc containing snippets of some of our gathered stories; mainly extracts as they were originally told to us, but Geoff Moore's diary, kept in a prisoner of war camp, is read by his son.

Many of our story-givers have said how fortunate Dunstable was to escape the worst of the bombing, and a number have fond memories of this time when they were children. For our story-givers, the recall of painful memories, sometimes for the first time, has been very emotional and we thank all of those who have shared their experiences, both good and bad, with us. We also thank everyone who loaned precious photographs and

TEA PARTY for 300 *(JY)*

those who have gifted items to the town. Modern technology means that copies of these items will be available for all to see at Priory House, Beds County Record Office and Dunstable and District History Society.

We received Big Lottery funding for our project without which we could not have made this permanent record of Dunstable and District at War. We also received Home Front funding and support from South Beds District Council that enabled us to run two weeks of local history exhibitions, tea parties to find our story-givers, WWII re-enactments and a VJ Day Commemorative Service involving many of the Services organisations. We commissioned a play, Victory at a Cost! written by Alex Baker and based on our Dunstable stories; it ran for a week at the Little Theatre. We asked for and got an extension to our Lottery Award, enabling us to complete the gathering of stories promised, but aware as we go to print that, even with the extra time, there are bound to be people and stories we have not recorded.

THE CHAIRMAN of South Beds District Council with Barbara Fryc *(JY)*

LISTENING TO THE SWING BAND in Grove House Gardens *(JY)*

THE BRITISH LEGION STALL *(JY)*

THE MAYOR OF DUNSTABLE with a Dunkirk Veteran *(JY)*

BRIGADIER PETER DALLY taking the salute with Jean Yates and Insp. Keith Jackson of Bedfordshire Police *(SK)*

THE STANDARDS as they are marched past the war memorial *(SK)*

BBC THREE COUNTIES RADIO interviews a war veteran. *(JY)*

We signed up as a partner with the BBC People's War project and that enabled us to make a Dunstable page on their website, www.bbc.co.uk/dna/ww2/U1075515. BBC Three Counties Radio has helped us to recruit story-givers as well as gatherers, and given us publicity for our projects.

STORY GATHERING – Sue King *(JY)*

So many partners have made this project successful and interesting for us to work on during the last two years. We hope you the reader find this look at Dunstablians and Dunstable and District in World War II as fascinating as we have.

*Jean Yates and Sue King*

## ACKNOWLEDGEMENTS

We would like to thank everyone who has taken part in the production of this book:

The following have worked for the project since the beginning and deserve a special mention:

Alex Baker, Marjorie & John Bavister, Paul Bowes, John Buckledee, Jill Calvert, Joan Curran, Vivienne Evans, Sheila Furnell, Barbara Fryc, Hugh Garrod, Len Harvey, Bob Hawkes, Dave Hills, Pauline Keen, Mick Partridge, Roger Pepworth, Neil Rees, Mary Roe, Sally Siddons, Alan Sinfield, Sarah Woodruff.

And members of – BBC Three Counties Radio, BBC Peoples War Team – Madeleine Forrester, The Dunstable & District Local History Society, The Dunstable Grammar School Old Boys Association, Manshead Archaeological Society, the Priory Church, many local War Veteran Associations, in particular the Far East Veterans Association.

South Bedfordshire District Council.

YMCA TEA VAN at the Dunstable At War event 2004 (JY)

## Individual contributors in alphabetical order:

Allison, Alex James

Ann, (Evacuee)

Ansell, Shirley

Barker, Denise

Basham, Una

Bates, Maisie

Bliss, Florence

Bonfield, Derek

Boron, Taduesz

Bourne, Colin

Brown, Olive

Bublik, Jaroslav

Buckle, Pam

Buckle, Phillip

Bundy, Brian

Cabut, Ludomir

Carpenter, Ulric

Carver, Jack

Cook, Morris

Corrie, J

Corrie, Mary (née
 Cheshire)

Couldwell, Dorothy

Cousins, Valerie

Cresswell, Mary

Croft, Peter

Crumley, Isobel

Curran, Joan

Cutler, Mary

Cutler, Rob

Czaczka, Stanislaw

Dawson, Arnold

Derby, Douglas

Dineen, Joan

Dolman, Mary

Dunbar, J

Evered, John

Evans, Vivienne

Forder, Frances

Fryc, Barbara

Fuller, Ilene

Garrod, Hugh

Gaskin, John

Geary, Reg

Gilbert, Derek

Grange, John

Grant, David

Hackney, Nellie

Haddon, Joyce

Haltiner, George

Hart, Monica

Hawkes, Robert

Heley, Paul

Henman, Catherine

Hing, Heather

Hodder, Keith

Holland, Arthur

Hughes, C L

Hull, Ted

Jones, Aubrey

Jorgensen, K

Kaye, Phyllis &
 Pauline Richards

Kelly, Mrs

King, Felix

King, Sue

Knight, Jim

Lewry, Margaret

Lock, Tony

Louda, Jiri

Luck, Phil

Malia, K

Manners, Dave

Maszadro, Zdzislaw,
 Dr

Mead, Carol

Michell, Hilda

Moore, Fred

Moore, G

Morden, Captain
 Herbert

Morden, E B

Morgan, Albert W

Morgan, Patricia

Morgownik,
 Stanislaw

Morton, June

Northover, Major
 H. R.

Novak, Miroslav

Oakley, Roy

Owen, Mary

Partridge, Jean

Partridge, Mick

Pendar, Lucy

Perkins, Harold R

Perkins, Pam

Perry, Doris

Polley, Bernard

Pullen, M. R

Purdon, John

Ratcliffe, Hilary

Raper, Ida &
 daughter Pat
 Carter

Read, Ann

Reason, J

Rees, Neil

Rudorf, Erwin

Rushton, Jean &
 John

Russell, John

Sadowski, Jan

Samuel, E

Samuels, Joyce

Scott, Christina

Sharp, M

Sinfield, Alan

Smithson, Joyce

Speller, E

Stafford, Len

Stevens, Bernard

Sutton, Gladys

Szumski, Meitek

Tarbox, Betty

Tibbett, Doris

Tingey, Marjorie

Tink, Roy

Tompkins, Betty

Tule, Kazmier (née
 Szikona)

Turner, Roy

Umlauf, Miroslav

Underwood, P

Ward, Joyce

Ward, Tony

Wheatley, Gerald

Wilsher, Alan

Winnik, Wojciech

Woolley, Bill

Woodhouse, Tony

Wooster, Yvonne

Yates, Jean

We would also like to thank the following people for allowing us to use their photographs:

Beds County Council (BCC)

The Dunstable Gazette (DG)

Dunstable & District Local History
  Society (DDLHS)

Dunstable Grammar School (DGS)

Historic Met Office, Dunstable
  (HMOD)

The London Gliding Club (LGC)

Luton Museum Service & The Luton
  News (LMS)

Manshead Archaeological Society
  (MAS)

Shirley Ansell (SA)

Una Basham (UB)

Florence Bliss (FB)

Olive Brown (OB)

Family of Lt. J Bublik (JB)

M Burnell (MB)

Ulric Craig Carpenter (UCC)

Mrs E F Clark (EFC)

B Fryc (BF)

Reg Geary (RG)

David Grant (DGR)

Mrs G Hurst (GH)

Miroslav Janecek (MJ)

Pauline Keen (PK)

Sue King (SK)

Phil Luck (PL)

Hilda Michell (HM)

Albert W Morgan (AWM)

Sonia Novak (SN)

Dr M R Pullen (MRP)

Hilary Ratcliffe (HR)

Alan Sinfield (AS)

Jaroslav Tauer (JT)

Gerald Wheatley (GW)

Jean Yates (JY)

Supported & funded by the Heritage Lottery Fund, the Big Lottery Fund and South Bedfordshire District Council

## NOTES ON RATIONING

The rationing of food lasted for 14 years, ending in July 1954 and varied as time went on. As well as food, clothing was rationed from June 1941. Each person had clothing coupons that allowed him or her one complete outfit a year. This ended in 1949. In 1942 coal, gas, electricity, sweets, chocolate, biscuits and soap were rationed. Petrol was rationed between 1939 and 1950.

Utility clothing was introduced in 1941 to control price and quality. The scheme was then expanded to include furniture and soft furnishings. It ended in 1952, but I know that there are many items in use today that still bear the Utility mark.

Recycling is not new. Everyone was encouraged to salvage as much as they could; tins and metal for weapons, aircraft and tanks; boiled bones for aircraft glue; kitchen waste for feeding pigs and chickens; paper, rags, and rubber for tyres. Old woollen items were unpicked and made into socks, sheets into bandages, shirt collars were turned when they became frayed and frilling was used to disguise worn cuffs and freshen up an old dress. Worn sheets were turned sides into middle so that you slept under an uncomfortable seam, and second-hand clothing was sold by many shops that had previously traded only in new items.

## A Week's Rations for an Adult in WWII

| | |
|---|---|
| Bacon and Ham | 4oz (100g) |
| Meat | to the value of 1s. 2d. (6p today). Sausages were not rationed but difficult to obtain; offal was originally unrationed but sometimes formed part of the meat ration. |
| Butter | 2oz (50g) |
| Cheese | 2oz (50g) rising sometimes to 4oz and even up to 8oz (225g) |
| Margarine | 4oz (100g) |
| Cooking fat | 4oz (100g) often dropping to 2oz |
| Milk | 3 pints (1.8l) sometimes dropping to 2 pints. Household (skimmed, dried) milk was available. This was 1 packet every 4 weeks. |
| Sugar | 8oz (225g) |

| | |
|---|---|
| Preserves | 1lb (450g) each 8 weeks |
| Tea | 2oz (50g) |
| Eggs | 1 shell egg a week if available, but at times dropping to 1 every 2 weeks |
| | Dried egg – 1 packet each 4 weeks |
| Sweets | 12oz (350g) each 4 weeks |
| Additions | There was also a monthly points system. The 16 points allowed you to buy one can of fish or meat, or 2lb (900g) of dried fruit or 8lb (3.6kg) of split peas. |

## Pounds (£), Shillings (s) and Pence (d)

£1 = 20s = 240d.

1 Guinea = £1 1s 0d

50/- = £2 10s 0d

1/- = 1s = 12d = 1 bob

2/6 = 2s 6d = two and six = half a crown

2d = tuppence

d = 1 ha'penny

d = 1 farthing

N.B. Private soldiers in 1944 earned £1 1s 0d in a week.

# Defence Precautions

## INTRODUCTION BY SUE KING

After the fall of France in 1940, it was felt that Britain faced a very real threat of invasion from the enemy. Church bells were silenced, only to be rung if an actual invasion were to take place.

On 14th May 1940 while the Battle for France was still raging, Anthony Eden broadcast to the nation asking for volunteers to join a new 'People's Army'. This new army would be made up of men from the ages of 17 to 65 who were either in a reserved occupation, too old to join the forces or too young to be called up. Within 24 hours a quarter of a million men had enlisted and by the time the Army had been evacuated from Dunkirk, nearly 750,000 had volunteered. They were called the Local Defence Volunteers (LDV), and on 23rd August 1940 Winston Churchill renamed this 'People's Army' the Home Guard. They formed platoons made up of men from their home towns, places of work, sports teams or clubs. Many were commanded and trained by former army officers who had served in the First World War. By the end of June 1940 over 1 million men had volunteered. The strength of the Home Guard never fell below a million men until it was stood down from active service in December 1944. The Home Guard was finally disbanded on 31st December 1945.

Men and women also joined the Auxiliary Fire Service, became air-raid precaution wardens (ARPs), carried out fire-watching duties or received first aid training to join the many medical units around the country.

Many women joined the Women's Voluntary Services (WVS) originally formed in 1938 to assist in the event of air attacks. On the day war was declared the organisation had 165,000 members. Their duties included allocating homes for evacuees, first aid assistance and distributing food and clothes for people made homeless through bombing raids. The WVS also provided mobile canteens, serving tea and refreshments to the ARP, Home Guard and military units.

## EXTRACTS FROM COUNCIL PROCEEDINGS

Air Raid Precautions had been discussed as early as 1935, and in 1936 Dunstable Borough formed part of the Luton and Southern Bedfordshire District. Volunteers were called for, and the organisation formed became known later in the war as the Civil Defence.

In late 1938 respirators were delivered across the county. Dunstable did not receive any and wrote and telegraphed about this omission. Further supplies eventually arrived about a month later and were distributed to the public free of charge.

Cleansing Centres for Decontamination Squads were constructed at the County Council Highways Depots in Dunstable, and at Kirby Road. First Aid Posts were constructed at the Maltings, High Street North, and later Park Farm in High Street North. Partitions were put up in the Assembly Hall at Britain Street School and at Northfields. The Red Cross provided staffing for these posts. In 1942 a Health Centre in Kingsway was erected and at that time a small number of full time, paid personnel manned the post. The Rescue Service developed and Rescue Party Depots were established at 23 West Street, Kirby Road Depot, Princes Street, High Street South and Brewers Hill County Council Highways Depot. The South Bedfordshire Area Control Centre for the County Emergency Committee was based in the Council Offices. There were 36 Wardens in the South Bedfordshire area.

On the night of 5th/6th December 1942 a combined exercise was held to test the defences of Dunstable, codename Watling, under blitz and invasion conditions. The exercise included bombing incidents throughout the night and an attack on the town. The Umpire gave Dunstable a favourable report for both planning the exercise and the co-operation between the services.

Regional competitions were held to maintain efficiency amongst the various services and the Dunstable Mobile First Aid Unit No.6 won the County Challenge Shield in 1941 and 1942.

Air Raid Sirens were positioned on the Police Station, Messrs Waterlow and Sons, AC-Sphinx Co. Ltd., Empire Rubber Co, Messrs Bagshawe, the Swimming Pool and Skefco Ballbearing Company Limited, Sundon Park.

Warden Posts were at 75 Tring Road, 22 West Parade, 270 High Street North, 7 Olma Road, Scout Hut Tavistock Street, 129 High Street North, 35 Edward Street, Old Museum and Library, Kingsbury Stables Church Street, 38 and 334 Luton Road, 180 and 65 Poynters Road, 32 Kingsbury

Avenue, 2 London Road, 154 High Street South, 43 Chapel Walk and 113 West Street.

## NOTES FROM THE BOROUGH OF DUNSTABLE, CIVIL DEFENCE

### *GENERAL SERVICES & WHAT TO DO AFTER AN AIR RAID*

### Gas Identification Services

If poison gas is used Wardens will immediately report the fact to the Control Centre and will also warn the public by using rattles. When all danger has passed the Wardens will ring hand-bells. Any problems arising from gas warfare will be dealt with by the Gas Identification Officer who is a specially trained chemist.

### Emergency Feeding for the Homeless

At the Rest Centres it will be possible to provide hot drinks, biscuits and light meals only, although it is hoped to make arrangements for giving breakfast to men who have to go to work. All these Centres are fully equipped and emergency stocks of essential foodstuffs are being kept in reserve.

For the first forty-eight hours meals will, if necessary, be supplied free of charge to homeless persons who produce a ticket which will be issued to them at the Rest Centres. After that period it is hoped they will have been able to make arrangements for accommodation with friends or relatives or been found billets.

### Domestic Shelters

The Council have spent many thousands of pounds in erecting baffle walls, strengthening private basements and completing trench shelters for persons who come within the prescribed income limits. Indoor table shelters have also been delivered and communal domestic shelters have been erected in Church Street, Victoria Street and Houghton Parade.

### Rest Centres

If your home has been destroyed, or you are unable to live in it, first of all see if you can go to a relative or neighbour. If this is not possible, go immediately to the nearest Rest Centre where you will be provided with hot drinks, light meals and temporary shelter.

### House Repairs

Many persons will be able to return to their own homes as soon as unexploded bombs are dealt with or as soon as repairs are carried out. If your house can be made habitable the Borough Engineer will, as soon as possible, arrange for temporary repairs to be carried out to make it wind and weather tight and later, in suitable cases, will see that more permanent repairs are done.

## Public Air Raid Shelters in Basements and Persons Accommodated:

| | |
|---|---|
| The Town Hall (Two Shelters) | 183 |
| 40 High Street (Cycles and Wireless) | 81 |
| 50–54 High Street North (Seldon's) | 100 |
| 177 High St North | 48 |
| 220 High St North | 45 |
| The Maltings (rear of Barclays Bank), H St N | 59 |
| 49 West St | 22 |
| Cordova, 137 West St | 43 |
| Rifle Volunteer, West St | 18 |
| Chew's House, High Street South | 59 |
| 43 High Street South (Rixson's) | 63 |
| Highfields, London Rd | 46 |
| 78 Great Northern Rd | 32 |
| Old Drill Hall, Church Street | 135 |
| First and Last, Church St | 40 |
| Halfway House, Luton Rd | 36 |
| Albion House, Albion St | 51 |
| Woodbine Cottage, 88 Union St | 20 |

### Trenches

| | |
|---|---|
| Bennett Memorial Recreation Ground | 216 |
| Grove House Gardens | 118 |
| Half Moon Lane | 50 |
| Northfields Recreation Ground | 192 |
| Luton Road (two) | 100 |

## Fire Brigade

The main fire station (now The Place) was opened in High Street North on January 28th 1939. In addition to this station the old fire station at Town Hall Yard was used as an auxiliary station, and trailer pumps were housed at five action stations across the town. Under the ARP scheme a further eight auxiliary units were equipped with trailer pumps.

*Source: The Official Guide to Dunstable and District, 1940–41*

## INTRODUCTION BY KEVIN JORGENSEN,
### Manshead Archaeological Project

Dunstable is placed on one of the main routes north that any invading army may take along the A5. Very few examples of the war time defences are left, but Dunstable was well defended. A pill box by the bridge at Station Road guarded the eastern approach to the town. A Spigot mortar emplacement was situated on the corner of Chiltern Road and West Street; the base of it can still be seen in the garden of the house on the corner. At both of these points there were portable anti-tank blocks, which at a time of emergency could be pulled across the road to slow any approaching armoured vehicles.

Green Lane was blocked with barbed wire and it is possible that there was also a pill box in place. There is also another feature behind the present-day Chinese restaurant at the bottom of the Downs that may date from this time, but we have not investigated this in depth, simply finding a concrete path leading to an oval mound.

THE SPIGOT MORTAR was an anti-tank and anti-personnel weapon with a range of about four hundred yards (c 365 m). It was first developed in 1941 and used by the regular army and the Home Guard. The Home Guard considered this a very effective weapon when concealed at road junctions and roadblocks. The Spigot mortar in the garden of Chiltern Road was a fixed emplacement as seen by the steel mounting pin set into the concrete. This would have had a trench around the base to shelter the crew operating the mortar. These emplacements were constructed by the Works service of the Royal Engineers. *(MAS)*

Dunstable Downs also had slit trenches that may have been used as a look out post. On the northern approach there were slit trenches at Puddlehill that the society found while digging the iron age site in the 1960s, and an anti-tank block at Watling Court. The centre of town was well defended with a gun emplacement in Grove House Gardens and slit trenches in Dunstable Park. Court Drive also had a small army camp with huts and a large Nissen hut canteen.

Fire defences were also sited within the town at the site of the ASDA supermarket in Queensway, where the National Fire Service buildings were located together with a large brick-lined water tank. There were also static water tanks at Church Green and West Street (somewhere near the Victoria pub).

AN EXAMPLE OF A PILLBOX, of which there were several located around Dunstable. Pillboxes were possibly located at Station Road and Chalk Hill but no evidence can be seen today. This example is a type twenty-four with modifications found at Stockwood Park in Luton. *(MAS)*

### Denise Barker – Fire-Watching and Sleeping in Priory Churchyard

When the war broke out I was working at Bagshawe's, in the wages office. Shortly after that I began fire watching on Friday nights for Priory Church in Dunstable. We were set up in teams of 3 and had to turn up at the Parish Hall. We had a training session on the green outside the church and were taught how to be proficient in the use of the stirrup pump. We had to sleep on camp beds; stretch canvas ones that were kept in the room at the side where the stage was. We took sleeping sheets with us (we didn't have sleeping bags in those days). The bed coverings were kept in a large chest in this side room and they were actually the curtains to the stage, which were very heavy and extremely dusty. I'm sure they gave me bad dreams because they were so heavy, but we would eventually settle down. There was a piano that wasn't in very good order in the corner of the room, and some evenings Harold, the lad from the grammar school, would give a little recital before we settled down for the night.

Now the church, in order to protect it or make access to it easier, had two large ladders fixed to the side from the ground up to the first roof, the aisle roof, and then another ladder from the aisle roof to the top. Some nights we had to do some sort of reconnoitre and would go up the ladders on to the roof and have a look round. Sometimes we would go up the tower just to check things out. In the summer months when it got very hot and it was really very uncomfortable in the parish hall, we would take these stretcher beds into the churchyard just over the wall and sleep out there. However, we had to try and get up early in the morning, because on one occasion I woke up to see a rather surprised person walking through Church Walk, shocked to see these three beds and three bodies lying there! We felt we were doing something for the church and something for the war, and it was really quite an enjoyable social occasion.

### David Grant – my Father, Arthur George Grant, in Dunstable Home Guard during WW2

My father joined the Dunstable local Home Guard unit and I recall him in his uniform, with big studded boots, rushing out of the house at night when the siren at the end of the road sounded, to check that the local residents were observing the blackout regulations. Some days my mother and I would

ARTHUR GEORGE GRANT *(DGR)*

stand at our gate and watch him and his uniformed colleagues as they escorted the prisoners of war under guard past the house and up to the 'Jerry built' housing construction sites further up the road.

My father used to go to a rifle range for shooting practice, which was in an old chalk pit hollow. He would take me there sometimes when it was not in use to collect up the spent brass shell cases for metal recycling. I remember there was a brass clip arrangement that we could slide five or six shells into.

### *Philip Buckle* - my Father, a Special Constable

I was born over my parents' shop in 1929. At the start of the war I was living in Downs Road, Dunstable.

My father volunteered to become a special constable and carried out general police duties. He dealt with black market smuggling and was called out mainly at night to deal with various other things. He was allowed a small amount of petrol for his car, because when on duty his car became a police car. In order to identify cars belonging to special constables, each car was issued with small white cardboard notice with the words POLICE written on it in blue. The idea was to put it on the windscreen when on duty, but the majority of people used to put it on the sun visor, so, when the visor was down, the special constable could be seen to be on duty.

The police station was on the corner of Friars Walk and High Street South in Dunstable. The air-raid siren was situated in the grounds at the back on a big wooden tower. My father used to say that, when on duty, they were allowed to go and have a nap. They would have a sleep in the car underneath the siren, and of course when the siren went off it used to wake them all up! Opposite the police station was Montpelier House, which became Montpelier Chambers. The basement of that building was used as either an air-raid shelter or a first aid post, and that's why the railings around it were not taken away during the war.

### *Celia Booth* – in the NAAFI & Fire Service

I joined the NAAFI in 1940, recording my age as 17 years when I was really 16 . I had tried to get into the WAAF but they wanted to see my birth certificate; the NAAFI didn't, that is until I had been at RAF Cardington for some months and then they let me stay.

The work was hard and the hours long, but the girls I worked with were a great crowd and I loved the freedom after being in domestic service with one half day off per week. Pat (my husband) came to Cardington with the Light Anti-Aircraft, Royal Artillery. They had lost so many men after Dunkirk that his old Regiment combined with other units. They were then stationed on a sports field in Bedford in the awful wet winter of 1940/1. Their guns sank into the ground, so their CO got in touch with the CO at Cardington to move their guns to another camp. Again the guns sank in the ground, but the soldiers didn't mind as they had huts to sleep in – heaven after so long under canvas.

Pat came into canteen number 1552 (I can still remember the number); there were other canteens on the camp – fate must have sent him to me! I took him home to Dunstable to meet my family; my mother thought he was 'the one'! We were engaged in September and married on 13th December 1941. We had white paper on top and around our wedding cake – we had no sugar for icing then. I left the NAAFI to get married and then went with Pat to Cambridge where he was then stationed.

I was 19 years old when I was called up, for although I was married we had no children. I was able some months later to get a posting to the Dunstable area in the fire service, which I found very boring after being at St Regis in Cambridge, the HQ for the Eastern Area. We were always busy working, 24 hrs on and 24 hrs off. Pat meanwhile had been posted to Norfolk; in October 1942 he was posted to Scotland and after a few letters I heard no more from him for about three months.

After contact with some of the other wives I realised there was something going on. He had been moved to North Africa with operation "Torch" (to back up the 8th Army) and it was 1945 before I saw my husband again.

### Fred Moore - in the Home Guard

The local Home Guard started off as the Local Defence Volunteer group, which I joined straightaway. We reported to the police station in the High Street, and I think we paraded at the ground at the back. We started off with just armbands before being issued with uniforms when it became known properly as the Home Guard. I was posted to the Empire Rubber Works on night duty. About 8 or 10 of us would carry out our duties 2 or 3 times a week; quite a strain to be up all night and then have to work all the next day in the shop. We had a rifle but not much ammunition but we were a jolly good crowd, had good fun and kept in touch with one another for many years.

### Betty Tompkins - Gas Masks

Gas masks were fitted for everyone in the town hall. They were placed in individual strong brown boxes with a cord attached to go over your shoulder. We replaced these with special leather cases, which we purchased from Wild's shop opposite Dunstable Grammar School. Ration books were issued and, in fact everything was done with tremendous speed. Every house had a bucket of sand and a bucket of water, which we placed by the front door in case an incendiary bomb was dropped. When the sirens went, we donned our dressing gowns and spent the rest of the night in a neighbour's cellar. Blackout material was issued for windows. Even if only a small amount of light was visible, you'd receive a knock at the door and be told to, "Black out that light!"

### Christina Scott - our Cellar

We heard a knock on our front door, "We would like to commandeer your cellar." We lived at 78 Great Northern Road. Large cellars were built under these houses, which also had a chute at the side where coal could be delivered. Father kept it whitewashed, but it was very damp. They shored the cellar up with extra wood and put in a floor. They then dug a tunnel from the side of the house across to the pavement so that there was an entrance on the far side of the street. There were various bits and pieces down there; a bucket, extra lighting, etc. It was meant as a shelter for people, but in fact it was never used.

### *Alan Wilsher* - **Troops and Guns**

I can remember in 1944, the hundreds of troops we had in the area. We had guns at the back of us in Castle Hill Road, Totternhoe, and there were also guns in the front of us in Sid Bates' field. We even had troops in the school playing field, which was only an acre in size. A family had a dog that was always chasing Bren gun carriers as they went through the village. The whole area was a mass of troops. They used to practise firing into the chalk pits on the right-hand side where the lane went down the incline. There were also a lot of troops down the Baulk and once a petrol truck was set on fire. The search light was down there. When D-Day came all the troops disappeared.

## RECOLLECTIONS BETWEEN
### *Mr Bill Woolley* (Chief Fire Officer in Dunstable during WW II) and *Hilda Michell* (Firewoman in Dunstable during WW II)

**Bill:** We were together at the new fire station – I helped build that. We were at the one near Grove House; we even had a loo there.

**Hilda:** It was posh there.

**Bill:** Part-time people were a pest really; you didn't know what to do with them.

I know when we left, they altered it to make living accommodation. Bill got a bottle and put all our names in it and dropped it into the cavity wall. He did the same when we built this new fire station.

**Hilda:** When the bell rang we took the message and shouted out to the men the location of the fire. When they attended the fire, they sent messages back and we passed them on to our headquarters in Luton.

HILDA MICHELL *(HM)*

**Bill:** We had to find the nearest telephone – often we looked for the nearest pub to use the phone.

**Hilda:** One officer always used to say when he booked in, "I'm going to see them at Toddington." We always knew he was going to the Angel. He did swear so much. I remember one night there was a fire at Houghton Regis and a message came through; we knew that when it came through as a 'fire glow', it was very important. This particular time it didn't say anything about a glow, so I passed the message through to Luton; they asked me about the fire, "Is there any glow?" I said well there wasn't any in the message, so he said, "Bloody hell, get yourself down to Dog Kennel Lane and find out then!" So I put my coat on and off I had to go. It wasn't a nice place to go at night, down Dog Kennel Walk.

We had no living accommodation at all. They didn't think we should ever need it (when they built it for part-time firemen). The men used to get their beds out and put them around the engine. We managed to get two of us in the control room but with two beds in there, you couldn't move if there was any action. Of course we slept in all our clothes but it never worried us at all, we were all young.

**Bill:** I was about the youngest fireman of the lot, I'm 90 now. (Hilda 89)

**Bill:** We had a bad fire at the rubber works, one at Flemon's & Marchant's in what used to be The Maltings and one opposite where the aeroplane parts were manufactured, but a good lot of them were lorry fires.

A lorry pulled up outside the old fire station one night. The driver said, "It's my back wheels," (back then, tyres often caught fire). Out we came with the water supply off the engine. A spark must have set fire to the canvas at the back of the lorry and the driver bolted. They put it out quickly and when he came back he said it had frightened him, as he had a load of high explosives in the back of his lorry. What a silly fool, pulling up in the middle of Dunstable with a load of high explosives!

A terrible thing happened to one of the part-time firewomen when we were very busy one day. Some girls were upstairs and one particular girl suddenly gave a shout; she'd been smoking and her coat had caught fire. I got into trouble over that. I was put on a charge because I should have known that it was happening. I had to go to Studley Road in Luton and see the manager over there and was reprimanded.

I went to Norwich once as a relief. Two years before the war we had a holiday in Norfolk on the Broads and went to the theatre in Norwich. The next time I saw that theatre a flipping bomb had fallen right on it.

Things were pretty peaceful around here. I went to London once on relief; I went with a firewoman from Luton as a standby to a fire station at the back of St Paul's in Red Cross Street. They were very good to us there. We went to a post office place where they trained us in telephony in the mornings and then we were free in the evenings. We went for walks; the roads were cleaned but there was nothing there except rubbish. It was just before Christmas, so of course it was dark and cold, but we walked as far as the West End with our torches. You had to point them (the torches) down on to the ground so you could just see your feet, but we got used to the dark.

There were about 10–12 people on a shift. Red, Blue and I think Yellow watch. I was on Blue watch.

**Hilda:** I was on Red watch. We got used to each other. Have you ever been naughty and got into trouble but it was worth it? I was outside the station one Sunday morning at 9 o'clock; the engine had been polished and the new watch were just going on. I was going in and I said to Stan (Gossy), "I'd love to go for a ride in the fire engine." He said, "Well go on then. There's nobody about." It was so quiet, a lovely morning, so I climbed up and off we went. We went up as far as the rubber company and I really enjoyed that, but when I got back the company officer had just arrived and he saw me. I couldn't have done anything worse. I hadn't got my hat on either. I was put on a charge for that. It was very wicked, but it was worth it.

When there were no fires, we polished the engine, tested the hose and swilled the floors out. There was a big concrete floor in the appliance room and we did that over with buckets and a broom.

We were supposed to know all the different smells of gas that could be used in wartime. There was an old garage somewhere in Friars Walk; we had to go in there with the doors closed and walk around and decide what kind of smell it was.

**Bill:** I had to go to Anstey Hall, Trumpington, Cambridge, on an officers' training course. I was there for 3 weeks; we had a written exam and it all came so easy to me. The officer said, "Are you having trouble, Woolley?" I said, "No. In fact sir, I've finished." So he said I could hand my papers in and leave, which I did and I passed.

In the evening one crew had to be on call to cover the place and on one occasion when it was my turn, I thought, I'm stuck here, I'd love to walk into Trumpington and have a pint. The chap I was with said, "I'll take your place on the crew." I said that I would change the names over on the board but he said no, he would do it, but he never did. One of the trainers that night thought he would take me out, so he went to change the names on the board, having got a replacement, but was told I had already gone to the village. Didn't I get into trouble for that!

For practices we had a 50 pump fire and you had to spring into action. I hadn't been there long and there was this 50 pump fire in Luton; I was frightened that night but I just had to get on with it.

Gossy was a great help; he looked after the station and drove. When we were in the control room trying to sleep, he used to snore. Dorothy used to get up and turn him over. I never think that the fire service had the recognition for what they did. On Armistice Day you see all these wonderful people who did all these wonderful things and at the end there's one or two firemen. In London they lost thousands of firemen. There was a fellow from Luton who was awarded the George Medal who helped out in London.

We had a fireman killed in a lorry fire. The traffic has been stopped but this lorry drove along and swerved right through into them. Percy was knocked all over the place but Harry was killed. I wasn't a driver. You had to know enough to move the engine but I was not allowed to drive.

Next door to the fire station was the mortuary. Quite often when we were in bed, we would hear someone knocking on the door in the middle of the night. The wall adjoined our room.

The men used to parade in the park in the morning and drill for exercises but most of the time was spent standing by and polishing. We carried 40 gallons, what we called the first aid. It was a fair amount of water. Towards the end of the war they started teaching girls how to run the small pump hose out. I left in the December; we decided that the war was nearly over, which it was, so we started a family.

The two on live watch were supposed to be awake all night but we used to drag a mattress on to a table in the recreation room. When we moved to the new fire station we had proper bunks and, when we had been out all day, we were glad to get into them. It was such a luxury. The control room was well built with bricks and reinforced walls, it was really smart – it backed on to the Sugar Loaf car park. There was a static water tank and we used to fish for newts on a Saturday afternoon when we didn't have a lot to do. A cotton reel with a little bit of worm tied on and these newts would come along and we would lift them out quick.

**Hilda:** We had quite smart uniforms; we had to keep one smart one to go outside in. We had to give them all up but they let us keep our overcoats that were very heavy, although we had to take the fire brigade buttons off. The ladies had a skirt and top for summer, an overcoat for the winter and great big clompy shoes. When we went to the Co-op at Luton to choose Iris's wedding dress, she disappeared into the room to try it on. When she asked me what I thought, I said I didn't think it went with the shoes, because she'd still got her firewoman's shoes on! They did save you from using your own coupons, though. The women weren't allowed to wear trousers; they weren't used then for ladies. We used to say 'Ladies first, except up a ladder!'

**Bill:** Percy was the water officer. He used to find things without coupons so I got my white shirts from him. I had a dark navy uniform with a double-breasted jacket and hooks at the side for your belt to go round and your axe to hang on. Equipment was the axe, nothing else – a hook one end, blade the other and a rubber handle tested up to so many volts so if you had to chop an electric cable you wouldn't get electrocuted. On the engine were hoses and foam. In those days there was a connection for the foam in the hose for a petrol fire. We had the pump escape and a 30ft ladder as well. On the tenders there was a 30 ft extension ladder, a smaller one, a spade, pickaxes, spare firemen's axes and tin hats. You had to wear your tin hat when you went to a fire.

### *John Rushton* – the Home Guard in Action

On one occasion we had a very bad accident in the town. From the brewery they used to march the guard down to the old drill hall, which was almost on the corner of High Street North and Tavistock Street. One dark night the guard were marching down the road when a lorry went straight into the back of these soldiers, many of whom were killed. Conditions in the blackout were quite frightening. People bumped into lampposts and telegraph poles and many were injured simply by walking along their own street.

I joined the Home Guard and was in the Gas Works Platoon and somehow worked my way up to being in charge. I had to organise the men and keep watch every night, patrolling just in case Jerry landed by parachute. We covered the Gas Works area and part of Brewer's Hill. We were joined by the platoon from the railway, which was based in High Street North. The next platoon was AC-Sphinx. As time went on they dropped so many incendiary bombs over London that we had to carry out fire watching as well.

There was a decontamination centre in Kirby Road. I remember going there with a fitter and helping to fit water heaters, sprays and showers in case there was any need to decontaminate following a gas attack.

### *Christina Scott* - **Dunkirk Days**

I left school in July 1940 and I remember Dunkirk so well. We couldn't initially appreciate the fact that the Germans had overrun all of France. We were led to believe that it was a huge heroic action we had fought. We were not informed, we were in the dark. It was a brilliant sunny morning when soldiers started coming back from Dunkirk; we didn't really understand. The streets were full of soldiers exhausted, driving, lying there fast asleep or going off to barracks.

### *Harold R Perkins* - **The Friday Gang**
### **- Fire-Watching in Priory Church**

After the initial air attacks on Britain, the government introduced a programme of fire-watching in an attempt to put out fires caused by incendiary bombs (mainly magnesium) before buildings were set alight. The mode of action was a bucket of water and a stirrup pump. We knew this would not extinguish magnesium, but the spread of fire could be limited, perhaps. Another important function was to alert the authorities to exactly where the bombs had fallen.

I served in the group that protected the Priory Church in Dunstable, belonging to the Friday gang. Every Friday for a couple of years until I left for university in late 1942, I was a fire-watcher. Our base was the Parish Hall, which, unlike the church itself, was blacked out. About four of us slept on camp beds, patrolling either for practice or in earnest if an air-raid warning sounded.

It was a strange experience to go round the empty church at night with only torches, and to climb the tower and learn how to reach the limits of the great roof area, most at risk if bombs had fallen. I can remember, probably in 1941, being at the top of the church tower and seeing an orange glow in

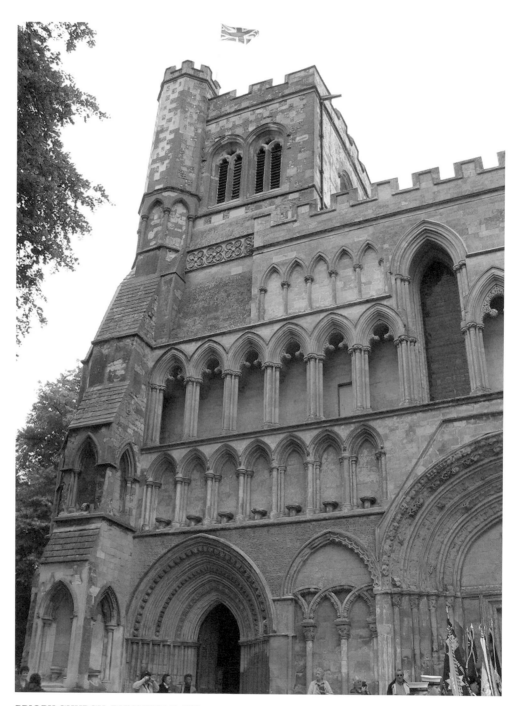

PRIORY CHURCH, DUNSTABLE *(SK)*

the southern sky. It was London burning, thirty miles away.

Each Saturday morning we were greeted by the Rector on his way to celebrate Holy Communion in the church. Holy Communion was celebrated there at least once every day throughout the war. Because blackout problems made Sunday evensong impossible in the darkest months, the Rector introduced a service of Compline, held at 7 pm in the blacked-out Parish Hall.

After a night of fire-watching it was home to breakfast, and then back for Saturday morning school.

The subject of fire-watching calls to mind the bizarre camouflage system that I remember seeing at Chaul End and Caddington. It was used to protect Luton and its vehicle factories from aerial attack, from about 1941/2 onwards. All the lanes on the surrounding hills were furnished with innumerable oil burners. They were cylindrical and black, with a wider part below for the fuel and a narrower chimney above, the whole rising to about one metre. There must have been hundreds of them altogether. They burned heavy oil and poured out black smoke. On clear nights, when there was a 'bombers' moon', they were all lit and the hollow in which Luton lies was completely covered by a pall of smoke. Whether for this or some other reason, Luton was never seriously bombed during the whole war.

### *Dr M R Pullen* – my Grandfather – a Full-Time Military Guard

My Grandfather, Andrew Cameron, worked as a full-time Military Guard at the combined AC-Sphinx and Delco, Remy and Hyatt site on Watling Street, Dunstable. These firms amalgamated after the war to form AC-Delco, recently demolished. Both firms were on the secret South Beds Region list of 'Key Points of National Importance', necessitating full-time armed guards.

He was included in the AC-Sphinx Home Guard Factory Unit with the part-time volunteers drawn from the work force, but operated in a rather different way. He wore the peaked 'Dress Cap' instead of the side (forage) cap worn by all (except staff) officers and men of the part-time Home Guard, and he carried a sidearm (a holstered revolver) instead of a rifle. Because his uniform differed in this way from the standard Home Guard type, early in the war he was once detained by the Dunstable Police as he walked past the old Police Station in High Street South, on his way home to

ANDREW CAMERON, a full-time Military Guard at AC-Sphinx in Dunstable *(MRP)*

Stipers Hill after a shift. They only released him after they had telephoned AC-Sphinx to confirm his identity and job!

He manned the Main Gate of each firm, on different shifts, for the entry of the workers. All passes had to be produced and checked and as a former Regimental Policeman in the Army he made no exceptions, even for the members of his own family that worked there! Once the gates were closed he patrolled the premises and did lookout duty on the roof of the main building. He was on the roof when a German bomber went past in October 1940, machine-gunning the High Street. My mother remembers him coming home that day and telling her about it; he took it very much in his stride. He also did lookout duty on some Sundays on the top of the north end of the Chalk Cutting, near the factory. My mother remembers walking there from Stipers Hill to take him his lunch.

### *Arthur Holland* – and the Army

There were a lot of army personnel in Dunstable, and the East Central Headquarters for Eastern Command was based at the former Bennett's Brewery on the corner of Chiltern Road. They also used the Territorial Army Drill Hall on the opposite side of the High Street.

### *Maisie Bates* – the Blackout

I did a certain amount of fire watching at the bank in Luton. I didn't have to stay all night but I did stay quite late. Walking to catch my bus after this was quite something, because during blackout periods you couldn't see your hand in front of your face! Occasionally it was worse than that because, when there was a moon, they used to set up a smokescreen to protect Luton.

### Colin Bourne - Fire-watching

We went to the Methodist Church on The Square, which took a big blackout effort. I remember carrying out fire-watching duty in this church. We bedded down in a couple of the small vestries, the lads and myself. I also did fire-watching in the dormitories at the Grammar School during the holidays. Things happened during the course of it; the odd aircraft went over and the odd bomb was dropped.

### Derek Bonfield - Rural Nights

I belonged to the Home Guard and occasionally we trained up on Totternhoe Knolls. Every Sunday morning and once or twice in the evenings we also trained, but we didn't have rifles. We also did a regular night at the mill in Edlesborough, up on the tower, and we did night duty on the main road by The Plough. A shepherd's hut was used as a guard hut. Any traffic was stopped, but there was very little. Parrot's lorries from Luton were the first things along.

### Reg Geary - ARP Duties

When war broke out I was working in my father's cafe in the High Street. I lived over the premises and had joined the ARP in the town as soon as it was formed in 1937. I found it very interesting and on one or two occasions I put my first aid training into practice. I then became a full time ARP warden; the pay was very good at £5 per week. I helped my father with his business during the day and carried out my ARP duties at night. It was during the 'phoney war' that I went to the recruiting centre in Edgware and volunteered. When I told my CO in the ARP, he told me that I'd signed a contract and that I couldn't join up. I replied by telling him that no-one could stop any man from defending his country and that I was to report back to Edgware in two weeks' time.

### Albert Morgan - Prelude and The Day War Broke Out

Sometime during 1939, we had to go to get gas masks. They were issued and fitted in a large room to the rear of the 'Cycles and Wireless' shop in High Street North, opposite Albion Street. The masks came in a cardboard box, to which most people fitted a length of string to carry it. A factory at the end of Matthew Street and Albion Street, I believe it was called

Grice and Young, which had manufactured gliders until the start of the war, produced a neat gas-mask case with solid wooden ends. They had a solid hinged lid and catch to fasten them. They were painted silver and came with a canvas strap. Mine lasted until the end of the war!

On the 3rd September 1939, the Prime Minister announced the start of the war and shortly afterwards the air raid warning was sounded. My mother told me many times that I had immediately said, "Where's my gas-mask?" After some minutes, most people in Edward Street, where we lived, went to their front doors and looked out to see what was happening. A few doors away, part of a house had been converted into an Air Raid Warden's Post. The wardens eventually emerged from behind their sandbagged doorway, dressed in yellow gas-proof suits with hoods, military style gas masks and Wellington boots. They each carried a large rattle that made a loud rasping sound when it was swung round and round; this was the signal for a gas attack.

I cannot remember ever seeing them dressed in these suits again during 'ordinary' air raids, although they did use them for special demonstrations, which were held on The Square in High Street South later on in the war. Quite an eye opener for a six-year-old. At various times during the war, we had to return to the depot for our gas masks to be updated. Additional filters were added which would protect us against 'new gases'. The depot would also repair masks that had a cracked 'window', usually caused by small boys throwing their masks into horse-chestnut trees to dislodge conkers.

My father was a member of the Territorial Army, and was called up for war service a few days before the outbreak of war. He was the Company Sergeant Major of the "D (Dunstable) Company", 5th Battalion, Bedfordshire and Hertfordshire Regiment. They had their H.Q. at the Drill Hall in

W.O. II ALBERT MORGAN off duty wearing the newly issued W.O. II Insignia. At this time he was with the Battalion Bedfordshire and Hertfordshire Regiment. *(AWM)*

Victoria Street, at the top of Clifton Road. On calling up the company, it was necessary to billet some of the troops with local families, as the hall was too small to accommodate all of them. My father was billeted to his own home!

Then came the blitz. It was possible to stand in the middle of the road in Victoria Street or Edward Street and see a red glow and flashes in the sky over London. Black-out boards were put up against the windows. We tended only to use the living room at the back of the house and the kitchen. It was easier to use one room.

When my sister was old enough she joined the ATS. Both the ATS and the Army didn't provide rations for weekend leave (they did for proper leave). If Dad was told a day or two before, he could usually wangle something from the cookhouse. My sister was stationed at Gower Street in London, and she could usually bring a little extra home in her gas mask case.

Shortly before the war, the Fire Station was moved from the rear of the Town Hall to a new station building adjacent to Grove House Gardens, next to Dog Kennel Walk. The town had a brand new fire engine that appeared with its predecessor in various parades. With the expansion of the air raid precautions, an enlarged fire station was built on the site now occupied by shops on the south side of Queensway. Roughly on the site of the present library, the fire service had a large 'static water' reservoir. This was fenced off, but we passed it whenever we went to one of our favourite play areas. It consisted of a maze of hawthorn scrub, crab apple trees and an avenue of larger trees. There was also a walled garden with some fruit trees. This was used as allotments. The whole area stretched back as far as Kingsway.

My uncle was recruited into the Auxiliary Fire Service soon after the outbreak of war and, during the 'Blitz', he told me that he and his colleagues took one or two appliances to Harrow or Edgware in North London every evening to await deployment to wherever bombs had dropped and fires had started. As the war progressed, he and his colleagues in the AFS were absorbed into the full time National Fire Service.

As part of the training of the general population in 'Air Raid Precautions', the Fire Service gave demonstrations and instructed householders in the skills of tackling incendiary bombs using either a stirrup pump with water or a sand bucket.

There were also larger demonstrations given either on the forecourt of the wartime station or on the Square in High Street South. For the latter a small building was erected near the main road in front of the Methodist Church. At the precise time an aircraft would appear flying low above the High Street. I remember seeing a Tiger Moth; an Autogiro and a Fairy Swordfish in this role. As the plane passed the Square, the small building would erupt into flames. Air Raid Wardens in their full gear of gas-suit etc. would appear on the Square and a few moments later a fire appliance would turn up to extinguish the fire. It all went like clockwork, and public belief in their Wardens and Fire Service was enhanced, helping public morale.

Their skill was tested to the full when Clark's Farm (Brewers Hill Farm) caught fire around one wartime Christmas. The farm pond did not contain sufficient water to tackle the blaze, so lorries with large canvas tanks on the back were used to transport water from hydrants in High Street North and Houghton Road. Brewers Hill Road was rather bumpy, so much water was lost as the lorries went over the railway level crossing and all the way to the farm. The Fire Service managed to save the farmhouse, but many of the other buildings and some animals were lost.

As the water mains would have become useless if damaged in an air raid, there was a need for water supplies other than the usual fire hydrants. This was supplied by 'Static Water Tanks' that were strategically placed at various points within the town. In particular, I remember one in Albion St., outside the Methodist Church premises near the junction with Princes Street. I passed this each time I went to and from school. It must have been about 8 feet wide, 24 feet long and have a depth of water between 3 and 4 feet. It was covered for safety purposes with a strong metal mesh and the whole thing was painted black.

## *Jack Carver* - in nearby Luton

I left Dunstable Grammar School in 1939, a few weeks before war was declared. For two years I worked in Luton Town Hall and served as a part-time firewatcher and enemy plane spotter. A colleague and I were attached to, but not members of, the Royal Observer Corps. If an air-raid siren sounded we raced to the top of the town hall tower with our binoculars, and if we thought we had spotted a German plane we pressed a button and sent all the staff to the basement. We were not popular if we got it wrong!

### Mary Corrie (née Cheshire) - Blackout Days

Father was in the ARP. I think he was in charge and wore a white tin hat. He went round to see if anyone had a light shining. We made blackout curtains and I remember putting them up every night. When father went out on his rounds, he sometimes had to say, "Halt. Who goes there?"

### J Reason - Gas Masks

As soon as war was declared – and I can see the front room in which we sat listening to the wireless as Neville Chamberlain told us that as from eleven o'clock that morning we would be at war with Germany – we busied ourselves with air raid precautions. A nice man called Mr Pillinger had a sweet shop in Prosperous Row, just at the back of the town square, and he made room available for the part-time volunteers to use as a base. My father was one of those local men who became involved. Gas masks had been issued, complete in their cardboard boxes, and it never occurred to anyone to raise their eyebrows and ask if they were ever likely to be necessary, which they weren't.

GOVERNMENT ADVICE on how to wear a gas mask *(DDLHS & UB)*

### John S Purdon - my Father was a Gas Identification Officer

My father was a scientist and since he was born in 1887 he was far too old for military service. So he was made a Gas Identification Officer for the ARP. As a result, the house was filled with strange equipment and even stranger substances that I was forbidden to touch. Father had a uniform and a steel helmet with ARP on it. We also had a telephone installed so father could be contacted if necessary and our number was Dunstable 197. The telephone was one of those stand-up black ones with the earpiece hanging at the side. To use it, you picked up the earpiece and waited until the operator would ask you, "Number please." Father used to go off in the evenings and on Saturdays and give lectures and demonstrations about poison gas. One thing I particularly remember was that he had to demonstrate the dangers of mustard gas. He used to fill a container with it and then put his hand in and tell his audience that they had so many seconds or minutes to wash it off before they were burned. On one occasion he was too slow and got his hand burnt.

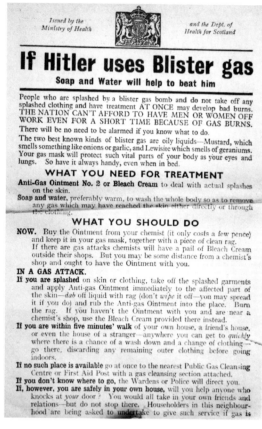

Issued by the Ministry Of Health (*DDLHS & UB*)

### Arnold Dawson - St John's

I was a member of the St John Ambulance Brigade and after the war started we formed a rescue department for the Dunstable area. We kept vehicles in the yard that is now occupied by Barclays Bank. I was on duty for 2 nights a week, during which time we would play cards to keep us occupied and awake. We were very fortunate however, as although there were many bombs dropped around the area, none actually landed in Dunstable.

### Mary Cresswell - Father in the Home Guard

We always wondered when dad would be called up. When he eventually received his papers he didn't pass his medical fitness test, which mother was very pleased about, but he served in the Home Guard instead. Luckily enough his unit was based in the golf club house on the top of Dunstable Downs; I think they quite enjoyed themselves up there!

## *Morris Cook* - **Home Guard Memories**

By the time I was 18 and due for call up, I was in a reserved occupation making components for, and later testing the engines for the Churchill tank which had been designed, tested, tooled up and introduced into production within 12 months – just imagine that in peacetime! I was therefore enlisted in the Home Guard. I was in H Company with headquarters in a shop near where the Book Castle (bookshop) is today. With Home Guard duties 1 or 2 evenings a week, weekend exercises and camps, night school classes at the Luton Tech 3 evenings a week and homework, it did not leave much time for anything else, but I lived in Friars Walk and was asked if I would turn out for fire watch duty during raids whenever possible, as many of the residents were elderly.

One Sunday morning we had been on manoeuvres on Dunstable Downs and the sergeant in charge decided he would march us back down West Street. He proudly marched in front shouting, "Left, right, left, right," to keep us in step, when two of our party decided it was time to do a tap dance with their studded boots. I think the sergeant was disappointed!

After about a year in the Home Guard fighting unit I was transferred to a new medical unit. We met every Thursday evening in a Nissen hut at Delco's where we more or less followed the St. John's instructions book. After these sessions we mostly trooped into the canteen for the 6d. Thursday hop. This was better than crawling through stinging nettles in wet fields, but we had to attend weekend camps and the firing range and do night guard duties.

I only had to apply my medical "skills" twice, once to put iodine and a plaster on an officer's leg after he got stabbed by a spike of barbed wire, when climbing over a fence, and once at the firing range, when another officer got grazed by a ricochet. I thought I was going to be busy one morning at the firing range, which was in a disused chalk pit at the top of French's Avenue, when a Sten gun had been acquired and members were told to take a single shot each at a dummy. One private's gun got stuck on "automatic"; he was holding it on his right and the force of the continued backlash was turning him round to the right. Those on that side very quickly scattered and luckily the ammunition ran out before anyone was hit.

The one-man night patrols were rather grim, as we had to keep awake and on our feet for most of them before and after a day's work. Some of

DUNSTABLE HOME GUARD marching up Church Street *(DDLHS)*

the places I guarded included the old Post Office in High Street North, the Home Guard headquarters, which were in the 'guest house' on Dunstable Downs, (the original golf club and now a residence), and the vehicle park at the Rifle Volunteer (later the Windsock and now housing), which was the headquarters of a film unit.

At the guesthouse I was allowed to 'sleep' on a straw mattress on the tiled floor with one blanket. Unfortunately it backed on to the old chalk pit used for rubbish dumping and the rats ran all over my blanket. Before I settled down one night the phone rang in the next room. I went and answered it but it was connected to a box full of terminals, which formed some sort of exchange. I had not been told of this and had not had a clue what did what. The only person I was able to speak to was the operator, who told me that someone from H Co. headquarters was ringing me. The HQ could only speak to the operator and so could I, so she passed on their message and my reply. Luckily that was in the days when there were human beings in the system.

At the Rifle Volunteer I had to stand at the gate with a loaded rifle with orders to point the bayonet at anyone who came to the gate and say, "Halt or I fire!" About 3 am in the morning the silence was broken by footsteps clonking up West Street. I got ready and waited; they gradually got nearer and eventually an army officer arrived and started to open the gate. I did my 'pointing of the bayonet and threatening to fire' performance, whereupon the officer continued to open the gate and said, "It's alright, I live here." I had not got the heart to shoot him, so I stepped back and let him in. I did not think to ask him what he had been up to until 3 am.

After the war I was glad to sleep in my own bed without having to listen for the siren and get up for fire watch duty. It was some years before rationing ended and when I got married in 1947 we could only have furniture, floor coverings, bedding and curtains etc, a bit at a time, as the coupons were released. Just as well, as we could not have afforded any more anyway!

### P Underwood - Gun Expert

Dad, being an ex officer from the First War, was put in charge of one of the Home Guard platoons. Their base was at the top of Periwinkle Lane near the water tower. Our house became full of guns and ammunition. They had the Ross rifle, some Lewis guns, all sorts of tin hats, hand grenades and ammunition. I became an expert at stripping down all these guns and putting them back together again. I was a great expert at pulling bullets off cartridge cases and getting the cordite out. My younger brother was in the Home Guard too. I had a very nice 9mm Luger gun myself, which Mum and Dad didn't know about.

### Valerie Cousins - Training Wardens

My father was too old to go to war, but he was an air-raid warden and carried out fire-watching. He patrolled from Poynters Road to Church Street in Dunstable. I can remember watching the wardens being trained. One day smoke came pouring out of a hut; the ARP wardens had to crawl through it so that they knew how to deal with smoke. I wasn't very keen on my dad going in there, but it didn't seem to do him any harm!

THE HOUGHTON REGIS HOME GUARD UNIT during the Second World War *(DDLHS) (DG)*

### *Tony Woodhouse* - **Father in the AFS**

My father was an auxiliary fireman in the AFS (Auxiliary Fire Service). He carried out fire watching and, as we had a large cellar, stored all the stirrup pumps for the service. One night he was called out to attend fires in London. During the course of this particular raid, a plate glass window exploded close to him and he ended up with several pieces of glass embedded into his skin. Years afterwards, little blisters would appear and he would get hold of a pin and dig out a tiny piece of glass!

# Under Attack!

## INTRODUCTION BY SUE KING

There were several reasons why Dunstable could have been targeted. A number of local factories had turned their production lines over to the manufacture of military supplies, the Meteorological Office was based here and, in the neighbouring town of Luton, Vauxhall Motors were producing Churchill tanks. Other bombs dropped in the area could well have been the result of German pilots simply lightening their load before flying home.

Many people recall seeing scores of enemy planes rendezvousing by the now extinct brickworks chimney in Houghton Regis before flying on to bombing raids in Coventry. Others remember the red glow over London at the time of the Blitz, and watching the sky turn black with scores of British planes flying over Dunstable on their way to the 'thousand bomber' raids in Germany.

## EXTRACTED FROM OFFICIAL COUNTY RECORDS:

The first incident in the county, which tested the defence planning and organisation, took place in brilliant sunshine on the afternoon of the 30th August 1940. A large formation of enemy aircraft dropped 63 High Explosive (HE) bombs over an area including Caddington, Kensworth and Whipsnade. The Control Centre in Dunstable received reports from warden posts and the police within a few minutes. Seven bombs failed to explode and the raid caused minor damage with no casualties.

## AN OFFICIAL REPORT OF A STRAFING OF DUNSTABLE STATED:

There were eight air raid warnings in the South Beds area on the 3rd October 1940 with HE bombs dropped on Barton and a cottage wrecked in Wingfield. In mid-afternoon a low flying plane travelling north to south over Watling Street, dropped several HE bombs at Hockliffe, causing casualties and damage to property. This plane later passed over Dunstable as low as 150ft, spraying the streets with machine gun bullets. Although the bullets penetrated roofs and windows there was only one casualty.

### Ken Malia – when the Germans Attacked Dunstable

The siren had sounded. So, abandoning tea, we all dutifully heeded the call to safety and headed for the back door. Just as we reached it we heard a loud roaring of engines followed by the sound of machine gunfire. Then we saw this German plane flying southwards along Dunstable High Street. Well it seemed like it was flying along the High Street but it was probably fifty feet up. The gunner was having a rare old time shooting up the shop windows. I think he managed to break some glass but did little further damage. He was probably doing this because he knew he was doomed and also in a fit of pique, as our local defence team had fired their machine guns at him from AC-Delco's factory roof. They also failed to do any damage. We were given to understand that he was eventually brought down somewhere further south.

As a thirteen-year-old at the time this was the only occasion I know of when the Germans actually attacked Dunstable. We watched the London blitz or rather the sky over London lit up by the fires but we were not troubled again. However, our ever-vigilant air raid wardens kept sounding the sirens regularly and our even more vigilant father kept on ordering us into the air raid shelter, and we and the neighbours all survived.

### Brian Bundy – Planes Overhead

I was nine years old when war started. I remember watching the flak at night when the Blitz was on. It was like watching a firework display. You could hear the guns and see the flashes and searchlights in the sky. One of my most vivid memories is the night they bombed Coventry when large numbers of planes flew over Dunstable.

I remember the thousand-bomber raids. We had an allotment in West Street where I used to help my father after school. One day I saw all these bombers flying over. The sky was absolutely black with planes – Lancasters and Stirlings. You could hardly see the sky. It seemed as though they met over Dunstable.

### Lucy Pendar – at Whipsnade Zoo

About 41 bombs fell on Whipsnade between August and September 1940. My friend and I were cycling down Incinerator lane, which runs from Whipsnade to Studham, so called because it was where the incinerator was located for all the zoo's rubbish. We then heard this terrific bang, looked up and saw this silver plane and a puff of smoke – we thought we were being bombed. We flung ourselves into the hedge. The bombs that did land in the park didn't do much damage; mostly they made craters that eventually turned into ponds. The only fatalities were the Spur Winged Goose, the park's oldest inhabitant, and a baby giraffe that panicked and ran itself into exhaustion.

## A CONVERSATION BETWEEN FRIENDS:
### Betty Tarbox, Heather Hing, Joy Smithson and Pam Perkins

**Betty:** There was a doodlebug at Dagnall about 3 miles away that split all the glass windows straight down the middle in shops in High Street South, and further along opposite Friars Walk. The glass stayed in the windows; we had to put sticking plaster on our windows.

**Heather:** One of the first shelters we had was under what is now the Book Castle shop. You can still see the slant of the run into the entrance. The sirens went one day and the warden couldn't undo the door; we all queued up and waited. That was the day when that fighter came and machine-gunned right down the High Street. It belonged to Rixon's, an antique shop so the shelter was full of antique furniture.

**Joy:** A gang of boys who were in our class went rambling over Ivinghoe Beacon. They found a bomb and took it home on the bus, as they lived in one of the villages, but there it exploded. One boy lost his legs, one lost a foot and his leg from the knee down and one had his face splattered.

Scores of German fighters and bombers went round the big tall cement works chimney on their way to Coventry. A German plane came down in the poppy fields near Canesworde Road and we ran up to see it. We also ran up to see one that came down on the hill in the woods at Dagnall near Ashridge.

**Pam:** We lived facing Blows Downs along the Luton Road and some nights the sky was a brilliant red over the top of the Downs; my mum told me that they were bombing London. When they dropped a string of bombs across a cornfield between Dunstable and Luton, my dad said they were unloading to get home quicker.

**Betty:** Do you remember the bombers coming back? They wouldn't have propellers going round, they'd have holes in the wings. I heard my mum say, "Dear God, let them get back." They weren't very high up, you could see the roundels and everything and the noise. We said, "Are they going to make it?"

**Pam:** My neighbour is Australian. He was on the Lancasters in the war and stationed at Wing. He came to Leighton Buzzard and that's where he met his wife. He said that over Luton all the planes from different stations used to rendezvous before going on to bombing raids together. Very like the German planes that came round the brickworks chimney; no different really.

### *Isobel Crumley* - Post Lady

I was living in Great Northern Road when war broke out. We moved there when I was 9. I married in 1945 and had 2 sons born at the end of the forties.

I was working at the labour exchange in 1939; I wasn't quite 16 and had to go and help out with the war effort. I went to the Ministry of Transport but I didn't like that job much. Afterwards I worked as a Land Girl reserve, just outside Bedford; I got a small wage plus board under tents.

At the end of the year I came back to Dunstable and started work as a post lady. I started at 6 am and had a large bag of mail to carry around. There were no circulars as there was no paper, I walked all around the High Street, Periwinkle Lane, Garden Road, Great Northern Road, then back to the post office to sort out the next lot; I did this 6 days a week.

I saw big long queues in the sweet shops. I didn't get anything myself, I was only there to deliver the post. I was a post lady for 3 years and didn't even get a jelly baby! I loved the job though. When it rained we had a big rubber sheet with a hole in the middle to go over our heads and cover the postbag; we got really wet but the post was dry!

At the weekends I would go up to London to spend the weekend with a friend. We stayed in Hammersmith and went to Regent Street, and saw a lot of awful things; it didn't stop us going up there though. We travelled by train, which took about two hours. We went to Lyons Corner house, to a large market and bought material from one of the cheap shops, even though we had no dockets. It wasn't too bad at all, I even visited Kew Gardens. We had no money for the shows but it was a lovely place to visit.

There were dances held in Dunstable; I rarely went out although occasionally we went to the town hall for concerts. The Methodist church had canteens where we could get chips, Spam, dried egg, slice of bread and a cup of tea, costing one and sixpence. We considered this the height of living! My mother, aunties and friends all used to go.

Whilst staying overnight with my future in-laws in Lewsey Road, we heard a sound like the world had exploded. All of a sudden we were thrown over and the room had collapsed.

It was a V2 rocket; you just didn't hear them that often. It had landed on Commer Cars and on the new canteen just down the road. Luckily the house wasn't completely demolished, I don't know how, but it wasn't. There were three walls standing and the roof was still on, but the internal damage was worst.

It wasn't long before help arrived. My mother and father-in-law got tossed about but landed all right; my injuries showed up the next day. We sat for a while and saw lorries of people going past covered in bandages, etc.

When I got home, I had tears streaming down my face from one of my eyes. I couldn't get any help that night but the next day I went to the eye man in Dunstable Road, Luton. It was damaged inside and I was sent to Welwyn Garden City to see one of the specialists. I got a lift from a friend; they had a look and told me that my eye was badly injured; it had exploded rather like a marble, which was caused by the blast.

I didn't think anything had hit it but I wasn't sure. I was sent to Watford hospital for 10 weeks; they couldn't operate and during my stay they kept prodding and poking, testing my arms and legs just in case any other injuries showed up. My other eye wasn't damaged but it was blurred.

I had to stop work and was totally incapacitated for the rest of my life. After the accident I went back to stay with my parents. I helped out in the canteen; I could dish up but not cook. I've never been able to see properly, but the camaraderie during the war was so great. Jim came home and he couldn't believe it, he had been all over the place and never got injured, and there I was with this.

When Jim came home and asked me if I was going back with him. I said no, not like this, as I was still having treatment, etc. Anyway I was just going to bed one Saturday night and my mother said, "Jim's coming down the passage." I said, "Don't be silly," and she said, "Yes he is, he's just parking his bike." Well, mention the word bike and I knew it was him, he lived for his bike. That was on the Saturday night and on the following Thursday we got married at the Methodist Church just down the road, and invited 50 guests.

### J Reason – Machine-gun Fire in the High Street

One foggy day, my father was home on leave testing a new and marvellously comfortable bed that he and my mother had bought for me. My bedroom was at the back of our house, which was not much more than 300 yards from High Street South. Like most schoolboys I could identify every aircraft flying at the time, British or German. My father was luxuriating on my new bed, and I was looking out of my bedroom window, when I saw a plane flying up High Street South, almost at ground level. I could see at once what it was. "Dad!" said I, "There's a Dornier flying up the High Street!" Father snorted in disbelief, but no sooner had he done so than we heard the unmistakeable rattle of machine-gun fire. The German aircrew were probably lost, and following the Watling Street. But as soon as they got past Half Moon Lane and saw the Empire Rubber Company down below them, they let fly with every machine-gun they could bring to bear.

My father leapt out of bed, but by then the Dornier was out of sight. All we could hear was its engines and machine-guns. Following the old Roman road was common practice for both friend and foe, and later we heard that when the Dornier got to Redbourn, it turned to the left, no doubt with the idea of finding the shortest and safest route to the east coast. However, it never got that far. It was brought down in Hertfordshire.

That incident was dramatic enough, but it did not compare with the huge flight of German bombers which I saw attack the Vauxhall works. The enemy must have known by then that Vauxhall were no longer making cars. They were making tanks. Anyway, quite by chance, I happened to be standing looking over the wall of the balcony of the California pool. It was a brilliant day, and as soon as I saw the size of the flight of aircraft, I knew they must be German.

I watched them fly over Warden Hills beyond Luton and then I saw them dive. Briefly they disappeared from sight behind the knoll of Blow's Downs, but we all heard the explosions as they dropped their bombs, and then I saw the towering clouds of smoke rising above the Downs.

The aircraft were Junkers 88s and they did not turn away. Instead they came straight on, directly over the California swimming pool. They were almost exactly overhead when they passed us and we could see that they were being harried by two lonely British fighters. The Junkers turned left as they went over Whipsnade, no doubt also to follow the Watling Street. We heard later that two of their bombers were shot down.

### Mrs Kelly (née West) - a Flying Bomb

At the end of 1944 a flying bomb fell one night at the end of Browning Road, which is just within the Luton boundary. Nobody was hurt. My father, an air-raid warden, got up to see what had happened. The bomb had fallen in a field, and thinking that no damage had been done, he went back to bed. A little later the chief warden of the ARP post knocked on our door and said, "Mr West, I think you'd better get up." The back door of the house had been blown off its hinges and a window shattered! (This incident was reported in the Gazette, though no place names were given. The report said that a hospital nearby had not been damaged – this was obviously the Luton and Dunstable).

### Jim Knight - in the Fields

A Blenheim bomber ran out of fuel and landed in Costin's field by the road to Eaton Bray. Two bombs dropped in the road near the Memorial Hall in Totternhoe, creating large craters which closed the road. An oil bomb dropped in fields between Totternhoe and Billington. It made a huge bang. I remember that my two brothers and I were in bed, and it seemed that in two seconds flat we were downstairs with our parents who were still up.

### P Underwood - Overhead

We had the occasional bomb, of course, although we were never really attacked in Dunstable. I remember some bombs dropping down Lancot Hill. We used to go searching for oil bombs. They were an incendiary type and filled with oil and other chemicals. Half of them didn't go off.

In 1940 we were getting more and more raids. Luton was quite heavily bombed, and 30th August was the day they bombed Vauxhall. That day I was in Half Moon Lane when the German bombers flew over. A whole squadron of them had presumably just bombed Vauxhall, and I was amazed that they weren't being attacked. There was no anti-aircraft fire but we had very few anti-aircraft guns round here, and they were just flying serenely on in a loose bracket formation. Heinkel 111s, I believe they were. The other exciting time was when the Dornier flew up the High Street and machine gunned us all. I was in Peter's house that afternoon in Blow's Road when I looked out of the window at the top of the stairs and heard this rattling noise.

When we had the doodlebugs, they were OK, because if the engine stopped and it wasn't too near, you were alright and if it flew past, you were alright, until the dastardly Hun started playing tricks. They started changing things; sometimes they would dive into the ground with the engine still running, sometimes when the engine stopped they would glide and sometimes they would go round in circles. One day shortly after June 6th doodlebugs came over and this thing was circling round us, and at one time it was pointing straight at us. Anyway it landed about half a mile away.

I was young and had no possessions to lose and in a way it was exciting, though sometimes frightening. I remember the first night they came over. We knew what German bombs sounded like and we knew what anti-aircraft fire sounded like, but the first night these things came over there was this different sound, and that was frightening.

Then the V2 rockets. One landed on Commer Cars in Luton and the occasional doodlebug came as far as Dunstable. I was standing outside what was the boys' club in High Street North, just north of the Town Hall, one weekend when a doodlebug came pop, popping up the high street and went all the way to Northampton, I believe. They did come this far.

In the summer evenings in Dunstable there were waves and waves of British bombers flying over. The fire raid in Hamburg was all good stuff for us, we hated the Germans. In 1943 we spent about 3 nights destroying Hamburg; we killed about 40,000 people. On the 60th anniversary of that raid I was in Hamburg. There were several exhibitions which I went to see with my German friends, and I asked to go to the mass grave in Hamburg. I have lots of German friends now.

### Patricia Morgan - a Big Scare

It was Thursday September 12th and Mother was walking up the high street, heavily pregnant with my sister. She met a friend outside what is now the Little Theatre and was having a bit of a rest when an aircraft came down the road – bang, bang, bang! There was so much tree cover she was lucky. When she went into labour that night, she was certain that's what brought it on.

### Albert W Morgan - a V2 Rocket Landed in Luton

After the summer holidays of 1944 when I was lucky enough to go on holiday with my mother to stay with some of my father's friends in the Manchester area, I changed schools and went to Northfields School. During my first term I had a heavy cold and was at home one morning. My mother had just brought me a drink when the whole house shuddered, seconds later we heard the sound of the explosion and all the windows rattled. It was some time later before the fact that a V2 rocket had landed on the Commer factory in Luton became public knowledge.

Photographs of local and national events as well as war stories were regularly displayed on boards in the Gas Company's showroom in High Street North. I cannot remember seeing any pictures of the damage caused by the V2 at that time. This was a regular source of information to us and we would often run down Regent Street to the showroom to see if the photographs had been changed. Sometimes they were not at all pleasant to see, especially those in 1945 showing the liberation of the Belsen Concentration Camp and the suffering of the inmates and piles of dead bodies.

### Phyllis Kaye - a Hospital Suffers

In 1940 I was nursing at a hospital in Finchley, North London. At the time of the London blitz, 6 pm was breakfast time for the night staff, and regularly we ate our breakfast with the drone of German aircraft overhead. Many a bomb whistled over us to fall near the hospital. Late one evening a string of smaller bombs fell on the hospital. The windows of the ward where I was on duty were blown in. It was a dark wild night, so all the beds had to be pulled into the middle of the ward, one having to be placed in front of a disused fireplace. Unfortunately for the patient, a little man, he ended up looking as if he was wearing a black cloak, with soot loosened from the chimney covering him. Daylight revealed two old trees decorated with items from the contents of the stores. Bars of yellow soap, all shapes of pots and pans, even ropes of sausages dangled from the trees. No one could have decorated them so well! A crate of eggs was also smashed. Hard luck! We were only allowed one per week, so there were no eggs that week.

### *Joyce Ward* - Bomb Blasts

When Dad was still doing his milk rounds in Luton he delivered along Bedford Road. He was walking with his small churn when Jerry came over machine gunning and he had to shoot up an alleyway between the houses. We had quite a few bombs in Luton but we never had a bombing raid on the town.

I was walking back from Cockernhoe when they dropped 2 land mines on the bus depot at Luton; it was a Sunday night and I had Rex the dog on a lead. There was Hubert, Betty, Sid and I, and we could hear this plane. Hubert looked up and said, "Get under cover quick, it's Jerry!" You could see the plane although it was dark, it was so low and we were on the high part of the road between Cockernhoe and Stopsley. We shot through a gate and got under the hedge as it came over, and the dog knew it was a German plane. He always knew when it was a German plane and was down in the shelter before we were. We always knew it was a German plane by the dog, and that night he snapped his lead as if it were a piece of tissue paper. So of course, never mind the German plane, I shot down the road after him and they were shouting at me because Jerry was very fond of gunning whenever they saw anything. We'd got along a little way when they sent this bomb down on the bus depot and the blast hit us.

They dropped a bomb at Farley Hill which didn't go off. There were quite a few that didn't go off. There was one hanging in the airport, swinging on the roof until they could get the people to deal with it. That night a terrific lot of damage was done around Park Street. There were streets blown up that night and someone who lived in Seymour Road said their piano shot across the room and out in the garden, there were keys everywhere. A huge number of people were injured by flying glass.

A V1 rocket came down in Old Bedford Road and a V2 on Commers. Various planes came down. I remember going to Breachwood Green and seeing the remains of parachutes up in the trees. They'd got the German pilot out of the plane alive. It had hit a huge tree but, if it had been one of ours, people wouldn't have got out to look. The villagers turned out and took the prisoner.

### Len Stafford – Lasting Memories

It was a very strange situation really because Luton didn't get a lot of bombs. A land mine came through the roof of the Vauxhall factory and killed lots of people and a rocket hit Commers. There used to be big paraffin type stoves that they lit at night; it created lots of smoke and provided cover from the German planes. When we lived in Beechwood Road, if you went upstairs and looked out you could actually see London being bombed; we saw it all lit up. I was in Luton one day with my Mum and after we got off the bus a German aeroplane came down and machine-gunned the street. There were shelters in local shops where you could run to, and that's what saved us when he came down from bombing Vauxhall. That memory is still vivid.

### Mrs M Sharp – Fatalities in the Garden

I was 13 years old on the day Vauxhall was bombed and living in Farley Avenue, Luton (now called Wilsden Avenue). I had not gone to school that day because I was feeling unwell and, as mother had to go shopping, I went to stay with a friend who lived further along the road. When we heard the siren we ran to the Anderson Shelter in the back garden. As we reached the entrance of the shelter a bomb was dropped from a German aeroplane. It landed in the next garden and the blast from the bomb threw my friend and myself into the shelter. This shelter was shared by my mother's friend and the next-door neighbour, and we couldn't understand why our neighbour had not come into the shelter with her two children.

I can recall we looked out to see if she was coming, only to see her little boy being thrown over the fences from the blast of the bomb (this little boy died in hospital later that day). When the all-clear siren went, my mother's friend went to see if our neighbour was alright, but found her and the baby dead. She had been killed as she bent to get the baby out of the pram.

My father was a Special Constable and was asked to break the terrible news to her husband when he came home from work. He told my father that he didn't know how he himself had escaped being killed at Vauxhall, only to be told later of this tragedy. I was a pupil of Surrey Street School and was off school for nine months with delayed shock.

### Paul Heley – the Town Targeted

Fortunately, and particularly when one sees photographs of the human misery caused by war, it must be admitted that Dunstable hardly knew that a war was going on at all. We had no factories of special strategic importance, so any bombs which landed on Dunstable were usually leftovers from whatever and wherever was the real purpose for the raid. There were a few attacks on Luton where the Vauxhall car factory (but more importantly, the Bedford and Commer truck works) produced vehicles for the war effort, so Dunstable got one or two throwaway bombs as the German planes returned home. I remember that one of our customers had her next door neighbour's roof tiles neatly piled up in her front garden as a result of one of these afterthoughts but, otherwise, no damage at all.

There was one occasion however, when Dunstable was the target. The town had two factories of minor importance; one known as the Sphinx Works and the other the Empire Rubber Works. Both of these produced components for military vehicles, so it was in Germany's interest that they should be knocked out.

I remember the day very well. It was a Saturday afternoon in late summer (most likely in 1943) and I was at the top of Bigthan Road when I heard the nearby drone of a plane's engine. Looking up I saw a German bomber flying very low; so low, in fact that I could see the pilot easily and could experience that strange sensation of direct eye to eye contact as we stared at each other for what seemed like an eternity but which was no more than a couple of seconds in reality. This was an eerie moment and I imagined he was going to shoot me – but he smiled at me instead. I wonder what he thought of the small boy gawping at him: I wonder if he had a small son at home as well. Such is the stupidity of war.

### Philip Buckle – Dangerous Days

I can recall going to Totternhoe Road after they had dropped a string of bombs in the direction of the Met Office. One of the bombs fell just between two bungalows. Many people thought the Germans were deliberately trying to bomb the Met Office but I think they were just jettisoning their load before flying home.

I was in Downs Road when a German plane came down and machine gunned High Street North and South. I remember hearing the rattle of machine gun fire although I didn't actually see it. I remember that it was a very bright sunny day when the Germans bombed Vauxhall (in Luton). I was at Dunstable Downs Golf Club. I could see the German planes high up in the sky like little tiny silver spots and a great pool of smoke around the area of Vauxhall Motors.

During the Blitz I looked out of my window and saw the glow from the fires in London, and later on when our forces were bombing Germany I can recall seeing our bombers, the Lancasters, Halifaxes and Wellingtons flying over Dunstable. The army built some temporary huts in First Avenue and some of the empty houses were used to billet other army and ATS personnel. One day my friend and I were treated to a ride in a Bren Gun carrier over the top of the Downs!

### Rob Cutler – the Searchlights

We had the first lot of incendiary bombs dropped at Dagnall, in a field about a quarter of a mile outside the village, which set fire to the hedge and part of the corn. My dad picked up some of the metal cases and brought them home. On the side of them it said they were manufactured by Krupps. He said that in 1918 he was standing on guard outside Krupps factory.

Not every week, but quite often, bombs were dropped, sometimes 20 or 30 in a night. I think it was because we had two, and then later three, searchlights at Dagnall, and as soon as the lights picked up the planes they used to hit us with bombs. Two searchlights were placed on the golf course and the other one was just across the road in a narrow lane from Dagnall to Studham. They had massive generators but no guns. You could read a newspaper when all three were on.

I remember 2 bombs were dropped between Dagnall and Ringshall and 2 were dropped near the church on the corner. They were dug out by Polish explosives chaps and the road was closed for two to three weeks. My sisters worked at the laundry cleaning army uniforms as well as ordinary clothes and had to cycle up to Four Ways Garage to get up to Ringshall, because the road was closed.

A doodlebug came over one night when I was with Bob, and just as it got level with us the two stroke motor cut out. We dived into a hedge but it carried on and crashed at the top of the hill coming out of Aldbury towards Ashridge. No one was hurt. Bombs were dropped all the way round the RAF Station. It could have been another reason why we had so many bombs. Some say that the RAF Station at Dagnall was a listening station for Bletchley Park. One day I went to the garage near there and all the hedgerows looked as if they'd been done up for Christmas; they'd been strewn with bits of silver paper. It was something to do with putting the radar out of action, but we didn't know what it was at the time.

A V2 rocket was dropped half a mile outside Dagnall at about 7 o'clock one morning. It blew the glass out of the window over my bed. The cats always sat on the windowsills in those days asking to come in but we never saw them after that. The Chapel looked a mess. I got my bicycle out and two of us went down and picked up an 18inch square bit of bomb but I had to drop it, it was so hot.

Liberators and Fortresses were at Cheddington when the Americans came. I've heard since that they couldn't take off with bombs from Cheddington because the runway was too short. So they took off and bombed up (filled up with bombs) somewhere in Norfolk. One night an American Liberator crashed into a wood near Dagnall. All four engines came off the plane and it was the first time I'd ever seen people in asbestos suits. They came up from Cheddington in massive four wheel drive vehicles and used foam to put the fire out. Tracers were shooting everywhere, deadly if they hit you. Some of the planes that got back were unbelievable. Sometimes the damage was so bad, you could see right through them.

My father and I went over to Wardown Park one day. As soon as we got just inside the gate, the air raid siren went and we all dashed into the newly built shelter. It was quite long and gloomy. We sat down on the left bench and everyone ended up on the floor. They had built these shelters in a hurry and, as there were no rawlplugs in those days, just nails in the brick work, every one of them pulled away from the wall. We all got up, sat down on the right hand side, and all ended up on the floor again!

### Shirley Ansell - Shot Down

We were told one day that a German plane had come down in a field near Brewers Hill, which was a cart track in those days; Barbara and I decided to go and have a look. We got to where the plane was; it had crashed into a hedge, its tail with a swastika painted on it sticking up in the air. We became a little nervous thinking that perhaps the Jerry was still in it, so we had a look, but they had taken him away.

When mum was working at the Post Office she would often take me out on the collection rounds with her. One day she stopped at the Rubber Works and went inside to collect the mail when the air raid siren sounded. All the women came out screaming and went down into the shelter. I was sitting in the Post Office van when I heard a V1 rocket (doodlebug) overhead, followed a few minutes later by two Spitfires. I heard later that it was shot down near Watford.

### Tony Ward - Watching the Skies

I remember my father held me up to watch the German bombers flying low over Dunstable, seemingly at the time in their hundreds. It was night time and everybody was looking; you could even see the swastikas and the pilots. I asked my dad if we should be doing this? He told me not to worry because they were off to bomb Coventry or Birmingham. Another thing I remember was being held up by my father one evening and seeing a glow in the distance – he told me that it was London burning.

### Valerie Cousins - Bombing the Zoo

In 1940 or 41 my parents took me for a birthday treat to Whipsnade Zoo! While we were there we heard the sound of an aircraft. My Dad got my mother and me under a bench. A few seconds after there was a terrific bang! I remember my dad getting up and walking off to see what had happened. Afterwards we found out that a German plane, after it had been chased by one of ours, had dropped a bomb to lighten its load and flown off. Mother panicked because she thought the lions might get out and run wild!

Later in the war we heard the rockets, the buzz bombs. We could hear the sound of their engines, everyone would be very tense, holding their breath, happy that we could still hear the engine but knowing that the minute the engine cut out, some poor soul might possibly get hurt.

## *Alan Wilsher* - **Plane Crashes**

One morning I was walking to see my father who was employed at the chalk pits when the air raid warning sounded. A few minutes later I saw German bombers in the sky. You could tell the difference between our planes and theirs by the drone of their engines. I ran home and we (the family) took cover in the pantry, the safest place in the house.

I can remember two planes crashing in Totternhoe village; one was a Blenheim Bomber that crashed on the right-hand side of Eaton Bray Road in Costin's field. I remember going down to the area soon afterwards. I believe the pilot was in the WRAC. She had been ferrying the bomber to another destination.

Later on in the war I vividly remember standing in my back garden at 32 Castle Hill Road watching a Spitfire, which was in trouble flying from the direction of Dunstable. It flew over my house and came down in Tom Turvey's field, which now belongs to the Dunstable Cricket Club. I understand the pilot was Polish and escaped uninjured. He made his way to what we used to call Bates houses at the bottom of Lancot Hill. The Spitfire was there for 3–4 days before it was taken away. I was there when they removed the machine guns and bullets from the wings.

I also remember one night when bombs landed in the middle of the road just past the Memorial Hall. Years later, we could still see where the road had been repaired and the telegraph wires were joined. That same night bombs fell in Totternhoe chalk pits near the lane to Sewell. Incendiary bombs also set Jessie Bird's chicken house on fire and a bomb fell near Middle Path at Eaton Bray. I always believed it was caused by a lone bomber who had got lost and was dumping his bombs before heading home.

I remember sledging up on Coxen hill, and night after night seeing the flashes of guns and explosions from London. Around this time, 5 or 6 lads from the village were awarded a certificate for putting out an incendiary bomb at the back of the chalk pits.

## EILEEN BERYL MORDEN
### Bomb Disposal, the Earl and the Secretary

Eileen Beryl Morden was connected to Dunstable by the fact that her mother, sister and her brother's family all lived in this town.

She was employed by the Ministry of Supply as secretary and personal assistant to Charles Henry George Howard, 20th Earl of Suffolk and 13th Earl of Berkshire, a qualified scientist, who was the Chief Field Research and Experimental Officer in the Directorate of Scientific Research of that Ministry.

Her passport shows that she entered France in early March 1940 and carried a visa from the French Ministry of Armaments. In order to carry out her duties alongside the Earl, she was granted an identity card that stated that she was attached to The Scientific and Technological Research Service.

Documents and newspaper cuttings from that period show that the Earl and Miss Morden were involved with the scientific elite in France and were responsible for some of them leaving that country to continue their work in the U.K.

The newspaper cuttings state that they were also involved in procuring a supply of a rare and valuable chemical, available only from Norway, and bringing it out via Paris for use in the U.K. This was 'Heavy Water', which was essential for atomic research. It was kept in the Tower of London with the Crown Jewels for most of the war. The Earl also had in his possession a great many industrial grade diamonds. He then commandeered a lorry to get them to Bordeaux, where he commandeered a ship to bring back to England a group of French scientists. This was happening at the time of Dunkirk and the relentless advance of the Germans. Miss Morden's passport shows that she got back to the U.K. and landed at Falmouth on the 21st June 1940; one report states that she escaped in a cargo boat.

Following their return from France, the Earl became involved in dealing with unexploded bombs during the 'Blitz'. He bought himself a large van and kitted it out with the necessary equipment. It was common for him to take his staff to Kempinski's, a smart restaurant in Piccadilly where he had a table permanently reserved in his name. He wore plus-fours and smoked a cigarette through a very long holder.

He led one of the earliest bomb disposal teams and was responsible

for learning the secrets of the German fuses and developing methods of making them safe. During this time, Miss Morden was at his side taking shorthand notes of his dictation as he worked on the bombs. Miss Morden had to be close enough to him to hear what he was saying, much closer than regulations allowed.

These notes became the basis of instructions to others involved in bomb disposal.

Their work continued into 1941 and on the 13th May they were called to deal with a bomb on Erith Marshes in Kent.

According to a letter in 1962 to the Daily Mirror 'Old Codgers', a Mr. W. C. Kempton, who was the Highways Superintendent of that area in 1941, states, *"I reported to him (the Earl) that all road signs had been placed and the roads roped off. I left him working on the bomb and had walked only a hundred yards when the bomb exploded. It blew my hat off."*

The explosion instantly killed the Earl, his secretary (Miss Morden), their driver/assistant (Mr Frederick Hards) and five soldiers who were there to assist in moving the bomb. The Account in the book "The Register of the George Cross" reports that they had been working on a booby trap device called the ZUS 40. The bomb was an old one that they did not expect to give them a problem.

The 'Daily Mirror' article states that according to Sir Winston Churchill's 'The Second World War', that was the Earl's thirty-fifth operation against unexploded bombs. It concludes with the statement that the Earl's pioneer work on bomb disposal techniques was recognised by the posthumous award of the George Cross. This award appeared in the 'Supplement to the London Gazette' published on Friday 18th July 1941.

In Churchill's book he also says that the problem of unexploded bombs was becoming critical. Volunteer squads were formed in every city and town and he remembered meeting the 'Holy Trinity', as the Earl of Suffolk, his secretary Miss Morden and his chauffeur Fred Hards were called. Fred Hards was described as a van driver, (one report says that they had a Pickfords van) and a clever originator of improvised methods.

In the same supplement, both Eileen Beryl Morden and Frederick William Hards were given the King's Commendation for brave conduct in Civil Defence. Eileen Morden was 28 years old when she died, the Earl 35yrs.

At 17yrs the Earl had sailed round the world before the mast of a sailing ship and then engaged in sheep farming in New South Wales. He took a degree in pharmacology and became a Fellow of the Royal Society of Engineers. He owned 10,000 acres in England and was married to Mimi Crawford, the actress. He succeeded to the title at the age of 11, when his father was killed in the First World War.

The exact nature of the fuse which killed the Earl and Miss Morden is not given in any of the documents to hand. However, it is known that a number of experienced bomb disposal crews lost their lives around that time due to the introduction of what became known as the '/Y' fuse. Externally this fuse looked like and behaved like the standard fuse, it had the same number except for the addition of the /Y suffix.

The normal German fuse was electrically operated and "charged" at the moment of release from the aircraft. After a short delay, a trembler

*opposite* Extracts from THE LONDON GAZETTE

## CENTRAL CHANCERY OF THE ORDERS OF KNIGHTHOOD.

*St. James's Palace, S.W.*1.

18th July, 1941.

The KING has been graciously pleased to award the GEORGE CROSS to:—

Charles Henry George Howard, Earl of Suffolk and Berkshire (deceased), Chief Field Research and Experimental Officer, Directorate of Scientific Research, Ministry of Supply.

For conspicuous bravery in connection with bomb disposal.

Albert Henry May, Higher Clerical Officer, Trinity House.

Miss Eileen Beryl Morden (deceased), Shorthand-Typist, Experimental Unit, Ministry of Supply.

George Frederick Murray, Member, A.R.P. Rescue Party, Birkenhead.

Jonathan Price, Member, A.R.P. Rescue Party, Birkenhead.

# Took Notes While Her Chief Examined Unexploded Bombs

## Mayor's Visit To Leyton Evacuees

Mr W. Jones, with the Farmer Road School, Leyton, party at Newlyn East, near Newquay, Cornwall, sends the following account of the visit of the Mayor of Leyton's visit to evacuees in the West Country:—

The Leyton children and staffs were very pleasantly surprised to have a visit from the Mayor and the Mayoress (Alderman A. G. Cochrane and Mrs. Cochrane).

The visitors met the parties at all the Leyton centres in the Duchy, calling upon St. Newlyn East; St. Mawgan; St. Dennis; Ladock; Cusgarne, and Perranporth.

Everywhere they were able to make personal contacts with sturdy youngsters full of cheerfulness and high spirits. The boys and girls were eager to talk about their lives in the country, and their smart and wholesome appearance showed how well the good people of Cornwall have looked after their charges.

Our Leytonians were a little bit proud to think that they and not the other evacuees had received a visit from a real live Mayor and Mayoress of their wn.

" hank you Mr. Mayor for the kindly of bringing a word of greeting home town.

**RENTS**

## POSTHUMOUS COMMENDATION OF LOCAL SECRETARY

### Helped Lord Suffolk In Vital Work

Killed with the Earl of Suffolk when an unexploded bomb which he was examining went off, the Earl's secretary, Miss Eileen Beryl Morden, aged twenty-eight, of Fairlop Court, Fairlop-road, Leytonstone, has been officially commended.

The award of the George Cross is made posthumously to Lord Suffolk in whose highly dangerous work Miss Morden shared.

She accompanied him on his work of examining unexploded bombs and would take shorthand notes of his observations and discoveries while he was actually engaged in dealing with the bomb, collecting data which has been of great value to bomb disposal squads. Thirty-five years-old, the Earl of Suffolk was chief field research and experimental officer to the Directorate of Scientific Research at the Ministry of Supply.

**EXAMINED BOMB AT LEYTON**

It may now be revealed that Lord Suffolk, some time ago dealt with an unexploded bomb which fell through a house and buried itself beneath the cellar of a house in Thornhill-road, Leyton.

He was interviewed by an "Express and Independent" representative while sitting astride the bomb, but reference to the fact was unable to be made at that time.

The Earl of Suffolk smoked a cigarette through a long holder which he would keep in his mouth until he was right on to a bomb.

### ARMY BLANKETS IN HIS AIR RAID SHELTER

Employed as a storekeeper at Woolwich Arsenal, a position he would lose if convicted, Frederick John Gibbs, thirty-one, of Maybank-road, South Woodford, was fined £5 at Stratford Police Court for being in possession of eleven Army blankets, believed to have been stolen or unlawfully obtained.

Gibbs admitted possession of the blankets, which were found in his air raid shelter, and said he bought them from a second-hand dealer.

By the KING'S Order the name of
*Miss Eileen Beryl Morden,*
*Shorthand Typist,*
*Experimental Unit, Ministry of Supply.*
was published in the London Gazette on
18 July, 1941.
as commended for brave conduct in
Civil Defence.
I am charged to record His Majesty's
high appreciation of the service rendered.

*Winston S. Churchill*

Prime Minister and First Lord
of the Treasury

THE CERTIFICATE OF COMMENDATION

switch was activated and this would detonate the bomb as it struck the ground. Occasionally, a longer delay was included, so the bomb did not explode on contact but would do so if the fuse were moved suddenly when attempting to remove it. This was countered by discharging the fuse with a short-circuiting plug before removal. The '/Y' fuse behaved exactly like the normal one when tested but it had an additional circuit that was isolated after activation. This circuit contained 'mercury tilt switches' which would detonate the bomb if the fuse were turned, even slowly. This was a 'Booby Trap' designed to kill bomb disposal personnel.

It was eventually countered when a fuse with a faulty connection was recovered and analysed by experts. They realised that by making a cup of 'Plasticine' around the fuse and filling it with 'liquid air', the mercury would freeze and the fuse would be rendered safe enough to remove for a few minutes.

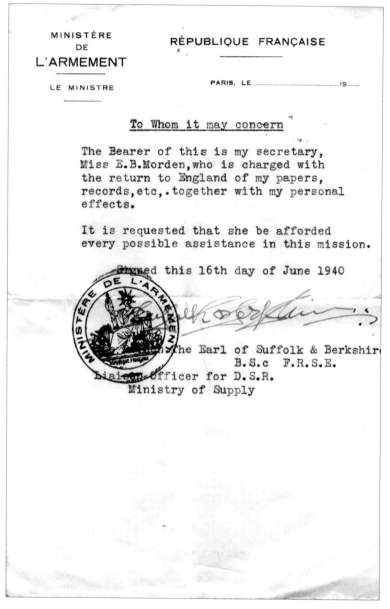

DOCUMENT ISSUED TO MISS MORDEN to allow her to take vital material (heavy water) back to the U.K. in June 1940. This was at the time of the French surrender.

f

XXXXXXXXXXXXXXXXXXXXXXXXXX
XXXXXXXXXXXX,
XXXX

Ministry of Supply,
Shell Mex House,
London. W.C.2.

16th July, 1941

Dear Mrs. Morton,

Your daughter lost her life while engaged on duties in the service of this Ministry.

And to you, her Mother, I send this expression of my deepest sympathy.

I send you also the news that your daughter's conduct will receive a Commendation in the Supplement to the London Gazette which will be published on Friday, July 18th.

I hope that this public recognition of her unselfish courage and devotion to duty will be a comfort to you in your great sorrow. It is a tribute to one who, willingly facing danger that the safety of others might be ensured, played a most splendid part in her country's struggle for justice and freedom.

Yours sincerely,

Beauchamp

Mrs. Morden,
34 Borough Road,
Dunstable. Beds.

LETTER TO MISS MORDEN'S MOTHER from the Ministry of Supply

# MINISTRY OF SUPPLY

## ADVISORY COUNCIL ON SCIENTIFIC RESEARCH AND TECHNICAL DEVELOPMENT

*Telephone :*
VICtoria 3811. Extensions 613 and 206.

*Telegrams :*
Secretary, S.A.C., SPLYCTS, LONDON.

*All communications to be addressed to the Secretary.*

*In reply please quote :* SAC .100

GREAT WESTMINSTER HOUSE,

HORSEFERRY ROAD,

LONDON, S.W.I.

May 31st, 1941

Dear Mrs. Morden,

The Scientific Advisory Council met yesterday for the first time since the accident to your daughter, and they asked me to express their deepest sympathy with you in your bereavement. Several members of the Council had the opportunity of seeing for themselves the nature of the work on which your daughter was engaged, and they realised how much her unsparing assistance and her disregard of personal danger contributed to the large measure of success achieved by the team of workers of which she was a member.

Not only did your daughter give her life for the national cause; she died also in her efforts to save life and property, which is an object denied to most of us in these times. This must be a source of consolation in your sorrow.

With deepest sympathy,
Yours sincerely,

*J. E. Lennard*

Chairman, S.A.C.

Mrs. Morden,
34 Borough Road,
DUNSTABLE.

LETTER TO MISS MORDEN'S MOTHER from the Chairman of the Scientific Advisory Council

EILEEN MORDEN (left) with her sister

*Above information, photographs, etc, courtesy of Mrs E F Clark. (EFC)*

# Home Front

## SHOPS AND SHOPKEEPERS
### Introduction By Vivienne Evans

Talk to anyone in Dunstable about wartime shopping and, well ahead of shortages, coupons and make do and mend, you will get a story about queuing. Surprisingly, these stories invariably reflect a great deal of humour, goodwill and the exchange of helpful information, some of which might turn out to be an unhelpful rumour.

Queuing really did become a way of life; if you saw a queue you joined it and asked questions afterwards. The story which circulated in Dunstable (and elsewhere) of the newcomer to the town who had queued for twenty minutes before she realised she was waiting for a bus may be an exaggeration. However, as the years went by and food became increasingly short, housewives became desperate. Not all of them were free to shop at different times of the day, many were on war work. It might be a child kept out of school for a few hours, an older relative or even a neighbour who had to be trusted with the precious ration books. This could lead to cheating; when off-ration goods appeared in the town, a husband and wife could go to a shop where they weren't known, join at different places in the queue and pose as two different families.

There are two versions of one Dunstable cheating story. In one version a husband and wife would be seen queuing together, one of them from time to time leaving the queue and going forward to see how well stocks were lasting. In the other version the old lady stood three or four places ahead of her husband. The two versions continue, either she sprinkled some pepper on his collar or he pulled out a hanky with some pepper hidden inside it. All versions then ended in the same way – an explosive burst of sneezing from the old man, the scattering of the queue and a new queue forming with the old lady one or two places from the counter! These deceptions were very few and far between. Most shoppers were scrupulously honest and only too willing to help their friends and neighbours. A child's birthday meant help from all the family, a wedding meant help from all the street.

There are stories of a wedding cake being made of white cardboard covered with a thin layer of decorated icing, but that was usually for a hasty wedding before the groom left to go overseas. Even then it probably sheltered a small currant cake or jam sponge underneath. A well planned wedding was far more ambitious. The 'wedding list' which was circulated wasn't for presents, but for items needed to make the cake, or a plate of sandwiches, sausage rolls or even a tin of fruit.

Kunzle cakes, small wrapped confections which came from a variety of different shops, were not on the ration. These were much in demand, but to get one, or even two, meant putting your name down on a list and waiting several weeks for your name to creep to the top. They kept well, and so for a special event, you put your name down in more than one shop and tried to get it down again, as soon as you had collected the first order.

Between 1939 and 1941 the whole nature of this form of business was to change. The shopkeeper became the middle man, between the anxious, sometimes desperate housewives, and the government department known as the Ministry of Food. No longer was it a simple equation of planning ahead the likely demands of the customers and making orders from the wholesaler to cover these demands, plus a selection of items with which to tempt people into a little impulse buying. Suddenly they had become civil servants, agents of the government, who collected coupons and points, filled in forms and attempted to convert these coupons into the next delivery of stock. If they had coupons, bombing emergencies permitting, they would get new stock, if not they and their customers went short. Rationed goods were quite straightforward, customers were obliged to choose a shop and register with them, but people could choose where they spent their points.

It was the skill of the shopkeeper to get as many different goods as possible into his shop to ensure he got plenty of customers. News of the arrival of fancy biscuits, tinned fruit, metal (not rubber) hot water bottles, even umbrellas soon spread round the town. Shopkeeper Mr Moore pointed out that the shortage of coupons to buy new clothes meant that there was a great demand for every type of decorative frills or lengths of artificial lace. Shortages resulted in a supply and demand form of rationing. The arrival of the evacuees left housewives very short of crockery. Various shops would open lists and accepted names knowing full well they were already down on a list next door. When the (usually pink or green) utility stamped china did arrive they would be only too grateful to get it.

The collecting of coupons was the relatively straightforward part of the business. Transferring them was another problem. 'Lost in the post' could mean just that, but in wartime years bombed trains could lead to letters and parcels being re-directed into an emergency warehouse where they stayed for weeks or even months. Fire bombs destroyed both mail vans and warehouses and the theft of coupons wasn't unknown.

Another problem was the need to get the 'off ration' goods into their shops and to find such emergency supplies as extra bedding for evacuees, or buckets for picking up potatoes. It was possible to obtain permits, (yet more paperwork), but then it was necessary to find a source of these goods and persuade the wholesaler to part with them.

Several of Dunstable's bigger shopkeepers solved these problems by delivering the coupons to their suppliers and not relying on the post. They also visited the manufacturers, made contacts amongst the staff and at times brought goods directly back to Dunstable.

### *Bernard Stevens* – at the Ironmonger's

I had my own business as an ironmonger during early war years at 45 High Street North, Dunstable. As soon as the war started it changed the demand for all sorts of items in the shop – e.g. black paint, and various other materials that people wanted to use for blackout purposes to try to make their houses more or less 'bomb-proof'. Rolls and rolls of adhesive tape were sold to put across windows and then of course materials started getting short. The only way you could get hold of supplies was to go to the wholesalers in London and Birmingham. I used to go up to the Birmingham wholesalers about once a fortnight. Other times we would have special permits from the various factories, as we supplied a lot of them with different materials. By getting these certificates you could get supplies from the wholesalers; there was one occasion when the army came to Dunstable and wanted 100 enamel mugs. So of course we were given a permit to enable us to go up to London and get the supplies. This also applied to other things that the army needed, such as shovels.

There were a number of army groups in the town; the Sugar Loaf was used as an officers' mess and several well known film people became officers and stayed there. Of course, there were a lot of huts situated where ASDA (supermarket) is now; also in First Avenue, Dunstable, a women's artillery group was based. Apart from soldiers being billeted in the town for short periods of time, trade in the shop decreased in volume generally. It was quite a job eking the stuff out and finding enough pots and pans for people to use. Many had evacuees and they needed more equipment to cater for them. Some firms were perhaps a little more generous if you went to their actual factory; they would look after you and try and find something for you. During the war years my wife and father kept the business going. We also had two girl assistants and a part time lady working in the shop and so did not involve any loss of manpower.

### Fred Moore – of Moore's Department Store

I was in accountancy to begin with, but my parents were in very poor health and could not run the business on their own (a small independent department store in Dunstable High Street). So I went in to help them, expecting to be called up soon – as it turned out I wasn't, so in the family business I stayed…

Although the introduction of the Delco factory increased the population of Dunstable, the biggest increase in residents came from a terrific influx of evacuees. Most of these people came from the East End of London; very good folk they were. At the beginning of the war, some of the most requested items in the shop included materials to make blackout curtaining. Every public and private building had to be blacked out and as retailers we had to hunt around everywhere to get hold of these supplies. (I don't remember having tape over our shop windows but we did have the old fashioned wooden shutters that were pulled down at night, which offered a certain amount of protection).

Rationing coupons were soon introduced and trading became very difficult as some goods were very difficult to find. Certain goods did not sell as people were only allowed to buy what they had coupons for. We struggled to find goods generally and other merchandise that did not require coupons. I think bedding was allowed to be purchased coupon free but it was a very rare luxury to buy a new suit or dress. We did manage to get hold of a tremendous lot of frilling. Ladies would use this to sew around the cuffs of an old dress to freshen it up. We also sold industrial wear; staff from the local factories used to buy their overalls from us. We also did a

MOORE'S DEPARTMENT STORE in High Street South, Dunstable *(DDLHS)*

good trade from farm workers – they would buy corduroys and so on. All the clothing then was very warm and hard wearing (brand names included Lion shirts and trousers).

A Utility brand was introduced; it was of very good quality really and on one occasion we were very lucky to get hold of a lot of linen flour bags, goodness knows where they came from! We had hundreds to sell. They were made from beautiful quality linen – it needed to be to hold flour – which could be turned into tea towels, table cloths and pillow cases; some people made sheets out of them.

We made constant journeys to the warehouses scattered all over London to try and keep up our stock of goods in the shop. We would then bring the supplies back with us on the train or we had it delivered. There was always a certain amount of pilferage, so some of the goods that we ordered did not always arrive! Many London warehouses would try to help small retailers by letting us buy goods in smaller quantities. We had to take the coupons that customers gave us to the supplying warehouses, and I think, when we ordered goods by post we must have posted the coupons. The mark up on goods was very low and very strict. Inspectors went round making sure that everything was marked up properly. We were given booklets issuing us with instructions as to the amount we were allowed to charge customers for goods. These tight controls meant that trading became very difficult and it was almost impossible to keep our premises up to date because of the lack of funds and materials.

There was a certain amount of petrol issued to business people and we managed to supply some of our customers in the surrounding villages, although not as many as we would have liked. Of course, this situation went on for some time after the war had ended. Public transport was very well used; there always seemed to be very long queues for buses, especially after 5.30 pm. We shut our shop at 5.00 pm in order that our staff could actually catch a bus to get home.

I remember a large army camp based at Houghton Regis and at RAF Stanbridge. As there were a lot of soldiers in town, we ran a canteen for them every night of the week at The Square in Dunstable. We provided them with hot food, egg and chips, sausages and so on, it was very popular and always full. Some men who were available helped out but mainly the ladies worked in the kitchen. That's how I met my wife; she was a sister of a soldier who visited the canteen. A lot of them came to the church and this particular soldier was invited to our home by my brother. My mother suggested that his sister came to Dunstable to say goodbye to him and that's how we met!

Then I was ill for about 3 months with rheumatic fever and could not join the army, which was expected of me. My brother worked as an accountant carrying out important war work so there was no question of him joining up. My other brother was a prisoner of war in Japan and worked on the Burma Railway. He kept a diary while he was there, which of course we all know now was very dangerous. His wife discovered it only about 12 months ago, written in pencil on rough paper; it's now held in the Imperial War Museum. Apparently he wanted to keep a record of what happened to his men so that he could inform their relatives. He recorded an incident when a Captain was beaten to death for having a radio. He also describes the hunger, starvation and the conditions that he was held under for 3 years. (This diary is printed in the Serving in the Forces Chapter). When he came home he went back to work for Vauxhall Motors, a job that he really enjoyed.

I stayed in the family business; I enjoyed the atmosphere and the relationships that we as a family had built up with our customers, many becoming our friends. The business could not have kept going without my wife and myself as my parents were in poor health and it would have been a shame to close the shop, which had been open from before the First World War. Nowadays we have many second and third generations of customers visiting the store.

## *Colin Bourne* - Family Grocers

I was born in Dunstable. My father had a family grocer's shop down at the northern end of the town; it had a provision and grocery counter, a red and white bacon slicing machine, flour and sugar packed in blue cartridge paper, etc. This is where I grew up; we had a lovely garden. Of course, he had all the problems of rationing and of counting out coupons, evening after evening, and recording everything. This created a lot of extra work for him, especially as he lost his assistant after he was called up.

Of course we had blackout procedures, and it was interesting how one very quickly got used to walking in almost total darkness, whether we ate carrots or not, as the Ministry of Food would have liked us to do!

When I was in the sixth form we went out into the country and helped on a farm near Houghton Regis and spent almost the whole summer holidays bringing in the harvest, which was great fun.

### Marjorie Tingey – ran an Off Licence

When we came down here Dunstable was a lovely little place, its high street full of little shops, and once people got to know you, they were quite friendly. There were stalls all along the high street where you could get greengrocery and stuff; that was all right, nothing was rationed there. In the ordinary grocery shop, food was rationed and you would have to wait ages in a queue to be served, and then perhaps when it got to your turn there would be nothing left. Next door to the sweet shop was an ironmonger's; he had everything in there including paraffin, which was rationed but if you weren't there on time when the paraffin van came in, you were just dead unlucky. On the corner of Church Street was a Home & Colonial. Now if you wanted cheese or butter or eggs from the Home & Colonial, you had to be there just after 9 o'clock. You may have to wait a couple of hours in the queue for the stuff to come in, or to be divided into your special portion but you had to be there early, and you had to queue. Further along was Hunts – that was an old-fashioned tobacconist shop and then there was Woolworth's and the Victorian Bun Shop. Now if you wanted bread or buns, again you had to queue early. They used to start serving at 2 o'clock in the afternoon, so if you weren't there by 12 o'clock you didn't stand an earthly. It was funny how people were cheerful, they would laugh and joke between themselves and you used to quite enjoy the queues in some cases.

On the other side of the road there was a fish & chip shop; if you were lucky you could get the chips but you couldn't get the fish. Further along there was a place where they sold furniture and of course it was all Utility furniture. We needed a new bed, so we had to go there and of course the mattress was very thin and the furniture was very poor really, but there was no chance of getting anything else. Further along still, we came to the local wet fish place. Mostly you could get what you wanted, although it was very expensive. Down the road was the Victoria, a little pub; a lot of people used to go there because they used to have little evening get-togethers.

Along West Street you came to Macclestones, another little bread and sweet shop; they sold a lot of bread pudding which was delicious.

Opposite where Woolworth's is today, was a grocer's shop and it sold cakes and everything. We used to have to queue there by 2 o'clock in the afternoon; there used to be a man and his wife queuing also. His wife used to be first in the queue and he used to be fourth and what he used to do, (he didn't tell us at the time but a long, long time afterwards he told us). He used to take a pepper pot and put pepper on to his hands and his knees and his nose, and he'd sneeze and sneeze and sneeze, so that people used to step back or get out of the queue because they were afraid of catching a cold during wartime!

When I came to Dunstable I had a baby of 9 months old and this was one of the reasons why I wanted to get out of London. Now, to bring a baby up in wartime was very difficult; you went to the clinic to get your milk and because I was in business and unable to feed my child, I had to go down to the clinic every week to get baby food, Oster milk and rusks. We had to have Terry towelling nappies; these were very scarce as well. When my child went to school in Burr Street there was no milk rationing; you could get orange juice, and in some schools they did have the little capsules of cod liver oil. What shall I say, the school days for the kiddies were quite good, the teachers were really qualified and they taught the children very well.

We had a van in which we made our deliveries, once a week only as petrol was rationed. The Off Licence we were in was a free house so we had deliveries once a week from Mann, Crossmans, Whitbreads and Guinness. We did not have enough to satisfy all the customers so you had to ration them. Wines and spirits were delivered to us once a month but the quota was very small, so again you had to have a rationing card. There were so many people who wanted whisky or wine all the time; you had to make sure they got their fair share.

## Doris Tibbett – Working in a Shoe Shop

I was living with my mother in Great Northern Road in 1940 and during the time I was there, the house three doors up was vacant – it belonged to my uncle, so I was able to purchase it and moved in July. The Monday after I moved into this house, my husband's call up papers arrived. I managed to stay in the house on my own but I took in evacuees. One older couple came

*above and opposite* Scenes in HIGH STREET NORTH, Dunstable, during WW II *(OB) (DG)*

from Clacton who worked all through the war at the Rubber Company in London Road.

I worked for Blindells shoe shop and while I was at the Harpenden shop, I was responsible for the black-out. I was called up by the police in the night; I had left the light on in the shop. They gave me a caution but it was ever such a small light, I'd forgotten to turn it off. We had criss-cross tape on the shop windows too. I went every day on the train to Harpenden whilst someone was away.

We always carried our gas masks and had practice gas attacks. I think it was 1942 and I had to wear my gas mask while I was serving people. It was very uncomfortable. There was no rationing on shoes.

At home we had a cellar – we had it shored up so it was safe; people who hadn't got cellars had a kind of table with mesh so they crawled underneath, or they had an air raid shelter in the garden. We grew our own vegetables

and we had an allotment; far more people had allotments then.

My first child was born during 1942 in a hospital private ward. I was issued with cod liver oil and orange juice from the clinic in Kingsway where they weighed the babies.

We had quite ornamental railings round our house and they were all taken down and went for the war effort. The cemetery in West Street had very tall elegant iron railings, and they were all taken away. I understood they weren't used which was a bit sad really. Someone came and cut them down and we had to build walls.

The cattle used to come on the train most Wednesdays, to go to Dunstable market. They used to walk them up Great Northern Road from the station and then to the market on the Square. I was terrified and ran behind the railings, so that must have been before they took them down.

**Advertisers** The Downs Guest House in Whipsnade Road promised hot and cold water in all bedrooms. G.A. Waller offered himself as a gold medal pie maker, Stotts Removal Service also sold furniture, The Commercial Hotel offered dining for 75 people, Franklin's tobacconist and confectioner also sold London theatre tickets and Costin's Coaches were making trips to the seaside and other places of interest.

Buckle's of Middle Row offered tailoring on the premises, 'Only the best is good enough for your suit', Charles Pritty, tailor to ladies and gentlemen and George Cox outfitters were both in High Street North. Herington's the chemist had 2 shops and 'The straight road to health and beauty' pointed to The Central Pharmacy. Moore's, General and Fancy Drapers, suggested to their customers that they should join their Drapery and Clothing Club.

The Dunstable Gas and Water Company promised 'an improved service every minute of every hour of every day'. 'If you require a Permanent Wave, Root and Point Winding' you could try Stoten Bros, or for an exclusive baby shop, Roberts of West Street. Opposite the Grammar School was the Hat Shop – 'Hats renovated, remodelled, made to order, Mourning Millinery and Matrons Hats a speciality'.

H. R. Smith advertised; 'Make sure your radio is installed by a competent electrical engineer. It will be to your advantage in perfect reception, reliability and efficiency'. Gibbs and Dandy supplied Ironmongery and Small and Son, Linoleum and Furniture. Baker's of Church St was a two floor store claiming to be Complete Household Furnishers and Ironmongers.

Rose Farm and Downs View Dairies offered a twice daily delivery of rich clean milk, cream and eggs. There were a number of butchers, including Tilleys at 4 High St South and a fishmonger, David Sewell in Middle Row.

My favourite advert has to be 'Don't Hope for an inexpensive snack or a good meal, Get it at – Transport Dining Rooms, The Square. Cut from the joint, two veg and Yorkshire 1/- (5p). Try our chips and taste the difference. All classes catered for'.

Under Local Institutions, two dance bands are listed, the Embassy and Fred Janes who has often been mentioned as the band playing at the Town Hall on a Saturday night in our stories.

Mention is made of the special mitred maple floor of the Half Moon Skating Rink as one of the best in the country.

*opposite and right*
Examples of
ADVERTISEMENTS taken
from The Official Guide to
Dunstable 1940/1

## DUNSTABLE LIVESTOCK MARKET
### Introduction by Vivienne Evans

Always busy and a great attraction for sightseers, Dunstable's livestock market became one of only four in Bedfordshire. Through the Ministry of Food, the government decided that for a number of reasons the sale of all livestock should be directed through their few designated sites, with a named responsible person to be in charge. Each certified market had a code; Dunstable's was EAH.

Charles Allcorn was for many years superintendent in Dunstable. His shop at 22 High Street North advertised 'Fat and Store Cattle every Wednesday at 2.00pm'. The exception to this was the great Christmas fat stock show which spread over two days and included turkeys, geese, chickens and, a most important part of the wartime meat trade, rabbits. Charles Allcorn held a very important position, he not only controlled Dunstable's market, but was for some time Chairman of the District Auctioneers Committee. This was made up of three Dunstable butchers and three local farmers. One of each had to be in the market to grade the potential meat for the Ministry of Food.

In Dunstable as many as 120 cattle were sold in winter and 350 or even more in summer. It was the duty of the superintendent to register their arrival and on the previous Wednesday to notify the Ministry of his expected sales of cattle, sheep and pigs and the number of lorries that he had ordered to handle them. In addition to the lorries, cattle being walked in from Hockliffe or up into the market from the stations was a feature of Dunstable life which continued during the war. The drovers and their well trained dogs as well as the men working in the market itself were all very experienced and reliable. Nevertheless, crowds would gather each Wednesday hoping that just one animal might escape and enter a nearby shop, providing entertainment for the crowd and enormous problems for the shopkeeper and market superintendent.

# WOMEN'S LAND ARMY

### *Mrs Catherine Henman* – at Marston Moretaine and Barton

I was working for Cross and Company at the beginning of the war but in 1942 I decided to join the Land Army. I went to an office in Luton, gave them all my details and was sent to Luton Hoo for my training. I was billeted with other girls in a big house, which had been occupied by the gardeners on the estate. Some girls wanted to do horticultural work and others wanted to work with animals, which was what I wanted to do. We did a month's training and then I was sent to Wood End Farm at Marston Moretaine. I went into Bedford to St John's Station and caught the train to Millbrook. The farmer sent his daughter to pick me up. I was billeted not at the farmhouse but at another house further up the road, Little Park Farm.

I'd been taught how to milk cows, so we had milking to do, pigs to look after, we collected eggs that the hens used to lay all over the place and helped with the lovely big farm horses. They used three horses to work on the farm. I loved those, and an old pony called Polly that we managed. On the farm there were two Land Army girls, Albert the cowman, Mick who did all sorts of jobs, Frank and 2 dear old gentlemen, Caleb and little Mr K; they used to look after us two girls. They'd been farm workers all their lives and were very good at their jobs.

We also had several sows and a boar. Then the farmer bought some goats but they were a bit of a disaster because they had fleas. There were about 30 cows in the herd and I was provided with an old sit up and beg bicycle to go down the road to fetch them in. Each cow knew just where to go in the milking shed and if another one got in the way, she would bump it out of the way. Very intelligent animals and, we knew them all. I didn't like rounding the animals up on a Saturday to go to Bedford market, because we made friends of them.

The farmer was also a butcher and had a shop in Marston Moretaine. Every so often he killed a pig and we'd have black puddings and he'd give me sausages to take home. Caleb kept a pig and our farmer killed and butchered it at the farm.

The first girl I worked with left to get married. Next came Edie for a few years before she also left to get married. All the women were single; you had to leave if you got married. Other farms in the area had Land Girls. Some

Land Girls lived in hostels and went out every day to different farms. Our animals needed looking after every day so I stayed on the same farm.

We started milking at 6 o'clock and then came home for breakfast. After that there were various jobs dependent upon the seasons. In the spring we spent most of our time in the fields, hoeing and weeding crops. We grew mangel-wurzels for the cattle and corn. Hay making was very hard work. The two old gentlemen didn't think girls should do this sort of work, but we got on ever so well with them, and they got used to us.

We didn't have combine harvesters then, we had the tractor and then the binder went round the fields. We had to go behind and pick up the sheaves of corn and put them in stooks, then we had to break off to do the afternoon milking. In the summer while it was daylight, we went back to do the harvesting. After so long the corn sheaves were gathered up and made into ricks. We helped put the sheaves on the carts and the men used to take them and build up the ricks. The ricks were in the yard at the back of the cowsheds. In the autumn the threshing machine came round and we'd see this old steam engine pulling the drum. It would come chug, chug, chugging along the road. The sacks were fixed on the threshing drum and filled up with corn and then the chaff went in another sack; we girls were in charge of that. We used the chaff for the animals' bedding. It was a very dusty job. To stop rats from running up our trousers, we'd tie them up with string. The farmer had four dogs so that helped. It was very tiring work.

Summer was the hardest and during the first year I got sunstroke. In the autumn we did potato and fruit picking. The winters were cold with snow and mostly the animals were kept in the yards. We had a big heap of cow muck in the farm-yard that the men used to bring out with a horse and cart and we girls had to spread it. We got used to the smell. A lot of time was spent cleaning out. We looked after Polly, she was harnessed to a cart and we used her for all sorts of jobs. She was ever so slow, but she was elderly and she was still there when I left.

We fed the cows on pellets. The mangel-wurzels had to go through a mangle. You turned the handle and chopped them up. We had sheep and they also had the mangel-wurzels. We used the pony for carting the feed to the sheep in the field. They used to stay out in the fields until lambing time. The lambs and calves were lovely. A man used to come walking round the farms with a stallion for servicing the mare. The men used to deal with that, as the girls weren't supposed to know about that sort of thing in those days. It was a long while before I saw a calf born.

German PoWs from Ampthill used to help with the potato picking. They were alright, they were just ordinary men. One or two could understand a bit of English and they had the guards with them to make sure everything was OK.

Occasionally in the summertime we used to walk over the open fields up to Cranfield to go to the pictures. Mick used to come along to look after us. In the evenings we were too tired to do much and we were a long way from the village. We had a bike each and we went up once or twice to the village hall. I used to come home once every other weekend. I'd get a lift to Bedford, catch the bus to Luton and then home to Dunstable. I'd leave on a Saturday and had to be back on Sunday night ready to start work on Monday morning.

We got some extra clothing coupons because we lived in uniform. We had 2 pairs of corduroy breeches, 2 pairs of khaki overalls, a pair of boots which nearly ruined my feet, walking out shoes, a hat, a green pullover, a tie and an overcoat for the winter. We wore felt armbands. We had a different one every year; they signified how long you had been in the Land Army. The early ones were green with red, and red was for 4 years' service. We wore the armbands all the time on our coat sleeves. I've kept my tie. We were supposed to wear them when we walked out. I think we had Aertex type blouses. The hat was felt and they were funny things, I never wore mine, I wore a scarf.

After I'd worked at Wood End for a while I wanted to be nearer home, so I got a job at a farm in Barton. It was a beautiful farmhouse surrounded by a moat. There was a small airfield near the farm which I understood belonged to the Luton Flying Club. The farmer had permission to send the cows out on to the airfield to graze. Again there were two of us girls and it was our responsibility to keep the cows off the middle of the airfield, because planes used to land there occasionally. So there we were in the winter, cold as could be, looking after cows. It wasn't my idea of farm work. I went back to Marston Moretaine.

I stayed until Christmas 1946. I then went home and worked at AC-Delco.

All the land girls from Bedfordshire assembled in Bedford when Princess

Elizabeth came. We marched down the high street and passed Princess Elizabeth who was standing on the Corn Exchange steps. We marched past her and then we were all invited back to the Corn Exchange for tea.

I've got a certificate from Princess Elizabeth, it reads;

"With the compliments of the County Secretary Women's Land Army, Harpur St. Bedford.

By this personal message I wish to express to you, Miss Catherine Bezant Women's Land Army number 74324, my appreciation of your loyal and devoted service as a member of the Women's Land Army from 11th May 1942 to 21st December 1946.

Your unsparing efforts at a time when the victory allied cause depended on the utmost use of the resources of our land has earned for you the country's gratitude.

Elizabeth R"

I have another certificate that grants my willing release from the Land Army after 4 years and 7 months and another letter which asks me to return my uniform. We were allowed to keep our shoes and I brought home a pair of our breeches. My sister was a lovely seamstress and she cut them up and made a pair of trousers for my eldest son.

### Ilene Fuller – at Kensworth House Hostel

When I was called up I did a month's training down in Luton Hoo before I was sent to a farm near Bedford. They wanted someone to look after 10 cows, milk them and everything, I just couldn't do that, I didn't know how; they didn't teach us that in Luton! They rang head office and sent me to see the person in charge in Bedford; she sent me to Kensworth House as they had just opened the hostel. There we did threshing, picking potatoes and brussels – any sort of work that the farmer wanted really. The threshing machine was operated by a steam engine and we used to follow it from farm to farm. The farmers used to hire the threshing machine out, you see. It was jolly cold in the winter – after about six months I developed paralysis in my face through driving in the open lorries so they put me in the hostel gardens. I helped to grow vegetables for the hostel; tomatoes, etc. There were also grape vines, peach trees and greenhouses. Kensworth was a very

KENSWORTH HOUSE *(BCC)*

big house; we started off with 20 Land Army girls and ended up with 40, mostly volunteers. Only 2 of us came from Bedfordshire, the rest came from London.

I was called up in 1942 when I was about 18 or 19 years old. I was in a reserved occupation working in the electricity offices at this time. My brother was missing in Singapore and I didn't want to be called up and moved a long way from my mother who took the news of my brother very badly, so I decided to join the land army and was able to get home on weekends. It was a lot of fun living with a lot of girls and I remained friends with one girl in particular. We sometime had parties (like little dances); the local boys and soldiers were invited along.

One of the worst jobs was picking brussels on cold frosty mornings – as soon as you picked them the frost would melt on your fingers. It was a hard life but very healthy. The food was nice and we had a good cook.

I was discharged in 1946. I had to come out to nurse my mother who was ill at the time.

## *Mary Cutler* - at Whipsnade and Leighton Buzzard

My father was working near London helping to clear land mines. When the situation began to get worse, we decided to move to Luton. I had an older brother and a younger brother and sister. As I approached my eighteenth birthday, my father told me to make up my mind as to what I was going to do, otherwise he said, "You'll be put into war work, and that won't be easy." I thought that, as I'm not the sort of person to take lots of orders, the best thing to do would be to find somewhere that was more relaxed.

I knew nothing about the country. The nearest we had to a cow was the churn in the dairy next door where we bought our milk. My family worked in the rag trade, we were townies!

Anyway, away I went to the town hall to join the Land Army. Once home, I decided to tell my family over tea. "By the way, I've joined the Land Army today!" They laughed. My father thought it was hysterical, "With shoes like that!"

The first place I was billeted was Whipsnade. We slept in a hut that was used by the waitresses that used to work at the Zoo. They had stoves in the middle of the room with pipes going up into the roof; very primitive but warm. For going out, we were given breeches, green woolly jumpers, woollen socks, hats and a great coat. For working we wore jumpers, dungarees, shirts and coat.

The war effort had taken over the land that was attached to the Zoo; the wild animals had gone and it was now used for growing food. Only the parrots were left and they soon learned to swear because the girls came from all walks of life. Many of them would say b**** off when someone came to the door! We enjoyed it although the job was very hard, especially working on the threshing machine. It was hell. I met Barbara on my first day. She was a giggler, although she stopped when mice came through the door and then the giggles turned to tears. That happened on our first day; we didn't like it very much.

We then moved to Leighton Buzzard where we did general farm work, brussel and potato picking, hay making, etc. The nicest place that we stayed in was Kensworth, a lovely house, altered to create more bedrooms and bathrooms. We enjoyed it there; it had a library with huge windows and a legend of the headless huntsman who used to ride by at night. Of course we loved all that. There was lots of fun attached to it.

Sometimes we would be let out in the evening but lights out was at ten o'clock. We would wait outside the hostel at half past ten, get a lift to Bedford Corn Exchange on the back of someone's motorbike and go jiving with the Yanks. Coming home, a friend would let us in but that stopped when someone told the warden what was going on. When we found out who it was, (what we thought was a dear old lady), we decided that we would dress up as ghosts. We put white sheets over our heads and knocked on her door making ohhhhhhhhhhhh noises. Well, the poor old dear left about a week later, so that worked! But we worked hard and played hard.

We were up at about 6.30 am and then given a packed lunch in a tin box before being dropped off at one of the farms. Some farmers were not very nice; they didn't want us girls there. We could appreciate that because they had lost good experienced farm-hands and in place they were given a couple of giggling females. They were at a loss because, as willing as we were, we didn't know much about farm work and none of us really wanted to either.

I learned to smoke as a land girl. This happened because one day we were given a cow shed to clean out. It was filthy, with lots of manure and the smell was terrible. One of the chaps in the shed told us that we would have to roll it up to get it out. So we rolled the manure up, just like a carpet! The smell got worse as we did this. He said, "What you need is a fag." I told him that we didn't smoke, he said, "You soon will!" He got out a little tin box and rolled cigarettes for us. It was marvellous! We couldn't smell anything else after that!

There was one particular farm where we dreaded going. We drew lots to see who would be sent. When our names were called we'd say, "Oh no, please not me!" One particular time, three of us were sent there, chewing gum and smoking cigarettes that we'd got from the Americans. We were cocky too, because we knew how to use the pitchfork. As we stood there the farmer came out, a gangling man, who stared at us. "Girls!" he said, tut-tutting away. We started to giggle. "Get your hands out of your pockets and you can put those fags out!" His wife though, was lovely. She used to feed us big slabs of bread pudding and give us hot drinks.

One farmer came from Somerset and had brought with him his own recipe for cider. When we went hay-making he would give us bottles of cider to drink, "Coming up, sunshine!" he would call. There were many good, funny sides to our work. On leaving one farm, the farmer told me that he would miss me. "You're the only woman I know that can handle a pitchfork." This was quite a compliment!

On another occasion I was sent to a farm with lots of pigs. Well, I love pigs, especially piglets. The farmer had told me that he had a little job for me working with the piglets. When I got there, the farmer told me to hold the piglets by their back legs. He then castrated them!

Spending a penny wasn't much fun when working in the fields either. We sometimes had to walk a long way to find somewhere that was out of sight of the men who were also working on the farm! Once we climbed into a field with a bull in it. My friend Barbara and I crept along, hoping it wouldn't see us!

Mrs Churchill visited us for the day at Leighton Buzzard hostel. She chatted to us, asking if we liked our jobs; of course we said yes! She was a very charming person. I must have enjoyed the work because after I had been doing the job for three years, I signed up for another year. It was a very free life.

During my time in the Land Army I learned a lot of things; how to notice wild strawberries growing by the side of a lane that no-one else would see, or birds nesting.

The Queen, when she was Princess Elizabeth, presented me with my four years' service green arm band, with WLA written across it. We had gang leaders; I was a gang leader eventually. There were new girls joining up all the time. They thought they would have a good time!

# FARMING

### *Derek Bonfield* – of Shepherd's Farm, Icknield Way

I was born on the 27th November 1924; so I was 15 when war was declared in 1939 on a Sunday morning, when my parents and I sat on the front lawn listening to the radio. I was born and brought up on Shepherd's Farm along the Icknield Way, when it was a poor time for agriculture. All the land had to be ploughed up and put into production. Up until then the ground had not been ploughed for many years, so father had to go and buy all the equipment to do this. The government paid you £2 if you ploughed up grassland and turned it into production, although I don't think they paid for the machinery and we didn't get any grants.

We had pigs, cattle, hens, a horse and of course we had a great infestation of rabbits. We also had 2 dairy cows – house cows, my mother used to milk those and look after the hens. On part of the farm near the road was a field called the Chute. Over the previous years they had quarried chalk from there to make up the road. Afterwards, the council in Dunstable tipped spoil and rubbish into it, hence it was called the Chute. We used to see a lot of blue butterflies – Chalk Blues. The best part of the farm was the apple orchard in the valley. We used to put wire mesh around each apple tree to keep the rabbits off. In 1940 we had a very cold winter when the snow was quite deep covering the top of the wire mesh – this killed many of the rabbits.

We were controlled by the Ministry of War who made us grow potatoes. On one occasion this was an absolute failure – the potatoes did not grow well because of the chalk soil. It was very poor and in places you could see the chalk on the surface. We used to grow corn and we'd under sow the corn with clover and then, when the corn was cut, we also had a crop of clover to plough back into the ground. The petrol we used for agriculture was coloured red. It used to leave a red stain round the carburettor so you couldn't use it in your car.

Times were tough. The first service we had was a telephone; our number was 38! We didn't have electricity or water laid on but we did have a well which was 80ft deep. We used a rope to pull the water up which was clear and sparkling, lovely water coming out of the chalk. If you drew the water from the well you couldn't drink it straight away because it was so cold. We used to get cyclists stopping to ask for a drink but we daren't let them; we thought they'd get stomach cramps, it was so cold. There was another well in one of the fields near the Chute; 60ft deep where the water was equally nice, we used it for the cattle.

There's a picture with me on the tractor and mother on the binder and the Downs behind. There's not a bush to be seen because Sharratts of Valence End Farm used to graze his sheep on the Downs right from the Gliding Club to Bison Hill.

Most of our groceries were delivered from the International Stores. Mr Pearson used to come round with a model T Ford and then later an Austin. I can see him slinging his money bag on his back now and cranking it up. He used to come late at night sometimes; I suppose we were last on his round. The baker used to come from Eaton Bray.

The biggest businesses in Eaton Bray were the glasshouses, growing tomatoes. My wife's relatives worked there in the war. It looked like a lake from up on the Downs. I think Mr Bates from Church Farm in Whipsnade grazed sheep on the Downs.

In 1948 father sold the farm and moved to Devon. I stayed here, I had married by then.

### Len Stafford – Potato Picking

One day, they asked us at school if we would like a holiday, well we thought that would be great but we ended up picking potatoes! We all worked like slaves but it was alright out in the field; every so often they would come along with some water for us to drink. They just conned you really when they said come on holiday; we were just slave labour but being children you didn't have an opinion in those days.

At Christmas we were given an apple and an orange and if there was anything else in your sock you thought it was wonderful! My Dad used to make a lot of our toys out of fire wood. He made me a wooden truck of firewood. I loved those toys as a boy.

## Harold R Perkins - Harvesting at Toddington

In the summer of 1940 the school had been asked to provide senior boys to assist in gathering the harvest. I was one of a group of volunteers who helped at a local farm owned by an 'Old Boy' of Dunstable Grammar School. Much extra land had been put under cultivation and he was reported to be in charge of some 3,000 acres – a huge area. The first part of the holiday was wet nearly every day and harvesting was difficult. After that the weather improved, and we were occupied every weekday from about 9 am to 6 pm. There was "Double Summer Time" as I recall.

Each day we cycled to the farm near Toddington, Bedfordshire, and were detailed our tasks by the farm foreman. We were taught how to gather the sheaves of corn that had been produced by a reaper/binder (horse or tractor drawn). The sheaves were packed upright in tent-like groups of six or eight, called locally 'shocks' (in some areas 'stooks' was used). It is worth noting that the headlands and other parts inaccessible to the reaper were cut by the foreman using a scythe. He then hand bound the product into sheaves, to be shocked along with the rest. Some of the fields were enormous; I remember one near Leagrave that was over 100 acres.

The shocks were left a few days to dry in the sun (too much rain meant that corn started growing on in the ears and would become useless). Then the sheaves were collected and taken to make a corn-cock, a round structure about 10 to 15 feet across and 15 feet high at the centre. For this purpose we used horse-drawn carts with extensions called 'ladders' at the front over the horse and at the rear to enable a larger load to be carted. The horse was led by an 'ogee' boy, an urchin of about 9 or 10 years old. The sheaves were loaded by us, being pitchforked up to a loader (another one of us), on to the cart itself. He arranged the sheaves to give the best stable cartload. Once at the corn-cock site, often in a corner of the same field, the sheaves were again pitchforked and placed to build the corn-cock. At first, the foreman did this but later we learned the trade and he was left with his specialist job of thatching the finished structure with straw. It was thus safely stored to await the availability of threshing capacity.

Threshing was done with a red-painted threshing machine, powered by a tractor fitted with a flywheel and connected by leather belting. Once more our task was to pitchfork the now dry sheaves on to the machine. I rather think a farmhand cut the strings. The threshed corn (barley, oats or wheat according to season) came down a chute at the side into a large sack, which when full of wheat weighed 2 cwt (100 kg). There was one farmhand who could lift such sacks single-handed. The straw was disgorged by the machine and had to be loaded on to a separate baler before being carted to a straw stack for later use.

At the end of the summer holidays in 1940 we were allowed a week of afternoons off from school so that the whole harvest could be gathered in.

The domestic side of our working days was simple. We took a drink in a bottle and sandwiches for lunch. Incidentally, no one wore sunglasses and barrier cream was unheard of. We just became browner or more freckled. At the end of the week we were given our pay packet – for each hour actually worked, for those under 14 years, 6d; for the older boys, 8d. It seemed a good reward in those days.

Before the war my father had, as a hobby, a smallholding at the back of our house in Luton Road, Dunstable, where he kept chickens. His main employment was at Vauxhall Motors in Luton. When the war began, in response to national requests for all possible food production, he extended his activities. He started keeping pigs, fed upon 'Tottenham Pudding', made from food wastage and delivered to the house in dustbins. It smelt pretty foul in hot weather. He also kept turkeys and, in due course, bees to produce honey and to ensure fertilization of the fruit trees he had planted. I had the task of doing some of the digging, picking fruit and extracting honey. Supplies of locally produced food were very popular with the neighbours. However, the main supply of eggs, bacon and ham went for central distribution via the rationing system.

# Industry

## INTRODUCTION BY JOAN CURRAN

Ever since the arrival of Waterlow's in 1891, industry in Dunstable had been continually expanding. At the outbreak of the war there were several large factories established in the town, mainly concerned with printing and engineering. At the beginning of the 20th century, following the collapse of the hat manufacturing trade, the Town Council had started a campaign to attract new firms to the area and early arrivals were Harrison Carter's in Bull Pond Lane, Bagshawe's in Church Street and Cross Paperware in High Street South. Some time later, in 1934, AC-Sphinx (later to become AC-Delco) arrived from Birmingham.

Another newcomer in the 1930s was the Empire Rubber Company (1938) in London Road and a firm started by a local man, Instruments and Movements, began in a small way, making precision instruments, in 1934.

From 1939 onwards all factories were subject to government control and most of the local firms could adapt their production lines to produce equipment for the armed forces. But the doillies and paper tableware made at Cross's were definitely not on the government's priority list, and most of the factory site was taken over by Henry Hughes & Son, a London based company making nautical and aeronautical instruments.

In 1942 Vauxhall built a 'shadow factory' in Dunstable, as a precaution against a bomb attack on the main factory at Luton. A year later the Erg Industrial Corporation was directed by the government to Dunstable and made electrical and electronic components at their factory in Matthew Street. (They moved to Luton Road in 1953 and have since closed down).

The new and extended factories all needed workers of course, and there was a great influx of men and women into the town. Some were billeted with local householders and some stayed in the hostels, which were put up in Meadway (where Pipers Croft is today), to house factory workers and some of the employees of the Meteorological Office. Women, of course, formed a large part of the labour force in the war and did many of the jobs previously done by men.

The list of things produced in Dunstable in the war is fascinating and ranges from 'bombardons' made for the Mulberry harbours used for the D-Day landings, caterpillar tracks for Churchill tanks, components for engines, instruments for Spitfires and parts for the famous Mosquito aircraft, to propaganda leaflets to be dropped over Germany, counterfeit currency and documents for the underground movements in Europe.

## INTRODUCTION BY JEAN YATES

Waterlow's opened a new factory in Park Royal, London, in 1936, specially designed to print the Radio Times. A commemorative newspaper gives us details of the company's operations up to this time.

In WWII Waterlow's produced 78 million ration books. They also produced large numbers of stamps and other postal stationery for the Belgian Government during the German occupation, survey maps of France and Belgium and other secret service work for the War Office.

In 1936 at Dunstable there were 1,500 employees. The plant had one of the largest photogravure machines in the world. This process was adopted to deal with British Treasury notes. A large section at Dunstable was devoted to manufacturing stationery as well as the printing. One of the main products was the manufacture of millions of envelopes each week, many of which went to H.M. Government. Enormous quantities of carbon paper, again the bulk used by the Government, was also produced

WATERLOW'S FACTORY *(taken from Waterlow's Commemorative Newspaper)*

at Dunstable along with pastes and gums.

From the Dunstable Official Guide in 1940 we learn that AC-Sphinx quality sparking plugs are made entirely in England. The range of AC-Sphinx quality products included air cleaners, air intake silencers, instrument panels, fuel pumps, oil filters, oil pressure gauges, petrol gauges, speedometers, windscreen wipers and car heaters.

Cross's advertised in the 1940–41 Dunstable Official Guide – 'Table Stationery of Distinction – A Local Product with a World-Wide Reputation.' Cross and Co Ltd., Bigthan Works.

### *Brian Bundy* – the Red and Black

When I started work at Waterlow's in September 1944, they had started to print propaganda leaflets and safe conduct passes for the government. They were red and black and gave the German forces safe conduct if they surrendered to allied troops.

### *Hilda Michell* – Leaflet Drops

I went into the fire service in 1940 until late 1944. I was at Waterlow's before that doing war work, producing leaflets to go over enemy territory, assuring them that all would be well and we would look after them. About a thousand leaflets, tied together with a hole through the middle, so that when they fell they broke apart.

### *Nellie Hackney* – Safety First

At the start of the war I was about 15 years old and working at Waterlow's. If we heard an air-raid siren go, we had to walk out of the factory and head to the brewery for safety. I remember saying, "Good grief, we could all be mowed down crossing the High Street!" Everyone laughed at that.

I then worked at AC-Sphinx before moving to the Speedo Line in the High Street, making speedometers.

### *Doris Perry* – Printing Stamps

I was an evacuee in Houghton Regis. In August I started work at The Empire Rubber Company. They manufactured service respirators, lines of communication, helmet protectors and earplugs! I still bear the scar to the top of my right middle finger from making the earplugs which were punched out of a strip of rubber with a treadle machine. At one point a German aircraft machine-gunned the spotting tower. It was over very quickly and no one was hurt.

I finally worked at Thomas De La Rue's. This I found very interesting. They produced foreign stamps and bank notes – on amazingly efficient German machines. I vividly recall the procedures, five operators to each huge machine, plus the machine minder. De La Rue's was near Waterlow's Ltd.

### *Jean Partridge* – Bomb Sights

I was 16 when the war started. I decided to go into war work rather than the Forces and joined Cross's, which was taken over by Henry Hughes of London. They made scientific instruments.

I mainly tested bombsights for aeroplanes. We had to line the sights up accurately and test them. Wounded airmen would often come down to see the work we were doing. About 40 of us worked in a separate prefabricated building near the water tower called The Hut on the Hill. Not everyone was local. Some people came from London and were billeted in Dunstable and some who were married took over property and then stayed here after the war. I was living with my parents at home and remained at Cross's during and after the war. We worked from 8 am until 5.30 pm Monday to Friday and sometimes on Saturday mornings. A lot of London firms came here and took over different places.

### *P Underwood* – Bomber Domes

At Cross's paper factory in High Street South they built plastic ray domes. On the bottom of some of our bombers we had a big ray dome which had a rotating thing in it. I saw them coming out from the side of the factory. Another little factory made aircraft compasses. I have one, it says on it – 'Inspected 18th April 1942, ACTS Dunstable'. I think that was one of the little factories at the Station Road end of Great Northern Road.

### *Jean Rushton* – Time Cards

I was living at home in Garden Road in Dunstable with my parents and sister. I worked for Henry Hughes who made nautical instruments. I worked in the office, dealing with employees' time cards.

### Carol Mead – **Thermo Plastics**

I lived at Chalk Hill and cycled into Dunstable. In the war I moved to 2
Waterlow Road. I worked for Thermo Plastics at the corner of Station
Road and Great Northern Road.

In the war Cross Paperware was divided into three sections – Thermo
Plastics, Hughes (aircraft instruments) and Cross Paperware. Some catering
materials were still produced, presumably for the NAAFI, and they made
filters said to be used in aircraft engines.

### Christina Scott – **Petrol Coupons**

There was very little petrol, making travelling very difficult. My father
was allocated petrol coupons during the war as he had a garage, but his
livelihood was restricted. He had made munitions in WWI. In WWII,
he turned the workshop of his garage into a training school. Some of his
employees who were too old to go to war, trained young men. It was very
dangerous because the petrol tanks for the pumps were underneath the
property.

### Arnold Dawson – **Tank Tracks**

I worked for a firm called Bagshawe's in Dunstable; quite a medium sized
engineering firm which made conveyors and fabrications amongst other
things. After the war started we became a reserved manufacturer and I
worked in a reserved occupation making tank tracks for armoured vehicles,
chiefly for the Bren Gun carrier. We made well over 2 million of those. We
had a good size machine shop and were fully employed with a lot of skilled
men in the factory, working 12-hour days from 7.30 am to 7.30 pm in the
evening. We also made very large containers – the landing stages for the
Mulberry Harbour, used in the D-Day landings.

### E Speller – **Training**

When the war started I was 14 and working at Waterlow's in Dunstable. I
was paid about £2 per week – good money in those days. Then I found out
that Bagshawe's needed war workers so I went there, fitting chains for tank
tracks. It was a skilled job; we had to oil and bang the chain links into each
other. I then worked in the stores and carried out inspections.

Being employed in a reserved occupation you weren't allowed to join up, so I joined the Training Corps. We trained in the evenings in the school playground and went camping over the weekends in Totternhoe, and had a great time on a farm there. On Sundays we'd march into church. My sister joined the corps but was flung out! She wouldn't do as she was told!

### Dorothy Couldwell - Gas Pipes

My father worked as a gas and water maintenance engineer for Dunstable Gas and Water Company. He repaired mains pipes, etc. When enemy planes were spotted over the coast a bell in our house used to sound, so that he could prepare to report to the works and repair any damaged pipes.

### John Corrie - V J Lights

I started work in Dunstable for a chap who had been at the Empire Rubber Company throughout the war. One of my first jobs (I left school in 1945) was to direct a light on top of a pole in Grove House Gardens, for the

A THANKSGIVING SERVICE held in Grove House Gardens to mark the end of the Second World War, August 15th 1945 *(DG)*

celebration of VJ Day. The fellow I was with, Dick, was erecting this light. We had a ladder up the flagpole in the middle of the green. He got to the top; the pole snapped at the bottom and down came Dick. It then snapped over him again. He wasn't very well for a long time. The Council turned up with a new flagpole, which was erected and a light attached to the top, all for the dancing and celebrations that took place that night.

### *Mary Cresswell* - War Work

My father received a letter telling him that he had to go and do some kind of war work and was allocated a job at the Empire Rubber Company. He was made a foreman in the industrial trimming shop but he also used to bring home stacks of rubber work. We'd help him trim windscreen wipers and all sorts of other things. However, in 1936 he'd started selling insurance, so my poor mother had to do this insurance round every week. Sometimes I went with her and we cycled from Dunstable to Totternhoe, Eaton Bray, Edlesborough, Stanbridge and Hockliffe. On Friday evenings dad used to go with her and call on Houghton Regis and on Saturdays they went to Luton. I used to have to look after my sister, do the housework and get the dinner ready for their return. Mum was a seamstress and took in lots of sewing, dressmaking and hat-work. For the hat making, she operated what was called a 17 Guinea machine. Straw plaits were delivered to our house and she would sew them together to make hats. They were then picked up and taken to Luton to be 'blocked' – they were very fashionable in their day.

I left school in 1943 and went to work for Percival's at Luton airport. They made Mosquito planes; it was quite exciting seeing these aeroplanes. I even managed to sit in the cockpit of the first Mosquito that was built on the production line! While I was there a V2 rocket came over and landed in Luton. It was very frightening because we could see the vapour trail just above our office block.

I'd had training in London to become a comptometer operator and in 1945 I found out about a job that was going at AC-Sphinx in Dunstable. As I was doing war work for Percival's they weren't allowed to release me, so I had to go to an industrial court in Luton. AC-Sphinx represented me and I won the day and began work in their comptometer office.

### Monica Hart - Herbs

I was 14 when I left school and went to work at the top of what was called Nicholas Way, in an office with my uncle. This was an old blacksmith's house that my uncle had taken over and either side of the building there were two yards where dried herbs were kept. Drying kilns and racks were kept further up the road. Thyme and mint were stored there.

Many people came to the yard with herbs to sell. The children used to collect dandelions and other herbs and bring them in; we had several loads during the day and we also bought them from the door. Pennies and tuppences in old money, I collated it all and then took it to the bank. I used to take it to Barclays bank in a blue bag and didn't think anything of it. I wouldn't like to do it these days, not all that money.

### Roy Turner - at the Assembly Shop

I left school in 1944 and went to work just before D-Day for a firm called Grice and Young. I worked in Nicholas Lane in the assembly shop. There was a small factory around the corner called the Boat House and that's where they made wooden 4 seater dinghies with oars for the Royal Navy. I was on assembly first, working on the undercarriage for Percival Proctors and then on the tail towing bars which fitted on the back of tractors and the front of the aeroplane; that's how you towed it along on the airfield.

I was an apprentice and had the job of going round and collecting people's lists of what they wanted from the shops – cigarettes and things. A new factory had been built opposite Albert Street on Kent's Meadow and my job was to go there. One day I pedalled up to the factory and no one was working, they were all sitting and laughing. I walked in to the canteen and a lady there called Doll said, "What are you doing here? Don't you know the war's over?" They forgot to tell our part of the factory. I pedalled back down and rushed in and told everyone. I bet nobody's pedalled down there faster than I did. One lady bawled her eyes out because her husband was away in the forces. I couldn't understand that at my age.

That evening I went to the youth club at Chew's House. Nothing was arranged but then we started to see people walking down to the town. A man came on to the front of the town hall playing a trumpet and everybody sang along to it. They switched all the lights on and opened up the gardens. Everybody was dancing; Dunstable was more relaxed that day than any

CHEW'S HOUSE, High Street South, Dunstable *(DDLHS)*

other that I can remember. I got told off because I was late coming home, but it was a fantastic feeling. The Union cinema switched all the coloured lights on and it was beautiful. The next day we went to Luton and stood outside the town hall where they put loudspeakers outside for us to listen to Churchill's speech. Afterwards we went to the pictures. It was a fantastic feeling.

### *Una Basham* - Machinery

Dad and numerous other men in the road worked at Harrison Carter's in Bull Pond Lane. They made disintegrators and crushing machinery; he was a wheelwright and did a certain amount of out-work at factories in London, the Midlands and the North.

## *Morris Cook* - **Buses and Bombs**

I started an indentured apprenticeship at Vauxhall, Luton, in May 1940. The weekly ticket for the bus from Dunstable town hall to Vauxhall cost 3 shillings and sixpence for 12 journeys of 7 miles. Petrol was rationed and so the buses were very busy. They were mostly rear-entry double deckers with a large low platform and a vertical grab rail. The bus did not always stop because passengers leapt on and off as the bus slowed, but I never saw or heard of any casualties. The homeward journeys were the most crowded and the bus was full when no more passengers could crowd into the gangways, upstairs or down or on to the platform. The platform would scrape the road on sharp bends and passengers sometimes felt the rear wheels bump the under body. The conductor was seldom able to fight his way through this crowd to collect fares, so for those without weekly tickets he took the money as passengers got off, no one waited for a ticket so it was up to the conductor how many tickets he issued afterwards.

I was caught up in an unannounced bombing raid in August 1940. I was in the apprentice workshop and was approaching the open doors to see what was causing all the rattling when I found myself colliding backwards with my workbench about 30 feet behind me. The commissionaire, whose hut was near those doors came running in shouting, "Don't go out, they're machine gunning!" So we crouched under our benches until assured all was quiet and then trooped out to the shelters. One bomb had fallen in the road, which our building fronted; the front entrance commissionaire was killed and some apprentices were injured by shrapnel and flying glass as the wooden shuttering over the windows was all blown away. As there had been no warning there was also no "all clear", so when it was time to go home we peered out, all seemed to be quiet so we headed home. My bus ticket and other items I carried were in my jacket in my locker and I wanted to change out of my overalls into my jacket. The entrances were closed and guarded as there were unexploded bombs around. I found a pair of doors which were barred and never used had been blown open and so I got through there and changed. We stayed home until the unexploded bombs had been cleared and then returned to work. On return I was informed that one unexploded bomb was found leaning against the wall behind my locker.

### Patricia Morgan – Tea Time

My Dad was at Vauxhall in a reserved occupation and was at work the night they were bombed. They hit the canteen and my Dad was so angry that he hadn't had a cup of tea. They had gone all night without a cup of tea because these \*\*\*Germans had dropped these \*\*\* bombs on the canteen, and he made a huge pot of tea, saying he didn't care how much he was using. After drinking his tea he went to bed, and then complained that he had to get up several times during the day, and our loo was out the back.

He was working in the experimental section at Vauxhall. They were producing 'Churchills' at the time when they were trying to stop sand affecting the engines. He was a machine setter but he was involved in technical stuff. He was also in the Home Guard and we used to try and get his Bren gun, so he had it chained into the wardrobe.

CHURCHILL RESTORED TANK (BCC)

### Mrs Kelly (née West) – False Alarm

My father worked for George Kent in Luton where they made steering gear for tanks. On the day when Commer Cars was bombed there were early rumours that Kent's had been hit, though this later proved to be untrue. I heard the rumour in school and was very distressed that I was not allowed to go home to be with my mother.

## *Mary Owen* – **Whiting Works**

At the outbreak of war I was living in Tring Road, Dunstable, on the corner of Totternhoe Road. My father was an air raid warden during the war, having retired from his business of whiting manufacturing; the same profession as his father and grandfather before him. The factory was based on the corner of Green Lane and Tring Road in Dunstable. Only men worked there; it was very manual and very messy. They used to get hold of a lump of chalk, mix it together with water in a vat, stir regularly and then leave it to stand for about a fortnight, emerging as a sort of pasty which was then rolled into balls or flat cakes in the men's hands. It was left to dry overnight and sold to various manufacturers, one of whom was the Fry's Chocolate factory. It was also used in the manufacture of domestic ware, baths I think, I'm not sure. After my father retired he sold his business to a gentleman who continued to use the same system until about 1949 and then it was just closed down.

I was working in Luton for a large insurance company, the Phoenix Insurance Company, when war broke out. I worked in a big sub office with two other men who were both eventually called up into the services. I took over the office for them and worked there all the time throughout the war on my own. When bombers came over Luton during the day and dropped bombs on the Vauxhall works (then making tanks) and on the town in general, we had to go down into the cellar underneath my offices. We shared this with 2 or 3 other firms; we all met down there and sat looking at each other for an hour or two, not very thrilling! I did some fire watching in Luton in the big factories there. Sometimes it felt very ghostly when you went inside some of the empty old buildings.

## *Arthur Holland* – **Aircraft Parts**

I lived in Totternhoe and started work at the age of 14 at the London Gliding Club. At the outbreak of war, then aged 16, I went to work at Grice and Young's, a small engineering firm who had a factory in Albion Street. They expanded rapidly during the war and also had factories or workshops on the corner of Matthew Street, Albion Street and in Nicholas Lane (between Charlie Cole's and the White Hart), and another factory, built towards the end of the war, near Garden Road. They also had a factory at Christchurch, near Bournemouth.

Eventually they had a work force of about 200 people in Dunstable, some of them travelling in from other places. One, at least, travelled up from London every day and some were recruited from the government training schools, which were set up in the war. The firm made parts for Mosquitoes, the Hawser Glider and other aircraft, including undercarriages for the Percival Proctor, a training aircraft.

Working in a reserved occupation I was not called up until January 1945. I remember the bombs falling near the Memorial Hall in Totternhoe and I remember a gas main being set alight at the bottom of Lancot Hill.

## MAJOR H.R. NORTHOVER OF BISLEY HOUSE, KENSWORTH
### Extracts from his papers by kind permission of Reading University and his family

During my First World War service in France I was awarded the Military Cross and mentioned in Despatches. I came back to England and worked at Enfield Small Arms factory on many machine gun improvements. I took over the modification of 2,200 Lewis machine guns for the Enfield Authorities. On completion of this work I was instructed to report to the RAF, in view of carrying out machine gun modifications for them, as they were in great difficulties over machine gun failures. I had 400 personnel working on machine gun testing etc., and was then promoted Major and Squadron Leader. The war ended and I was awarded the O.B.E.

I received financial awards from England and Canada to help perfect my various inventions, but needed to find employment to supplement my pension. I thought of clay pigeons. These were all imported from the USA, so I experimented and invented machinery and started a small works employing ex-soldiers, or their boys. It was a hard struggle, my money gradually dwindled and then I asked another man (a big user of clay pigeons) to come in and help. He agreed, and we started a factory at Perivale and gradually built up an output from one to four million clay pigeons a year. I was selected to go on a team to shoot clay pigeons at the 1936 Olympic Games in Berlin. Whilst there, I saw all the German preparations for war. I came back and said to my partner, "We have to move from Perivale, there is going to be a war; the Germans are working for it. We must build a new works away from London and be ready for it. If war comes, the RAF will need clay pigeons for training."

He opposed me, but I acted alone and borrowed £8,000 from Barclays Bank in Hanwell. I came out of London to Kensworth, near Dunstable, and built a larger and up to date works for clay pigeon making. I finished this in May as war broke out in September. In less than one year we were working round the clock to supply the RAF, Ministry of Supply, the S.A.A.F., and later the American Air Force. My foresight had without doubt placed Great Britain in the position to use these targets, which they would not have been able to do as the old Perivale works was bomb wrecked, and I was the only maker in the Empire.

The Home Guard was formed but with no weapons. I was told to attend a lecture and hear instructions on the making of Molotov Cocktails. The best a man could throw was across an ordinary road. I saw the futility of this and started to invent, design, make, and put to trial a weapon that would do this. Then came the S.I.P. or phosphorous bomb. I fired the first of these from my weapon at the request of the wartime Prime Minister and War Cabinet. I was ordered to go to the War Office early one morning, and from there I was taken to No 10 Downing Street with my projector. I had the honour of showing and explaining it to the War Cabinet. I can remember Winston Churchill and Anthony Eden bringing Mr Morrison and Mr Bevan along to me, and I explained the weapon to them. Mr Churchill said, "What do you expect for doing this?" I said, "That is in the hands of the government." He said, "You won't be forgotten." Mr Bevan said, "Can you get all the labour you need?" I said, "Yes." He replied, "If you have any labour troubles, write to me personally." (I had none). Mr Morrison told me to write to him personally if I could not get enough materials. The weapon was put on trial before the War Council. I put a tank out of commission with a single shot, and 21,000 of these weapons were made. Some went to Africa, the others were issued to the Home Guard all over the British Isles; it was the most popular and efficient weapon they had.

### David Grant - my Father, Arthur George Grant, in the Drawing Office

My father moved us from Newcastle-on-Tyne to 15 Borough Road, Dunstable, in the early days of the war. He was in a protected occupation as a design draughtsman for Spillers the flour millers, and was involved in the war effort designing the flour mills that were being constructed around the country. This proved to be useful during the food-rationing period, as he often brought home some freshly baked bread samples from the flour manufacturing trials at the mills.

My father worked in a drawing office situated in the old laundry of Beechwood House (near Markyate). Beechwood House was a large mansion in extensive grounds and he would sometimes sit me on a seat on his bicycle crossbar and take me to his work. I recall there were aircraft, Spitfires I think, parked underneath the overhanging branches of the large trees so that they were hidden from view from the air. I believe there was some sort of aircraft repair works going on there and I was

ARTHUR GRANT *(DGR)*

told there were some 'wooden mock-up' aircraft parked in the open, away from the real aircraft to act as decoys to the enemy aircraft flying over. He had lots of work drawings, not all of them flour mills, as I suspect they may have been involved with drawing 'other items' to do with the war effort as well. The drawings were on a linen type of cloth for stability, which I think may have been recycled from used flour bags, as paper was in short supply at this time.

## *Derek Bonfield* – the **Lime Lorry**

My father had a haulage business, and in 1940 his driver left to work for Robins, the whiting people. Father at the same time was taken ill with rheumatic fever, so at 16 I went on the lorry delivering lime from Totternhoe to London and various other places. At night I worked on the farm, helping my mother. The lime was used to build surface shelters, as cement would crack because it wasn't flexible, but with a lime mortar mixture, it held. They also used it to repair buildings that had been bombed.

I drove through Dunstable with the lorry every day in the war, but didn't really stop in the town. I used to take a lot of lime around the area of

Cheshunt, Hoddesdon and Goffs Oak. The lime came from The Greystone Lime Company, which was very busy during the war with all production spoken for. The lime has very high silica content and makes good cement. They used it mixed with horsehair to make their own plaster on the building sites. It was live lime – quicklime. By the end of the war there was gypsum – plaster in bags.

One night one of the lime kilns exploded. The fire door was quite large and heavy and worked on a pulley; it weighed 2 or 3cwt and blew out about 100yds. Fortunately the chap on duty was barrowing the ash away from another kiln that night and no one was hurt. They had to rebuild the chimney. In 1947 they acquired their own transport at the lime works.

The German planes used to fly up the (Thames) estuary towards Ford's (a huge factory manufacturing vehicles, and a prime target). The Becontree estate, made up of roads and roads of houses built for the Ford workers, regularly had slates blown off their roofs. It was more dangerous in the latter stages of the war. I had a near miss with a rocket in London, it did my ears in. Everybody carried on though. There'd be a warning but everything would be operating, buses running and so on.

### *Colin Bourne* – **Index Printers**

Back in Dunstable, the town hadn't changed much. I went back to my old job at World Books but found it was completely different and didn't enjoy it. At that particular time Index Printers, who were timetable specialists in Dunstable, started a new publication in June 1946 called the ABC Air Guide. I joined them in January 1947 and stayed there for nearly 40 years working on the Air Guide, the history of civil aviation and scheduled services across the world, on a monthly publication that grew from a journal of 200 pages to one consisting of 2,200 pages.

Further reading:

'Old Trades of Dunstable'

1 Dale's Dubbin & Flemon's Herbs by Colin Bourne

2 Shops & Markets by Fred Moore & Don Kemp

3 The Whiting Works by Joan Curran

4 Bagshawe's & Cross's by Colin Bourne

5 Straw Hats and Bonnets by Joan Curran

# Childhood Memories

## INTRODUCTION BY SUE KING

Life was a mixture of emotions for children growing up during the Second Word War. Memories of those times remain with them to the present day.

Scores of children grew up with fathers absent for long periods of time while serving in the armed forces. Read Shirley Ansell's reunion with her father, who had been away from home for so long she could no longer remember him. Many mothers volunteered to perform fire-watching duties or worked in factories making weapons and munitions and children were expected to help out much more in the home.

At the start of the war many toy factories turned their assembly lines over to the manufacture of military supplies and as a result, children learned how to make their own playthings. Other hobbies included spotting both British and enemy aircraft, trips to the California swimming pool and collecting the parachutes from flares that were tested up on the Downs. Other 'treasures' to collect consisted of shrapnel, badges, even incendiary bombs! During 1942/43 the build up of American troops in Britain continued and a popular pastime, as convoys passed through the town, was chanting, "Got any gum, chum?"

The BBC radio programme 'Children's Hour' hosted by 'Uncle Mac', was one of the most popular shows broadcast, entertaining children with plays and stories, of which 'Toytown' was one of the best loved. Despite paper being rationed during the war, comics were still published as they helped to brighten up the lives of children. The Dandy and another popular comic The Beano helped the war effort by showing their favourite characters coming out on top in encounters with the Germans and their allies. Other popular comics were the Wizard, Rover and Hotspur for boys and Crystal for girls. Books were popular and in 1942 the first of Enid Blyton's 'Famous Five' books was published.

From 26th July 1942 sweet rationing was introduced. Ration coupons were issued to children allowing them to buy a few ounces a week. There were many varieties of boiled sweets to choose from, such as pear drops, sherbet lemons, floral gums and acid drops. Toffee was available, as was chocolate, but it was 'Ration Chocolate' and by all accounts barely edible.

A visit to Whipsnade Zoo was considered a special treat, and many stories tell of paying to sit in the cockpit of a captured Messerschmitt in Grove House Gardens. Numerous children joined the Cubs, Brownies, Scouts or Guides, army or air training corps and sang in local choirs. Miss Olive Brown created the first Girls' Training Corps, Nautical Training Corps and a Dunstable Girls' Club. The Dunstable Girls' Training Corps band of drums and cavalry trumpets was believed to be the only one of its kind in Britain.

Memories of the end of the war are particularly vivid. Don't miss the stories of long-awaited celebrations, the Edward Street VE Day street party and the return of bananas!

### Rob Cutler – I saw the King!

The Second World War was an exciting time for us boys in the village of Dagnall. If truth be told, we would have been disappointed if war hadn't been declared; we were really looking forward to it in one sense, although I suppose we shouldn't have been. I remember Sunday school was disbanded for the day and we didn't go to church at night in case we were bombed.

At the beginning of the war the ARP wardens used to blow a whistle to warn of an impending air-raid before the sirens were put in place. If the wind was in the right direction we could hear Dunstable's siren but the animals at the zoo didn't like the sirens; you could hear the lions roar. At school, when we were all talking in the shelters, we never did hear the all clear go.

My school in Dagnall was situated at the crossroads and one day we saw lots of army chaps with massive radios. They said, "If you stay here and behave yourself, you'll see someone important." That was the first time we saw the King. He was on his way to Ashridge, where the hospital was situated. I thought how small the King looked when I saw him in the back of a massive black Rolls Royce, with Army dispatch riders on motorbikes. A year or two later I saw him again in Ashridge, just after Arnhem I think. A lot of men were sent to Ashridge for convalescence and we had to stand back in a gateway as he went past. General Charles de Gaulle stayed near there, just past Ashridge House, for most of the war.

### Shirley Ansell - on the Train

We would often visit London during the war as mum wanted to see the family and she would take me with her. We would get the bus to Luton Station and then catch the train. I was always very frightened when the train came puffing and rumbling into the station and would hide behind mum. The train was always full of troops and there was never any room to sit. Sometimes a soldier would give up his seat so that we could sit down. When we arrived at St. Pancras station we would catch the no. 73 bus. This would take us along the Thames embankment and past Big Ben and the Houses of Parliament. Everything looked dull and dismal; covered in camouflage with barrage balloons in the sky to stop the buildings being attacked from the air. I would look at the bomb sites with wild flowers growing out of the brickwork. On one occasion when we visited my Nanny Howard towards the end of the war, we were sitting talking by the fire when there was a terrible explosion. All the windows rattled and somehow we ended up under the table. We heard later that a V2 rocket had blown up a few streets away. I was so frightened that I never went to London again until after the war.

Once, when we were coming home from one of these visits, the train came to a halt in one of the tunnels a few miles out from St Pancras Station. We sat in the carriage in the semi-darkness for a very long time, when a Guard came along to tell us that there was a bombing raid going on overhead. I think mum thought that it was too dangerous for me to go again, so I would stay with Uncle Sid and Auntie Win.

One day mum said that the war was over and that my dad would be home soon. Several weeks went by and we had a street party to celebrate the end of the war. Mum received a telegram to say that Dad was on a bus in Luton and would like us to meet him at the bus stop opposite the Grammar School in Dunstable. Mum was at work, so Auntie Win dressed me in my tartan skirt and red school blazer and Uncle Sid and I went to the bus stop. I was very nervous as I could not remember him at all because he had been away for so long. After a while a bus came along and stopped at the bus stop and a soldier got off. I knew it was my dad as his number was on his kit bag and I had memorised it. As we walked up Union Street I felt very proud of him; everybody was clapping their hands and saying, "Is this your Dad, Shirley?" Auntie Win was waiting for him and had prepared a boiled egg for him. He would often say, "I had just come home from the war and all I got was a boiled egg!" I don't think he realized that eggs where very hard to come by and food was on ration.

SHIRLEY sitting next to her mother, with a picture of her father beside them *(SA)*

## J Dunbar – the White Lion

My dad, Kenneth James Dunbar, was a clerk of works at the Air Ministry Works Dept. He had four postings and I think he was sent from Bentley Priory to cover up the White Lion at Whipsnade. He had to lay miles of chestnut fencing on to the Lion, flat on the chalk. Then they covered the fencing with topsoil.

## J Reason – Memories of the California Swimming Pool

I had a season ticket to the California swimming pool up on the Downs. This had been built in 1937. It was an open-air pool and it was straight out of the 1930s American concept of what such a facility should look like. The pool was 33 yards long and 11 yards wide. A high diving-board was in the middle with a spring-board on one side and a set board on the other. Those two boards were the same height, at about four feet.

On one side of the pool, just out of the shallow end, was a water chute. Set back from the side of the pool were two stepped terraces, and those were comfortably furnished with solidly built wooden benches each capable of seating four people. There was a lot of land around it too, much more than an acre. It had been a chalk pit but work on that had been stopped for environmental reasons. This made it possible to concrete an area big enough for basketball or netball, and the ground rising up to the Downs beyond was terraced for sunbathing. On a good Sunday in the summer holidays, the California pool attracted more than a thousand swimmers and sunbathers. Some even found their way to it from France.

## Pat Morgan – to the Party

I remember the fun. I lived in Great Northern Road and we used to go up on Blow's Downs and play, we were away all day. Mum gave us sandwiches and a box of Ministry of Food orange juice. If the Home Guard were on manoeuvres we had to go home. To us, the war was quite good fun because we had no restrictions.

We went to the VE party in Great Northern Road and we also went to the VE party in Garden Road because we had two aunts living there who had no children. Park Road, Grove Road and Downs Road all had their own VE Day parties.

## EXTRACTS FROM OLIVE BROWN'S ALBUMS

### Founder of the first Girls' Training Corps, Girls' Nautical Training Corps and Dunstable Girls' Club

**No 186 (Dunstable) Company – Girls' Training Corp's** first parade was on 1st May 1942, the corps having been formed in March. Miss Olive Brown was the Commandant.

At the first enrolment ceremony of the 1st Dunstable Company Girls' Training Corps in the grounds of the Catholic Church, the Mayoress Mrs Sharman, president of the unit, presented 11 badges. The Mayoress said that at their first public parade on United Nations day, their appearance evoked much favourable comment.

Reporting on the month's activities Miss Brown said that 5 parades had been held and classes included drills, lectures in anti-gas training, fire fighting and incendiary bombs and training in despatch carrying had begun. The Dunstable company was the first such unit in Bedfordshire and was affiliated to the national body. It was a pre-service corps for girls aged between 16 and 18 and provided a semi-military training. Later a junior section was formed and girls of 14 –16 were allowed to join.

About 80 people enjoyed a dinner in the Catholic hall to celebrate the 1st birthday of No 186 (Dunstable) Company Girls' Training Corps in April 1943. The dinner was cooked and served by the N.C.O.s.

On July 27th 1943 the GTC paraded at Burr Street School in front of their president, the Mayoress. After the parade, "the girls performed various evolutions in one of the playgrounds, under the command of a Home Guard N.C.O. The Company now comprises 14 cadets and six officers."

Various fund raising events were held to raise money to start a band. The first public duty for the drum and trumpet band was at Cadets Day on May 6th 1945, when the band headed the parade to the drumhead service held in Grove House Gardens.

## Girls' Nautical Training Corps No 15 (Dunstable) Unit

Commanding officer: Miss O M Brown
Administrative officer: Mrs E M Love
Headquarters: Training Ship Preston, The Old Mill, West St, Dunstable

A bottle of champagne crashing against the sides of Bedfordshire's oldest windmill marked the transition of the old structure into the Sea Cadet and GNTC training Ship, 'Lionel Preston'. Admiral Sir Lionel Preston said, "Dunstable has never launched a ship before!" when he addressed the units of Dunstable, Luton, Biggleswade, Welwyn and Edmonton. The Sea Cadets and GNTC had been using the Mill for 18 months before this opening.

In the same year as the Olympics were last held in London the cadets and GNTC had paid off £500 of the original mortgage after purchasing the Mill two years previously for £1,500.

## 1946 press cuttings: Old Mill in Nautical Dress

The Old Mill in West Street has survived many vicissitudes since it performed its original function 300 years ago when, as Admiral Sir Lionel Preston remarked in opening a fete there, "The old miller was grinding grain when it was more plentiful without the trouble of controls, queues and B.U.s."

In an article entitled 'They were not at Sea, Fete Aboard the T/S "Lionel Preston" ', Dr I Foster, recently back from the Navy, judged the ankle competition which attracted about a dozen entrants. The prizes were fully-fashioned silk stockings. This was a fete where the Girls' Nautical Training Corps joined forces with the Sea Cadets.

The GNTC band established just over two years previously made a BBC recording in early 1946.

Also in 1946, Miss Brown escorted a GNTC party to Norway and then wrote in an article, "The shops were full of goods and though many were on coupons they were somehow available if one was English. Lack of coupons was no obstacle and all the party of 20 Dunstable GNTC managed to get silk stockings." They had a most uncomfortable journey on a Dutch troopship but enjoyed a marvellous holiday.

## Dunstable Girls' Club

3rd March 1943 – Dunstable Girls' Club elected a new committee. 'Riders to the Sea' and Irish drama was performed by members of the drama class at the Drama Rally held at the Town Hall on Friday. A social was held at Burr Street School on Monday and another will be held next Friday.

'To any would-be members I would like to explain that the club meets at Burr Street School on Monday and Thursday evenings and is open to girls between the ages of 14 and 20. Activities include dancing, rambling, hockey, net-ball, drama, P.T. etc., and we are always glad to welcome new members.'

In August 1943, 20 members went Youth Hostelling in the Lake District and in September the drama section produced a three-act play, 'Quiet Wedding', under the auspices of Dunstable Association of Youth Organisations. A month later the play was performed again at Britain Street School for two evenings and £40 was raised for the Dunstable Borough Gazette's Readers' Forces Fund.

Under the heading 'Girls' Club's Happy Year' the Borough Gazette reported on their AGM. The club leader Miss Olive Brown presided. The secretary's annual report mentions the athletic sports activities when under D.A.Y.O., "the club won the challenge cup for the second year running and also the triumph of the play. Not only did it raise money for the Forces fund but also produced £24.10s for the Merchant Navy Fund. Since then the club had also won another cup at the D.A.Y.O. Drama Rally."

On 12th May 1944 the Borough Gazette reported that a very interesting talk on American youth had been given by Sgt Hugh Hawkins of the U.S Army. Club members had been for a cycle ride to Ashridge with members of the Pioneer Boys Club. They had performed their play 'O.H.M.S.' at Whipsnade on 29th April in aid of their 'Salute the Soldier Week'. Fancy cookery classes were started at Britain Street on Wednesdays under the instruction of Miss Murgatroyd and continued until early June.

The second annual Empire Youth Rally took place in May 1944. Various youth organisations marched along the High Street to the Union Cinema. Miss Olive Brown was the District Youth Leader. In July 1944 the A.T.C won the boys section trophy at the D.A.Y.O. sports held at Waterlow's Sports Field. Priory Social Club won the girls championship with the Girls' Training Corps coming second and the Girls' Club third. In the Schools Relay Race Acland Central, a school evacuated to Dunstable from London, came second.

In August 1944 a choir was started known as 'The Girls' Choir' under the conductor Mr R Allen. It was proposed to hold a crooning competition at a social in November.

In September it was off to North Wales Youth Hostelling, and October saw the start of doll making classes. This was to help provide articles to sell at the bazaar on 11th December. Enough money was raised at the bazaar to buy a radiogram for the club. The annual Christmas party was held on Thursday 28th December.

In 1945 to celebrate victory the Girls' Club invited 62 of their smaller friends to a tea in Burr Street school hall. In August 1945 the first athletic sports meeting promoted by the Dunstable Youth Council was held on Cross & Co.'s sports ground.

# A COLLECTION OF PHOTOGRAPHS DONATED FROM THE ALBUMS OF OLIVE BROWN

*above* COMMANDANT OLIVE BROWN *(OB) (DG)*

*opposite above* WATERLOW'S SPORTS DAY *(OB) (DG)*

*opposite below* GNTC *(OB) (DG)*

PRIORY CHURCH *(OB) (DG)*

GNTC BAND *(OB) (DG)*

PARADE *(OB) (DG)*

GTC marching to Whipsnade *(OB) (DG)*

Sports BURR STREET SCHOOL 1944 *(OB) (DG)*

GTC September 1942 TANKS WEEK *(OB) (DG)*

YOUTH RALLY May 1943 *(OB) (DG)*

# D·A·Y·O
# First YOUTH RALLY

### in the UNION CINEMA, DUNSTABLE
### SUNDAY, MAY 23rd, 1943

## *Souvenir Programme*

The Procession, marshalled by Major S. Cadman, Home Guard, will pass the Saluting Base at the Town Hall at 2.45 and should arrive at the cinema for the Programme to commence at 3 p.m.

1. CHAIRMAN'S REMARKS

2. PRESENTATION OF D.A.Y.O. AWARDS by HIS WORSHIP THE MAYOR (Alderman A. E. Sharman)

3. FLAGS OF OUR ALLIES. An Ensemble presented by and Narrative spoken by F. L. WELCH, ESQ., Hon. Organiser of the British Council

4. THE NATIONAL ANTHEM

5. HIS WORSHIP THE MAYOR will introduce the Speaker,

6. SQUADRON LEADER SEABOURNE, R.A.F.

7. ALLIED YOUTH REPRESENTATIVES of the following Countries will speak : (1) AMERICA, (2) CHINA, (3) FRANCE, (4) HOLLAND, (5) INDIA, (6) NORWAY, (7) POLAND, (8) RUSSIA

8. MALTA SPEAKS

9. CANON G. W. CLARKSON, Rector of Dunstable, will lead up to

10. THE ROLL CALL

11. BUNYAN'S PILGRIM HYMN (*see back of Programme*)

---

*Music by an Augmented Band of Dunstable Salvation Army*

---

As you leave the Cinema, you are invited to put your hands in your pockets and deposit your loose cash with Members of the Girls' Training Corps who will be at the exits with Collecting Boxes. Any surplus, after defraying expenses, will be handed over to the International Red Cross, so please give liberally.

DUNSTABLE YOUTH ORGANISATIONS

Present

# QUIET WEDDING

A COMEDY IN 3 ACTS

by ESTHER McCRACKEN

on

## WEDNESDAY, JANUARY 5TH 1944.

and

## THURSDAY, JANUARY 6TH 1944.

Doors open 7.15          -          Commence 7.45

at

BLE TOWN HALL

AID OF MERCHANT NAVY FUNDS.

AMME   THREEPENCE

D.A.Y.O PROGRAMMES
– various (OB)

D.A.Y.O. invites you to their

# Youth Rally

## UNION CINEMA,

## Sunday, May 21ST, 3 p.m.

Speakers :

# LORD LUKE of Pavenham

## Corpl. L. A. HUNT

Canadian Army

## GRAND PROCESSION OF YOUTH

(Marshal : Lt. Col. S. Cadman, Home Guard)
will start from Great Northern Road at 2.30;
Salute will be taken outside the Town Hall by
Lord Luke of Pavenham.

Admission free to the Cinema—Give your support to the Youth of
Dunstable.   Collection in order to defray expenses.

ENTERPRISE WORKS, DUNSTABLE.

GNTC *(OB) (DG)*

GNTC Training Ship 'Preston' *(OB) (DG)*

*above* GTC BAND Drummers *(OB) (DG)*

*opposite above* GTC BAND Trumpeters *(OB) (DG)*

*opposite below* GTC UNITED NATIONS DAY 1942 – first public appearance *(OB) (DG)*

### Tony Woodhouse - the First Firework

Most of my toys (tanks, guns and ships mostly) were wooden, made by my grandfather who was an ironmonger by trade. He was a foreman at the foundry at Harrison Carters. He retired in 1938 but returned to work throughout the war years after many skilled men were called up. Part of the foundry was closed and was used by the war department (WD) for storage. The remaining part was used exclusively to produce castings for the Admiralty

On VE night I sat on the entrance to the public air-raid shelter near the town hall and watched people dancing in the street. Someone found an enormous Catherine Wheel. It was wonderful. The first firework I'd ever seen!

WEDNESDAY 15TH AUGUST In this picture, children are queuing on Keep's Corner at the junction of West Street, to buy fireworks to celebrate VJ Day. *(DG)*

### P Underwood - an Accident

I was always interested in aviation and the increase in air activity was quite phenomenal but we boys knew them all. If you wanted aircraft recognition, you didn't have to ask an expert, you could go to a 12-year-old boy. We knew just what mark it was, when it was made, how many guns it had, what colour it was and we didn't have to see them, we could tell by the sound. There's something about aircraft recognition – the way it sits in the air, its poise. There was plenty to do, plenty of airfields, we all had bicycles. We used to go to Luton airport; Napier's and Percival's factories were up there. Later we used to cycle over to Woburn where they stored a lot of bombers – Stirlings and Halifaxes all in the park. I think they were there to scrap.

In 1943 I went to college in London, coming home at weekends. I was in digs and the mini-blitz was on. Nothing like the 1940 blitz, but it was an exciting time with a lot of noise and air raids. I woke up one morning to see a bomb sticking out of my next door neighbour's garden that hadn't gone off. I went to college and when I went back, it had gone.

We used to pick up incendiary bombs off the street. We were all adept at unscrewing the nose-cap and shaking out the magnesium powder and then they're fairly safe. However, there were accidents. One night there was an air raid and an incendiary bomb hit the house I was in and started burning in the loft. It was fizzing away and we needed to put it out before it set the house on fire. For some reason we hadn't got a stirrup pump, and while this was fizzing away in the roof, we were rushing up and down the street asking people if they'd got a stirrup pump. It was like Dad's Army, absolutely true. Eventually we got a bucket of water and put the bomb out, just as it burnt through the ceiling and fell through on to the floor of the bedroom beneath.

I often stopped in central London overnight on my way home to Dunstable from south London. I slept in Green Park in the summer. London at night in the war was quite fantastic when there wasn't a raid on. It was so full of servicemen and women. I was in London wandering around Leicester Square in the middle of the night when I heard a piano. I followed the noise and there was someone in the middle of the road playing Chopin on a grand piano. It was an incredible experience in the middle of war.

Trafalgar Square was always so full; I loved it. Servicemen from all over, Americans, Canadians, Indians, men, women, all so young. I was 15 or 16, just wandering about watching what was going on. When I go to Trafalgar Square now, I still see these ghosts, they're still there.

### *Pam Buckle* – Celebrations

We were all delighted when VE day came and there were many celebrations. However, a great friend of ours had a husband who had been a Japanese PoW and we still had no news of him at all. Our concerns were for him and for other PoWS. We had a very big celebration for VJ day. I went with my family and stood in front of the old town hall with lots of other people, very happily waving flags. The Mayor and councillors came out and cheered along with us.

### Paul Heley – the Romance of Battle

We studied photographs, pictures, diagrams and sketches of guns, ships and planes on both sides and spoke knowledgeably amongst ourselves about Spitfires versus Messerschmitts, Lancasters versus Heinkels, and so on. We knew the badges of the different regiments and branches of the armed services; the equivalent ranks between the Army, Royal Navy and Royal Air Force; the roles of the 'hybrid' services such as the Royal Marines, the Commandos, Fleet Air Arm, and RAF Regiment. We heard the propaganda broadcasts given by the infamous traitor Lord Haw-Haw; we joined in the singing (awful when one looks back) of songs about Hitler and Goering and Goebbels, (they were always deficient in some physical attribute, I remember) and about White Cliffs of Dover and Meeting Again Someday.

For much of the earlier part of the war, Britain could easily have been beaten and the situation was pretty grim. But we kids didn't appreciate such subtleties; we were too engrossed with the romance of battle.

We collected anything vaguely connected with the war. In particular, every boy had a shrapnel collection in which any twisted piece of metal would be attributed to some German bomb or a bit of blown up Italian tank – the stories were fantastic and completely fanciful. But who was to know what was right and what was wrong? And who cared anyway?

We also collected badges, buttons, fragments of uniform, a forage cap or a piece of uniform with stripes on it – especially prized. We would polish the badges until they shone much more than the original owner had ever made them shine. Of particular curiosity, and therefore value, were German badges – anyone with anything like that was envied out of all proportion. I don't know if girls collected anything to do with the war or even if girls were in the slightest bit interested in the war. All I know is that we wouldn't have been seen dead with a girl and such creatures were to be avoided at all times. Girls played soppy games and fantasised about being married and having babies and (horror of horrors) love and kisses. Yuk! Girls were definitely not part of our scene.

Another offshoot of the war which impinged on our lives in the St Peter's Road area was to do with the station. As part of the drive to make war time machinery such as tanks and planes, scrap metal was very valuable. From the earliest days of the war, the iron railings which traditionally decorated people's front garden walls were systematically removed, which made access much easier when retrieving footballs or whatever, and taken to places like Freddie Carter's scrap dump at the station. As well as garden railings, this dump had all sorts of exciting bits and pieces which we just had to see and investigate. After a while, this dump grew to mountainous proportions and we would climb all over it without ever thinking of the potential dangers associated with such an insecure structure. There were all sorts of things worth having (to us at least) and I have no doubt that many of the pieces of German tank in someone's shrapnel collection started life on Freddie Carter's dump.

There was a large crane which was used to transfer the scrap metal from this dump into waiting railway trucks. This crane was obviously an object of great interest. We wanted to climb it, but the spoil-sports at the station (as usual) didn't see it like that. There was always someone around during working days to chase small boys away and threaten them with some fate worse than death if ever they were caught. But not at weekends, so that was when we did most of our foraging and even climbed part way up the crane – only part way because this was a very tall crane and we weren't really as brave as we liked to pretend.

On one Saturday afternoon, however, Ian decided to give it a go and climbed and climbed until he discovered that there were lots of people watching him from the allotments which used to lie next to the station and along the Luton Road. One of these public spirited types thought the station master and his entourage ought to know about this escapade, and the station master thought the police should be informed at once. In a comparatively short space of time there was a reception committee awaiting Ian's descent – and their body language suggested they weren't altogether friendly. Ian gradually climbed down and when he got to about six or eight feet off the ground, he suddenly jumped and tore off like a scalded cat.

### Robert Hawkes - Newsreels and Lead Soldiers

As a young boy living through the 1930s I was very aware of the grave situation in Europe from newspaper reports, the wireless and cinema newsreels. There always seemed to be photographs of goose-stepping Germans and one could turn the knobs of the wireless and often hear martial music and Hitler's rantings from some Nazi Party rally.

My favourite toys were the splendid lead soldiers, produced by W Britain & Co., and many mini battles were fought among the cabbages, with those of my friend Paul. As the European crises deepened gas masks were distributed to the population and on September 3rd 1939 I listened with my parents to the Prime Minister's solemn broadcast, announcing that Britain was at war with Germany. Air raid sirens sounded soon afterwards and we all returned to our Anderson Shelter, newly erected by my father and myself and positioned at the end of the garden.

One memory of this time is watching a lone aircraft drop bombs on Luton. It was rumoured that Midland Road (Luton) had been hit. This was where my father had his office. In alarm I cycled to the scene to find a number of houses down but thankfully my father's place was still standing. I was told he had been using his St John Ambulance skills and had just left for home.

Apart from first aid he was a very conscientious fire watch warden. I remember him gazing up at the night sky and remarking, "They're over," as he identified the re-occurring throb of German aircraft engines.

### Roy Turner - Messerschmitt in Grove House Gardens

I was in church attending the Sunday morning service when the verger went to speak to the Reverend. The Reverend climbed into the pulpit and explained to us what had happened. The National Anthem was played on the organ and we all came home. That was how the war started for me. I was a choirboy

My father worked at the Empire Rubber Company and the only thing I noticed was that he worked longer hours. My mother had a part-time job with the same company and they used to bring work to the home. Mother had terrible problems with her fingers, after using the scissors to cut pieces of rubber to fit inside tin helmets.

We always used to laugh, my mother and myself. There was a saying about 'enemy raids last night and they dropped their bombs at random'. One day the news was on and they said it again. I said to my mother, "There can't be anything left of that place." She said, "Where?" I replied, "Random." I thought it was a place.

We used to hear the planes. The night they bombed Coventry, we heard it all night long. They must have followed the A5. The lion on the side of the Downs was camouflaged during the war to try and stop the Germans knowing where they were. I only saw one enemy aircraft and that was the one that came up the high street. It must have been a Monday because Eric and I were taking the school milk money up to the bank. The only other one was in Grove House Gardens. They had a Messerschmitt 109 fighter in a tent, and you paid so much money to go in plus extra to have a sit down. We couldn't work out why, when you got in it, you dropped right down into the aircraft, but then we worked out that the Germans didn't have seats, they put their parachutes in the hole and that acted as a seat for them. I looked at the Messerschmitt and saw it had Dunlop tyres. Apparently the company made them for both sides under contract.

We weren't allowed any petrol for travelling to football matches, so Britain Street School played Acland School nearly every other week. We lost one of our football pitches at school because it was dug up for the school to grow vegetables. A lot of people went potato picking and we went round the hedgerows picking rosehips before it was discovered that they rotted our teeth. One day I went for the impossible, a pound of poppy petals. They made some medicines from them. We used to take them to Flemon's and Marchant's, on the other side of the White Hart in Nicholas Lane. Some people used to put stones into their bags of flowers and herbs to make them weigh heavier. We also used to collect elderberries. I spent my money on the Picture Post and War Illustrated.

I went to watch Luton Town Football Club. They kept going through the war. I used to go to football with a chap called Bill, a butcher by trade, who'd had to go into factories to carry out essential war work. He used to take me to London for ever such a lot of matches. There was a team called Clapton Orient. Their ground was bombed, so they played all their home games at Wembley. (Clapton Orient became Leyton Orient in 1946).

I still have a lot of football programmes, the first is for Saturday 6th June 1942, the Football Assn XI versus the RAF XI at Luton Town's Ground. All these players were internationals although the referee was a local man who refereed a cup final after the war. The second one is Luton Town versus the South of England Anti-Aircraft XI. That was Luton playing the Army XI. All the Army players were professionals from some of the big clubs. Then there was Eastern Command versus South Eastern Command at Luton.

I never missed a game from 1940 until the end of the war. Mostly it was The Football Association versus the Civil Defence XI, or the National Fire Service, Met or Lancs Police. On 15th April 1944 a cup final; Chelsea v Charlton. I went just to see Joe Payne, who used to play for Luton before playing for Chelsea. Another cup final, the Football League South, April 7th 1945, Chelsea v Millwall. When you went to Wembley during the war, you'd see people standing on top of the stands with machine guns. One particular programme is my pride and joy. It's for the Victory International, England v France at Wembley 18th May 1945. The war didn't finish until May 8th, so this was arranged in a few days. They drew one each. It was the only time I saw Montgomery, Eisenhower and de Gaulle, who all came and sat in the back of an open car and drove around. Bands from the Irish Guards, the U.S. Army and the First French Army were all there. It was one of those days when history was made. I'd never seen the three leaders before.

### Tony Ward – Got any Gum, Chum?

I have a memory of going with some friends on to the Downs to see a crashed Messerschmitt fighter. I also remember that there were these little rockets that exploded on the Downs and small silk parachutes used to come down – we used to collect those. I believe they were either markers or flares. I remember that all the signposts in the area were removed. At the top of Chiltern Road there were loads of concrete tubes piled up on the corner ready for pushing into the road if German tanks were to come along – we used to play on those of course. Also at the top of the road in Chiltern Crescent on the junction with West Street was a gun emplacement but without a gun. At the bottom of the Downs at the junction of West Street opposite what was then the whiting works was a pill-box. I also remember in those days the entrance to the Met Office up Worthington Road; it was caged off – there were guards on the gates. We all expected it to be bombed constantly but it was rarely targeted.

TOFFEE APPLES! *(OB) (DG)*

Going back a year or two, probably just before the war started, when people were disappearing because they were being called up, I remember being taken to the Co-op in West Street as it was; I used to sing Roll Out the Barrel. There was this chap behind the counter who used to throw sultanas into my hand, so every time I went in there, I struck up and expected sultanas. One day they didn't come – he wasn't there, he'd been called up.

So many things were in short supply, anything you wrote down on a piece of paper had to start right at the top left corner of the page and finish at the bottom right; no margins and you used the back as well. Books that you could borrow were also in short supply. As a special treat, we used to get odd-bods coming round, I don't quite know who they were; suddenly a chap would be in the room with some chocolate powder and we would have a spoonful of that. Someone would also come round with dolly mixtures and we would probably get one or two each! There were no ice creams or bananas of course and, as you've probably heard, people's health was almost certainly better than ever.

Sweets were heavily rationed but I knew an elderly couple down the road who were members of the Priory; the man was a member of the Church of England Men's Society, of which my father was Secretary at the time. I used to go down and do little jobs for them and they would give me their sweet coupons!

In our spare time in the school holidays we used to run around the countryside. Access to parts of the Downs was unfortunately restricted during part of the war with barbed wire, but we used to go to Wellhead to catch tadpoles and up to Totternhoe Knolls. Sometimes we would be away all day during the holidays. Our parents wouldn't need to worry; we had no problems at all. As time went by we played in the relics of war such as the pillbox at the bottom of the Downs. We often played war games.

During the war I joined the Cubs, and eventually the Priory Choir. We used to meet up with various lads in the area and walk down together. During the winter and with the blackout, you could hardly see anything. The Choirmaster Harold Deacon, a hard taskmaster, lived two doors away from us, so if I missed choir practice, there would be a hammering on the door and I would have to account for it! He was a very good organist and his choice of music was rather different, which I thought was better in those days. As choirboys we used to sing in the mornings and evenings; we got a shilling for weddings and funerals. As a treat during the war we were taken to Whipsnade Zoo. We used to walk all round it and be given an ice cream and walk back – our day out!

There were very few cars in those days. If you had a car you were a doctor or solicitor. No telephone either and you walked everywhere. Most buses went to Luton; Luton Corporation buses were brown and white and Eastern National were green. Some of the old Luton buses were commandeered from about 1920 I think, as they had wooden slats as seats; a huge sit up and beg thing. They had to be careful what route they all took to get under the bridges.

Towards the D-Day situation we had huge convoys coming through the town. Masses of British and American troops; some of them marching in columns and others in long lines of transport; tanks chewing up the road and airplanes on the back of trailers. Going all ways in fact, I think the idea was to confuse the enemy as to where they were going to some extent. Coming out of school, if one of these convoys were going past and they were American, we used to shout, "Got any gum, chum?" They would throw us packets of gum and maybe a packet of rations as well. When they decided not to, we were most hurt.

I remember the celebrations at the end of the war, probably VE day. The church bells rang – we hadn't heard them for a long time, in fact I hardly knew what they sounded like. People danced in the street, literally; I wondered where they had all come from. We had a street party; all the children went to that and their parents provided the wherewithal for it. There was a conjuror – I remember this vividly as he wasn't very good!

### *Ann Read* - Fun and Games

I was 3 years old at the beginning of the war and do remember many things that happened. I lived in Garden Road in Dunstable with my mother, father, sister, brother and my grandmother who slept in the front room downstairs. My father worked at Harrison Carters at the top of the road as a wheelwright and also carried out fire watching duties. It must have been quite an effort doing fire watching all night and then going back to work the next morning. I think my father was in a reserved occupation or maybe he was too old to go to war because he was born in 1900, but he often had to work away from home repairing machines.

I had my tonsils out in hospital when I was 7. I travelled on one of those old buses to the Children's Hospital. We were shut away without visitors for a week. It was very painful and I felt very homesick; the only good thing was that we were given ice cream to eat!

My aunt in Luton Road used to give us 3d a week and I think we had 6d (2 p) from Mum and Dad. My aunt would buy us stories by Enid Blyton and the Girls' Crystal but that was a bit later on, so we had plenty to read. Mum and Dad had lots of books, one in particular mother liked, Hunters Marjorie. There was a colouring competition in the Daily Sketch every week. On one occasion I won a prize – it was one of those books that open up with animals inside it.

Those funny old buses going to Luton were so luxurious with leather seats. We didn't go that far really, just to Luton, and when going to Hastings, we went by train. We went to St Albans sometimes to the Abbey and then down by the lake, so we did have a few treats. For games, we played skipping and hopscotch. We used to draw hopscotch on the path and occupied ourselves with lots of different games rolling hoops down the road. I belonged to the

GLB, the Girls Life Brigade. We used to meet at the Methodist Church in Victoria Street, now the Polish Church. We used to listen to the radio a lot; it was the highlight of our day to listen to Children's Hour when we came home from school.

We had street parties at the end of the war when flags would be brought out but I've no idea where the food came from! A lot of people were still in the East; my sister's father-in-law was in the East and it was a while before he came back home.

### Keith D Hodder – Flying with the US

As a 15-year-old in 1944 I joined the ATC and kept a flying log – my first recorded entries were to record flights in Stirlings from RAF Chedbourgh during a week's camp. These were night flights lasting 20 minutes for the first, and 3 hours 15 minutes for the second. I recorded the numbers of all the aircraft that I flew in; these were LK499 and EF466. I well remember these flights as on both occasions I occupied the bomb aimer's position, not only during the flight but also during takeoff and landing. I was unaware at the time of the somewhat fragile nature of the Stirling's undercarriage! Later on I had flights in Oxfords, Dominies, Ansons and Dakotas.

I also used to visit local US airbases in my ATC uniform and found them more than happy to fly me around the country. Some of the most interesting of these flights took place from Cheddington. In January 1945, I flew in Liberator 250483, a J type, from Cheddington to Woodbridge in Suffolk. This was one of the emergency landing airfields with a runway three times the normal width and seemingly enormous length. As we landed and taxied in, a Mustang that had landed in front of us rolled to a stop beside us, and I could see that the prop was bent back for about 2 feet of its length; the vibration must have been tremendous.

At the far side of the airfield was the most enormous pile of wrecked aircraft, a real heap, something that today's restorers would give their eye teeth for. The purpose of our trip then became apparent; we were collecting another Liberator, this time an H type 25217, and as I write this I see that it was one of the early aircraft, for return to Cheddington. On climbing in via the bomb bay I realised that it still had its bomb load, a bit of a shock but all part of the excitement of war time flying. The flight home, journeying through the tops of the clouds with me occupying the right hand seat, rounded off a magical day.

One day as I was leaving Cheddington I was spotted by an ATC Officer and soundly berated for having the audacity to visit a US base unauthorised. Sometimes initiative is unrewarded, but it did not stop my regular visits.

I would finally add that to avoid conscription into the mines or whatever, I volunteered and spent 7 years in the FAA, but that's another story…

### Mrs Kelly (née West) – just before D-Day

During the week leading up to D-Day a vast army of lorries, trucks, gun carriers and tanks were parked along both sides of the roads around the Poynters Road area in Dunstable. The soldiers were British, American and Canadian and they brought with them chocolate which they gave to the children, wonderful to an 11-year-old girl. There was an air of expectancy and excitement everywhere, a feeling that something important was about to happen, though nobody knew exactly what. Then one morning, everyone got up to find all the vehicles had been driven quietly away in the middle of the night and the streets were empty. I believe that the men just camped out in their vehicles while they were there.

### CONVERSATION BETWEEN THREE FRIENDS: Pam Perkins, Betty Tarbox and Heather Hing

**Pam:** On the Luton Road recreation ground, the grass grew and grew way above us, so we made these tracks; it was like a maze because there was no one to cut it.

**Betty:** The triangle of land by Church Street Station is now apparently of scientific interest as a special migratory bird place. It was all ploughed up in the war and harvested, the land army girl Bessie used to give us a ride on the tractor.

**Pam:** Along the main Luton Road we had big Yankee convoys, one after the other. They'd all come to a stop on the big grass verges and jump out to have a bit of a rest, Mum gave them tea and they gave us gum. They were coming in droves for weeks and weeks and obviously they were trained up north before heading south.

**Betty:** All the troops were in Bennett's Rec, it was choc-a-bloc. Josie and me used to go up on our bikes; we went up in the lorries with them and my dad gave me 6 Sexton Blake books at a time to give them. With hindsight they were waiting for D-Day. The tanks used to come up Church Street from the factory, turn round, scrape all the tarmac off the road and go off to London.

**Heather:** There were Nissan huts full of troops where the Queensway Hall used to be at Park Farm.

There used to be a path from the Royal Oak through the middle of them to Houghton Regis, probably down Dog Kennel Lane.

### *Christina Scott* – a Dash Home from Brussels

I was in Belgium in August, just as war was becoming imminent. I was still at school and staying with a girl of my own age in South Belgium, on an exchange visit in a minute village just a few miles from the French border. I was at the Cedars School in Leighton Buzzard; this girl had stayed with me for 3 weeks and then I had 3 weeks with her.

We listened to the news avidly every day and by the time the guns were out in the streets in Brussels, it looked as if I would have to come home before my time was up in the last few days of August. On the night of 31st when the radio in Belgium announced that the Germans had invaded Poland, the farmer said to me, "Christina, it's time you went home." On the morning of 1st September, we left at 6.00 am and the farmer very kindly took me as far as Ostend. It was a long journey with several changes of train; the farmer said goodbye and I caught virtually the last Channel crossing from Ostend.

The sea was dead flat calm, a 4 hour crossing, and as we came into Dover I remember seeing a sub surfacing. I arrived at St Pancras station, and in those days you could put your suitcase on the train, go and have a cup of tea or coffee (tea was 6d a cup) and when you came back your suitcase would still be there. As I sat down at a table an older man came and sat next to me and said, "I am going to buy you a cup of tea." He then told me, "There will be war. War is coming. If we go down, we'll go down fighting!" I've never forgotten that. We said goodbye and I got back to Dunstable. War broke out on the 3rd, so it was a pretty close shave.

I lived in Great Northern Road in Dunstable and we would all sit round our large kitchen table waiting for news on the radio. It came through just about 11 o'clock when Neville Chamberlain said war had broken out. I had never seen my father break down before, but he simply put his head in his hands and cried. He said, "I can't take this again, we've only just got over 1914–18." Understandable, when you consider it was only 21 years after the First World War. My father did not go to the front in 1914–18, he did munitions work here. By WWII he was too old to go to the front, so as a family we came off extremely well.

I left school in July 1940 and I remember Dunkirk so well. We couldn't initially appreciate the impact that the Germans had overrun all of France. We were led to believe that it was a huge heroic action that we had fought. We were not informed, we were in the dark. It was a brilliant sunny morning when soldiers starting coming back from Dunkirk; we didn't really understand. The streets were full of soldiers exhausted, driving, lying there fast asleep or going off to barracks.

## *David Grant* – Long Evenings

I remember all sorts of war stuff about the house, including tin helmets, gas masks, spotters aircraft type silhouette books and operational maps (including some Ordnance Survey maps of England printed in German with target areas marked on, obtained from the captured PoW infiltrators that had parachuted down). We were in one of the target areas for enemy bombing, as there were factories near us manufacturing equipment for the war effort including Delco and Vauxhall Motors.

We had a Morrison type shelter which some of us would get under when the siren went. The steel angle girders of this made a very useful workbench in later years at the end of the war. My father was a keen cricketer and snooker player and he still managed to play the occasional games during weekends at Markyate.

Things were hard in those days with a shortage of coal to heat the house in those very cold and snowy winters. The only consolation was being taken on a homemade sledge to slide on the snow down the hillside. The long cold dark evenings would be spent huddled around a Bakelite radio set listening to Uncle Mac and then Dick Barton Special Agent. After this I would twiddle with the knobs to find other stations such as the Voice of America overseas forces broadcasts, which started my lifetime listening passion for jazz and Glenn Miller, much to the annoyance of my parents who were more into the Luton Girls Choir and Tommy Handley's ITMA.

(The name of the programme derived from a topical wartime catchphrase. Whenever Hitler made a new territorial gain the newspapers of the day would headline, " It's That Man Again".)

I remember the crowds on VE day where everybody went down to the High Street to celebrate the end of hostilities. It was good just to go for long walks over the Downs to Whipsnade Animal Park or just to watch the kites and gliders. We appreciated the masses of wild flowers and listened to the skylarks that seemed to predominate in those days before insecticides had decimated our open spaces. We looked forward to summer holiday trips on the steam train down to Porthcawl Pleasure Park and to see our relatives in Tondu. Their house in Shepherds Bush, London, had been destroyed when a bomb exploded and destroyed the Telegraph Hotel next door; luckily the family were not at home at the time but had to be evacuated to Wales.

### *Derek Bonfield* - Launching Gliders

As a boy I used to go up on to the Dunstable Downs to watch the gliders. Before the war we used to help launch them with an elastic rope. As many as we could muster pulled on the rope and somebody would hang on the back of the glider. We used to walk, and then they would tell us to run, and then, run like hell! They would let go of the glider and you would fall in a heap. They were very basic things. They used to land with an enormous bump. They weren't gliders as such; they had a tubular frame and a bucket seat. I can picture the pilots now with their Oxford bags flapping in the breeze.

### *Brian Bundy* -Playing with Danger

When we heard the air-raid siren go we went and slept on top of the reams of paper at the printing works in George Street, where my father worked. Why we went there, I don't know, because when I think about it now, although it was a very large building and my parents probably thought it would be safer, it was however a factory, and therefore more of a target! A lot of people who came from Waterlow's factories in London to work in Dunstable, also lived underneath the printing department in the cellar. They lived and worked in Dunstable during the week and went home at the weekend.

For a boy aged from 9 to 14, it was quite an exciting time; there was always something going on with troops in the town. Sometimes we'd be up on the Downs looking for strips of foil that German planes dropped to try and interfere with the radar. Or we'd be messing about in bomb craters looking for shrapnel and souvenirs that we could find, but my mother threw all my finds away! They used to fire large and small flares up on the Downs. The large ones were about a foot long and about 3 or 4 inches round, full of magnesium. To test these flares, they'd fire them up over towards Whipsnade and the flare would drift to the ground on a parachute. We'd get up on a Saturday morning and if the weather was right we'd be there, running about, ready to collect the silk parachutes. I used to go fishing, so I'd take a fishing rod with me and catch them on the end of my rod. One day we found one of these mortars, unscrewed it, took it to bits, removed the magnesium and took it to the back of Tavistock Street, placed it in a tin lid and put a match to it. It created a huge flash and burned my cousin's eyebrows and eyelashes. He ended up in bed for a week with the injuries to his face. We both got told off for that!

A Liberator aeroplane crashed into the woods, taking the wings off the body of the aircraft as it crashed into the trees. It was an American air force plane but by the time we got there they'd dragged it out and we found, lying on the ground, all these half inch .5 bullets. We picked them up, took some of them home, put them in a vice, pulled the tops off and got the cordite out. We were banging them like caps! We didn't realise then just how dangerous it was.

I used to go fishing in the canal with my friend Dickie, and one hot day he decided to take a swim. He had only been in there for a couple of minutes when some WAAFS from RAF Stanbridge came and sat down on the towpath. We had to take his clothes down to him as he walked further down the canal, so that he could get dressed!

We used to go by the canal and watch the Liberators limping home with engines damaged and smoke trailing. I kept a diary and on D-Day I wrote – invasion of France. Next day – played cricket in park, because life went on almost as normal for us.

My father had been in the army in the First World War in the Beds Yeomanry, but was too old to go to war again, so he became a special constable. We took in two people that had been bombed out in London. After a few months my mother had a row with them and threw them out but, when my father came home, he went mad. My mother had bought a lot of things from them, silk underclothes and suchlike. They were trading in black market goods and he was keeping an eye on them for the police. So that was the end of that!

### *John S Purdon* - **Battles with our Gas Masks**

The threat of gas attacks by the Germans was very real from the day that war broke out. In fact, the Government had been planning how to deal with this threat for some time before actual hostilities broke out in 1939. The result was that very early on everyone was issued with gas masks. For us children they were initially something of a torment and even a horror. I was frightened of the nasty thing that smelled of rubber and the idea of putting it on filled me with revulsion. However, we had to do it and we did. By law, everyone had to carry their gas mask at all times, and you could be fined if you were caught without it. When they were issued they came in a pretty flimsy cardboard box with a strap so you could hang it from your shoulder. After a time firms began offering for sale more elaborate satchels, since the cardboard soon wore out. By 1942 I was eight and I had

Examples of GAS MASKS used during WW II *(SK)*

to carry not only a gas mask to school but also a satchel for my school stuff. But the great thing about the gas mask was that you could slip it off your shoulder in a second and it became a sort of weapon. We children used to have battles swinging our gas masks at each other on our way to and from school. If we had ever been required to put them on for a real gas attack it is doubtful that they would have still been of much use. But fortunately and sensibly, the Germans did not resort to using gas on England.

Because of the war, toys were largely unavailable and you had to make do with what you had. I was very fortunate since I had two older brothers and inherited many Dinky toys and a very large Meccano set with clockwork motors, together with the necessary nuts, bolts and several screwdrivers and spanners. From this I made all manner of things. I even managed to make a truck, which I could steer from above by means of an extended rod with a steering wheel attached to it. With this I toured the house in and out of rooms, all the time accompanied by suitable motor noises. I am sure my parents must have found this more than a little irritating. One other inherited toy that was very tantalizing, was a train set which had been Marcus' and David's. It was double O (OO) gauge, German made system, but it would not work because it needed this vital spare part, and of course they were unavailable. But I did have a large supply of O gauge track, with one clockwork engine. Tony also had a large supply of track and one engine, and we used to set this up in his garden. It must have covered a total of well over 100 yards with crossovers and points. We had great games trying to set the two engines running, so that they would almost crash at the crossover, but not quite.

Once I had grown out of my little red pedal car there was a tricycle that I inherited from my older brothers. It had large wheels, with solid tyres and a leather sprung seat just like a big bicycle. It operated much like a regular bicycle too, with pedals and a chain that drove one of the rear wheels. It also had brakes that operated on the front wheel. This front brake system meant you had to be a bit careful, as they could grab and cause a sudden tumble. The 'trike', as it was called, was my staple until I graduated to a two-wheeler when I was about fourteen.

I well remember May 1945, when the Germans surrendered. I was allowed (at the age of 11) to go to the centre of town to view the celebrations. There was much dancing and singing and a lot of drunkenness. I was particularly fascinated by an old man (he was old to me), walking around complaining in a very drunken manner "I've lost me teeth!"

In about August 1945 my father was made a Colonel in the British Army and sent to Germany to examine Hydrogen Peroxide Plants. He went to both the British and American zones and came back with a small suitcase full of American candy – Snickers, Hershey bars and chewing gum, some of which had a very curious flavour, like an antiseptic ointment we called Germoline. But we chewed it anyway.

I had two older brothers; Marcus was in the Royal Navy and David was working on a farm and as such, was not called up into the forces. He was, however, required to be in the Home Guard. My Mother and I visited him in the country and one day there was a big alarm and the Home Guard was called out at night. In fact, this was to cover for the impending D-Day landings (June 6th) and I recall that every narrow lane was full of British and American lorries (trucks), loaded with men and equipment heading south for the invasion. We small boys especially liked the Americans as we used to call out to them at traffic stops. "Got any gum chum?" Sometimes we got a stick.

On the whole I remember the war as fun, much as a young boy might, since we were not really aware of the dreadful events that were unfolding. It was no doubt much different for people on the Continent in occupied areas and for our poor parents. My mother had, I believe, a particularly difficult time, as did all mothers. They had to handle the rationing and arrange to put meals on the table and keep the family and, in particular, feed a young growing boy. But for me there were plenty of interesting and exciting things to do.

### Lucy Pendar – My Life at Whipsnade Zoo

I was eleven years old when war broke out; my father was a resident engineer at Whipsnade Zoo and as a result we lived in the park grounds with my parents, my mother's mother, my father's brother's wife and her nine month old baby. I was sitting on some steps playing marbles with some friends when a very important gentleman came up to us. Most people would have just told us to get out of the way, but this gentleman asked us to move very politely. When he came out we were told that war had been declared and we went home to get our gas masks – contained in little cardboard boxes held with string. The first thing to happen was that the policeman was sent round on his bicycle informing everyone that the park would be closing. As we had nothing to do we were offered riding lessons on the Shetland pony!

Two elephants were sent to Whipsnade while a new elephant house was being built in London Zoo. They were soon joined by another three evacuee elephants from London together with the senior elephant keeper and his wife, who were housed in a cottage in the village. Three giant pandas arrived at Whipsnade during the summer and were kept in a pen where the new chimp island has now been built. They chewed on bamboo, which was grown especially for them in Cornwall. Four chimps and two orangutangs were sent down with the senior chimp keeper and his family who were housed in a cottage in the car park. Wives and children of the Zoological Society were also evacuated and housed in old army huts in the village.

With all the evacuees in the village, the superintendent's wife formed a Guide company. We were taught Morse Code and were so good that we won the district award for it. Of course guiding meant service so we collected rubbish and filled sandbags. I was sent to look after toddlers in a nursery behind the Catholic Church but I didn't relate to small children very well and spent my time chatting up the Catholic priests. I didn't know at that time they had to be celibate and I wouldn't get anywhere!

The Guides belonged to the Dunstable Association of Youth Organisations and held swimming galas at the California pool in Dunstable. I was lucky enough to be the swimming champion. My little highlight of the war at the California happened when a man was in difficulty, his wife was shouting and I plunged in, grabbed hold of him and pulled him out. When he thanked me for rescuing him, to my astonishment he was dressed in a sailor's uniform!

We went on parades in Dunstable with the army and air cadets. We had Warship Week and Wings for Victory week and would stage plays and concerts in Whipsnade village hall to raise money. We also had a National Savings competition. We did so well that they put a flagpole up in the grounds of the village hall and we children took it in turns to go and hoist this flag. It wasn't very long before most of the wives and children evacuated went back to London but there were still enough children for us to have parties and a social life, which was totally non existent before the war.

The government regulations stated that a certain amount of grassland should be set aside for growing food. The park had always made its own hay but now the old farmland (because the zoo had been a farm before it was a zoo) found parts of itself back to its old use. Potatoes and root crops were used to supply the restaurant and used as animal feed, the grass made hay, domestic animals were bred on the farm, pigs and sheep were sold to the Ministry of Food while some pigs were sold to the Herts and Beds Bacon Factory at Hitchin.

During the time of rationing, if local people could afford it, they would come to Whipsnade for Sunday lunch for the price of 3 shillings and 6 pence. It meant they could save their coupons and I remember one of the people who came was Phyllis Calvert, the actress. She had a house in Kensworth and would walk with her husband and their children to have their lunch at Whipsnade.

Our meat ration as a family was supplemented by rabbits; there were colonies of them on the Downs. The overseer used to go out on a regular basis so we had rabbit at least once a week, roast rabbit or rabbit pie, which was absolutely gorgeous. My father kept bees, chickens and ducks and not only for the eggs but for the hens as well. We also grew runner beans and tomatoes. I have never tasted tomatoes like the ones he used to fertilise with elephant poo! Tomato sandwiches were absolutely delicious! My mother always mixed the two rations of butter and margarine together and it wasn't until I was at college that I realised what butter tasted like on its own!

We used to go out into the fields and gather in the grain, put it into sheaves (there were about seven sheaves in a stook) and splay the legs out so that the rain would run off them. We worked late into the night and ended up with very scratched arms. The dry stalks were cut off and used as animal straw while the grain was taken to the works yard thresher. My job was to fill the oat sacks; I never thought that I would encounter a rat or a mouse; otherwise I probably wouldn't have done it. They were then taken down to Eaton Bray with me standing on the back of the lorry for a ride!

In January 1940, a black rhino and an African elephant both died as a result of a very severe winter. The ground was so hard they couldn't dig to bury them so they were burnt in one of those flint pits that used to run along the front of the Downs; it took a week for the carcasses to burn. Food was very scarce and during the first Christmas of the war a polar bear had a cub and its father ate it. A litter of tiger cubs and a giant panda all had fits and Boxer, the two-year-old giraffe, became ill. Visitors to Whipsnade were encouraged to bring food for the animals. They were asked to bring lettuce, cabbages and carrots for the herbivores, buns for the bears and sugar and buns for the elephants – I always had acorns in my pockets, they loved those. The one animal that didn't need feeding was the wooden horse; it stood on the top of the Downs. It was going to be broken up, but a group of admirers saved it and brought it to Whipsnade in 1937 where it stayed until 1947.

Whipsnade was an air-raid warning post; warnings were phoned to the estate office (which was also the headquarters of the Home Guard and the Civil Defence) and passed to Kensworth and Studham. There was a hooter on top of the water tower which always sounded at five o'clock, so that wherever the works department were, they knew it was time to knock off and go home. That now became the air-raid siren and every time it sounded the wolves howled in unison!

We had a bonfire on the common when the war finished on the 8th May. I finished the war with an absolute flourish, because on VJ night I tipped Gerald Durrell headfirst into a cowpat, not knowing how famous he was going to become.

The war was a very exciting time for me; the only really serious parts were the shortages of food for the animals; animals that had to be burned at the beginning of the war, and seeing the bombing of London.

## Jim Knight - on the Buses

One of my earliest memories of the war is being taken to Luton by my mum. She told me that we had to leave well before 5.00 pm, as all the buses were classified as 'workers priority' and were often full up as they called at the factories before arriving in the town centre. I was also told to hold on to her hand very tightly when the bus came because everyone pushed forward and fought their way on (no queues then).

Some of the older single-decker buses were converted to 'standee vehicles', i.e. seats were placed around the sides of the vehicles, facing inwards, to allow more standing room so that single-deckers could carry the same number of passengers as a double-decker bus. On the rare occasions we came home on the bus in the black-out there were no street lights. The blinds were pulled down over the windows at the front, so you had to keep a sharp look out to see where you were. The interior lights had deep shades fitted, making it very gloomy inside the vehicles at night. The conductors were provided with a little light in the ceiling, shining vertically downwards, also fitted with a deep shade, which could be pulled along so that fare collecting was made easier.

Ivinghoe Beacon was used during the war for firing ranges and gun practice. Some boys from Eaton Bray went shrapnel collecting there. While waiting for the bus home a live round they had collected exploded, severely injuring some of them.

### *Albert (Bert) Morgan* – Savings Weeks, Competitions, School Parties and Messerschmitts

We were encouraged to save regularly at school by purchasing 'Savings Stamps', 6d for a blue one and 2s 6d for a red one. These were stuck into our savings books and on reaching a total of 15s or later 10s, they could be exchanged for a savings certificate.

There were regular 'Savings Weeks' in which the town was given a target. In 'Spitfire Week' the target was £5,000 for each Spitfire and a higher figure was requested in 'Warship Week' where several towns were asked to contribute. Competitions were held in which school children were asked to draw a picture and write a composition depicting the savings theme of that time. Winning entries were displayed, together with the child's name on large boards in the window of the 'Gas and Water Company' in High Street North. The prizes awarded were National Savings Certificates and Savings Stamps. Other activities were to be found in various parts of the town. One was the display of a captured Messerschmitt Me 109 in Grove House Gardens, it was in a large marquee. An entrance fee of 1d was charged to go in and for an additional sum, one could sit in it and work the control column, levers and switches. To small boys such as myself, this was something special.

Others were:
(i)    A 'Link Trainer' (we would now call it a flight simulator, albeit rather simple) used for basic and blind flying tuition by the R.A.F., this was in the showroom of Scott's Garage in High

Street South. We could take a turn as a trainee pilot for a few minutes by buying a savings stamp.

(ii)     A rig consisting of a small Bomb Rack mounted above a cloth model of 'Adolf', the rack contained small dummy bombs and as 'Adolf' was pulled along beneath the rack we could watch through a 'Bomb Sight' and drop the bombs on him by pressing a button. This was in the 'Water Company' showrooms. Again a 1d or buying a savings stamp secured a turn.

This was all fun and took our minds off the war. However, one afternoon we were promised a party at school. I must explain that an evacuated London school shared the premises at Burr Street and we only attended for half days, mornings one week and afternoons the next. On the afternoon of our party, the 'Air Raid' siren sounded an alert shortly before we were due to go to school. The rule was that we should stay at home until the 'All Clear' sounded and if this was after 2.30 pm, we should not go to school that day. I anxiously waited, hoping the 'All Clear' would sound so I could go to the party. My mother and I heard the sound of a low flying aircraft together with the rat-a-tat-a-tat of machine guns. We both ducked down in our living room. The siren did not sound the 'All Clear' until it was too late to go to school. The next time at school we were told that Miss Boyes would bring our party food after morning break. We had a bowl of jelly, a small fairy cake and a drink of orange juice, then back to normal lessons.

There were various places that we liked to play, Grove House Gardens with the swings, slide and roundabout, or Bennett's Rec. One of our favourite places was the old car park, a walled garden all overgrown with apple trees, hawthorn bushes and wild roses.

One of my school friends lived in West Street and his back garden backed onto the grounds of the 'Old Mill'. There was a skating rink in this area with small goal posts and nets that had been used for 'Roller-skate Hockey' prior to the war. This was ideal for us to play football until two army motorcyclists arrived and told us to leave.

A few minutes later we saw them remove the goal posts to one side and ten to a dozen Bren-gun Carriers roared up the entrance drive and parked on the skating rink. This was the end of our football pitch for the duration. The Mill eventually became the home for the Royal Naval Cadets.

Toys weren't that easy to come by, so we made our own, perhaps had a stick and a rim of a bicycle wheel. One lad had a steel hoop and a hook and we had whips and tops. We made little tanks out of cotton reels, an elastic band, a slice cut from a candle and a matchstick; we had races with those. It was all good fun.

Most weeks, bright lights that left a trail of smoke behind them could be seen over the Dunstable Downs. These were parachute flares that were fired from mortars situated near the entrance to the Golf Club. There was a concrete base with pipe-work and other fittings that was used to support the mortars. The bombs were fired high into the air above the slope of the Downs; as they reached the zenith of their flight, the end cap flew off and the parachute flare was released. They drifted on the wind as they burned for about two minutes, after which time the parachute slowly descended to earth, often as much as a mile from the Downs. The empty bomb cases fell onto the bottom path along the foot of the Downs. The soldiers that were in attendance may have collected some up, but we often found cases that had been missed. In retrospect, I believe they were quality control tests of flares manufactured locally.

If we saw these bright lights when we had an afternoon off, we would dash off, get downwind, and hope to find one. The smaller size were about half to two thirds of a metre (of pure silk) in diameter, whilst the larger were about one metre. Neither was quite big enough to make an adult skirt or dress but both could be used for children's undies, and the larger had sufficient material for an adult slip or knickers. They would perhaps be firing them off all day, and I remember wandering to Kensworth once, and there was a great crowd of children in the field. The big boys used to run underneath the parachutes as they floated in, they could jump higher than us and grab them.

On one occasion when larger parachutes were landing in a field somewhere near Kensworth Church, two older boys wearing gloves roughly barged smaller children out of their way and, having grabbed a parachute, took it to a man and woman who proceeded to cut off the strings and put the silk canopies into a carrier bag. This was obviously an organised group out to make money!

I had a collection of two different sizes of empty bombs, the smaller had four fins fixed to a tube with about twelve holes in it and a striker at the rear end, the case was quite heavy and seemed to be made in one piece. The larger was fabricated from several pieces of thinner metal and had a conical nosepiece in contrast to the flat end cap of the smaller bomb.

My father used to buy aircraft recognition books. They were about as big as a notepad with about 20 or 30 aircraft in them. British aircraft were covered in about 4 or 5 books, German similarly, I think. Sometimes we'd see aircraft that we didn't know. We were in Grove House Gardens one day and some planes flew very low towards Leighton Buzzard; I found out later they were Westland Whirlwinds. I only saw them once but they were a striking aircraft. There were posters around the town and in the school about butterfly bombs. These were anti-personnel bombs that the Germans dropped. A policeman brought the only one I ever saw into school. He was very worried about children collecting live bombs from the Downs, so he brought one in to warn us but he accidentally dropped it on the table and it fell onto the floor. It made such a clatter. Nobody thought there was anything in it. We knew he wouldn't bring a live bomb into school!

There were live AG Mortars fired at the back of Ivinghoe Beacon. After the war a few boys from Eaton Bray collected some. They were waiting at the bus stop and one went off. I worked with one of the lads who survived, I think 3 were killed and 2 survived. The bus was coming, they put the boys on, and it went non-stop to the hospital. With my father being in the army he always said, "Don't pick anything up, always look to see if it's empty." We'd seen the empty ones with the nose-cap off and I don't think I ever saw one with the cap on.

Just before the war, my maternal grandfather retired from his work at the Waterlow's factory. Soon afterwards, my grandparents moved to Black Notley, near Braintree in Essex. They had a thatched cottage called St. Andrew's in Baker's Lane. My cousins and I visited them for a few days on several occasions. We got to know the area of the village very well. Just down the lane was a slaughterhouse, mainly for horses, where my grandfather helped out for a few days each week. He told us that each horse was examined; most carcasses were put into a vat of purple dye and used for pet food in London, but some from fit young horses had their lower legs removed and were put in a cold room before being sent to Birmingham. He thought they would be turned into meat pies.

One day, probably in 1940, we had this suitcase delivered. It had come

BERT with his uncle, 'digging for victory' *(AWM)*

all the way from Essex by train and was full of damsons. They were a little bit ripe but there was some sugar available, so damson jam was made.

Eventually my grand-mother persuaded her husband to move back to London in 1941. Their first home was in Clarendon Crescent that backed onto the Regent Canal in Paddington. They had a second floor flat. The visits we made there were rather like holidays as we could not, of course, go to the coast because of wartime restrictions.

I liked these visits as it was possible to go to Royal Oak station and watch the trains running into and out of Paddington. There was a turntable opposite this station and there was a great deal of activity as engines were watered and turned for their next duty.

Once when my father was coming from Hereford, my mother and I went to Paddington Station to meet him. There were a lot of armed soldiers waiting for the train and before the passengers were allowed off the platform, they marched up the train. They returned a few minutes later escorting some high-ranking German officers; my father eventually came through the barrier and told us that they were captured generals.

No matter where you lived, one was asked to save metal, paper and cardboard for recycling. The collection of such materials was known as a 'salvage drive'. My grandmother said there was such a drive whist we were staying with her. On that afternoon, we heard the sound of a Scottish Pipe and Drum Band. They were not dressed in traditional kilts and plaids but in black ARP uniforms. They wanted children to help with the collection so my cousin and I joined a group of local children. We followed the pipers for two or three hours and thoroughly enjoyed ourselves collecting salvage.

We gave it to the men whose job it was to load the lorries and carts, after roughly sorting the material that we had been given by the householders. There was a sense that we were all helping out.

A footbridge crossed the canal at the end of the road and the path led to Warwick Avenue and 'Little Venice' where there was a junction with another canal. Warwick Avenue was exciting to us as there was a barrage balloon stationed there. Each evening, the crew would send the balloon into the air and bring it down the early the next day; we liked it especially when they were practising raising and lowering it during the day.

My grandfather, although over 70 years of age, helped with the clearance of bomb-damage just off Warwick Avenue. We used to go and meet him. They had a light railway to reach the far end of the site and the rubble was loaded into tubs that were pushed by two men. A motor winch was used to pull them up the final ramp for loading into the waiting lorries.

In early 1944, my grandparents moved to Penfold Street, which was near to Edgware Road station. I missed seeing the engines at Paddington but a consolation was that I could go to a shop in Church Street, Marylebone, where I could buy 'Kiel Kraft' balsa kits for model aeroplanes. I saved my pocket money as the small kits cost 6d each for planes such as a Spitfire or Hurricane up to about 1s 6d or 2s for bigger aircraft such as a Lancaster bomber or Sunderland flying boat. In retrospect, I realise that my friends and I did not shape the wings and fuselages very well when making them. This was brought home to me when I saw a set of similar models displayed at 'Bletchley Park' museum; these too had the same child-like faults in their construction.

Early in the war someone in authority feared that enemy aircraft and gliders might use large fields as emergency landing grounds. Consequently, suitable meadows had redundant lampposts and other poles erected in them to prevent this occurrence. Unfortunately, it also prevented our own aircraft from making emergency landings in those fields most suitable for that purpose. A large meadow between Clark's Farm and the railway must have had about a dozen posts erected in it.

One morning break-time we saw a Blenheim bomber circling low over the town with its wheels down. We came out of school at lunchtime and other children told us it had landed at the top of First Avenue. We ran through 'Bennett's Rec' and along to the end of the avenue where we could see the Blenheim on top of the hill (now to the south of Queensbury School). Policemen stopped us from going any nearer. The next day we rushed out of school to find that the bomber was now close to the road and guarded by airmen. There was a large aircraft transporter nearby and presumably the aircraft was dismantled and loaded onto it as it had gone by the next day.

We had heard on the radio that a cease-fire was imminent and that church bells would be rung to celebrate. My friends and I were playing football on the Grammar School Sports-field when we heard the bells ringing at the Priory Church. Everyone was really pleased and a few days later we had a street party.

After VE day, what was called the Women's Tea Committee from the Congregational Church in Edward Street, decided to have a street party. The party was held outside the Congregational Church. The church had a supply of trestle tables as well as cutlery and crockery. When the Territorials had departed from their drill hall in 1939, my father arranged for some items, which included flags and bunting, to be stored at our house. These were got out, the street was decorated and every one who had a flag of some sort suspended it from their upstairs window. The street looked really colourful.

My mother, my Auntie Maggie and the lady next door went round asking people if they could spare a little margarine, butter, or a few points, because the shopkeeper had said, "If you bring the points, you can have food for the party." At one house, which was occupied by 'The Hospitality Ladies' as they were known when mentioned in front of us children, they struck gold. There were 2 young ladies there and they gave them tins of corned beef, a wooden keg of butter and some large tins of fruit cocktail. These were duly taken back to the Congregation. When a couple of maiden ladies saw them they said, "We can't possibly have those! They are the wages of sin!" They were all marked U.S Army. Maggie and my Mum said, "The children don't know about that sort of thing, they'll enjoy it." Of course it was a marvellous spread. It was a fine day and trestle tables and chairs from the church were put outside. Red, white and blue bunting was laid down the middle of the tables, all the church crockery was used, the Reverend officiated, said Grace, gave thanks for the end of the war and then we all tucked in.

We heard that my father was returning from India and, about the same time, I had a form from school about another try at the 11+ examination. My mother sent this off and shortly afterwards I went to Luton Technical College to sit the exam. My father came home and on the day before the term ended, we received notice that I had won a place at Dunstable Grammar School. My father was pleased and bought me a bicycle from Halford's in Luton.

During the summer holidays, the war with Japan ended and there was another party, but somehow the great 'Euphoria' of V.E. Day was not there. In due course I started at the Grammar School and the post war period with even more stringent rationing began.

### Mary Corrie (née Cheshire) - VE Day

On VE day, I'd never seen anything like it. People brought pianos out for street parties, everyone was in a good mood and there were crowds everywhere. At the town hall there was a wonderful band called the Embassy Band who played on the balcony. Everyone in the street cheered.

VE STREET PARTY in Skimpot Lane 12 May 1945 (DG) (LMS)

## *Betty Tompkins* - **Street Party**

At the end of the war I remember the street parties. Edward Street had a lovely street party and a girl called Lilac pushed her piano into the street and sat playing. My mother rushing in at the end of the war shouting, "Bananas! There's a shop in town selling bananas!" We hadn't seen any for so long!

EDWARD STREET VE Street Party *(AWM)*

# Further Childhood Memories

## INTRODUCTION BY SUE KING

You would have thought that wartime would have been traumatic for children, but generally the memories are happy ones. With wartime rationing, quite a lot of recollections revolve around food, but not the lack of it; certainly, sweets, sugar & meat were rationed, imported fruits such as oranges and bananas were almost non-existent. Children helped their parents 'Digging for Victory' in the gardens and allotments, so vegetables and garden fruits were available, and most households kept chickens and rabbits to supplement meat rations. As clothing was rationed, a lot of children relied on 'hand me downs' and government advice to 'make do and mend'.

For treats there were visits to the cinema to see Pathe News followed by Walt Disney's Fantasia and other films. Another activity was collecting salvage; there were many avid children in Dunstable looking to win badges for the amount of salvage collected. In March 1941, a huge amount of money was collected by local people during War Weapons Week; enough, said the Luton News and Dunstable Gazette, to buy three destroyers.

## EXTRACTS FROM COUNCIL PROCEEDINGS

A Ministry of Food scheme ensured distribution of fruit juices, vitamins and Cod Liver Oil throughout the war to expectant mothers and mothers with children under five years.

There were three children's Day Nurseries in Dunstable. Space for 40 children was available in West Street with an average attendance of 25. Luton Road could take 80 children and Douglas Crescent 40.

The WVS began an emergency meals organisation. A cooking depot was set up in Houghton Regis and provided hot meals for agricultural workers and later for schoolchildren. They were also involved in organising a pie scheme for field workers.

In the County Council records we find that Bedfordshire set up Holiday Farm

Camps at Blunham, Ampthill and Sharnbrook. They opened each summer from 1942 and were designed to give families a break from London by working on a farm. Accommodation was available for 250–300 people at each camp. Facilities included a cinema and two dances per week in return for working on the farm. Families were urged by the Minister of Agriculture to help with the agricultural harvest in 1945. The target for adult volunteer land workers that year was 200,000.

## DUNSTABLE CHURCHES IN WARTIME
### Introduction by Hugh Garrod

The churches of Dunstable were at the forefront of the town's response to the war time situation. Individual priests, rectors and ministers were deeply involved in the many human tragedies in which the war resulted. Many families were comforted by their church families in times of despair at a member reported missing or killed in action. Attendance at services rose during the wartime. Churches and chapels were places of familiarity and reassurance in a world which seemed to have changed forever.

All the churches were involved in the many charities and fund raising initiatives, both local and national, which were supported throughout the war. It was one of the many ways in which the nation and the town united against a common enemy. The list of wartime Charities shows the diversity of these collections. Many were aimed at supporting the British armed services abroad and reflected the churches' on-going concern for the poor and destitute.

The churches were also involved in the town's effort to raise money for military hardware, such as naval vessels and RAF Fighters. Money was earmarked for individually named vessels or aircraft.

Normal restrictions applied to all church buildings. They were expected to observe the blackout regulations and were subject to the same ARP inspections as domestic houses. At the start of the war, the Priory's evensong was moved to the church hall. Later on, the service was moved back to the church when blackout curtains were installed in the Lady Chapel. The nails can still be seen on either side of the windows.

The churches and chapels mirrored the ebb and flow of the war. They organised services of prayer in the dark days and services of celebration when the nation had cause to rejoice. Remembrance Sunday, initiated in

1919, was marked each year throughout the war by survivors of the First World War and by service men and women who were in Dunstable on leave.

All the churches and chapels organised services of thanksgiving at the end of the war, to mark VE Day and VJ Day. There was a new optimism at the end of the war. The churches and their congregations had learnt to collaborate in times of hardship. From this grew the ecumenical movement, which is represented locally today by Dunstable Churches Together.

## WAR TIME CHARITIES

During WWII, the Registers of Services show the charities which were being supported by the Anglican, Methodist and Congregational congregations.

| | |
|---|---|
| Domestic collections | The Fabric Fund |
| | Mothers' Union. |
| | |
| Mission and Outreach | Pretoria Sunday |
| | Aid To China |
| | Church Mission To The Jews |
| | Society For The Propagation Of The Gospel |
| | Waifs and Strays |
| | Farthing Breakfast Collections for the Salvation Army |
| | National Children's Homes |
| | Women's Work Overseas |
| | Overseas Mission |
| | United Mission to Central Africa |
| | The Bible Society |
| | Church Army Flag day |
| | |
| Wartime | King George's Fund For Sailors |
| | Mission to Seamen |
| | ATS |
| | L & D Hospital |
| | British Forces Benevolent Fund |
| | Red Cross |

RAF Benevolent Fund
The Bishop Of London's Appeal for the
    Reconstruction of Churches in Europe
The Royal British Legion
Earl Haig Fund
'Our Own Soldiers' Xmas Appeal

The first Sunday in September was designated the National Day Of Prayer in all churches. Civil Defence Sunday was the Sunday after Remembrance Day.

### *Joyce Haddon* – Fetched Priory Loaves

On Sundays I had to go into Priory Church at about one o'clock to collect a loaf of bread for my Gran. There were many loaves there but I never met anyone else collecting a loaf at the same time as myself. You can still see where the shelves were at the back of the church today.

### *Maisie Bates* – Canteen for the Troops

In Dunstable we ran a canteen at the Methodist Church in the Square, when we had a regiment of soldiers stationed in Dunstable. It was tremendously popular. The Church parlour then was absolutely choc-a-bloc with soldiers. We opened the canteen early in the evening and were given extra rations (from the ministry, I suppose) to produce hot meals for them. I had never seen so many dried eggs in all my life; we cooked them until we looked like them! We had plenty of coffee, tea, milk, cheese and bread, so cauliflower cheese was a popular item on the menu! There was also a piano in the Church parlour that was put to good use on Sunday evenings after the church service. It was quite a successful time for the church. We met quite a lot of soldiers and in fact a member of our congregation married one of them. They were a good crowd and presented us with a bible when they left.

I used to help out in the canteen every Friday and stayed overnight in the church premises fire watching with another girl, Sylvia. There was one young man who slept in the church parlour but what use any of us would have been if there had actually been a fire bomb, I don't know because I could never work that stirrup pump! I don't know how many times we were shown how but I could never quite manage it. I don't remember feeling nervous or frightened during the war. I think it was youth to some extent, also a lack of knowledge and a fatalistic attitude.

## Denise Barker – 100 ways to Cook a Potato

We never went hungry. I feel that we ate well; there were even books that told you how to cook 100 things using potatoes! We certainly grew things at home as I think everyone did. We had a large garden in Princes Street and grew rhubarb and potatoes in abundance. I think at one time we kept chickens and a rabbit but everybody refused to eat it, so we didn't try that anymore. We ate a lot of rabbit from Mr Barley's at the corner of Princes Street; he had them hung up outside and even now we drool about those rabbit stew casseroles.

For entertainment of course there was the cinema and occasionally we went to The Old Palace, but most of my spare time was spent in the Parish Hall where I belonged to the Priory Guides. The Priory Youth Club was extremely active and had a drama section that would enter for the Annual Youth Drama competition.

## Ann Read – Railings Dumped at the Bottom of the Garden

One thing that sticks in my mind was the big blast wall that was built outside the back door and living room. It must have been built by the Council; it was about 7ft tall and at an angle quite close to the house. I suppose it was to stop the windows blowing in and was taken down after the war. At the bottom of the garden we had a big dump, well we called it a dump because it was in the field. All the old railings that were taken down were put there; there were tyres and all sorts of metal; it was a really dangerous place but we used to get out at the bottom of the garden and go and play in there, we had great fun!

My aunt lived in Luton Road with her husband and my grandfather, and I can remember that when my mum used to go shopping for meat with her sister, she would take a knife with her and chop some meat off her ration to give to them. My father had an allotment and grew potatoes, beetroot, onions, parsnips and radishes. Potatoes mainly though; they helped to fill us up. We used to go blackberry picking as mum did lots of bottling; we always had a dessert with our meal and had a few apple trees in our garden.

We used to pick those and then mum would store them down in the cellar. We were always warm and well cared for. I can remember my sister and I had two very pretty dresses, I don't know where they came from, they just appeared. I think they were someone's bridesmaids' dresses; you were just happy that you had a pretty dress.

There was an old copper boiler in the corner of the kitchen and on a Monday morning mum used to light the fire underneath. The house would fill up with steam. Mondays were always wet days and I don't mean outside, I mean inside! I can remember the gas lighter coming around to light the gas lamp outside our house. (Lit very dimly towards the end of the war, as blackout ceased).

### *David Grant* - **Make Do and Mend**

I had a long walk to school, down Park Road passing a baker's shop on the corner, where you could buy a warm bun for one penny, then a short cut through an eerie churchyard and across Luton Road. We had little furniture and would often go to a big second hand saleroom in Luton to see if father could afford to purchase anything that we needed. Food was rationed and we would grow fruit and vegetables in the garden, helped by the instructions by Adam the gardener in the newspaper articles. My mother, who was previously trained as a milliner, would make some of our clothes, as they were in short supply during this period. She would also spend her time making jam, bottling fruit in Kilner jars and pickling eggs in brine in big stone flagons, as a change from the dried egg we received from overseas, while we

GOVERNMENT POSTER encouraging the general public to 'Make Do and Mend' *(DDLHS)*

would be making rugs out of hessian sacking and scraps of cloth. Toys were few and usually crudely home-made of wood, or tin cars and trains made from recycled baked bean cans, with the original printing still visible on the inside, but my brother and I would spend many happy hours playing in the sand pit with a few old bricks.

### Gladys Sutton - my Sister Married a Soldier

When war was declared over the wireless our neighbour came round and asked my father, "Is it true, is the war on?"

I was living at 67 St Mary's Street, Dunstable, at the time. The next thing I remember was having to go with my family to get measured for gas masks. We had to take them with us everywhere we went.

My aunt and uncle lived in Croydon and were very close to a lot of bombing, so my Mum offered to have their three children. There were 7 children in our house, all older than me (three brothers and three sisters), and then we had three more! We always slept three in a bed because our house wasn't very big. I remember the dried egg but we never really went without. Mother cooked good plain food; she was a very good manager. She was always very hard up, my Mum, but she would give her last ha'penny away.

We used the cellar as our air raid shelter. When the sirens went we used to clamber out of bed, grab our coats, (we never dressed), go down, sit there and wait. When it was quiet we worried and then when we heard anything it was frightening. My brother started knitting a dark green scarf. One night for some reason he wasn't there, and I was. I saw it and thought I'd put some sleeves on and make a doll's dress. He was a bit annoyed when he went down there the next time.

As I got a bit older I used to hear the older ones talking about the soldiers and the Americans, they'd say, "You be careful." My Dad didn't really want my eldest sister to get in with any army man, but of course she did, and he nearly went mad. He wasn't American, he was from Devon. It took quite some time before she was allowed to bring him home. One day Mum said, "Albert's coming today so be on your best behaviour." I was playing in the street with 2 or 3 other children when I saw this tall soldier coming up the road. He came up to me and asked me if I knew where Winnie lived. I felt so proud to show him the house. I was pleased he'd asked me but I didn't go in the house for a while. As it happened he was a really lovely man; they courted and got married. The wedding was held at the Priory Church in Dunstable. She had a white dress and Ave Maria for her song. The reception was at home; we had food but I can't remember having a cake. My dad was in the Home Guard and he was very merry that evening when he went out.

My eldest brother was a toolmaker; he couldn't join the army but he was in the Home Guard. My other younger brother was called up which upset my mum. He was a stop at home boy, so it was a big wrench. He was posted to Sheringham for a while before going abroad. He used to write to us and one day I came home and my mother was crying. I couldn't bear to see her crying. I said, "What's the matter?" She gave me this yellow piece of paper to read. I didn't really understand it, but he was a prisoner of war in Germany. They came out in 1945. The day he came home I didn't recognise him one little bit. They'd starved him. It was awful, he was skin and bone. My Mum nursed him back to strength but it took some time. He met a girl eventually and then they got married. He deserved a bit of happiness.

A WARTIME WEDDING August 1943 – Private Morgan (ATS) of Dunstable with her father, now commissioned in The Pioneer Corps. *(AWM)*

I was really spoilt by my family because I was the youngest. "We beat the Jerries!" my brother in law said in one of his letters. In every letter I have, it said, "I can't wait to get home and see you all and Mum's smiling face." Everybody thought about coming home to Mum. We had a lovely, loving family. I have a Christmas card addressed to me from my brother-in-law who was in Italy – it's a map of Italy turned into a Christmas stocking.

My father had served in the First World War and was in the Home Guard. He also worked at a garage. Winnie and Ivy were at work and my brother George worked at the garage with my Dad. We used to do little things, we'd go to the Salvation Army on a Monday night and have a cup of pea soup for a penny. I was in the choir when the Mayor asked us to join the Dunstable Girls' Choir; we turned it down, how silly. We had a new dress each year for the anniversary when we sang. George came home from the Sally Army with this enormous trumpet to learn. It was really funny. We girls used to like playing the tambourines, but we weren't in the band.

My dad loved Vera Lynn and the old songs, and he'd say, "Let's have a sing song." We listened to the wireless quite a bit. Our back garden looked on to Prosperous Row next to the Queen's Head. It was a very narrow garden with a wide path and an apple tree. Dad had the barn and used to mend shoes there. We had a street party in St Mary's Street at the end of the war.

### Jean and John Rushton – had a Honeymoon in London

**Jean:** We had a very fine organist who offered to teach me to play on the organ at West Street Baptist Church. I belonged to the St John Ambulance brigade and went on parade in Ely and shook hands with Lady Mountbatten. John and I got married in 1943.

**John:** I knew I was coming home on leave so we decided to get married. I had to get a special licence but this could be obtained through the forces quite cheaply.

**Jean:** I went to Luton with my mother and bought a green dress. Your mother cried all though the ceremony because she was losing her boy! As a honeymoon we spent two days in London and then John was away for the next two and a half years.

### Jean Partridge – Danced at the Town Hall

We used to have dances every Saturday night in the old Town Hall. There was a local band called Fred Janes and sometimes there was a dance at the Drill Hall near Tavistock Street. You didn't go far because of the blackout but you weren't afraid to walk about on your own. I walked home at midnight from the dances and it was quite safe to do that kind of thing then.

If you wanted to go to the dances at the George Hotel in Luton, you sometimes had to walk home as the buses stopped at about 10 o'clock. During the day you could get buses but they weren't very frequent. If you wanted to go anywhere you went on your bike.

### *John S Purdon* - Childhood Tales

I was born in 1934 and was only 5 when war was declared. So these WWII memories are those of a young child. Despite my young age, many of my memories are quite vivid and quite naturally many are associated with food and food rationing.

My Father, who was a chemical engineer, was a keen gardener and we had a 'Dig for Victory' allotment to supplement our already quite large vegetable garden. I used to help my father on Saturdays and Sundays carrying tools to the allotment and bringing back produce. What he grew became quite extensive and included the general run of vegetables such as cabbages and carrots and Jerusalem Artichokes, which are potato-like tubers but with a very distinctive taste. In the garden extension at the bottom of our garden were several apple trees and two magnificent cherry trees, which in season used to supplement the very small ration of sweets and chocolate.

As I grew older I remember entering into the serious business of swapping pieces of war related debris that we could find in the countryside. Nearby was an Army artillery range and we used to find bullets, bullet cases and even pieces of shrapnel. Towards the end of the war, when radar jamming was in operation, we would find small slivers of the aluminium foil that was used by Bomber Command to mislead the enemy as to the size and direction of the RAF night-raids on Germany. One day, probably in the summer of 1940 when the Battle of Britain was at its height, there was great excitement when a German Messerschmitt fighter was shot down just half a mile from our home and I went with every other small boy to see the debris. We hoped to see the pilot but he had been captured long before we got there.

Another great activity for small children was 'Salvage Drives'. We had to

DUNSTABLE BOOK DRIVE *(DG) (LMS)*

collect everything useful for the war such as paper, tin cans, aluminium and bottles, all of which represented very valuable materials in very short supply. The Mayor would organise 'drives' and badges were offered as a reward for being a good 'Salvage Collector'. Diana, my wife, was a very enthusiastic Salvage Drive collector and she won several badges.

The Government also organised exhibitions of tanks and aircraft to support their campaign to get people to donate their aluminium pots and pans to make more aircraft. They also used to ask people to make donations in cash, in a campaign to 'Help Build a Spitfire or Tank'. I used to give part of my very precious shilling a week pocket money. Of course I believe the real reason for the request for cash was to apply a kind of voluntary taxation, to sop up extra spending power and reduce inflation, because people may have had cash in their purses but there was little to buy.

Another food not rationed were rabbits. Dunstable was quite small and you could get to the country in minutes on your bicycle. Some farmers would sell rabbits they had shot and the fishmonger had them hanging in his shop. We had rabbit pie and also stews. But when eating rabbit you had to be careful of the small lead pellets from the guns that you would find in your mouth. Mushrooms were also an important supplement to our diet as they grew quite plentifully in season in some of the nearby meadows. They were often quite enormous and most delicious. Another supplement was beechnuts that as children we would gather from the ground where they had fallen. Beechnuts are tiny and it took a lot of work to collect even a cup full. Nothing that could be eaten was wasted. In the hedgerows were often brambles (blackberries), big, black and juicy, and these we would gather for my mother to make wonderful pies; but there was no cream and certainly no ice cream!

### Joyce Haddon - Collected Nettles for a Ha'penny

I was born in Church Street, Dunstable, and attended Ashton School. We had a very large garden backing on to Ashton School House and that of a corn merchant in High Street North. We kept chickens and rabbits and went to him for our bundles of straw, which cost us 6d. Those with cellars had to make them as safe as possible, so that's where we sheltered. My Gran, Dad and Uncle set up beds, food and other supplies just in case we had to shelter there for some time.

Gran used to go to the butcher's in Church Street for offal to make brawn. On Saturdays we had bread with dripping and salt, a lovely tea. We had swimmers; little suet puddings dropped into hot pans of water and served with margarine and sugar. We ate such a lot of fat in those days. We used to go wooding – we went to the fields to fetch wood to burn on the fire. We also collected nettles, poppy petals, dandelions, etc. We were only paid a ha'penny or a penny for collecting a huge sack of nettles but we had a great time!

My Dad was in the Air Force and was sent away to India. While he was there, Mum made us stand on a sheet of paper and drew around our feet. She then sent this paper pattern to my father who posted pairs of shoes back to us. Real leather with lovely designs!

A well loved person in Dunstable was the man who had a second hand shop on the corner of Britain Street. It was like an Aladdin's cave where people went in hard times to sell their wares. He was kind enough to take in almost everything. In fact, my doll's pram was sent there.

### Joyce Smithson - a Bomb in our Garden?

I was 7 years old at the beginning of the war. I remember our next-door neighbour had her radio on when it was announced that war had been declared on Germany. My mother was in a terrible state and fainted because my brother, who was 12 years older than myself, would have to go to war. This upset her greatly. My father had been in the First World War and was reported missing three days before the armistice was signed. Fortunately, he was alright but my mother still had lots of memories of that time.

My parents belonged to the Salvation Army and we lived at 5 Kirby Road in Dunstable. We didn't have a shelter ourselves but the family across the road from us did and although we always had the opportunity to go there, my mother told us to go and hide in the cupboard under the stairs and put a cushion over our heads!

Once soon after the siren had sounded my mother heard this loud explosion. She was sure the bomb had dropped in our back garden so she fetched the ARP down. My father found them digging up his vegetables! She was convinced the bomb had dropped in the back garden but of course there was nothing there!

My father was a stoker at the Dunstable gas works and cleaned Lloyds Bank to make a little extra money. He also had an allotment near the cemetery in West Street. Dunstable had some very good shops then. My mother used Barleys butchers in Princes Street and the Home and Colonial on the corner of Church Street. For entertainment we went to the cinema in High Street North and played quizzes and games in the Salvation Army. My father and brother were also in the band.

## CONVERSATION BETWEEN FRIENDS:
### Betty Tarbox, June Morton, Heather Hing and Pam Perkins

**Betty:** You couldn't buy handbags then. My sister used to make hers out of strips of felt she used to plait. She used to keep big pots of Pond's cream in the corner of her bag in case one of the Yanks came near her. They used to stand in the doorways all the way up the street.

**June:** The rationing didn't stop until the 1950s; we didn't have any childhood or teenage time, we had Utility clothing, you couldn't be fashion conscious.

**Betty:** My father was a coal merchant and that was rationed. If you had a baby or someone was very ill you could get a permit for extra coal. Our Mum tried to kid us that we had butter but it was margarine. My job was to write out the coal round books. Bread was rationed after the war. We had 3 rashers of bacon a week and in those days everyone had a cooked breakfast, so it didn't go anywhere. We had a stuffed rabbit one Christmas day. We kept chickens and we used to sit on the doorstep and pluck them.

We cultivated our entire garden and were never without vegetables. My mother had hens; she had a great big pot of these stinking potato peelings on a trivet by the fire that she used to mash up with bran to feed them. They were kept in a fence my father made.

**Heather:** My dad kept pigeons and he raced them. We had pigeon eggs and if they didn't race well they were on the table the next day. He was allowed to race them despite the fact that we used pigeons for war work.

**Betty:** We had double summer time in the war; my uncle had a farm and if you worked on the farm harvest you got an extra petrol allowance. Of course then it was horse and carts mainly. Petrol was dyed so you couldn't pilfer it.

**Pam:** I was sent into Dunstable every Saturday morning to queue. If you saw a queue, you joined it, it didn't matter what it was. I queued at Bata's for sandals. You used to stand in these queues and at the end you'd get a packet of curlers.

**Betty:** All the town railings were taken and put in a field in Bull Pond Lane. They were there through the whole of the war. That field was full of chains and railings, even from graves and from the church; I never did see the point of that. They said it was to be melted down for munitions for the war effort but they never used them. Fred Carter was the scrap metal merchant here, so he had the contract for all of Vauxhall's scrap. We were led up the garden path.

We were all encouraged to join in and do something. I joined the St John Ambulance and in February 1944 I got my preliminary first aid certificate.

**Pam:** Father dug a great big hole and bricked it up as a shelter; the Dad next door had to go to war so we had a hole in the fence so that our neighbours could come in with us, and you'll never guess who was always first down the shelter when the siren went off! It was the dog that was always first in; as soon as you opened the back door when the siren went, he was gone.

**Betty:** There was a big thermometer thing on the town hall. This used to show how much had been saved for a ship or an aeroplane, something for the war. The totals used to go up.

I was in the Priory hospital because I had scarlet fever. You weren't allowed to have visitors to start with. When you did get to have visitors you had to go to the tennis court and look through at your parents. I was 10. You couldn't look through the window where I was because it was sandbagged up. All four of us got it. We went to the isolation hospital and it was so full my brother, who also caught it, had to sleep at the bottom of my bed. I had to help teach my brother to walk again; we were in bed so long. I was there 6 weeks.

If we saw an ambulance we said, "Touch my collar, never get the fever, pass it on to a dog!"

**June:** We used to go to the Cali swimming pool in the summer and skating in the winter.

We were given jam sandwiches and bottles of pop by mum and were over in the fields all day long.

**Heather:** We went up on the Downs and just sat and talked and played rounders. A word you never heard when we were young was bored; we were never bored, we spent most of our summers out of doors.

**Betty:** Nobody had watches; I used to run home when I heard the town hall clock chime 9 o'clock.

We left school in 1946 and now we have reunions. We go out to dinner twice a year. We had a special one at the Old Palace Lodge for 50 years and are planning one for 60 years.

## K. Malia – his Father Patrolled the Garden in case they were Invaded

The air-raid siren sounded. The usual family activity followed. That is to say father, in his role of family protector, issued his instructions, "Quick, into the shelter." The only thing was that the time was wrong. These instructions normally came when it was dark and when we were already in bed. But this was teatime on a lovely summer afternoon.

The air raid shelter had been dug and created personally by Dad. It was properly lined and totally underground. Under the far corner of our garden to be precise; it was fitted out with bunks, seats, a table and lights.

No scrambling down makeshift ladders because it had a stairway leading down to an inner door into the shelter proper. My father's name should have been Anderson, except that Anderson could not have been as good as he was at building shelters!

Certainly our neighbours thought so, because several of them were invariably ensconced there by the time we arrived on air raid nights. All were welcome of course – for what would be the point of survival if we were alone, especially as one of them was doing his best to teach me to play the piano!

Sitting or lying in the shelter we were all periodically informed on the progress of the war as it affected Dunstable by my father. He, having built and maintained the shelter, was the only one who never used it, except for my older sister who could never be awakened and so lay blissfully in bed throughout all the raids that never were. How envious the rest of us were. So despite his Herculean efforts, if Jerry decided to drop a bomb on 27 Kingsway, all the neighbours would have been saved but only four out of the six in our family would have joined them. My sister would have happily continued her rest permanently and my father would have joined her, as he patrolled the garden making sure we were not invaded.

### Maisie Bates – One of the First Lady Bank Cashiers

I was 20 at the time, living in Friars Walk in Dunstable and working at Barclays Bank in Luton. I was either on ledgers, statements or securities; all that sort of thing. After many men working at the bank were called up, the assistant manager asked me how I felt about working on the counter. Well, the Chief Cashier was horrified. He thought the world would fall in if women started serving on the counter! I was the first woman to serve on the counter in that bank; that was quite a change in occupation. It was quite daunting to begin with but I enjoyed it immensely. Eventually more women joined the staff although, when I was there, there were only 5 women in a very large company. We were second class citizens! But of course everything changed during the war.

In 1942 I was sent to the Bletchley branch. Of course we knew that there was something going on in Bletchley Park but it was all very hush, hush. I was there for 2 to 3 months. I didn't enjoy that very much because I was the only woman there and the other gentlemen were a little on the elderly side. I also worked in Leighton Buzzard carrying out counter work. I then went back to the Luton branch.

I had an extraordinary experience in Luton before I started work on the counter. It was quite early on and I was sitting at a desk working on some ledgers when there was an almighty crash; it seemed to come from outside the bank. Everyone grabbed their ledgers and shot downstairs into the vaults. Everyone disappeared without a word! About ten minutes later the gentleman in charge of ledgers came down and in a very sarcastic voice said, "What are you all doing down here?" Someone told him that we'd heard a bomb or something, he said "You heard wrong, that was a lorry that crashed into Fishers butchers shop across the road!"

## *Margaret Lewry* – Stitched the Pleats into her Skirt every Night

My father had two allotments where he grew vegetables. He used to ride a big bicycle behind which he attached a cart, basically a sturdy wooden box mounted on an axle with two wheels and long handles. He would somehow fasten this behind the saddle to carry his tools and/or produce from the allotment. I used to go with him sometimes to help with the weeding and watering. We kept chickens and rabbits in the back garden at home. My sister and I would be sent over the open fields at the back of Ridgeway Drive, to a farm in Houghton Regis to buy day-old baby chicks at a penny each. We put them into a deep round basket to carry home where they would be reared at the hearth until they could go into the garden.

I can remember sweets being rationed. My sister and I would go to a shop along the Luton Road on a Sunday morning to buy sweets for the family. My parents hadn't a tooth between them but my mother always had toffees and my father had Mint Imperials. I had either Chocolate Beans which are now called Smarties or, my real favourites, Floral Gums because they were tiny and you were given lots for your allowance.

When outside, we played hopscotch and skipping. We wore gymslips for school; I think my mother bought them from a tallyman who called at the house. Every day when I took off my school skirt, I would put big cross stitches in the pleats of the skirt to hold them in place. I probably wore a lot of hand-me-downs outside school, after all I did have five sisters and one brother.

### Mary Dolman - Just One Banana

I worked at the Totternhoe Lime Company in the office and one day a chap came in with a banana and gave me half, I thought it was marvellous. I didn't ask him where he got it from. Probably on the black market.

### Mary Corrie nee Cheshire - Marrow Jam and Suet Puddings

People all looked out for each other and morale was good. My parents used to listen to the radio news and we used to sing along to all the war songs. Mum did very well, she made marrow jam and suet puddings. There was a big surge to get tinned fruit when one of the shops had them. Mum used to make some of my clothes, or we were given hand-me-downs. I don't think we went ragged but things were a bit make do and mend.

### Mary Cresswell - Town Hall Dances were 1/6d

We had superb dances in Dunstable Town Hall. That was a lovely building and they had wonderful bands playing there. It used to cost one shilling and sixpence to go in, (7   p), but my uncle was sometimes on the door and very often I got in for nothing!

We were short of food in some ways but my dad had two allotments so we were never short of vegetables. Mum would cook potato and onion pie and we always had chickens in our garden and kept a cockerel for Christmas. Rabbits could be bought from the local farm. A man came from Luton on the bus who used to come round to the back door of our house with a big suitcase full of things. I can't remember what was in his suitcase, but I don't think he sold black market goods.

### Arnold Dawson - Growing Swedes

I moved into the area in 1937, got married and rented (what was then a very rare) new house in Houghton Regis for 15 shillings per week. As our house was surrounded by fields, I was able to take a small plot of ground to grow vegetables. It was very hard work to dig the soil as it had never been dug before and I decided to grow swedes – they all came up! But how many can you eat? I gave most of them away.

### E Speller - Rang Totternhoe Church Bells

I lived with my parents and sister. Dad's sister had died, leaving a baby who lived with us as well. We also had five Irishmen billeted with us all through the war – they worked at Bagshawe's but they never spoke about their work. My Dad was in the Home Guard and carried out fire watching in the old police station at the bottom of Friars Walk. I met my fiancé when I was 18 in the Queen's Head in St Mary's Street. He was then shipped out to Burma. Dunstable had some very nice shops during the war; I bought a lovely gold lamé wedding dress in West Street. My mother's relatives were older than me so I was given a lot of hand-me-down clothing.

We used to gather herbs. We took them to the herbalist where the Quadrant Shopping Centre is now and got paid a very small amount of money for a lot of hard work! We went to the Picture Palace in High Street North. In another cinema we saw the Crazy Gang and other films.

At the end of the war, all of us in the Training Corps went along to the Totternhoe church and rang the bells! It was really hard work!

### Mary Owen - Cycling with no Lights

Compared to the present day, Dunstable was sparsely inhabited. We had an acre of garden which father looked after although I had to cut the grass. We grew all our own vegetables, and kept chickens, guinea fowl and a donkey. I had a pony, cats and dogs; it was very much like a smallholding, very useful for mother in the kitchen. Meat was rationed of course, but father somehow managed to obtain a little bit extra at that time, such as pheasants.

I travelled to work by bus mainly, although if I was going to be late home at night (because I would go to a dance or the cinema in Luton), I used to cycle, as there were no buses after 9pm. I was very nervous to begin with as I only had a tiny lamp to shine on the ground but I soon got used to it and found it quite exciting at times! Locally I went out with a group of RAF people stationed at the Met Office on Dunstable Downs. We spent our free time going to local dances and the cinema, a very happy crew.

To mark VE Day we had a big fete held at the back of Bagshawe's grounds in the town, with stalls and fireworks – quite exciting! There were also a lot of street parties. I went to one or two; it was very exciting seeing everybody sitting down at the long tables, eating nice food or better than it had been.

### Jean Yates - Camping at Whipsnade

My aunts, Phyllis and Vera, were young married women at the outbreak of war. The two sisters and their husbands were fortunate enough to each own a small car and with some friends they regularly enjoyed camping weekends around Bedfordshire. Tents were heavy canvas with large flysheets, which at the outbreak of war were camouflaged.

As petrol became more and more precious they devised a scheme where they could continue their camping weekends. They kept their tents in a barn, one raised high on stones to keep it dry and free from vermin, at Church Farm, Whipsnade.

Both husbands worked at Vauxhall in Luton and had reserved occupations so were not called up, and so summer weekends could still occasionally be enjoyed under canvas on Bates's farm. On these weekends they cycled to Whipsnade from Luton.

On one weekend the young women heard a low flying plane and ran out of the tents to see what it was. They looked straight up at a German plane and could see the pilot looking at them. He flew off having seen these young women in their summer dresses; they thought that if they hadn't run out, or the men had been outside, they may all have been killed, as the pilot would have thought that their camouflaged tents belonged to the army.

### Mrs Nellie Hackney - Patrolling in a Tin Hat

There were seven children in our house, plus my mother and father. Dad worked on the railway and didn't earn a lot of money, so mother took in washing, helped to deliver other women's children, laid out people who had passed on, in fact, she did anything to help the family budget. One day returning from work, my sister and I came into the house and found that my mother had taken in a lady and her four children (evacuees). She'd found them wandering around the town. My sister and I looked at each other; we looked at the evacuees and saw that they were in our clothes! We nearly went berserk! We then had mattresses on the floor to sleep on. That was Mother! Although we had a rough time we had a wonderful mother and father.

We lived on the Northfields Estate in Dunstable and had to patrol the area in our tin hats, making sure that no lights were visible, but to be quite honest my sister and I were terrified. When our father found out that we had to take our place on the rota he said, "I can't see what good you two are going to be. You're walking out of here like frightened animals!" But we did our duty and we had quite a few laughs one way or another.

We loved to go ballroom dancing with a group of girls. We'd go home lunchtime and put dinky curlers in our hair in readiness for the evening. We went to the town hall in Dunstable about 2 or 3 times a week. I also used to go to the Sugar Loaf hotel; that was out of this world because it had long mirrors placed all around the room – I felt like a princess. Sometimes during the interval, we would club together and just about managed to buy half a shandy each at a little pub round the corner but we were very happy in those days. We used to swap and loan clothes because they were rationed and very difficult to buy. We also used to go dancing at the George Hotel in Luton (6 miles away). Unfortunately there were no taxis and we had to walk all the way home, singing and carrying our dancing shoes. One day we were challenged by the Home Guard. We were scared to death! All of a sudden we heard. "Halt! Who goes there?"

My husband joined the RAF. He served for three and a half years altogether, but he was based in Gibraltar for two of those. We got married on his embarkation leave. We had already decided to get married and had our banns called but he came home earlier than expected, which left me in a panic. With no coupons I thought that I'd have to get married in just a little dress that I already had, but his sister knew of a neighbour prepared to loan her wedding dress. It was a bit short but quite nice. I had what you would call a Utility wedding! I had three bridesmaids and it was stated in the local newspaper that I had a rainbow wedding because each bridesmaid had a different coloured dress (they were all borrowed). We had no wedding cake or honeymoon. However, I had a Utility wedding ring which cost £1 10s 0d, and we were happy and in love.

When my husband was in Gibraltar we used to write to each other every day. One day I told him that my younger sister had been taken to the children's hospital there. Unbeknown to me, he sent a bunch of bananas to the hospital but none of the children knew what a banana was and they had to be shown how to eat one!

When my husband went back to Gibraltar I thought that I would never see him again. I was fortunate though and when he came back, because we had no money, we lived for a time with my mother.

### P Underwood - Collecting Scrap

One of the things we kids did was to go potato picking. If I remember rightly you got time off school to go. I did it once at Sewell.

We also went looking for scrap, because scrap was needed for the war effort to make tanks. It was a great excuse for wandering all over people's farms and property. I don't think we ever collected any but it was great fun. The countryside was right on our doorstep. You just walked up Periwinkle Lane towards Beecroft Farm. We lived in 219 High Street South opposite Cross's factory.

We kept chickens and there were pig bins at the corner of many streets for people to put their kitchen waste in. This was then carted away for the pigs. Once we needed to kill a chicken but no one could bring themselves to wring its neck so I shot its head off.

Entertainment – it wasn't all doom and gloom. We had the radio and we all went to the cinema practically every week. We watched Pathé and Gaumont News and the propaganda about how wonderful we were and how awful the Germans were. Tommy Trinder, the Garrison Theatre, Elsie and Doris Waters, the sisters of Jack Warner. There was a lot of enjoyment to be had.

### Pam Buckle - Sharing a Cupboard with the Neighbours

Soon after war was declared, an air-raid shelter was built underground in Bennett's Recreation ground. That came along near the back of our garden. The first time we had an air raid during the night, we ran around to this air-raid shelter and stayed there for about an hour. We did that about 3 times but we very soon got very tired of that, and from then on we would go and sit in a large cupboard under our stairs. Later we joined forces with a neighbouring family and the two families would share one of the two cupboards which helped to pass the time!

### Philip Buckle - had an Identity Bracelet

We were issued with an identify card and I can still remember my number today! Some people had a bracelet made with their identity card number printed on it; all our family had these bracelets made. I've still got mine.

On one occasion I was given a banana. Now before the war I acquired a taste for them and I hadn't had a banana for several years. A friend of ours had a sailor billeted with them and this chap brought back a bunch and gave me one. I treasured it, eating it bit by bit. I kept the skin in my bedside table for months, just to be able to smell a banana!

### Rob Cutler - and the Mars Bars

A chap called Arthur was getting some straw out of this straw rick when he came across 48 Mars Bars. We were told that if we found anything, we weren't to touch it, pick it up or eat it, as it might poison us all. Some adults had a discussion and decided that they would give an old dog a Mars Bar and if it was alright in the morning, then they'd know they were alright for the rest of us to eat. Well, the dog was alright the next morning and I think we boys were given half a Mars Bar each. Wonderful, when you were on rations.

### Roy Turner - and the Pomegranate

One of the places we couldn't go was the gas works, but why, I don't know. I've still got some ration books. Certain people seemed to get extra if they had bigger families but we always managed. I can never remember feeling hungry; my father had an allotment and chickens, everybody did. Once a ship got through and we were told that children could have a pomegranate. I've never been so disappointed in all my life; all you got were seeds! I remember when we first had bananas. Some of the children had never seen them before and didn't know what to do with them.

Dunstable used to have Weapons Week or Wings for Victory Week, where everyone tried to save as much as they could to buy Spitfires; I remember Dunstable bought 5. I used to take two shillings and sixpence to school every week. It used to mount up and when we'd saved fifteen shillings we were given a certificate.

### Shirley Felice Ansell - Squares of Newspaper and Christmas

The thing that I did not like was the lavatory or the 'lav' as we used to call it. This was situated in the yard; it was a brick building with another attached for next door. It had a wooden seat with a hole in it and a cast iron cistern with a long chain, which you would pull when you had finished. It was dark, cold and draughty and the door had peepholes in it. I would be frightened to stay in there for very long because there always seemed to be

'SALUTE THE SOLDIER' – a military parade in High Street North, Dunstable, during War Weapons Week in March 1941 *(DG) (LMS)*

spiders lurking around. Auntie Win would scrub the lav out every week but the spiders always returned. In the summer I was much braver and would sit and play with the newspaper squares that were threaded through a piece of string that hung from a nail on the wall. There was no toilet paper in those days and sometimes I would sing and kick the wooden box for the music. We didn't use the lav at night-time; we had a pot under the bed. In the winter it would freeze so we would have to take a bucket of water with us to flush it down. We never spent long in there; it was freezing cold!

Auntie Win kept rabbits. I used to play with them but when she had fattened them up she would kill them and I would watch while she gutted and skinned them. She would sell the skins for a shilling and she would make rabbit stew and rabbit pie. Auntie Win was a lovely cook; I can always remember Christmases when I lived there. In October she would start to prepare the fruit for the Christmas cake and Christmas puddings. She would then collect the big bowl from the bedroom and mix the puddings in it. We would all have a stir and make a wish. She would then put the mix in basins with a cloth on top and they would be boiled for hours in the brick copper that you did your washing in. She would keep the fire going under the boiler while they cooked. She would bake the Christmas cake in the big black range. Another thing Auntie Win did was to pickle eggs. She would get the big jug down from the bedroom and pickle eggs in isinglass. They would keep for some time but didn't taste very nice.

The preparation for Christmas was lovely; about a week before Christmas we would make the chains to decorate the room. You could not get Christmas trees so Auntie Win would get me a branch and put it in a pot. We would then make bells to hang on the branch from milk bottle tops and pompoms out of odd bits of wool. When no one was in, I would go into her bedroom and look under the bed to see what they had bought me for Christmas. Mum and Auntie Win always managed to get me something; a toy Post Office, a Snakes and Ladders and Ludo game, sweets, an orange and a Rupert Annual. One Christmas I had a doll's house. On Christmas Eve, Auntie Win would be busy getting food prepared. She would make mince pies, prepare what meat she could get hold of and light the fire in the front room. On Christmas Day, Auntie Win would cook the dinner. Mum would be delivering the mail, as there was a delivery on Christmas Day. Uncle Sid would be round the pub, then came home so drunk that he could not eat his Christmas dinner. We would push him up the stairs to sleep it off, before he went to the Post Office to put the blackout up. Some Christmases Auntie Win's brother Ron and his wife Flo would come and spend the day with us. After tea they would push the table back, get the gramophone out and I would have to turn the handle and play Bing Crosby singing *White Christmas* while they danced.

Summer was also a lovely time; I would play out with my friend Barbara and sometimes I would be allowed to stay for tea. Her mother would always let me have salad cream on my eggs and salad; I thought it was delicious as my mother never bought anything like that! Sometimes I would be allowed to sleep the night. Barbara's father had the use of a friend's car and they would often take me with them when they went on an outing. We would visit Ashridge, and Barbara and I would wander through the woods while her parents stayed in the car and read.

Barbara and I joined the Brownies. We could not get uniforms because of the war, so Barbara's Mother used an old brown curtain to make us both Brownie uniforms. The tie was made from a triangular bandage dyed yellow. We had lots of fun at Brownies and later went up to the Girl Guides. I also joined dancing classes doing ballet and tap and I was in several shows.

In the summer on a Sunday, we would have an early tea and go to the cemetery to see the graves of Auntie Win's relatives. Sometimes we would go up to Dunstable Downs and on the way home we would call at the Globe pub for a drink. I would have to sit outside with my lemonade and packet of crisps.

### *Tony Ward* – Sheltered behind the Piano

The blackout of course affected everybody. There were air-raid precaution wardens, ARPs, who if they saw a chink of light would come hammering on your door. In part of the war, my father, who was concerned with the printing industry and wasn't called up at that time, used to have to carry out fire-watching duties on the top of a factory. Also, I remember that sometimes during raids, you could see searchlights at the northern end of the town in the Watling Street area. I don't think they actually fired at anything though. You could hear gunfire and bombs, in Luton in particular. Eventually we used to take refuge behind the family's piano. That was the government's advice. The idea was to put it against a load-bearing wall, with come cushions, and hide behind it. So if the house was brought down, you had something to protect you! I had lessons on this piano and in fact I've still got it! It used to belong to an uncle and aunt; they left the area and gave it to my parents.

The cinema was very popular. My parents took me to see Walt Disney's Fantasia and Bambi – things like that. We also saw the newsreels showing Germans troops and Hitler and so on.

When we went to visit relatives in Henlow who had a smallholding, this would involve several bus rides. A couple of times we visited relatives in Sussex. We had to tell the authorities where we were going and for how long and get permission to go; partly to avoid general chaos and also, if your house was bombed, the authorities needed to know if you were in there or not.

Food-wise I remember powdered egg and milk, having perhaps half an ounce of butter a week and the Co-op milkman coming round; supplies of milk didn't seem to be too bad. My grandparents lived near a local dairy; they had their milk delivered in a churn, ladled directly into their own containers. Often the milk would still be warm, absolutely fresh! Bread and fruit were short. Rations for meat – there used to be queues at the butchers'. I don't know if you saw Dad's Army, where people try to keep friendly with their butcher Corporal Jones, in order to get a few extra sausages. Well, that was definitely reminiscent of wartime! There were many small general stores about in Dunstable and as a child I was often sent with a list of groceries to go and collect, but the only time you saw an orange was at Christmas, when you had one at the toe of your stocking. At the end of the war ice creams started to appear; locally ice-cream vendors would come round on their special bikes shouting "Icey, Icey!"

Not only did we grow vegetables in the garden but my father also had an allotment in Worthington Road, which I used to help him with on Saturday mornings. I remember a chap who used to sit at the corner of Chiltern Road with an easel, painting pictures. I believe he was arrested as a possible spy because he was painting pictures of RAF personnel walking about.

### *Tony Woodhouse* – Listening to Messages

My father was a butcher and had a shop at the top of George Street in Dunstable. We lived above the shop and watched endless convoys of tanks and lorries winding their way along the High Street. After school, I used to listen to these weird messages that were broadcast over the wireless such as, 'My mother's aunt has dropped her cup,' or something similar, which of course was a coded message for someone in Europe!

### *Una Basham* – did the Hokey Cokey when War Ended

There were six of us, Mum, Dad, Grandma, and three children living in the same house. We had a good roomy cellar in which to shelter. Also a blast wall was built opposite the sitting room window. Several of the houses had to take in evacuees; some of these children attended our school, Burr Street, Dunstable (now Icknield School). Older girls living in our road took us to school and frequently during the winter months the lane was so muddy, we had to go the 'street' way.

At the rear of Harrison Carter were allotments and a static water tank for use in the event of fire. Dad had one of these allotments and we also had a large garden at home to grow vegetables. Dad would take us in the wheelbarrow into Church Street to buy potatoes and seeds.

Our coal was delivered via a chute in the passageway down into the cellar. A baker would come from Smith's in Church Street in his horse and cart and sometimes I would get a ride up to the Stipers Hill area.

At that time National Savings were introduced; mum had a float of about £5 and sold stamps to whoever wished to buy, as a means of saving. They would canvas a road and then find someone to collect. She loved to go out on a Friday night; hearing the local gossip was an added bonus!

In order to buy meat you had to register with a butcher; Mum got her meat from Lonley's in West Street. Furniture, rugs and other goods came from Baker's in Church Street and Durrant's. Things were often bought on approval and paid off week by week.

We bought our dress material from Monk's. At the bottom of our garden (now Hawthorn Close) was the dump, containing old tyres, scrap metal and iron railings. In fact one day, the doctor came and looked out of our window and said, "There's my gates!"

There was a chap who had a smallholding off Bull Pond Lane at the top of Garden Road and kept pigs. There was a pig bin half way down the road and we'd put in our peelings and kitchen waste for him to collect. Rose's and Burdett's had a dairy nearby and the Post Office and corner shop was on the other corner of Garden Road. On the corner of King Street was Roberts', another grocer, further down there was Lynn's, and on the corner of Lover's Walk, Parkin's, which Mum patronised. I didn't know anyone who owned a car until the late 1940s. An ice-cream man would come round on a tricycle with a container for the ice-cream.

Once at school we took a jam jar and got an amount of drinking chocolate which was scarce. Milk was beaten into marg or butter to make it go further and we'd have a stick of rhubarb and dip it in sugar as a treat. Sometimes we made toffee in a tin. At the end of the war I remember dancing the hokey cokey with my friends near the Town Hall!

### *Valerie Cousins* - had Outings in the Car

We lived on the Luton Road in Dunstable. In our garden we had an underground air-raid shelter complete with 2 sets of bunk beds, electric light and an oil stove. It was very damp and we didn't use it very much, although from time to time it became our playhouse. Like lots of people we got used to the air raids and would just get underneath the dining table.

We didn't travel very much but my Dad did get a petrol allowance because he worked for a firm that made flying helmets for pilots and he had to visit a firm in Amersham every now and then. My Mum and I went with him; that was an outing for us!

### *Mick Partridge* - Dancing

We went dancing most nights at the Old Town Hall, AC-Sphinx (Delco) or the Drill Hall. They were all in High Street North.

### *Jim Knight* - in Search of Food

My Dad worked from 6am–6pm Monday to Friday and 6am–4pm Saturday and Sunday at the Totternhoe Lime Company. As a lime burner on the kilns he was in a reserved occupation. In addition we had a large garden and two allotments down Stanbridge Road at Ditchlong. We boys helped with the digging in spring and picking potatoes in the autumn. Dad kept a lot of rabbits which were killed to make pies and stews. We boys had to fill 2 sacks of food which we picked up on the Knolls for the rabbits each day after school and before tea in the spring, summer and autumn. Many people took allotments to 'Dig for Victory', which was a slogan in the war, although they knew very little about vegetable growing and would ask the seasoned gardeners for help. On summer evenings later in the war, as we toiled on the allotment, the sky was often filled with bombers going over. I can remember my Dad taking me to the look-out post when he was fire-watching and showing me the glow over Dunstable Downs as London burned.

Some village boys like me, got jobs helping with the harvest. I used to lead the loaded horse and carts from the field to the farmyard. Bigger boys pitched sheaves on to the carts. Later when the threshing machine came, wire netting was put on posts a little distance from the ricks being threshed. It was put all round us boys who were given sticks; the farmer's terrier dog was also put inside the netting. Our job was to kill the rats. We also went stooking – putting the sheaves of corn into stooks to dry as they came off the binder.

## *Alan Sinfield* – Starlight Street Lamps

120 High Street South was the family home, having been built for my Grandfather at the end of the 19th century. The house had a large cellar used as a fuel store. With the start of hostilities, this was converted to part fuel store and part air raid shelter. Fortunately, I cannot recall it ever getting much use as the latter. My father and I did make up some large screens from old pieces of plywood mounted on 2 x 1 inch battens. These served a dual purpose of protecting the glazing in the event of a bomb exploding in the vicinity and providing an effective black out for the windows. Also, as an additional aid to prevent the window from splintering, a diamond pattern of adhesive tape was applied to each pane of glass. My father worked for the London and North Eastern Railway at Luton and when he received his call up papers in 1941 I shall always remember the words of my cousin, "Things must be getting really bad, if they've got to call up Uncle Walter!"

Around this time married women were directed out to work and I recall that my mother was sent to the Index Printers which was at that time located behind the shops in High Street South from Woolworth's to Moore's.

The blackout was very effective as there were no streetlights, which made driving at night extremely difficult. Vehicle headlamps were covered by a screen with a tiny horizontal slit which had a downward shield over it to prevent any light rays going upwards. At some point during the war, it must have been 1943–1944, a new form of street lighting for main roads was tried out in Dunstable. The tall lamp standards had been introduced in Dunstable some time prior to the war, but only along the A5. The lamp called a Starlight was fitted to the existing standards and was a fairly low wattage tungsten lamp completely enclosed in a lightproof case, except for the base which had a star shape cut out. When driving down the High Street in the dark, you were guided by the Starlights above you.

# Schools and Evacuees

## INTRODUCTION BY HUGH GARROD

By the time war was declared, plans were well advanced for the evacuation of children from London and other towns and cities which were vulnerable to bombing. The railway system was to be the means for mass evacuation. Parents had to give their consent for their children to take part. When war was eventually declared, the evacuation programme swung into action. All the reception schools had been identified but the children and their parents were not told in advance where they were going. There were, however, no plans as to which homes they would stay in.

All the Dunstable schools were involved. Initially, evacuees and local children were educated in the same classes at the same time. It soon became evident that this was unworkable. One solution was to find separate accommodation for the evacuees, under the control of the host school. The other was to educate the local children in the mornings and the evacuees in the afternoons.

The evacuated children had a range of experiences. Some found a home from home, others were desperately unhappy and homesick. Some local people viewed the evacuees as uncivilised and assumed they knew little of hygiene or good manners. Some of the evacuees viewed Dunstable as a journey back in time, lacking all the excitement and amenities of London.

When the expected bombing did not immediately materialise, many evacuees went back to their homes in London. When the Blitz eventually started in earnest, the children were re-admitted to their Dunstable schools. Most evacuees went home after the war; a few are still with us.

All the schools in Dunstable seem to have been involved in educating the evacuees who arrived at the beginning of the war.

The Secondary schools were the Grammar School, Britain Street and Northfields. The Primary schools were Ashton School, Burr Street, Chiltern Road and Evelyn Road.

The Headteacher of Ashton St Peter's Lower has kindly allowed the war-related items from the Ashton School Log Book to be reproduced. The Log entries are typical of those that would be found in any similar school log of that time. They give a good indication of the changes in routine which the war caused.

The analysis of the Highfields (Evelyn Road) School admissions registers shows how there was a large influx of evacuees in 1939 and 1940. Many of these children returned with their families to London over the next few years. Many were then re-admitted in 1944. This is typical of most schools across the country who took in evacuated children.

## WAR EXTRACTS FROM THE LOG BOOK OF DUNSTABLE ASHTON JUNIOR MIXED SCHOOL

### 1939

| | |
|---|---|
| June 14th | Headmistress absent from School in the afternoon to attend meeting at Britain Street School in connection with ARP and dispersal of children. |
| June 23rd | Headmistress absent from school to attend a conference of Head Teachers re ARP and evacuation of children, at Shire Hall, Bedford. |
| July 10th | Air Warden to supply gasmasks to those children who had none. 1.30 pm. |
| July 11th | Gasmask drill taken in school 11 am. |
| July 13th | The Director of Education, HE Baines Esq., called at 10.10 am to discuss measures for dispersal of children and ARP preparations. |
| July 28th | Air raid dispersal practice. 3.45 pm. |
| September 11th | School did not open as usual, owing to the arrangements having to be made to accommodate evacuees from London. |
| September 18th | School reopened with a double shift, owing to war conditions. |

Placed here are: -

| | |
|---|---|
| Hargrave Park Infants | 89 |
| St Luke's Old Street Infants | 91 |
| Edinburgh Road Infants | 4 |

|                |              |     |
| -------------- | ------------ | --- |
| Dudden Hill    |              | 1   |
|                | Total        | 185 |

|                                |       |      |
| ------------------------------ | ----- | ---- |
| St Luke's Old Street Jn Boys   | 55    | + 18 |
| St Luke's Old Street Jn Girls  | 58    | +  8 |
|                        Total   | 113   | + 26 |

On the Ashton School registers are 307, making 631 children in all, attending this school.

September 26th — Mr. Birkett, HMI, visited school to enquire into accommodation for visiting schools. He also considered how the double shift would work when the weather became colder and more inclement. He was surprised that the Head Teacher was supposed to be responsible for a class.

October 3rd — Headmistress absent from school in morning to consult with D of E concerning several problems that had arisen connected with school under the double shift arrangements.

October 10th — Mrs. Locke, HMI, called to enquire concerning the progress of the trenches, 4.30 pm.

October 19th — Off shift did not assemble as Church Hall was required by the Freemasons.

November 1st — Chairs and tables arrived for Hargrave Park School.

November 8th — Mr. Pinnock called in afternoon to ask for plan and numbers, to show how children were distributed during on and off shifts.

November 17th — Chemical lavatories (4) arrived for Air Raid Shelters.

November 28th — Dentist and Nurse paid second visit to finish Inspection and to inspect the London children.

December 12th — Air Raid Drill taken. Children all out with outdoor clothes in 2 minutes.

## 1940

February 19th — Twenty children in the top classes attended a musical recital given at the Wesleyan Church by Mr. R Jacques,

| | |
|---|---|
| | Musical Advisor for LCC, at 2.30 pm. |
| February 27th | The Director of Education called at school about 2.30 pm to make enquiries re Dispersal for Air Raids. |
| March 4th | Mr. Pinnock called to enquire concerning distribution of London Scholars over the school during their on session. |
| March 5th | The Director of Education called in the morning to make enquiries re the proposed formation of a Sunday School at Evelyn Road for evacuees. |
| March 6th | Mr. Pinnock called again re numbers of Hargrave Park Scholars. Mrs Locke called re ARP dispersal. |
| March 13th | The Director of Education called to enquire concerning Air Raid Dispersal. |
| April 2nd | Mr. Pinnock called re this school having two more rooms for the off shift. |
| April 4th | Mr. Pinnock called again re Air Raid Drill. |
| April 5th | Air Raid Practice. A child slipped in the corridor and dislocated her thumb. |
| April 8th | Mr. Hall called to enquire the greatest number of children in school at any one time. (328) |
| April 9th | Air Raid Practice, morning on shift. All clear in 80 seconds. Off shift all clear in 120 seconds. |
| April 12th | Air Raid Practice in concert with other schools in the town at 11.45am. Children all in homes or billets within prescribed time. |
| May 14th | School reopened after Whit Holiday, a day earlier than usual owing to the international situation. |
| May 21st | Visit of Mr. Irons, SAO for Luton, to verify attendances of border children. |
| June 6th | Visit of attendance officer for returns re evacuees. |
| June 10th | Visit of Mr. Pinnock to consult with London Head Teachers and Dunstable Head Teachers re organisation in September. |
| June 11th | Attendance officer called for evacuees returns from Mrs. Deane. (St Luke's) |
| June 21st | Letter received from Bedford ordering all schools to be |

| | |
|---|---|
| | closed, but teachers to stand by from 9 am till 1 pm and 2 pm till 5 pm, to receive officers of the LEA who might come to decide what should be done to the building to afford protection for children, in the event of an air raid. The policy of dispersal to be abandoned. |
| June 26th | About 1.45 pm the Director of Education, the County Surveyor and AN Other visited the school and decided that the cloakrooms and corridors should be used for shelter. The windows in these were to be bricked up and all other windows in the building to be covered with muslin, stuck on to the glass. Windows at the eastern end of the Church Hall to be bricked up. |
| June 29th | Letter received authorising all schools to be closed while the above work is being done, that is for a fortnight, and this fortnight to be considered the children's summer holiday. Some teachers to take the fortnight's holiday, but the Head Teacher and some of the Staff to remain behind to help cut up the muslin for the windows. These teachers are promised a fortnight's holiday later on. |
| July 5th | Work of bricking up the windows and replacing glass in the screens with boards begins. |
| July 15th | The above named work finished, but no muslin for windows yet to hand, and no work begun at Hall. |
| July 23rd | Protective work finished at school. Cleaning begun on 22nd and still in progress. |
| July 31st | Hall now in use. The Director enquired re ARP work and dispersal of children in school. |
| August | Mr. Hay, HMI, visited school to enquire re Hargrave Park numbers. |
| September 11th | Air raid siren 12.10 pm. Dinner children only on premises. |
| September 12th | Air raid siren 10.50 am |
| September 13th | Mr. Marshall called to bring two torches for use in Refuge Room should the electric light fail. |
| September 18th | Air raid siren 3.20 pm. All clear 4.10 pm. |

| | |
|---|---|
| September 30th | Mr Pinnock and Mr. Hay called in the afternoon. On their suggestion, 20 Ashton children will in future be taught with St Luke's children. |
| October 3rd | First Air raid Siren sounded at 9.30 am. With the exception of about 15 minutes at 11am, the children were in the refuge and the shelter all day. |
| October 9th | Siren from 3 pm to 3.30 pm. |
| October 10th | Siren from noon till 12.30 pm. |
| October 14th | Sirens twice this morning, all clear at 12.40 pm. Siren again at 1.05 pm, all clear not till 1.55 pm. |
| October 21st | Alert Signal sounded at 11.32 am and All Clear at 1pm. |
| October 25th | Siren went at 2 pm. Children in shelter and refuge rooms till 3.30 pm. |
| October 31st | Alert signal at 1 pm. All Clear at 3.10 pm, therefore school did not reassemble this afternoon. |
| November 6th | Siren at 9.30 am. All Clear 9.40am. Siren about 2.40pm. All Clear 3.15 pm. |
| November 11th | Siren sounded 2.45 pm. All Clear 3.50 pm. |
| November 12th | Mr. Pinnock called to enquire re off shift and children staying home. Repairs to shelters and additions to corridor lighting discussed. |
| November 14th | Mr. Lilley called concerning lights and repairs in air raid shelters and refuge rooms. |
| November 15th | Alert signal at 3.45 pm. All Clear 4.30 pm. |
| November 22nd | Alert warning from 2.20 pm to 2.50 pm. |
| December 2nd | Mr. Dew, SAO, called re Evacuee returns. |
| December 4th | Alert Signal from 11.25 am till 11.55 am. Alert signal from 2.10 pm till 2.25 pm. |
| December 5th | Alert Signal from 2.10 pm till 2.25 pm |
| December 6th | Alert Signal from 11 am till 11.45 am. |
| December 11th | Headmistress off duty, beginning the second week of her 'summer' holiday. |
| December 12th | Mr. Goodman, County Surveyor and Mr. Lilley, clerk of the works, called this afternoon re improved lighting of Air Raid Refuges and Shelters. Lighting in refuge corridors begun. |

**1941**

| | |
|---|---|
| January 6th | Alert Siren at 10.15 am. All Clear 10.50 am |
| January 7th | Alert Siren 9.05 am. All Clear 9.20 am. Alert Siren 12.10 pm. All Clear 12.25 pm. Alert Siren 2.20 pm. All Clear 2.45 pm. |
| January 19th | Alert 4 pm. All Clear 5 pm. |
| January 20th | Alert 9.55 am. All Clear 10.45 am. Alert 11.30 am. All Clear 12.25 pm. Alert 1.43 pm. All Clear 2.15 pm. Alert Signal 3.40 pm. All Clear 4.15 pm. |
| January 23rd | Alert Signal 10.40 am. All Clear 10.50 am. |
| January 28th | Alert Signal 11.05 am. All Clear 11.30 am. Alert Signal 3 pm. All Clear 3.20 pm. |
| January 29th | Mrs. H absent from duty on account of her husband having seven days leave. |
| January 31st | Alert Siren 1.57 pm. Less than 20% of children were in school. These were dismissed at 3.30 pm when all clear was given. |
| February 5th | Alert Siren 2.35 pm till 2.50. |
| February 18th | Alert Siren 3 till 3.30 pm. |
| February 27th | Alert Siren 10.35 am till 11.30 am. |
| March 5th | Alert Siren 11.25 am till 11.50 am. |
| April 22nd | This morning the Director of Education called to enquire re the possible AR Shelter at the Town Hall be used for Country Dancing and other such activity work. The Director of Education called again re the Country Dancing at the Town Hall and also discussed the possible re-arrangement of the schools by which St. Luke's should have entire use of the Church Hall, and one classroom in school; and the Ashton children entire use of the other seven classrooms. By this arrangement all the children would be accommodated in school for full time education. After consultation with Mrs. Dean this arrangement was agreed upon, Miss H being allowed the use of the largest classroom for her Infants. |
| April 28th | The scheme for accommodation described above was |

|              | put into operation today, and bids fair to work satisfactorily. |
| May 8th      | The Director of Education called re Country Dancing at the Town Hall. |
| June 9th     | Mrs. H absent without leave from the Committee. Her husband has seven days leave. (She was dismissed 6 months later.) |

## 1942

| January 23rd | Instruction in Needlework, which, though in accordance with war time restrictions in materials, shall give the children full benefit of the subject was started today. The course includes four sessions, and is held at Britain Street Senior School. Six teachers from this school have applied for the course; three attend this morning, and three this afternoon. This procedure will be followed for the next three successive Fridays. The remainder of the Staff share the classes between them. |
| May 19th     | Air Raid Wardens in school testing children's gas masks all morning. |
| July 16th    | M. O. I. film shown to children in the afternoon. |
| October 14th | Member of County Constabulary spoke to children re unexploded bombs and water tanks. |

## 1943

| February 18th | Visit of Mr. Pinnock, and Miss Laycock (of LCC), to discuss changes to Staffing and transfers of Unofficial Evacuees now in St. Luke's School, to the Bedfordshire Schools. Six of these are to come to this school. |
| February 28th | Mrs. Constantine (LCC) ceases Temporary duty here, and is to start at Burr Street School on Monday next. |
| March 1st     | 7 children admitted from St Luke's. These are now Dunstable residents. |
| March 2nd     | SAO called again re two children from St. Luke's who should have gone to Burr Street, but have not yet presented themselves there. |

| May 6th | SAO called re transfers from Burghley Road Evacuated School. This week has been 'Wings For Victory' week. The school contributed £125.15.6d. |
| September 15th | Mr. Pinnock called to say that Mr. Bennett (LCC) would be in during the afternoon to check furniture belonging to St. Luke's School. Mr. Bennett did not come. |
| September 20th | 12 children transferred from Church hall (St. Luke's Old Street evacuees) to this school. |

## 1944

| January 11th | Gasmasks tested by Air Raid Warden, and new containers issued where required. 247 children present. |
| June 30th | Alert Siren 8.58 am. All Clear 9.15 am. |
| July 11th | Alert Siren 1.05 pm. All Clear 1.30 pm. Only about a dozen children were at school; these were joined about three minutes after the Alert by the children who were escorted back from the dinner centre. (Britain Street). All these children were accommodated in the indoor shelters. Air Raid practice taken during the afternoon. All children in shelters in 1 minute 15 seconds. |
| September 15th | Mr. Stew and Mr. Kemp visited the school to talk to the children about the Book and Salvage Drive. |
| October 24th | Miss M. (LCC) reported for duty, very disgruntled over loss of week's holiday in London and school not type she was accustomed to. At 11 am went to Billeting Office, re billet, finally settled at 4 pm. |
| November 20th | Miss M. sent word that she has returned to London. |
| December 19th | Mrs. Clowry (LCC) left today. She has to report in London tomorrow. |
| December 21st | Mr. Dew visited school today in the morning re American gifts to Kent children. |

## 1945

| January 30th | Attendance 113 + 17 out of a possible 251 + 26 |
| February 2nd | Miss Dobbyn called to discuss the Needlework Scheme. |
| May 8th | The school did not assemble today as a holiday was |

|            | allowed until Friday 11th May to celebrate the end of the war in Europe. |
|------------|-------------------------------------------------------------------------|
| May 18th   | A police sergeant called to talk to the children of the dangers of road accidents and accidents due to playing with live ammunition, bombs etc. |
| July 13th  | Mrs. Chattoe was recalled to London. |
| July 27th  | At the closing Assembly, the Headmaster presented Miss Walker and Mrs. Warren each with a cheque and an autograph album containing the names of the Staff, Managers and children as a memento of their five years stay in England. They are returning to Guernsey. |

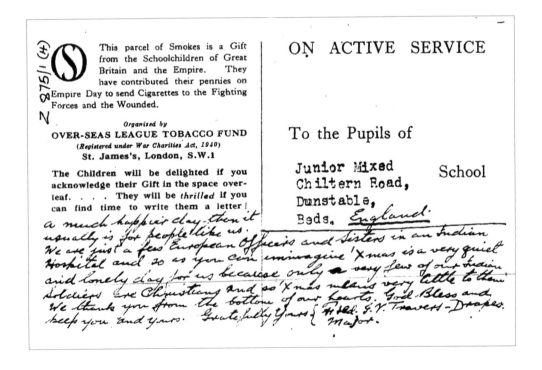

This parcel of Smokes is a Gift from the Schoolchildren of Great Britain and the Empire. They have contributed their pennies on Empire Day to send Cigarettes to the Fighting Forces and the Wounded.

*Organised by*
**OVER-SEAS LEAGUE TOBACCO FUND**
(*Registered under War Charities Act, 1940*)
**St. James's, London, S.W.1**

The Children will be delighted if you acknowledge their Gift in the space over-leaf. . . . They will be *thrilled* if you can find time to write them a letter!

ON ACTIVE SERVICE

To the Pupils of

Junior Mixed      School
Chiltern Road,
Dunstable,
Beds, England.

The children of Chiltern Road School collected to send cigarettes to the troops. Above and opposite are letters received by the school, thanking them. *(DDLHS)*

U. S. Transportation Corps
Dunstable, Bedfordshire
November 28, 1942

Miss R. Walker, Headmistress
Dunstable Chiltern Road, J. M. School
Dunstable, Bedfordshire

Dear Miss Walker,

It's needless for me to try to tell you how much I enjoyed meeting with you and the children on November 26, our Thanksgiving Day.

In behalf of myself and my boys, may I say "thanks" to all of you for the cigarettes that were sent. They not only brought us more pleasure on our holiday, but added to the many things we have found to be thankful for, since arriving in your great country.

Yours sincerely,

Richard Kimball, 1st LT.

Clarence Marlowe 2nd Lt.

Angus M. Brewer, Tech Sgt.

Benjamin Aranoff S/Sgt.

Robert F. Lynch S/Sgt.

Gerald D. Stone Sgt.

Harold F. McCullough T/4

James Vant Hul

John C. Bold

Leonard A. Lyons

## DETAILS TAKEN FROM A GOVERNMENT EVACUATION SCHEME INFORMATION LEAFLET
### Selected by Sue King

Instructions to Mothers and Women in charge of Children:
- If it should be necessary to put the evacuation scheme into force, you will receive announcements by radio and in the newspapers.
- On a day which will be announced, go to the school named at the top of the form where you will be registered. Take this form with you. A notice outside the school will tell you the time to assemble.
- Take with you the children named on the form who are going to go with you. Each child must have a label giving his name and address and the party number.
- Take only the luggage which you can carry. There will be no one to help you carry anything. The other women in the party will have their own children to look after.
- Besides the clothes which the child would be wearing (and these should include a coat or mackintosh), a complete change of clothing should be carried. You should also take towel, soap, toothbrush and if possible, an extra pair of shoes. Blankets should not be taken.
- For identification purposes the rucksack or haversack should have attached to it a linen label with the name and address of the mother and the name and number of the party.

### *Alan Sinfield* - Past Chairman of Dunstable Grammar School Old Boys Association

Through the Second World War many of Dunstable's sons and daughters were called to do duty for their country. Among these were ex pupils of Dunstable Grammar School of whom forty-five gave their lives and seventeen received decorations for bravery.

The Dunstable School Old Boys Association, of which there is a current membership of nearly five hundred, was able to contact those members who were either at school during the war or who had left and were serving their country. Their reminiscences resulting from this enquiry are contained within this book, especially this chapter and 'Serving in the Forces'.

LEAVING FORM, Dunstable Grammar School, 1943 *Photo by Kenneth N Collins, donated by AS (DGS)*

### *Bert Morgan* – at Burr Street School

We had a school billeted with us at Burr Street and soon settled down to attending mornings one week and afternoons the next. Two Polish boys were billeted near us; they could speak German and used to do imitations of Hitler. They put one finger under their nose, held their right hand in a Nazi salute and jabbered away in German. It was all very amusing. Some children went back to London but others billeted in Victoria Street stayed all through the war.

### *Tony Woodhouse* – Hosting Evacuees

I was born in Dunstable in 1936. I remember going to school in Chiltern Road with my gas mask, which we used to hang on a designated peg in the cloakroom. We wore short trousers with long grey socks, grey shirt and a school cap.

My mother took in evacuees, most of whom came from the Acland School in London. At one time we had six evacuees and a lodger because we had about five bedrooms. Our lodger worked for a plastics company in Dunstable, which made canopies for Spitfires and Hurricanes.

## Dave Manners - an Evacuee

It was a bright sunny day for late autumn. I don't know the date; dates aren't of much interest to a six-year-old boy who was on his way to school. School was St. Luke's Church School in Finsbury, and to me it was just an ordinary day, I had no idea what was in store for me or my fellow pupils. I knew something was up when lessons didn't start, instead we were organised into groups and had red GPO postbags put round our necks. In my bag there was a drink in a glass bottle, a pack of sandwiches and an orange. I then had a stiff brown label tied with string to the buttonhole of my coat. I suppose it had my personal details and possibly my intended destination written there but I was not aware of any of this at the time. I was just filled with apprehension; the air was tingling with anticipation, excitement and for my part, dread.

We children were marched out in twos, holding hands. A long snake of bewildered children walking from the school yard into the roadway, a sea of faces each side, grown-ups, desperate to see; to touch a certain child, as though it was for the last time. Some children began to cry, I was confused and withdrew into a protective shell trying not to see or hear. I suppose my mother was there, I didn't see her and I didn't look, I was afraid, this was not normal, something was wrong. We walked several hundred yards to Old Street underground station. I can't remember all the details of the journey; it was a blur to me. Perhaps something had been said to me the day or night before the exodus, warning me of what was going to happen. If so I can't remember, perhaps nothing was said in order not to cause upset or worry, either way I felt very alone.

How we got there I don't know, we had been on a train and now we were in a hall, a Chapel, I believe. We were given tea and something to eat. People, strangers, ladies with big blue hats (WVS), were milling round carrying clipboards, calling out names. We were organised into groups; some of the groups, ready early, disappeared (never to be seen by me again), children I had known, just gone, where, why? Then a surprise, my brother Richard was suddenly there by my side, what relief, why did I not know he was with us? I can only construe that we had been grouped and travelled together in classes. Richard was ten, so would have been in a class above mine and presumably travelled separately to us six-year-olds. Amid what to me was total confusion, somebody was well enough organised to reunite family members before the next phase began.

Once again a snake of children was taken out through yet another door. Surprise! It was totally dark, the ladies in big blue hats were milling round like sheep dogs keeping us in line, some had torches and were reading from their lists. The line stopped, we were in a street with rows of terraced houses, the big blue hats would go to a house and knock, there was furtive whisperings, "How many will you have?" "We haven't any room," or "We will take a girl." It seems that girls were in popular demand, for as the snake dwindled it was mostly boys who were left. It seemed to go on for hours, I had no idea of the time but eventually it was Richard and I at the head of the line. More furtive whisperings and Richard and I were hustled into a warm and cosy sitting room; a grey haired couple fussed round us and we were given cocoa and something to eat. We were then put to bed, it was late and we were very tired.

We were lucky, we had found a home and we were cared for with love and attention as though we were their own. Richard fell ill and was moved to a hospital leaving me alone, I didn't mind; I had a room and a bed to myself. Coming from a home where I was the youngest of nine children, living in three rooms of a three storied terraced house, this was heaven. Don't misunderstand, my mother cared for us children and she did her very best for us but she had a very hard time. My father was blind and unable to work, so mother had to go out to work to keep us, as well as tend to a large family, so you see my change in lifestyle was dramatic and I liked it.

The Chapel I mentioned earlier was at the junction of Victoria Street and Albion Street and, as I found later, I was living in Victoria Street. Once the local children had got used to me, I was accepted into their group and made some very good friends; soon it was as though I had been born and bred in Dunstable. I regret deeply that I cannot remember the names of these very nice people and their parents who welcomed me into their homes. I would love to mention their names and express my gratitude for the kindness shown to me.

There was one blot on my experience of living in Dunstable, which I must mention because it made such a lasting impression on me; this was to do with schooling. I attended three different schools, the last being Northfields High. I remember that from the playing fields I could see the Blue Circle cement works with its tall grey chimney putting out grey smoke.

Some of the older girls would go through the wire fence to meet Italian prisoners of war who were working on adjoining farmland or the quarry; they threatened us younger boys with 'death' if we 'split' on them. But I hated that school, there was one teacher, who had taken a dislike to me, I don't know why, perhaps I had upset her in some way, but she would humiliate me in front of the class at every opportunity she could. I gave her plenty of opportunity for I was not a good scholar, she would pull me out in front of the class and say things like 'Manners maketh man'. I didn't understand what she meant and I suspect neither did the other children, but they all laughed anyway. What made it worse was that the children in the class then began to tease and bully me outside the class, as though encouraged by her treatment of me and I became very reclusive. I feigned sickness and I remember my poor guardians being very worried and taking me to the doctor who, not finding anything physically wrong, said I must draw lots and lots of houses using pencil and paper. He showed me how to draw three-dimensional pictures of houses, ah! The power of psychology. I never said what was really wrong, I was too afraid.

Notwithstanding my school experience, my time in Dunstable was good for me; it showed me a side of life I would never have known existed. Dunstable was the catalyst that was to change my life and I shall be forever grateful to the kind people of Dunstable who took me in and made me welcome. After evacuation I could not settle in London, in fact I hated it and I left when I was nineteen years old. I made a new life for myself living in country places.

I was evacuated because of the war, the war caused terrible things to happen but out of that I found a new way of life, a good way of life. They say "It's an ill wind............"

## EXTRACT FROM CONVERSATION BETWEEN THREE FRIENDS:

### *Heather Hing* - Teatime

How far back can we go? Well, all my friends sat next to one another at Ashton Infant's School all the way through the war. They didn't have shelters built when the war started, so we were allocated a house to go to on our way home, should the sirens go off. I remember going to one; we walked up Church Street and up to the High Street to Downs Road. They lived upstairs above a shop and one day, when we were there for a long time, we had tea with them. Afterwards, everyone had to take their own things out to the kitchen to wash up except for the father; someone else did that. We didn't do that in our family.

### *Betty Tarbox* - in the Cellar

Josie and I had to go to a cottage near the Royal Oak. A little old woman used to put us in the coal cellar on 2 chairs. I can confess it now, she couldn't hear the all clear siren but we could hear the Priory Church clock, so if it was meal time we used to tell her the all clear had gone so we could go home. She used to make us a cup of cocoa.

### *Francis Forder* - in the Shelter

When Ashton School had shelters built, we had to go across the yard to a corner, up a ladder and over a wall; the shelter was on the other side. I remember sitting there with our feet on the duckboards. Evelyn Road was a brand new school when I went there, but within a year we had to have all these lovely cloakrooms turned into shelters and barricaded up. One teacher used to twiddle her wedding ring all the time in class; she didn't know where her husband was.

### Dr M R Pullen - Certificates

My grandmother, Janet Cameron, took in several evacuees throughout the war, including sometimes the parents of children 'bombed out' from London. She received the Queen's Certificate for this. She also organised collections for the Penny-a-Week Fund for the Red Cross and St John Ambulance and received the Duke of Gloucester's Certificate in recognition of this work.

### Jim Knight - Evacuees Arrive

One Saturday afternoon my friends and I were playing on a grassy bank at the junction of Eaton Bray Road and Castle Hill Road in Totternhoe, when an Eastern National double-decker bus came from the direction of Stanbridge, (which they never did normally). It was filled with children, many leaning out of the window shouting, screaming and waving. Later at about tea-time, a village lady came knocking on the door with a little boy in tow. She told my mum that she had to take the boy in. He was an evacuee. Mum said we had no room in our small two up, two down cottage, with Mum, Dad and us three boys. After an argument with the lady, Mum gave in on the understanding that he only stayed until another house could be found. He actually stayed with us for several months before returning to London.

The older boys and girls who had moved up to Britain Street School in Dunstable came back to Totternhoe School for their final summer term, to ease congestion in Dunstable schools. Many children evacuated from London schools had moved to Dunstable. The Acland schoolchildren were based at Britain Street. These older children were often sent unsupervised on to the Knolls for walks in fine weather. For our safety we had to practise evacuation from the school in case of air raids. One teacher, herself a refugee from Jersey, would read to us in the afternoon as we sat around under a tree in the school playing field. The weather always seemed to be fine in the summer.

### Shirley Ansell - Away from the Blitz

September 3rd 1939 – and little did I know that it would change my world completely. I was living at the time in Ruskin Buildings, Millbank, Westminster, London, SW1. I was two years old, my father was in the Army and my mother and I lived in this top flat on our own. All my grandparents lived within a few minutes walk, so I would often visit.

A few days after war was declared, we were evacuated to Wokingham but did not stay for long as nothing was happening in London and mum missed her mother, sister and brothers. We had not been back long when the bombing started. When the bombing was heavy we used the air raid shelter. One night our flat in Ruskin Building was hit by an incendiary bomb; we lost everything. I can remember seeing the flat the next day when my Uncle Joe, who was in the Fire Service, went up the long fireman's ladder to see what he could save. Sadly, there was not much left; all the curtains were hanging out of the window and everything was burned. We went to live with my Nanny Howard who lived in a flat at Tothill House, Page Street, Westminster. We would sleep in the sofa bed and sometimes Auntie Eva would sleep with us. She was deaf and would not hear the siren, so mum would shout at her, "Get up Eva and get down the shelter!" Then we would use the surface shelter; it smelt of sweat and dirty washing and it was damp and horrible. The bombing was very bad; one night, the sheds in the yard were bombed and I lost my pram. We had a searchlight and a big anti-aircraft gun at the end of the street and all night long you could hear this being fired; it was very noisy with the gun and the bombs dropping.

During this time of the Blitz on London I began to get a very bad cough. I think that it may have been caused by our nightly sleeping conditions. Mum called it shelter cough and eventually took me to the doctor. He said that if she did not get me out of the shelters and away from the bombing he would get me taken away, so she made arrangements for us both to go to Dunstable. Dad was stationed at Tring on the guns with his brother Teddy. We went to live in Ridgeway Drive but were not there very long. We then moved to Blows Road and lived with a couple and her father, whom I called Uncle John. Mum got a job at the Post Office where the man worked; Auntie Mary (the wife) looked after me. My Dad would sometimes visit but he was sent to North Africa and I did not see him again until after the war. We were very happy there; I used to play in the garden and look after my own chicken called Snowball. One day, Snowball was missing; Mum said it had gone away but I found out in later years that it was our Christmas dinner! Auntie Mary became ill so we had to leave.

Mum told the caretaker at the Post Office that she was looking for somewhere to live. He said that he had a spare room at his house and perhaps we would like to go and meet his wife and look at the house. We went to live with them in Union Street and I was to call them Uncle Sid and Auntie Win. Mum tried to get me into school but because I was only four and a half they would not take me, so she managed to get me into a private school called Aberfeldy. It was a fee paying school and cost four pounds a term. The school was run by a woman and her daughter. I didn't like going to school; I would cry and grizzle when Auntie Win tried to get me ready for school and I seemed to do nothing but cry when I was there. They then decided that Auntie Win should collect me at 12 o'clock instead of 1 o'clock for dinner and return me at the usual time of 2 o'clock. This went on for some time and as I began to settle down, Auntie Win allowed me to come home on my own with the other children at dinnertime. One day I decided that I was not going to school and would not get ready, so Auntie Win locked me in the bedroom. When I thought that every one was at school I asked to be allowed out to play. Auntie Win said that I must stay until Mum came home from work at dinnertime. I then called her an 'old bugger' and when Mum came home I got a clout!

SHIRLEY and her mother in her post office uniform *(SA)*

## P Underwood - Crafty Cockneys

I was 11 when the war broke out and living in Dunstable at the time. When I was born the Great War had only been over for 10 years and I was aware of this big shadow over the country resulting from the losses of the First War. My father served in the trenches and was wounded in 1917 and each Armistice Day we all gathered, all the traffic stopped, the guns came, fired and we had a two-minute silence, so war was always there in the background.

In the summer of 1939 we were on holiday in Clacton. My elder brother was in the RAF at the time and on leave but was then recalled. Around the 31st August he went to France before the war broke out. I have never heard any mention of any serviceman going before September 3rd, but he did. And so we came back from holiday and Mum joined the WVS. The particular reception centre for evacuees that she was associated with, was based up at the roller skating rink.

We have a family album in which Mum wrote: "When war was declared, I was in charge of one of the rest centres where we were alerted to be ready to receive 250 children from London. We were prepared and after 2 days of hectic searching had found homes for almost all of them. Imagine our dismay when someone or something had sent us 250 mothers and children. Almost half the people who had agreed to take the children alone would not have mothers and tiny children and babies, so we had to start all over again. By 9.45 pm on Sunday evening (probably September 3rd), we had succeeded in housing 200 of them. We fed the remaining 50 and bedded them down in the centre. On the next day at 10.00 pm we had reduced the number to nine, one mother with 4 children and one with 3. I took the 4 and one of my helpers took the 3. They were with us for 18 months or so, eventually getting a house in Hadrian Avenue."

We had this little family staying with us for 18 months. Alfred was one of the children, they called him Alfie; they were Cockneys. Occasionally we had a soldier billeted with us. One I remember was either Canadian or Australian and that was quite exotic in those days.

I started at the Grammar School in 1938 and was still on summer holiday when these evacuees arrived. I ran errands for Mum, dashing here, there and everywhere. I remember Chamberlain's broadcast on September 3rd, unforgettable. So we were at war and we had to get on with it. It didn't make a whole lot of difference to me as a child; Mum and Dad had always been busy. Dad was headmaster at Northfields, Mum with her WVS and the Operatic Society. I was always very much free to do what I wanted on my own. I don't remember any problems with the evacuees, they were quite exciting, they were Cockneys, bright, crafty and streetwise compared with us country bumpkins. A lot of the mothers and children went back because the bombing didn't start.

Two of our masters went into the services. An old gentleman came out of retirement to teach us but he couldn't maintain discipline and we made his life hell. Not very proud of that.

I joined the ATC in 1942 when I was 14; the 460 Squadron. Our CO was H J B, the sports master at the Grammar School. That was good, we used to go to lots of airfields, Wing, Stradishall, Waterbeach and flew in bombers and Hansons. We used to meet at the ATC HQ in Chew's House and paraded at Britain Street School.

### Maisie Bates – our Russian Evacuees

My father was a billeting officer and I can remember some of the evacuees that stayed with us. We had a headmaster and his wife from London; they stayed with us for quite a while and became very firm friends. Then we had a doctor and his family (his wife, two children and the grandma) also from London, whose house had been bombed. He was Russian by birth and his family had to escape Russia because his father was a Rabbi. The extraordinary thing about the grandma was that she could only speak German. She was also stone deaf, so she had to report to the police station every week. Now why she only spoke German I never worked out!

### Ida Raper & her daughter Pat Carter – Adult Evacuee Story

**Ida:** I was living at the time in Colliers Wood, London, when war was declared during the middle of the day. I'd got Pat, she was just about two years old and in no time at all we heard the sirens go and thought this was it. My husband had already been training for over a year as a fireman and so of course he went and enlisted straight away. Then all the neighbours didn't know what to do, saying, "What do we do, what do we do?" We just settled down to it. I can't recall exactly how we carried on for the next few months where nothing much seemed to happen; people were getting very, very lax and laid back over things. I remember going out to Hyde Park once and saw men digging trenches; I wondered what on earth they were digging trenches for, what a waste of time, but there you are, they didn't realise it was a waste of time then.

We carried on through that first year when nothing much happened. My mother and father were living at Fulham, which is next to Battersea, and one night we had a very bad raid. I can't recall how I got over to Fulham with Pat and some others. At that time there was lots of bombing at the docks, where it was very, very bad; of course my husband being a fireman was there (at the docks). I went over to mum's with Pat and whilst I was there (I was there for about a day), my brother turned up who lived in Dunstable. He had heard that the Battersea Power Station had been hit and knew that we might be in danger, so he came up to fetch mum. Of course when he got there, he found I was there with the baby, my grandmother who was 78 and my husband who had just come off duty with the fire service.

The Thames was alight and my husband was resting in the bed when my brother went in to see him. He just said, "Take them away, take her and the baby away – if I never see them again, please take them away. They can't stay here." But neither my grandmother nor my mother would come. "No, we're staying here," they said, and they did. My brother brought me straight away in the car with no spare clothes, nothing, to his home in Dunstable. My grandmother came later and we stayed with my brother in Great Northern Road. We were made very welcome for a whole year I think, before Dad came down permanently to live.

He was a fireman for a very long while and when we came to Dunstable I remember saying that it felt like it was the place that God had forgotten. All the local people talked about was Vauxhall and how many raids they'd had. I know for them it was dreadful but for me it was peanuts, they hadn't seen anything. I remember going past the Fulham hospital in the car and seeing that the whole place had been bombed, the whole place was down, wards torn apart, dreadful. Pat had fits over that; she was really worried about it. We went for a walk one Sunday down Friars Walk in Dunstable and saw some partly finished houses there. The builders had just walked away from it and they had put the Army in. My brother was holding her (Pat, my daughter) and she was screaming her head off, she was absolutely terrified. Afterwards, we realised that it must have been the memory of what she had seen in Fulham.

**Pat:** It was a long, long while until I was happy to go anywhere near a half built building. To me, it was like a half demolished building. I was only two and a half but I do have a long memory.

**Ida:** So once we got to Dunstable that was it, it was a completely new life; it was wonderful, nothing ever seemed to happen. However, I found it very difficult to get on with the Dunstable people; I suppose it was terrible for them. What with parents coming from London to be with their (evacuee) children, sometimes just for a day, it added to the general atmosphere, it was a burden for them. I know the people next door said to me once, "Well if you don't like it here why on earth don't you go back?" As if I had just come for an outing.

**Pat:** Did they think you were clean?

**Ida:** Oh no, many people remarked that Londoners didn't bathe; they kept coal in the bath and thought we were a dirty race of people. Little things like that, you know.

**Pat:** Did you put them right?

**Ida:** No I didn't! There was one thing I found strange – they didn't want you to knock at the front door; I wasn't used to that in London, we were all friends together and this made you feel as though you were different. We used to shop at the International, which was more or less in the centre of town. We never shopped very far from home because we had to carry all our shopping home with us. We grew a lot of our food ourselves. Dad took to gardening and grew potatoes, carrots, beetroot and parsnips. He also kept chickens and rabbits. We had everything more or less because we had a fairly big garden, which hadn't yet been cultivated.

My brother and his wife started to look for a house of their own in Dunstable. As soon as they found a house in Lister Road, a direct requisition order was made on the house in Great Northern Road. He was unable to sell the house so we stayed on there. At first we were given a family from Blackheath, they had been bombed out and took over the three empty rooms, which left us with the two front rooms. Then two girls in uniform arrived, very posh, very clever. We had two camp beds delivered for them to sleep on but my husband said, "They can't sleep on camp beds like that!" So we gave them our bedroom! It was so cold, trying to sleep on the camp beds in the spare empty room; we didn't know what to do. Then we realised we had some rugs that we had made ourselves before we got married. So we put this rug on the camp bed first for us to lie on to stop the draft!

It was all very hush, hush. We were told not to converse with each other; they left early every day, just saying, "Good morning," and came in every night at about 8 o'clock. This went on for quite some considerable time; we hardly every saw them and we never did know what they did or where they went.

### *Monica Hart* - Lodgers

I lived with my parents in Great Northern Road. We had lodgers from firms that had been evacuated to Dunstable. One or two came from the new Delco Remi and Hyatt factory that was moved here. It was under the railway bridge in Church Street where McDonalds is now. One of the lodgers had a band called S & B (Staines and Blake) and he used to do quite a lot of dances and play for them.

### *Roy Turner* - at Ashton Junior and Britain Street Schools

I was 9 years old and living at 6 Albert Street in Dunstable. I went to Ashton Junior School in Church Street and then on to Britain Street School leaving at 14, as you did in those days. Things changed. Schools were evacuated and very often we went into the parish church hall for lessons, and when there weren't enough teachers, we used to watch films. Towards the end of the war we only had 2 male teachers, all the rest were ladies. Many teachers were brought out of retirement to educate us.

I was 14 when I had my first pair of long trousers. We had caps at school but no uniform as such. Acland's (London School evacuated to Dunstable) colours were the same as ours so when the two football teams went out there wasn't much to choose between them. I still see some of the people that were evacuated from London.

We had a girl evacuee billeted on us in our 2 bedroom cottage. My mother said, "I've got a boy," they said, "That's easy," and they put a curtain up in the middle of the room. The girl slept one side and I slept on the other. She was Ethel from Tower Bridge Road, Bermondsey, and was about 2 years older than me.

We also had 2 lorry drivers billeted with us from Smithfield Market.

They used to get up very early in the morning and drive off. I believe Smithfield got hit, so the cattle market in Dunstable became the main collection centre.

## Tony Ward – Displaced Persons

I was about three years old when war broke out. One of the earliest things I remember was that people had to stick tape on their windows and dig air raid shelters in their gardens; all the neighbours helped each other to do that. Another early memory I have is that almost from the beginning of the war, we had lodgers. We started off with some 'displaced persons' – an Hungarian gentleman, very distinguished; no one knew what he did. He gave me a mouth organ made in Prague, so I held him in high esteem. We then had a Pole who got arrested on the Downs because he went up there for a walk without his papers. We had a French lady and various RAF personnel. One evening in particular I remember, we had a knock on the door during a blackout; there were loads of RAF personnel all over the place with clipboards, trying to get lodgings for these blokes. They were pleading with people to take one in. They asked us to take two and my mother said yes; we had them for some time. Then we had WAAFS and a string of people who worked in the Met Office. Some of the military personnel that we had used to leave suddenly and you didn't know where they were going. We only managed to keep in contact with two people that we had as lodgers during this time.

I started school in the early part of the war in 1941. Initially we only went half days as they did not have enough teachers – half the school was taught in the morning and the other half in the afternoon. I quite liked that, as my friends and I would go roaming the countryside – bearing in mind that Dunstable was a country town at the time. So we enjoyed our freedom and then all of a sudden we had to go full time – we didn't like that at all! A gross infringement of my freedom! The school was called Burr Street. I think they dragged one teacher out of retirement because she used to teach my father. There were very few male teachers, as many men were being called up.

### Mary Owen – our Polish Colonel

At the very beginning of the war we took in 2 children evacuees from London. I didn't see very much of them as I was working full time in Luton. They only stayed for a matter of months as they wanted to go back to London. Many evacuees stayed in Dunstable throughout the war but the majority soon went home. Later on we had a Polish Colonel; he was the lawyer for the Polish Army in London and he came to Dunstable to get away from everything at weekends. He spent his time sleeping, reading and chatting to us. He was a very pleasant person and rather handsome. On the few occasions that I took a cup of tea up to his bedroom he often had a hairnet on!

### Ann – from Hostel to House

I was aged five and my sister aged seven at the start of the war. We were first sent to Dunstable after having been in two earlier billets in nearby villages, in the second of which we were inadequately fed and clothed. Our mother insisted on having us moved because we had become so thin; I think that the family had agreed to take evacuees in order to get more rations which they kept for themselves. My sister and I were so hungry that we ate leaves and berries from the hedgerows and also acorns. We also stole and ate the family's store of pears. So we were taken to a 'short-stay' hostel in Dunstable High Street; it was a rather elegant building, the front door up stone steps, bay windows. There was a basement area so that the railings round the building had not been removed for the war effort, as had most others. I visited Dunstable in the seventies—a sort of trip of curiosity— and the house was then an antique shop. It was on the same side as what was, in our time, the public library and opposite what I remember as the police station. Near to the police station was Periwinkle Lane, a name that I thought quite enchanting. Further down from Periwinkle Lane was the cattle market. I adored the cattle market! I would stand for ages watching the animals being led up rickety wooden ramps and into carts. Does that ring any bells? The hostel was a well-run place and there were six girls there, including us, and a matron and nurse were in charge. I'd have been quite happy to stay there for the duration. But as I say, it was a short-stay place until something more permanent could be found.

So after a while we were transferred to a small house immediately opposite the hostel where we lived for about six months (I would estimate) with a man and his French wife. They spoke to each other in French and hardly ever conversed with us; they had no children. It was a small house, its front door directly on to the pavement outside and with stairs from the main living room hidden behind a latched door. The owners kept rabbits and hens in the backyard to provide extra food and eggs. They looked after us very well; we were content there.

When we left here we were sent to a large, extended family at the other end of the town and there we remained until the war ended; we were very, very, unhappy for the four years or so we were at this last billet. By the time we went back to London I had spent more than half my life away from my mother and this had a damaging effect on our relationship, but it soon reverted to normal, happily. I loved my mother dearly; she was wonderful. But whilst we were away from home we were always in fear of her getting killed and, consequently, having to remain with the family in Dunstable. Many of our evacuee acquaintances ran away back to London, but they were always caught at King's Cross and returned. My sister and I hadn't the heart to do the same, as we were aware of the anxiety it would cause our mother.

As far as schooling is concerned, we were first of all sent to Burr Street School, then I was sent to Northfields or Highfields (can't remember which name it was). By the time war ended I was eleven and started in secondary education when I returned to London. My sister, though, at age eleven was transferred to the evacuated Acland School. We returned to London at different times; I went after VE Day and she returned after VJ Day. It was all to do with being sent home with our schools.

### *Pam Buckle* - **Moving to the Avenue**

My family moved here in 1937 when I was 6 years old, so I've lived in Dunstable for most of my life. We moved into a house in First Avenue that had just been built. At that time we could look out across open fields right up towards the Downs.

I went to a small private school in Great Northern Road, which had about 30 pupils and taught the basics of English, Maths and elementary French. The highlight of summer was playing croquet on the lawn at the back of the house. We had great fun playing little contests and tournaments.

We were on holiday in Norfolk when war was declared. In the fields opposite our house portable huts were built and the ATS girls were billeted there. In the few empty houses that had not yet been sold in First Avenue, officers were billeted for most of the time of the war. My father was too old to join the forces but he had been in the civil service and was given a reserved occupation in various parts of the country, including Reading and Southampton, preparing for D-Day. We didn't see very much of him during that time.

A few months after war was declared, some evacuees came to live with us. We had a brother, 13, and a sister, 8. They came from the East End of London, John and Sylvia. Sylvia was terribly homesick and missed her mother although John, being just that much older, took it in his stride. They stayed with us for about 14 months. Their mother came to visit them as often as she could. She was very concerned about Sylvia, as she was so very homesick. When John turned 14, their mother took them back to London. After that my Auntie, who lived in London, came to live with us for the rest of the war with her daughter until it was safe for them to return home.

I took the entrance exam to Cedars School in Leighton Buzzard and passed. I stayed there through the rest of the war and until 1949.

### *John S Purdon* – **Polish Evacuee**

We lived in quite a large house with five bedrooms and as a result we were always having people billeted on us. There would be a knock on the front door and a policeman would hand over a form that told my parents that a person would be arriving, and we had to put them up. We had some very interesting people. One I recall very well. He was a Polish airman who managed to get to England after Germany and Russia invaded Poland. He had been transferred into the RAF and he had a hush-hush job at the Meteorological Office. He was very tall and was always standing to attention, bowing, clicking his heels while he used to kiss ladies' hands.

He hated the Germans almost as much as he hated the Russians. He married a young English WAAF (Women's Auxiliary Air Force) who, under the laws as they stood at the time, became Polish and was transferred to the Polish Air Force! Since the Polish Government in exile had little money she had a bad time. After the war he and his English wife went to Australia, in order to be as far from the Russians as possible.

## *J Reason* – at Dunstable Grammar School

In 1939 I sat the entrance examination for Dunstable Grammar School. When I took the exam I was only nine years old, and the formidable headmistress of Burr Street School quite rightly thought that it would be better if my father held me back for another year. But my father demurred, "It will be good experience for him for next year."

So I sat the exam and was awarded a scholarship. This was a mixed blessing, because it committed me to surviving in a group of boys who physically were much bigger than me, and inevitably one or two of them were bullies. I asked for a set of boxing gloves that Christmas and the practice I had with them served me in very good stead. Luckily my swimming earned Brownie points!

The realities of age and physique became all too apparent in that first term because the school had a cadet corps, which was formidably well equipped. It had a whole range of firearms. These were kept in an armoury built alongside what were then called the New Buildings. Looking back, I suspect that at that time, Dunstable School was one of the best-equipped fighting units in that part of Bedfordshire. They had enough .303 rifles to arm a platoon. They had a rifle range complete with large butts and they had a selection of .22 rifles for practising marksmanship. They also had all the necessary ammunition.

The firepower was kept under the watchful eye of Sergeant Major Odell. He was a veteran of the First World War and his uniform was what he would have worn fighting in France. He had a peaked cap, rather like that of a present day officer and he wore puttees, which came up to his knees. No one pronounced the "g" in sergeant major, either. So his rank came across as 'sarnt-major'.

The corps drilled on the school quadrangle. This was between the main school building and the fives court and the swimming pool. New boys were nowhere near old enough to join the corps but some of those that were, those in the sixth form, knew that within a year they would be in the Army and fighting in France.

At the beginning of the war, the ground underneath the school's rifle range was tunnelled to provide a network of underground air-raid shelters. These were capable of housing the entire school, as well as the boys in the prep school over at Ashton Lodge.

In the early months of the war, the headmaster organised practices in the drills necessary to evacuate the classrooms, the gymnasium and the boarding house, so as to move more than three hundred boys and masters into relative safety.

### Gerald Wheatley – Nazis on our Playing Field!

My brief military career began when I joined the Army Cadet Force of Dunstable School on 1st September 1939. Two days later, the Second World War commenced.

We might have been mere schoolboys but we knew the serious nature of the situation. For years our weekly visits to the cinema to see such favourites as Charlie Chaplin and Laurel and Hardy were spoilt by the newsreel coverage, which reported the expansion of Hitler's Nazi regime.

One by one, formerly independent nations were taken over until finally, in 1939, Hitler's army invaded Poland. After years of appeasement our government decided that this was the final straw and war was declared. Germany was well equipped for war; for years her military strength had been built up to unacceptable peacetime levels. Apart from the newsreels, the first Nazis I actually saw were a hockey team, which came over in 1938 from Düsseldorf to play against our school. At the end of the match our team captain called for 'three cheers for the visitors'. To our amazement and horror, the German team sprang to attention, gave the Nazi salute and shouted 'Heil Hitler'!

Later when the war was under way, the Luftwaffe were able to pinpoint important industrial sites such as Vauxhall Motors at Luton. They were able to do so because their visiting 'hockey team' had expressed great interest in the London Gliding Club, which operated from Dunstable Downs. They were treated generously and were taken up for flights over the area. When we were eventually at war, it was clear that their innocent interest in flying and gliding had a more sinister nature.

I shall never forget the sense of horror and outrage that I felt when I witnessed their barbarian demonstration on our English playing field.

By the time I left school in 1943, I was a cadet sergeant in the corps and was equipped with a War Certificate 'A', which testified to a basic knowledge of musketry, field-craft and map reading.

After leaving school, I worked for a few months as a junior assistant in

Luton Public Library and at seventeen and a half years of age I volunteered to serve in the Army for the duration of hostilities, and was enlisted in the General Service Corps in September 1943.

### *Mary Cresswell* – at the Church

When the war started I was attending Luton High School. I had to go on the bus every day from the stop near the cemetery in West Street, Dunstable. My first recollection of the war happened when I was sitting under the trees in Grove House Gardens. I heard a bomb explode and saw a plane circling around; I think it hit the Vauxhall plant in Luton.

I used to attend the church in Union Street where many evacuees were sent before being billeted around the town. I lived with my parents and we had evacuees and several people staying with us that worked at the Met Office, in fact, we're still in touch with some of them now.

### *Rob Cutler* – Harvest Help

At school we had to try and do some lessons with our gas mask on. This was really difficult because they used to get all steamed up and made funny noises, so it wasn't very successful.

We had evacuees at our school for a while. We had 118 pupils and couldn't all sit down together, so some went out gardening in the mornings and others in the afternoons. The farmers would come to school at 9 o'clock and ask for a number of boys to help with the harvest. The first job I had when I was about 11, was turnip and poppy pulling – those poppies smelled terrible!

### *Douglas Darby* – in a Rush

After fixing the blackout covers on our car's headlamps on the weekend the war started, my father and I went to the old skating rink at the top of Half Moon Hill to await the arrival of evacuees from London. By early evening most of them had been accommodated. After the first rush, those that were left had a meal and spent the night on camp beds or mattresses on the floor.

Next morning, members of the Committee checked their list of appropriate offers and I was asked to go to Markyate, where a lady had a spare bedroom. Ready to drive off I did not look to see who was in the rear seat and sped off. Arriving at the house in one of the side streets I jumped out, knocked at the door and returned to find my only passenger was a woman. The lady of the house having opened her front door looked as concerned as I was – and then the truth dawned. She said she had offered to take a boy or a girl but, at this point the evacuee broke into tears and they put their arms around each other and went indoors.

Part way along the High Street a policeman and a warden stopped my car and asked me who I was and where I was going. Being satisfied, they said they had just had warning of a possible air raid and I'd better get back home as quickly as possible. I didn't stop to ask any more questions and covered those four miles back to Dunstable in almost as many minutes. However, as we know now it was a false alarm that time!

### *Dorothy Couldwell* - Arriving by Bus

My maiden name was Dorothy Middleton and I lived in Houghton Regis in Bedfordshire. It was a warm summer's day when the evacuees arrived in the village. They arrived by bus and were taken to one of the nearby schools. The local school children were told, "Not to go in and stare at them." I was 11 at the time. People of the village were asked to take in one, or perhaps two children and to go to the school to collect them. I was the eldest of 4 children living in a modest terraced house, so we hadn't put our names down for any. Anyway, my father went for a stroll after tea and came back with 3 evacuees. There were only a few left to be placed in homes and these 3 were proving difficult, because they were related and had been told before leaving London, to stay together. There was Charlie aged 6, Roy 5 and Peggy 12. They were sad, bewildered and a little frightened. They each had a bag with their belongings and gas masks. Beds had to be made up on the floor of the front room, which was only used on 'high days and holidays'. When we all got to know each other we got on quite well. We used to sing 'Charlie My Darling' and he used to go all shy and hide behind the chair, but it was all in good fun. Our neighbours had an evacuee girl called Joan and we became very good friends.

The bombing of London didn't happen for a while and as many parents missed their children and vice versa, the majority of them drifted back, including Roy, Charlie and Peggy. When the bombing really started, my mother was asked if they could come back but by then, my aunt and her daughter had come to stay from Tottenham. Some of the children's mothers managed to get a house in the village to be with their children

Many lasting friendships were made with the evacuees. I was glad to be a child of the village and not an evacuee; it must have been a very frightening experience for them and heartbreaking for their parents.

We never forgot our evacuees but didn't hear any more about them. I hope they all made it through the war.

### Mary Corrie (née Cheshire) – Sharing a Big House

I can remember the milkman coming into my parents' house and listening to Mr Chamberlain on the radio telling us that we were at war.

I was 7 years old and living in Dunstable. I had three brothers, John who was in the army, Colin 17 and David 9. We had evacuees, Frederick and Joseph and 2 sisters, Maud and Kitty. Later, Kitty was billeted to number 9 Victoria Street. They stayed with us for about 18 months before moving to Poynters Road so that they could all be together. Later, Charlie came from London before moving to Surrey to join his father who was a policeman, because the bombing wasn't so rife there.

We went to Burr Street School but I think our evacuees went to Britain Street. We only used to attend school in the mornings or afternoons because of the influx of evacuees from Acland School in London. We had air raid practices and had to go into the cloakroom. Every day we took our gas masks to school in a cardboard box with our names on it. They were horrible things and we had to practice wearing them for so many minutes a day.

There seemed to be a lot of comings and goings at our house at Victoria Street. Mum's friends were already with us from Kent when the evacuees came, and stayed for 4 or 5 years because they were being bombed. My parents got us out of bed one night because they thought the bombing was a bit close. We sat on the stairs at Victoria Street, Dad at the top, Mum at the bottom and the children in the middle.

After the evacuees we had soldiers billeted with us, as our house was quite big. One of them, George, was in the ROAC and stationed at the brewery (now the Priory pub in High Street North).

## Len Stafford - Outcasts from London

I don't remember when we were first evacuated. I know we all had to assemble in a hall and had little things pinned to our coats. I came out of London from St Pancras on the train and arrived in Luton where they lined us all up. People walked along saying, "You go there. You go here," and we just stood there with our gas masks. I remember being very unhappy because I thought someone had pinched my Mum and Dad. I wasn't at all happy in the house where I was placed in Dunstable and in the end my auntie came to take me back home.

My dad found a job in Hatfield and my parents rented a place in Luton but we used to go back to London every weekend. That was the funny thing; all these bombs and rockets were around but it never really stopped the people having an ordinary life.

We rented a house in Beechwood Road in Luton and went to Beechwood Road School. We were sort of outcasts really because we came from London. There was a lot of prodding and pushing and I can remember I used to get beaten up almost everyday. I was punched in the ear and had 6 months off school. But I went back and gave the other bloke a punch on the nose. We weren't really accepted because we were strangers but it did settle down when people got to know us, though.

## Christina Scott - Smithfield Market was Evacuated to my Father's Garage!

We were summoned back to school early at the Cedars in Leighton Buzzard and had a whole week to collect clothes and underwear to send to evacuees. We all dug out clothes we could spare because we thought that there would be shortages, but initially there wasn't; it was really quiet in the first 12 months. I went back to school for a third year in the sixth form as I was hoping to go to university. I should have gone to France as I was studying French, so I had to stay on at school and do what I could to keep my language skills going. I remember that year there was an outbreak of German measles and most of us caught it; we were kept off school for a week, ironic really.

We only had half time schooling at the Cedars because we shared our school with boys evacuated from William Ellis, Highgate, quite a high class Grammar school. We were a mixed school so it didn't make life very easy.

The numbers doubled and so the staff had a difficult time. We went in the mornings and came home at lunchtime. These boys were put into billets in the town. The same thing happened at Luton High School, with a girls' school from Edgware. William Ellis was a bigger school than ours; we had only just over 200 in those days, however we survived.

I went by Eastern National bus to the Cedars at Leighton Buzzard, but they were not very frequent and it could be very inconvenient if you missed the bus and didn't get home until 7pm. Father didn't believe in running me to school although he had a car. The Cedars took girls from Bletchley, Wolverton, Linslade as well as Dunstable. The playing fields are in Mentmore Road, which was a long way from the school then but near the station. The school has moved from there now.

As war broke out, people were made billeting officers. One our local officers knocked on the door and said, "Mrs Scott, how many rooms have you got and how many people can you billet?" We had a couple of spare rooms and we thought we were going to have some schoolchildren. In the event because my father owned quite a slab of land on the west side, which was an area of lockup garages, and a huge shed, Smithfield market came down. The government commandeered it and people had to be turned out of their garages. They proceeded to put a big set of doors on the front of the shed meant for meat storage. Shortly afterwards the meat came down from Smithfield. A well known meat trader at Smithfield and his wife wanted to get out of London, so they came down and needed a billet. My father agreed that they could have the big back bedroom in our house. The lady had a pet marmoset and that was billeted as well! Sometimes we looked after it. She used to walk around with it on her shoulder and then it went into a box wrapped in flannel and put by the pipe near the boiler. That didn't last long, the couple were called back to London and so was the meat. It was at the time of the phoney war. We still had the empty bedroom and I was off to university.

One day in summer of 1940 a customer came to get petrol from my father's garage; a chauffeur driven car with a lady and gentleman in it. They said, "We are desperate to get out of Blackheath." My father, knowing we should have someone to stay in the bedrooms, told them to see my mother. The man was a pearl merchant in Hatton Garden with his sister, and for 8 months we shared our house with them. They came back for another 10 months when the doodlebugs came. In between times we had officers from the barracks in High Street North, Royal Engineers I think, and then a series of colonels. They paid, of course. When I came home from university, I had to sleep in the little dressing room but there wasn't much room. We also had the box room and we were open house to mother's relatives. One Sunday night my cousin and I shared a single camp bed; I was at the top and she was at the bottom, and in the end I put my head in a drawer because I couldn't put my head anywhere else. It was quite dreadful. It was very hard work for my mother providing meals on rations but we were so full of people, we just had to help each other out.

### *Doris Perry* – **Evacuated to Houghton Regis**

On the 1st September 1939, with war imminent, all London school children were assembled at their various schools for immediate evacuation to the countryside. War was announced two days later after Chamberlain's ultimatum to Adolf Hitler was ignored.

I was amongst those children. I was just thirteen years of age. I remember we travelled light with a case, our gas mask and a few items to eat. We arrived late afternoon in Luton from St Pancras Station – my home area. We finally came to Houghton Regis. I recall a large pleasant village green and a long dark coloured hut. From here we were given refreshments, much kindness and told to wait until our foster carers chose us.

The youngest children were chosen first. Being amongst the eldest, my school friend and I were chosen by the licensee and his wife to go to the Chequers Inn – opposite the village pond. They had one small boy and we stayed happily with them for several weeks. It was then announced that evacuees should not stay on licensed premises and we were moved to Park Avenue and lived with another nice family. By this time we had started our schoolwork at the old village school situated at the top of the High Street, Houghton Regis. After tests we were placed in various forms at Northfields School. Life took on a very rural style. As I was drawn from a Church of England school, Sundays meant regular worship at All Saints Church. I loved the checkerboard effect of the stone-craft. It was from this church under the instruction of the vicar, that we were later confirmed at the old Priory Church, Dunstable, on 10th December 1939.

It was a very happy existence in Houghton Regis. The winter of '39–'40 was extremely cold but the summer of 1940 is well documented as one of the hottest. After school the village boys and girls would take pleasure in walks and rambles over the fields. Often Spitfires and Hurricanes flew low, practising for what lay ahead.

Until early 1940 there were regular meets on the village green. There were many hounds all with different names. The riders looked picturesque in their 'pink' riding habits. A certain Colonel, we were told, owned much of the surrounding countryside.

On Saturdays with schoolwork done we would head for the excellent roller skating rink in Dunstable. It was called the Half Moon Rink. We would skate around to the popular tunes of the day and feel well exercised, then either bus, or walk home. Another popular entertainment was the Union Cinema in Dunstable. Judy Garland, Deanne Durbin, Mickey Rooney and all the big stars could be seen in the classic films of that era. The radio was very important and as the war lengthened it became more so. It was an evening event to catch up with the latest news on the war front.

By May 1940 Hitler's forces had invaded the low countries of Holland, Belgium and Denmark after the fall of France and our retreat from Dunkirk. Bombs began to fall on us. A stick of bombs fell near us at Easthill Lane. I was now living in Easthill Lane, off Drury Lane, with a wonderful family with whom I am still in touch. I remember those bombs falling and running to the Anderson shelter in the garden, as they seemed to come nearer. There were many factories in Dunstable now into war work. Sphinx, Bagshawe's, The Empire Rubber Company, and Luton's car plant made tanks.

Spring was lovely and often the family and I would rise very early and gather mushrooms from the surrounding fields. These would be cooked on return with gammon rashers – my first introduction to this delicacy. Rationing of all foodstuffs was not as severe as later on. A clutch of wood pigeons would be brought to the door by a travelling supplier and the husband – an excellent cook – would cook these in a flaky pastry. I can taste it now!

By September my widower father said I could return home. I said my farewells to the family and boarded the train. The date was 7th September 1940. As the train drew into St Pancras station the sirens began blaring, warning of imminent danger. The time was 5pm. I emerged from the station on to Euston Road and everyone began to scatter. Above me there was noise of gunfire and trails of vapour in the blue sky. It was the beginning of the Battle of Britain, and our young airmen were taking on the enemy aircraft high above. I was warned to take cover. There was no one to meet me as my father was unsure which train I would be on. Fortunately, I lived only a few minutes walk to our London flat in Church Way, Euston and I was reunited with my father who was very anxious.

All night long the bombs rained down on the East India Docks and around. The residents and myself took cover in the brick built air raid shelter in the grounds of Wellesley Buildings. The blasts rocked the shelter and hurt our ears. The 'All Clear' did not come until dawn. My father said I must return to Houghton Regis. Broken hearted he put me on the train back to Luton. All around me were servicemen with full kit returning to their units, ships and aerodromes. I cried all the way.

Back in Easthill Lane we watched the glow in the sky on winter's nights as London burned at the height of the blitz. I returned to the Empire Rubber Co. I remained there during the winter. Many times we would walk across the dark frozen fields to 'clock-on' by 7.30 am. Meanwhile the family found space for extra evacuees, notably a family of three Jewish people. I remember the terror they spoke of, afraid of what might happen. The lady of the house was still in her twenties, a superb cook and a very competent housewife. Her three children were slightly younger than myself. Her husband worked at the cement works. They later had their share of sadness.

Houghton Regis was a pleasant, peaceful place. Dances and community interests were held in the halls there. I still remember the sunlit day I finally arrived back in London in June 1941, two weeks before Hitler invaded Russia. Another four years of war before peace came in 1945.

### Bernard Polley – at the Grammar School

In May 1940 I was evacuated with my mother and younger sister to Bedford to stay with relatives. In July my father was serving in REME and was posted to Luton, so he arranged for us to join him there and we rented a house in Oakley Road. This was a few yards from the Shaw and Kilburn garage, which the army had requisitioned with father, the Commanding Officer.

My schooling had been sadly neglected since leaving Colchester and as

I had reached the age of eleven something had to be done to rectify the omission. Eleven-year-olds at this time could take an entry examination into the grammar school, and it was arranged that I should take a special sitting at Dunstable School for this purpose. I remember the very warm day in August when I met the headmaster and sat in the school dining room to do the exam on my own, accompanied by an alarm clock with a loud tick! I didn't do well enough to enter the appropriate class, but was accepted for the class where I was a year older than most of the other pupils.

At the height of the Battle of Britain in the middle of September, I joined the Prep School, which was based in Ashton House. Normally the uniform at Dunstable was Eton collars and dark suits but because of wartime clothing restrictions we were able to wear short trousers, blazer and a soft-collar shirt with a school tie.

Every morning we joined the main assembly seated in Big School. The prefects, who like the masters always sat in lines of descending seniority, took up their seats in the front row. Then the gowned masters walked in from the back of the hall and took up positions on the stage with a master at the harmonium. All stood as the headmaster entered and took his place at the central table. Using the Public School hymn book we'd sing a hymn (quite often, 'Dear Lord and Father of Mankind'). The headmaster said two collects and then we sang a psalm from the hymnbook. After a pause, the head put on his mortarboard, indicating that we could sit, before giving the daily announcements.

On November 22nd the Grammar School celebrated 'Founder's Day' with a service at the Parish Church conducted by the Rector. In the afternoon, Speech Day took place in Big School with prizes presented by Lt General Sir John Brown. He asked for the traditional half-day holiday, which was enthusiastically received. Then we all sang the school song – 'Hurrah for Dunstable, the best of all schools!'

In the summer term of 1941 we were able to swim in the school bathing pool, and it was always made out that it was a great privilege to be allowed time to go there on Wednesday afternoons.

Dunstable had a Glee Club attended by several masters and senior pupils from the school. I remember attending one of their concerts in the Town Hall when Mr B (my Geography master), performed an item wearing a variety of comic hats.

My second year at Dunstable Grammar commenced in September 1941 when I moved into Shell A class in Big School with a form-master who was a Colonel, an elderly gentleman called out of retirement to replace a classics master who had been called up for service. Several new boys joined the class, many of them Jewish, whose families had been turned out of their homes in Poland.

As young schoolboys we probably didn't appreciate the full implications of war. It was only when the siren sounded on Waterlow's factory next to the school, would we take to the air raid shelters built in the school grounds. These were long tunnels with benches on either side so that we could continue lessons whilst the alert was on. Fortunately, I don't remember these situations happening too often.

Sporting activities were curtailed because of the lack of young, physically fit masters, so unless a pupil was keen to play football, hockey or cricket and get into one of the recognised teams, you weren't pestered to take part. My sporting ability was not recognised, so cycling to and from school was the only exercise I received!

In May 1942 we had a school photograph taken. It was one of those long horizontal prints where the photographer pans with the camera. I still have this photo framed, sixty plus years on; I can remember most faces but many names escape me.

Just before Christmas mother was taken seriously ill and it was decided that the family would have to return to Colchester, so that she could be nursed by my grandparents. My schooling at Dunstable Grammar came to an abrupt end, no time for goodbyes and it was arranged that I would be transferred to Colchester Royal Grammar School.

Looking back on those wartime days spent at Dunstable School, I have fond memories of both masters and schoolmates and am pleased to be kept in touch with the Old Boys' Association newsletters.

### *Harold R Perkins* - the School Shelters

At the Dunstable Grammar School there was a grassy area behind the swimming pool. Normally it was used by the boarders for *ad hoc* games and included the firing range for the rifle butts at the back. At the beginning of the war air-raid shelters were built there. They consisted of underground corridors cut in the chalk and covered with mounds of spoil. If the air-raid warning sounded, which it did frequently in the very early days of the war, we all trooped out from the classrooms and into the shelters where we sat on long wooden benches. There we were supposed to continue our lessons but really not much work was done. Of course, we were all obliged to carry our gas masks at all times (there were penalties for being without). Mine was in a tin canister with a screw lid. It survived the war.

### *Robert Hawkes* - Cadet Corps

I followed the progress of the war closely, cutting out photographs and subscribing to a new publication, 'War Illustrated'. By this time I was a pupil at Dunstable Grammar School although we lived in Luton. Air raid shelters were built at the school but were seldom used, as the town fortunately received little attention from 'Jerry'.

I joined the School Cadet Corps and learned the rudiments of military training, even day dreaming of the Corps defending Dunstable in the event

AN INSPECTION of Dunstable Grammar School Army Cadets by Lieutenant Colonel AC Wadsworth and Captain Brock in December 1943 *(DG)*

of invasion, except of course our ancient carbines were quite inoperable. We were encouraged to help the war-effort by assisting with the harvests on local farms and with the post at Christmas. A small group of us worked on a farm during several school holidays.

## Joyce Ward – a Variety of Children

Phyllis, my sister, had three evacuee children who wouldn't be parted. They were friends from the same school and their parents had asked if they could be kept together. Two were all right, but one came from a very poor family. Her mother never wrote to her or came down or anything, her older sister used to come and bring her things. The little one didn't see much of her parents, but the middle one had been brought up nicely and the parents used to come down every few weeks to see her. To start with, Phyllis had to de-louse the oldest one and youngest one. You collected the powder from the depots where they brought the children in. Two of them had never sat down to a meal or used a knife and fork.

Phyllis wasn't well and the doctor told her that she would have to send the children back. She didn't for some time but then got in touch with the evacuee office and, as nothing was happening in London, they all went back. When the bombing started, the youngest one's family wrote to Phyllis and asked her if she would have them back, but Cyril said no, they'd had them enough. They were a trial. She had to teach 2 of them as if they were tiny children. The middle one was nicely dressed but the other two, I think the parents were glad to get rid of them. The eldest one was about 12, the middle one about 9 and the little one, 7. If they'd all been like the middle one it would have been alright, all they knew was a bit of food in their hands and sit on the doorstep. The children didn't want to go back. They were quite happy; I suppose they had a better life being evacuated.

## Betty Tompkins – School Uniform

I was sitting in the dining room with my parents and younger sister as we listened to Neville Chamberlain on the radio announcing the start of the war. In September 1939, I went to the Luton High School for Girls. On the first day of school we all assembled in the hall and had to paste brown sticky paper over the very long windows. School uniform had to be worn at all times. In winter it consisted of a navy blue serge tunic with a white blouse and tie, a badge, winter coat and rain coat in navy blue, hat, blazer, beige stockings, black shoes with laces, indoor shoes with soft soles, black plimsolls for gym and hockey boots. For summer, a dress, panama hat and white tennis shoes for sports.

We caught the bus to school but often there were no buses home, so we'd have to walk, carrying our satchels, gas masks and all the other things we had to take with us. In the end my father purchased a bike for me from Charlie Cole's but he couldn't get one for my sister because the shop had run out, so he made her one. Nothing was wasted. We even had to save tacking cotton that we used in the needlework room at school. We knitted balaclavas for Russian sailors. The wool was navy blue, oiled and very thick.

While I was at school each form had to go in turn to work on the farm. After we'd changed into suitable clothes, an open lorry used to come to collect us, and off we went. When we got to the farm in Tilsworth, we had to stand in lines in the field and wait for the gym mistress to blow her whistle for us to start. We then began by scraping the earth off potatoes that had been dug up and sorting them into buckets.

We didn't take in any evacuees but my father, who was a haulage contractor, would bring home all sorts of odd people that he found on the road when he was driving his lorry. People would have to walk miles because there was very little transport. He brought a gypsy girl home once, carrying a newborn baby in a shawl, very hungry and tired, trying to make her way to Wales! He brought her home and she was fed, rested and went on her way. He also brought home a young doctor, also on his way to Wales to see his parents.

### *Alan Wilsher* - at Totternhoe Church School

I was seven years old when the war started and one of my earliest memories is going to school with a biscuit tin sealed with tape. This contained a supply of biscuits and other food, just in case we were stranded at school during an air raid. This had to be taken and kept at Totternhoe Church School, Castle Hill Road, until the end of the war.

# Prisoner of War Camp

## INTRODUCTION BY SUE KING

The London Gliding Club, based along the Icknield Way at the foot of Dunstable Downs was established around 1929/30. As soon as war was announced, the club's manager Tim Hervey was ordered to stop all flights, as the club was 'in an area of Fighter Command'. Later on in the war, instructors from the Gliding Club began training military pilots.

The club was then requisitioned by the War Office as a prisoner of war camp for Italian and German prisoners from 1941 until 1945. This PoW camp consisted of living quarters, a guardhouse, bakery, exercise field and it even had its own chapel. Many people recall PoWs helping to build new houses and working on local farms during the latter part of the war.

In his book 'Take Up Slack', Edward Hull informs us that soon after the club was requisitioned, 'Farmer Tom Turvey converted one of his barns at Totternhoe for use as a clubroom. Throughout the war Mrs Turvey provided snacks and teas for Club members who gathered at weekends to talk over old times'.

After the war, civil flights were still prohibited. In his book, History of The London Gliding Club, Dudley Hiscox tells us that he and F/Lt Stanley

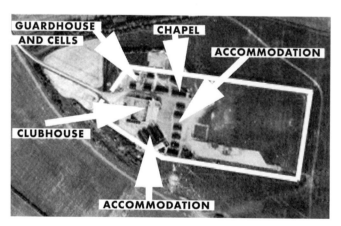

POW CAMP at The London Gliding Club (*LGC*)

Sproule resisted this ban and flew their gliders for the first time after the war on 2nd September 1945. They had in their possession a document issued by the RAF, stating that 'gliders were not aircraft in the meaning of Kings Regulations'. They informed the local newspapers and were consequently contacted by the Chief Constable of Bedfordshire, instructing them that he 'would take action if there was a repetition'. Dudley Hiscox goes on to say that they 'hoped to be taken to Court for the sake of more publicity'. However, civil flying restrictions were lifted soon after.

Before the London Gliding Club was commandeered as a PoW camp, one of its members, an estate agent, carried out a 'schedule of dilapidation'. This was very fortunate, because after the land was returned to its members, the club was awarded a claim of £5,000. After an enormous amount of restoration work the club was finally reopened on 1st January 1949.

*right* A GLIDER over the Downs *(LGC)*

*below* ITALIAN POWS at Dunstable *(LGC)*

## INTRODUCTION BY KEVIN JORGENSEN,
### Manshead Archaeological Project

There are several of the buildings left today, including a row of barrack huts and kitchens, which are now used as workshops for gliders. You can still see where the flues for the ovens go through the roof, and the drain gulleys for sinks run along the floor at the far end of the building. Outside you can also see the postholes for the perimeter fencing and telegraph poles.

Fortunately as the war went on, the threat of invasion ended, so many of the defences were demolished, some by the prisoners from the Gliding Club, and as a result very few examples are left today.

The buildings are, from left to right, THE CLUBHOUSE built in 1936 and THE BARRACKS from the prisoner of war camp. *(MAS)*

The building was THE HANGAR AND WORKSHOP built in 1937, now used as a Flying foundation. *(MAS)*

THE GUARDHOUSE and lock up which is now used as a paint store and a storage area. It is still possible to identify the interior walls. *(MAS)*

The front view of THE ORIGINAL CLUBHOUSE built in 1936 *(MAS)*

THE KITCHEN, which is now used as a workshop for repairing gliders. Inside the building you can see the cut outs for the flues in the roof which run about two thirds of the way down the centre, and in the bottom left corner is the drainage gully for the sinks. *(MAS)*

THE PRESENT DAY CLUBHOUSE and facilities *(MAS)*

POST HOLES for the compound fencing and telegraph poles *(MAS)*

THE BOILER HOUSE which supplied the kitchen with hot water for cleaning and food preparation *(MAS)*

A REAR VIEW of the boiler house *(MAS)*

## INTERVIEW – BBC THREE COUNTIES RADIO
with *Erwin Rudorf*, a former German PoW,
and *Ted Hull* from the London Gliding Club

**Interviewer:** Ted – How come so little is known about the Club's history?

**Ted:** The Club was closed down during the war but members did manage to fly until Feb 1940 because they just ignored the order that private flying should stop. No one told the Club officially, so they carried on! Most men joined the forces and just weren't around.

    The local farmer Tom Turvey, who had sold us the airfield early in the thirties, had provided a barn for the storage of gliders during the war. There was also a little clubhouse where people would go at the weekends and Mrs Turvey made them tea, but no one really knew what was going on behind the wire.

**Interviewer:** Gliding was a very different sport in those days. Were the gliders launched off the top of the hill then?

**Ted:** Yes! They were launched by an elastic rope. They used to drag the gliders up the hill with an endless rope driven by a winch at the bottom, and then they'd recruit a few people from the on-lookers, half a dozen on each side of the bungee rope, and they'd catapult them off the top of the hill!

**Interviewer:** So, the PoW camp, do we know how or why it was put there?

**Ted:** Before the war we were training the air defence Cadet Corps, which later became the ATC. There were 2 army huts built behind the clubhouse for their accommodation. Presumably the air force knew about this and someone decided that it should be used as a prison camp. In the meantime Vauxhall had been using the hangar to store cars.

**Interviewer:** The Club itself was also used to train German pilots before the war?

**Ted:** Yes. But there is a bit of a myth grown up about this. There were only 16 of them on a fortnight's course in 1937!

**Interviewer:** You have a couple of photographs, what do they show?

**Ted:** One is a group of Italians prisoners standing in front of a hut. The other one is an RAF aerial survey that shows the camp, compound and buildings.

**Interviewer:** It must have been very small, capable of holding about 20 or 30 prisoners?

**Ted:** When Erwin was there, they had about 200 German prisoners.

**Interviewer:** Who were they guarded by, the Home Guard?

**Erwin:** The army. In Luton, we had Pioneers as guards but they were dangerous!

**Ted:** There is a little story about three club members who were in Totternhoe having their tea, when they decided to go and have a look at the Club. They drove up to the gates and bawled at the guard in German that they were going to organise an escape. The guard was a bit nonplussed and pointed them in the direction of the sergeant. He didn't speak any German either and there was no officer there at the time, so they shouted at him for a bit, walked around to see what state the buildings were in, which they didn't think much of, walked out and bawled out the guard for not saluting them!

**Interviewer:** Erwin, how did you come to be in Dunstable?

**Erwin:** I was in Great Offley as a cook; just over 80 men came to Dunstable. A cook had to accompany them, and that was me!

**Interviewer:** How old were you then?

**Erwin:** 19.

**Interviewer:** Where were you captured?

**Erwin:** In Luxemburg. I was with the Americans for 10 months before being sent to England.

**Interviewer:** It must have been quite frightening for an 18-year-old?

**Erwin:** No. It was worse when I was 17, in a working group in Estonia.

**Interviewer:** How were you treated?

**Erwin:** The Americans, I'd rather forget about it.

**Interviewer:** Obviously, we tend to focus on the bad side of things but you decided to settle here after the war?

**Erwin:** It's as good a place as any!

**Interviewer:** Did you not want to go back to Germany?

**Erwin:** At that time there was no work there. I was in the camp for about 4 months. I worked on Hill Farm in Wingfield and stayed with that farmer for 4 years. We were allowed to stay on for 12 months in Civvy Street. I thought I'd stay for this time to buy some clothes to go home in!

I have now two boys and grandchildren.

## *Albert W Morgan* – the **Prisoner of War Camp**

The London Gliding Club Headquarters was used as a 'Prisoner of War' camp for much of the war. The main hangar and clubhouse had a steep drop on each side of it. The barbed wire fences ran along the top of these drops and out towards the Downs where they enclosed a football pitch. On the apron of the hangar were a number of huts. I understand that until Italy made an armistice with the allies, the camp inmates were Italians. After this date, they were allowed to come into Dunstable during the evenings. However, a contingent of Polish soldiers were stationed in the camp situated to the rear of Dr Binns' house, now the site of Argos etc. There were fights between the Italians and the Poles so the Italians were replaced by German PoWs. The Germans remained there until after the war and were then employed in building work on the Beecroft estate where they were photographed by the local press. The 'Nazi' emblem of eagle and swastika can be seen on the right breast of several of them.

POWS DIGGING THE FOUNDATIONS of the Beecroft estate *(DG)*

When the estate was being built, there was a wooden cabin at the end of what is now Maidenbower Avenue with the junction with Chiltern Road. This had a notice 'Foreman' on the door and beneath was one in German with the word 'Arbeitsfuehrer' on it. I had just started to learn German at the Grammar School and our teacher, Mr. R. F. Broadfoot, confirmed that this was indeed the German word for foreman.

### Pat Morgan – the Bambinos!

The Italians were working on the fields at the bottom of Blow's Downs and we used to spit at them. They used to get very upset, cry and say, "Oh, the bambinos!" We were 5 or 6 years old and horrid. The evacuees were worse than us. I started school in 1943 and they were amalgamated with us. We did 3 days one week and 4 the next. The Londoners didn't like the Germans or the Italians, and encouraged us to do these awful spitting things.

## EXTRACT OF A CONVERSATION BETWEEN THREE FRIENDS:
### Pam Perkins, Betty Tarbox and Heather Hing

**Pam:** My uncle had his own lorry and used to go to the Gliding Club to pick up PoWs, take them to work and collect them at 5 o'clock; sometimes we used to go with them. We had a great time. All the prisoners used to sit on the back of the lorry on benches and the Home Guards used to sit on the tailgate. Nobody wanted to escape; they were having a lovely time.

**Betty:** Opposite the crematorium in Luton is Putteridge Bury; we had prisoners of war from there working for us. Pieter, a German, used to come for dinner and tea on Sundays. Dad used to sign a form for him to come.

**Heather:** They dropped a load of PoWs off in the morning to work for us; they were very good to us, especially the Italians. They had their own shed with a stove and made their own coffee with creamy milk, which we didn't have. Mum used to cook them a big saucepan of potatoes every day and we worked alongside them where Frosts is now at Woburn; my dad managed the place then. After the Germans and Italians we had Land Army girls helping because our men were still away.

**Betty:** In the middle of where the prefabs were built, there was a displaced persons' camp. There were two lots of prefabs in the town, one where

Pipers Croft is now (called Bennett's Close then) and the others at the bottom of Blow's Downs in Half Moon Lane. The German PoWs built the prefabs. They carved us edelweiss out of chalk and made us bats with chicken shapes that pecked.

**Heather:** They made my needlework box, which I've still got, and they found willow in the village and made baskets.

**Betty:** They used to show us photos but the grown-ups wouldn't have anything to do with them. My Dad was in the 1st World War and he told me that there is good and bad in everyone.

### John Rushton - the Fence

There were a lot of PoWs in Dunstable during the war. Many of the Italians were given leave at the weekends. My father employed a couple of them to creosote his fence and look after his garden. He then gave them a meal before they went back to the camp at the Gliding Club.

### Lucy Pendar - in the Snow

In 1945 I remember falling off the snow plough and was caught by an Italian PoW. We had 2 Italian PoWs helping out at Whipsnade.

### Marjorie Tingey - Clearing the Roads

The Gliding Club had Italian prisoners of war there and at one time the roads were so thick with snow, buses couldn't get down the road, so they got these Italian prisoners of war to come and sweep the streets and keep the roads clear. Some people took the prisoners of war teas and coffees because they did work very hard. Some of them remained behind and married local girls.

### Derek Bonfield - Italian Airmen

In the later part of the war, the gliding club was turned into a PoW camp. We had 2 Italian PoWs to work on the farm and eventually we converted one of the stables so they could live on the farm. One of them had been in the Italian Air Force and was educated at Oxford while his father was a miller in Rome. His English was perfect with an Oxford accent, and he assured me that he used to fly very high and drop his bombs in the sea. We had no contact after the war.

## *Joan Dineen* – the Portrait

My father worked for Hill's Transport. They had a contract to collect PoWs from the camp and take them to their respective places of work in the morning and return them in the evening. When I was 16 years old, a German PoW painted a portrait of me taken from a photograph my father kept in his wallet.

PORTRAIT of 16-year-old Joan Dineen, by a German PoW *(SK)*

### *Mary Corrie (née) Cheshire* - **Italian Workers**

The Gliding Club was totally out of bounds and surrounded by barbed wire because the Italian PoWs were being held there. The PoWs worked at the cement works or at the lower railway station in High Street North.

### *Betty Tompkins* - **German Voices in the Kitchen**

Part of my father's job was to move PoWs from one place to another. We didn't tell one another very much, so I can't tell you where they came from or where they went. On one occasion during a very severe winter, my father's lorry broke down. He managed to get it home, put all the PoWs in our house and carried out a repair.

Unbeknown to me, I came home from school and saw guns in the back porch and I could hear German voices. I was terrified, until I recognised that one of the voices belonged to my father. He had been in the Royal Flying Corps during the First World War and was sent to Germany after the war had ended. He was looked after by an old German lady and learned how to speak German. The German PoWs and British guards were all standing around the fire in our living room, with my mother making them coffee.

# Bedfordshire's Secret War

## INTRODUCTION BY JEAN YATES

I have heard Bedfordshire described as the spy capital of Great Britain. Was it chosen because the A5 was the route from London to Birmingham and beyond for the main communication lines? Was Bletchley Park chosen as the code-breakers' home because it was within reach of London and next to a main line railway station? Were other places such as Milton Bryan, Woburn, Dunstable's security printers and the Met. Office just happily in the right places at that time, or was it all part of a big security plan? The more we uncover, the more you realise that the latter was true.

Some of our stories seem extraordinary now, but more than sixty years ago Bedfordshire was a very different place. Petrol rationing, few telephones, no television and restrictions on newspapers meant that people were working in complete isolation and ignorant of what was happening on their doorsteps. Add to this the constant messages of 'keep mum' and the Official Secrets Act, which so many people signed, and we can begin to understand why some of these stories are only now coming to the surface and many will never be told.

Dunstable played a part in Britain's Secret War, the war of propaganda, both 'white' and 'black', written and broadcast, listening and decoding, and the placement of those involved in the various Bedfordshire secret locations. A number of the places mentioned here relate in some way to Dunstable. Other information is included here because it has recently come to light as a result of work in the county carried out for the BBC People's War website in which I was involved.

The operations in Bedfordshire were part of a new secret department, the Political Warfare Executive (PWE), set up to control all 'white' and 'black' propaganda, which in turn was part of the Political Intelligence Department. The PWE 'white' section was based at Woburn Abbey, which became known as Country Headquarters.

The BBC broadcasts to Germany and written items bearing HM

Government's imprint and dropped by the RAF were 'white' propaganda. The other propaganda activities classed as 'black' were operations that would have been impossible for the BBC to be involved with. It was imperative that the BBC's credibility for truth and fact be maintained. New venues were therefore built or rented for the 'black' operations as the war progressed.

Sefton Delmer ran the 'black' operations, which he wrote about in his autobiography, 'Black Boomerang'. The 'black' written operation was carried out at **Maryland, Woburn**, and Ellic Howe was responsible for this. In his book 'The Black Game', he reveals the extent of the 'black' printing, some of which was carried out in and around Dunstable.

**Milton Bryan** (**MB**) studios were built to house the 'black' broadcasting section on a five acre site, opened in 1942, closed in 1945, the site now being derelict. As well as the studios there was a record library, intelligence files and newspaper and radio newsrooms. There were some three hundred people living in the compound at one time. Some of these were prisoners of war, some defectors, some refugees, others like Sefton Delmer, British, but educated or living abroad before the outbreak of war. There were many aerials erected on the site and at the related Potsgrove transmitter. MB was guarded by uniformed special constables and patrolled by dogs.

In 1943 Sefton Delmer was promoted and appointed as 'Director of Special Operations against the Enemy and Satellites' (black). His 'black' assault now included Hitler's satellite countries as well as Germany.

This caused an increase in barracks at Milton Bryan to house the new teams from Italy, Hungary, Bulgaria and Rumania. Fresh stations and campaigns were launched directed towards Italy. Radio Livorno pretended to be broadcasting from an Italian warship at Livorno base. Each night the station ordered the Italian navy to do nothing without orders from itself. The navy was told that negotiations were being held for its liberation from the Germans. On September 10th, Radio Livorno from MB gave the Italian navy the order to sail. The ships did as they were told and sailed for Malta, to the Livorno broadcast rendezvous, and surrendered.

Records and newspapers were smuggled into neutral Sweden from occupied Europe and were then flown to Britain by RAF Mosquitoes. They ended up at Milton Bryan where Sefton Delmer's unit read them word by word and extracted every last piece of information that could be used or stored for future campaigns.

Motor cycle dispatch riders rushed aerial photographs of bomb damage inflicted by the RAF to Milton Bryan. These photographs were brought back by RAF Mosquitoes that followed the bombing raids, and enabled Milton Bryan staff to pinpoint streets and buildings affected. This information was then broadcast back to Germany. Because the station built a reputation for truth on the accuracy of these and other reports, the fictional propaganda reports were accepted by the listeners.

On April 14th 1945, the Soldatensender West station broadcast its last programme and then just disappeared.

MILTON BRYAN STUDIOS *(BCC)*

## *Phil Luck* - Transmitting Programmes from Potsgrove, all over Europe

PHIL LUCK in WWII *(PL)*

My friend, who had a cousin in the Foreign Office, had been recruited into SCU1, Special Communications Unit number one, which was really the communication section of MI6. He phoned me and told me that they were looking for someone else to join his unit. "You've never told me anything about it," I said. He said, "No, I'm not allowed to." "Is this a reasonable job?" "Yes," he said; I replied, "Well OK, I'll be interested."

I was working in a reserved occupation for a limited amount of time before I'd have to join the forces, so I jumped. I found out later a man had been killed, electrocuted by an equipment malfunction at Potsgrove.

It was all carried out on the phone. I had to give notice and after about a month they told me that I would be met at Bletchley railway station. I had never seen the guy and he had never seen me, and we were supposed to meet at 1.30pm. I was standing there with a suitcase on a very busy station. Eventually this guy, Lieutenant, later Captain, Fuller came, and was 2 hours late, I wondered what was happening with this outfit; that's how I was recruited.

I worked as a civilian; this was in Oct/Nov 1943, because I'd been trained and they just needed to get me into their way of working, and I took over a shift position fairly quickly. Operation and maintenance of high-powered transmitters was my expertise. They transferred a man to replace the one who died from Gawcott to Potsgrove, and slipped me into Gawcott.

PHIL LUCK (JY)

The two stations, Gawcott and Potsgrove, each of them had two short wave transmitters, and at first we were broadcasting from discs that were all cut on a machine, transported (from Whaddon and Wavendon) by a civilian driver and broadcast at various times of day and night. I also worked on the Potsgrove transmitter, which was about 3 miles from Milton Bryan (MB), but I never knew anything about MB at the time. (Never allowed to go there).

One hut at Whaddon was allocated to the black propaganda group but nobody knew that there were also people working there doing Morse code tapping for Bletchley Park and another village nearby. Bletchley Park was only one link in the chain. You never asked what people did, but you did ask where they were based. Whaddon Hall was HQ of SCU1, they dealt with all the communications at Whaddon, but they got a bit nervous about this black stuff and so they took over Wavendon Towers. Powers that be, high up, wanted to be prepared to wash their hands of the secret war and that's why they moved it out of Whaddon. They shipped the disc cutting and machinery to do it to Wavendon Towers and then they purpose built the studio at Milton Bryan because Wavendon Towers wasn't big enough. It's ruined now but there are still some huts there. We've since put up a blue plaque.

COMMEMORATIVE PLAQUE *(BCC)*

The code word for Wavendon was Simpson. A man arrived, a civilian driver with a wooden box of discs in a Hillman Minx. I was told never to shout, "The records are here." If someone was working in the field, always use the codeword – Simpson is here.

It was black propaganda. The BBC did all the white propaganda – the above board stuff – and we did the sting in the tail. When they built the MB studios they were running live programmes, then it came down a landline and it was 16–18 hours a day of broadcasting.

The programmes were in all kinds of languages – French, German, Greek, Scandinavian and they were broadcast to resistance organisations in various countries. One programme was made for transmission to the Africa Corps.

The main German programme was called Soldaten Sender Calais. It started as Kertsveller Sender Atlantik, it was for the U-boats and was a German forces programme, with segments for the army, the Luftwaffe and the Navy. I now hear that they had U-boat commanders there (at MB) at that time who were taking part in these programmes. Sefton Delmer was a genius: he organised it all but I never met him.

Times have moved on and this doesn't sound so bad now, but we had this girl who used to be like a forces sweetheart, billing and cooing into the microphone, sending kisses to soldiers. She had a regular slot where she would come on and one day she called this commander of U-boat no.Y who was in sector X in the Atlantic; we had good information. "I am pleased to tell you that your wife's delivered a son and he weighs... mother and child are doing well and waiting for you to come home." The sting was in the tail, because he hadn't been home for 2 years. That wouldn't have much impact now, but then it was different; he was an officer and he couldn't believe his wife was playing with his fellow officers. It destroyed him; he took his boat into Ireland about 3 months later and surrendered after this had worked in his mind.

I had little grasp of languages then. They had a captured military band and they took them to Milton Bryan to play. They had 3 air force crew, who flew over to Manston with the latest German aircraft. They could never be described as PoWs, because they had come over of their own free will, landed there and held their hands up. The plane had all the latest night fighter equipment. They came as a result of these broadcasts that were done so well and so thoroughly, they surrendered because they thought we knew more than we did. They came and added to the knowledge, they were turned around and those three pilots went to M B.

We didn't get feedback then, even Sefton Delmer didn't get a lot of feedback during the war, and at the end nobody was very interested. At the end of the war they burned everything; they had 40 gallon drums burning for days. There is one log book which I have seen from Wavendon Towers still around.

I used to work three shifts. The transmitters ran day and night and I worked with three or four men during the day when we did most of the maintenance. In the evening and at night there was just me in charge of the transmitter and 2 or 300 yards down the road there was another transmitter with another engineer and a Home Guard man who floated between the 2 buildings. This was only after the other died, when they realised it was dangerous to have one man there on his own. There were no more than 20 people, all men, at each of the stations to man them. We got 7 days off every 3 months. We covered the 24 hours but if you were on nights you were on until 8 in the morning, 8 am – 5 pm was a day shift and 5 pm – 10 pm, so the evening shift was short. There was an overlap.

I was at Potsgrove several times and once I was billeted with the Woburn farm manager on the estate. He lived in the buildings where the garden centre is now. Initially we used to have lodgings in the villages. I lived in Gawcott with the local carpenter and undertaker and his wife. Then we were told we were moving to live in Bletchley, which was great because there were cinemas there and then we were transported to work each day.

Bletchley Park (BP) had two sides, the radio side and the code-breaking side. BP got their information via radios. It was all intercepted by a huge organisation of people listening on headphones. It all began with what were called volunteer radio interceptors – all radio hams. At the beginning of the war they realised they were going to need this help and they didn't know where to look. Somebody in government was friendly with the head of the radio ham society and asked him to help.

They recruited all these people, didn't pay them, took away their transmitters, and said you listen on this segment of the dial and you listen on this one and they had to write down everything that they heard. (These were Y Stations). Information was all being sent in 5 letter groups of code and they had to take it down, put it in an envelope and send it to Box 45. If the Germans had stuck to the telephone line or if they had sent postcards, Bletchley Park (BP) couldn't have existed.

When it came in to BP from intercepts, it went via Box 45, and then BP received and broke it. When it was decoded, Churchill or the War Office needed it and it would go on a tele-printer in a British code, or it went by dispatch rider to Whaddon Hall where again it was put into a British code.

They used a one-time-pad (see Leo Marks), which was the same pad at each end, and tore it off each day, because it can't be broken. There would be a man in Whaddon in an army hut and he would have a Morse key and a transmitter. He would be told to send the message on this frequency. At the other end SCU1 had equipped some special liaison units. A Special Liaison Unit was a truck with a transmitter and receiver built in and four men.

Windy Ridge was the name for the Whaddon transmitter station, because it was in the grounds, not in the Hall. A friend was attached to General Patton's army and they had a special liaison vehicle and messages would come from Whaddon in code. They took down the message. Attached to their unit was a decoding section, 4 RAF personnel and an officer in another truck, and the message went from the receiver into this next truck where it was decoded. The officer had the right to see Patton any time of the night. Messages were coded in Xs. If it was a 5 X message he could wake him up, a 1 X he could relax until morning.

In Aspley Guise the houses there were rented or requisitioned for the Sefton Delmer organisation. They provided accommodation for the foreign artistes. The names of the houses were Dawn Edge, Larch Fields and the Rookery. A variety of nationalities were housed there. Larch Fields housed the man who presented the programme, Gustav Siegfried Eins (GS1). Peter Seckelmann, I think was his name, he was quite coarse and swearing, but he was dropped when they started the Soldaten Sender Calais programme which then moved on to music and news bulletins.

They used private cars to pick people up and transport them. Sefton Delmer had his own car. They used to go to Wavendon Towers (before MB was built) to make discs. We weren't too fussy then in England about how we achieved the objectives. They had 2 French sections, (one Free French), and at Wavendon Towers one group heard the other group, and they were incensed and quit in a huff and never went back. It's in a hand written log from the shift at Wavendon Towers. "Mr Robin said F3 overheard F2 rehearsing and big investigations followed after one of them quit in a huff."

They played jazz, but not too American, as it was meant to be a German forces programme. They used to get the latest music hits in Germany; they brought them up through Sweden and flew them over here in a diplomatic bag. They had the German newspapers flown over too. That's how they got the commander's details.

Delmer had almost a daily delivery of these newspapers and they had a huge card index filing system. They had a room full of German speaking girls who scoured the papers and kept the filing cards. A room at Milton Bryan was used for reading and storing papers. When the German news service at the beginning of war abandoned their offices in London, they left a machine, a Hellschrieber, like a telex machine that worked on the radio, so that when Hitler made a speech, it would be picked up by the machine and came out, in tickertape. Delmer got hold of the machine and had the official German news agency proclamation when it was made; it was on his desk as it was broadcast. It was so valuable they had the machine copied in America; they had several of them in England, one of the machines was based at Milton Bryan. The BBC had a huge monitoring service at a place called Tatsfield and everything was monitored and collated. It was a huge organisation.

The discs were labelled F for French or G for German etc., not a very sophisticated code.

The Gustav programme was being transmitted 18–20 hours a day. The set up was, there would be news broadcasts and items of interest and music, but there would be news broadcasts every half hour, excerpts for the Luftwaffe and Navy, then Vicky came in and did her stuff, akin to 'Hello Hank it's your birthday.'

The discs were solid like an old 33 record and played from the inside out, they were American. We were the original DJs. When the discs used to come they had a card with them, F3 or something, whatever type they were, the time they were supposed to go out and the antenna that was to be used, as the antennae were directional. If it was going to Norway, Africa or the Atlantic they all had different antennae and they were all switched inside the building.

You would set up the frequency and then the antenna and then you'd get a disc as soon as they arrived and you'd listen on headphones and make a mark with a wax crayon where it started, perhaps one, two or three turns. You set the needles and they were needles, not diamonds in those days, on the mark and start it rotating and listen and count the wax mark going round. The programme would begin and then you stopped it and marked it 3 and three quarters, if that was where it needed to start. The object was that the enemy had to believe that it was a live broadcast, not recorded, so it was important that there was no hiss noise. When the time came to radiate the programme we had a fader and you would put it on about 2 minutes beforehand. We had a chronometer and an electric clock and you watched it tick up, and you would start it, and with practice you would hit it right and fade in and throw the switch and hear it on the headphones. A long programme could run for 20 minutes.

The only mishap was when they decided to finish Gustav as they needed the Soldaten programme on that frequency. Gustav always said he would be back at a certain time, all things being well, to give the feeling that he was in danger. Then one night you heard boots kick the door in and submachine gun fire and you heard noises and he was dead. That programme went out at 1850 hours and 2050 hours every night and they forgot, and it went out twice. Delmer was listening! That went out from Potsgrove when I wasn't there.

An American radio station had a transmitter made by RCA at 500kw instead of 50kw and it was in a warehouse for 2 or 3 years. A salesman here asked Gambier Parry if he had use for a 500kw transmitter, and Churchill said get it. Harold Robins went to see it and asked for it to be 600kw. Harold took the cheque to pay for it, and it was all shipped back safely except the antenna, which was sunk and a new one was made. It was known as Aspidistra and was so powerful that it could swamp German transmitters.

We had 150ft high steel towers with the aerials strung between, 6 at Potsgrove and 6 at Gawcott. Short wave radio bounces off the heavy side-layer, Medium wave relies on ground waves and when it gets so far it drops off the end, the power runs out and you don't get it. If you're in the middle of England and you put the transmitter here, you have extended it by 100 miles, so Harold Robins said no to Aspidistra being in Bedfordshire and put it near the coast at Crowborough. They wanted to put it underground but all they had was one excavator. Fortunately a Canadian unit was stationed nearby and over a drink in the pub it was agreed that they would dig the hole for beer money, and that's what happened. Churchill did not get along with the BBC and they were not allowed to run it.

The Germans had one programme made in Berlin and lots of transmitters that broadcast it over Hamburg, Frankfurt, Cologne, etc. The local transmitters went off the air about 30 minutes before the RAF reached an area. [The Germans switched off the transmitters on the RAF route to prevent the bombers picking up signals and homing in on them. − JY]

Harold Robins devised a method whereby Aspidistra came on the air and took over these German stations as they were switched off, and they trained people at Milton Bryan to sound exactly like the presenters, and played games with them (the German people). They made announcements like, 'there'll be an extra ration of meat distributed from the railway station at 8 o'clock tonight'; and then they bombed the station. Everything was allowed; anything that would bring the war to a close was fair game.

Ellic Howe, he was at Marylands, Woburn, the cottage hospital, he operated from there and was responsible for dropping leaflets etc. The editorial was written there and they experimented with various typesets. A lot of them were printed at the newspaper people at Dunstable. They printed fake ration books and even false stamps for the agents to take out.

It was all centred around a very small geographical area just crossing the borders of Beds into Bucks. Ellic wrote a book about this. At Woburn Abbey they only had the riding school to start with; the Duke offered them that as long as he didn't see any of them.

VE day came as a surprise to us. Our station and the Soldaten programme stopped in April 1945, and VE didn't come until May 8th. We thought, what's going on? No transmitters were going, we went to work and carried out maintenance on the transmitters and sat around and played cards. They were never ever used again.

One or two discs were broadcast telling people in the outer reaches of the 3rd Reich that the war was over, where to report and surrender, but the main Soldaten programme was finished. Sefton Delmer called people together at Milton Bryan and said, why would the Germans who hardly have 2 stones left on top of one another, the place is a wreck − why would they have a forces programme still going, when they haven't a kilowatt to cook a dinner with? Tonight just pull the plug, don't say goodbye.

The last 2 days of the programme, the engineer Harold Robins asked Sefton Delmer if he could record, and so the last 2 days were on big discs, about 47 discs − about 25 minutes on each disc and he stored the discs in his attic for 37 years on the understanding that he dare not bring them out as he had signed the Official Secrets Act. Those last 2 days of transmissions can be purchased from the Imperial War Museum. They knew at the studios that things were coming to an end. Potsgrove, Gawcott and Milton Bryan all stopped at the same time.

Nothing happened at the end of the war, you saw people started getting demobbed. We ran the transmitters up once a week, not with a programme, just power into the aerial. Eventually they said we want you to go and work at Cresslow near Whitchurch, Aylesbury, the transmitters for Hanslope Park. They were tapping the keys at Hanslope Park and it was coming down the line, Diplomatic Wireless service, and transmitted from Cresslow.

I was in uniform and everyone else was in civilian suits. At this time it was a transition period and people were transferring from uniform to civvies and keeping their same jobs. It was offered to me and I said no thank you. I drank tea for days and days and got myself back to living at Tattenhoe camp, travelling to and fro on the bus. It was a waste of their time and mine. It was a chaotic time. I wanted to get out, there was a sense of anticlimax, nobody told you anything, then they said they we were going to offer me a job at an embassy maintaining the equipment, I said no. I asked to be demobbed and this was when I realised I hadn't really been in the army because they demobbed me the next week, just on request. If I had been in the army I'd have had to wait until my age plus length of service number came up.

It was so secret that I just did my job and went back to Tattenhoe camp to sleep where I was billeted. It was an experimental camp, all ranks were in there, there was one dining room, no sergeants' or officers' mess. I had to wear Royal Corps of Signals uniform. SCU1 was a Royal Signals branch. We didn't get paid from the army, it took me a long while to figure out that I wasn't in the army because we had army pay books, but we were paid from the Foreign Office. Bedfordshire was alive with all this.

## INTRODUCTION (CONTINUED) BY JEAN YATES

At **Aspley Guise** many of the larger houses in the village were taken over by various different nationalities involved in the propaganda war. The German contingent took up seven. They were all told that they were not to go out, they were collected by car for their various broadcasts and recordings, but rumours abound of them meeting in the village pub.

Sefton Delmer lived at The Rookery, Aspley Guise, with his wife and a variety of members of his team throughout the war. Sefton gave his 'guests' false names and perhaps the most famous one who lived with him at the

Rookery was known as Oskar Jurgens, real name, Dr Otto John. Otto was one of the men who had tried to assassinate Hitler in July 1944 and the only one of the group who managed to escape from Germany. Otto John returned to Germany after the war and later disappeared into the Russian sector. The Germans believed he had defected but Sefton was sure he had been kidnapped and eventually Otto did return to the west.

In May 1941 Sefton reported that his unit did not have the correct German typefaces and newsprint to satisfactorily forge a page of a German newspaper. However by 1943 he said that his own printing unit was capable of producing counterfeits of any German document from army orders to postage stamps and ration cards.

In the 'Black Game', Ellic Howe (also known as Armin Hull), says at the interview for this new position he was asked three questions, one of which was, "Could he forge the current French postage stamp design, Petain's head, because it would be cheaper to print them in England than buy them in France?"

He goes on; 'In 1942 the first of a series of French philatelic forgeries was put in hand. Like all the later German ones they were executed by Waterlow and Sons Ltd.

Also in 1942 'Special Operations Executive (SOE) agents were able to mail black propaganda booklets within Germany using forged postage stamps.'

One of the MB 'black' campaigns was to cause a rift between Himmler and Hitler and to that end a number of operations were carried out. The most intriguing one for me was the production of counterfeit German postage stamps bearing Himmler's face instead of Hitler's. They were attached to letters and cards and posted by agents all over Germany, and much to everyone's surprise no one noticed the new stamps.

Sefton Delmer credits Ellic Howe as the genius behind the counterfeiting organisation, even using a convicted forger serving time in Wormwood Scrubs to carry out one operation.

Ellic's department carried out forgery work in 1942 for the Free French, Belgian, Dutch and Norwegian governments in exile. He stated, 'we could supply almost anything from a few forged letter-headings to several million forged German ration cards.'

'White' leaflets were dropped over Germany by RAF bombers. To accurately place the forged posters and post the counterfeit letters to German addresses, the 'black' campaigns mainly depended upon the underground agents. RAF air-drops were used however to distribute forged German ration cards. Initially counterfeited for S.O.E. agents to take on missions, they were later mass produced and thousands were used by the German population to buy extra food.

The American pilots of the Special Leaflet Squadron worked with Sefton's unit from April 1944. The 'leaflet bomb' that they dropped from their Flying Fortresses was sixty inches long and eighteen inches in diameter; it contained 80,000 leaflets. At 1,000ft the container released the leaflets and they were dropped with some accuracy.

These planes were dropping yet another Milton Bryan/Maryland production, a German daily newspaper jointly produced by the British and Americans. The lay-out was done at Marylands and the printing carried out at Home Counties Newspapers at Luton, printers of the Dunstable Borough Gazette. Some two million copies a night were produced, with page proofs being sent to Sefton Delmer at 3.00am every morning for approval.

It is possible that these leaflets were flown from USAAF **Cheddington**, as the 406th (Bombardment Squadron) Night Leaflet Squadron was based there from 5th August 1944.

A number of items of written black propaganda can be seen in the Imperial War Museum. Waterlow's at Dunstable, security printers, played their part in this operation as did Home Counties Newspapers. De la Rue, security printers were also involved in this operation and worked with Waterlow's during wartime.

Local rumours of cars and coaches with blacked out windows leaving the Sugar Loaf at Dunstable for places unknown, but thought to be connected with the secret war, are partly confirmed by Ellic Howe. He tells us that a number of people who had their own transport were instructed on Friday 1st September 1939 to go to the Sugar Loaf Hotel at Dunstable, 34 miles north of London on the old A5 London – Holyhead road. 'Upon arrival at Dunstable they were told to ask for Mr Gibbs-Smith, who had been appointed Administrative Officer at Country Headquarters. After checking each new arrival's identity Mr Gibbs-Smith whispered the name Woburn Abbey and provided a rough sketch map showing its location.'

### Bill Woolley - **Dunstable's Fire Officer**

A lot of people who went to Bletchley Park must have come through Dunstable. We had a lot of codes that we had to record in the occurrence book; the fact that this person whoever it was, had passed through. We passed this information on to Luton, who passed it to London. I think they were important people. It was a busy road and there wasn't the communication then.

### Derek Bonfield - **RAF Edlesborough**

The nearest farm to us was at Valence End, the next was Ebenezer's, where the RAF place was based at the Travellers Rest. It was a signals station but we never knew what its function was, mostly it was underground. We found that out when we carried out a raid in the Home Guard. The exercise was to capture it. We managed to get over the fence and we came across what we thought was an air-raid shelter, went down, fell over a dispatch rider who was asleep in the passage way and found it all happening! We had achieved what we wanted. They were connected with the Stanbridge RAF station, a kind of sister station.

### Tony Woodhouse - **Coded Messages**

After school I used to listen to these weird messages that were broadcast over the wireless such as, "My mother's aunt has dropped her cup," or something similar, which of course was a coded message for someone in Europe!

### INTRODUCTION (CONTINUED) BY JEAN YATES

**The 'Y' Service** was the wireless receiving operation, or 'signals intelligence', and was the ears of Bletchley Park. There was an Army 'Y' Station at Markyate, listening to and locating enemy radio stations. It was part of a network of fixed receiving and direction finding stations. (Bletchley Park Reports, Funkers and Sparkers, by John Pether).

**Chicksands** was an RAF 'Y' Station. At one time it had 200 receivers intercepting the German Air Force strategic wireless network.

**Hockliffe** had a secret radio station run by the Czechoslovakians who were communicating with their president and government in exile. (See separate chapter).

Many rumours abound about the **Paris House** at Woburn. We have heard stories that it was to be used as an interim safe house for the Royal family if Britain was invaded. The plan was to get them to Liverpool and on a ship to Canada. The Woburn house would have been an overnight stop. Several sources have reported that the Queen's brother, David Bowes Lyon, stayed there.

The Paris House at Woburn was used by Sefton Delmer to house an SS Officer, code name Dr Nansen, real name Zech-Nenntwich, who had deserted. Sefton never trusted the man and kept him away from MB although he used him as a speaker on a radio station aimed at the SS.

Woburn Park and Markyate Cell Park were used as storage for planes – all hidden under the trees.

Leo Marks, inventor of 'one time pads', was trained at the English School for Cryptographers in **Bedford**. Some of these pads were printed on silk and sewn into the linings of SOE agents who were undertaking missions in occupied countries. Leo Marks influenced the world's secret service organisations with his code developments. One time pads were uncrackable!

The BBC did many broadcasts from Bedford Corn Exchange stating that the programme came from 'somewhere in England'.

SOE Agents were trained at Howbury Hall, Bedford, Station 40. Another SOE Training School was based at Chicheley Hall, Newport Pagnell. SOE Sections were of various nationalities – Albanian, Belgian, Czech, Danish, Dutch, French, German, Greek, Iberian, Italian, Norwegian, Polish and Yugoslav. Each occupied country in Europe had a government in exile in Great Britain, with the Czechoslovakians nearby and General de Gaulle living at Rodinghead on the **Ashridge** estate after France fell.

Many SOE Agents were flown from **Tempsford** in Lysanders, including Violette Szabo and Odette Samson. By April 1945, 29,000 containers, 10,000 packages and 995 agents had been flown in and as many personnel flown out.

## *John Grange* – Bedfordshire's other Secret War

Much is already known about the World War Two clandestine activities of organisations such as the Special Operation Executive (SOE) and others, who conducted their secret operations from various parts of Bedfordshire to good effect against the enemy at that time. What is perhaps not quite so well known, is that there were other highly classified installations located in, and adjacent to, the county as a part of the conventional war effort. For example, the then GPO (General Post Office) was asked to provide a standby Operations Room for the Royal Air Force (RAF) Fighter Command HQ located at Bentley Priory, Stanmore, in the event that the Priory became destroyed. This alternative operations centre became operational in 1939 and was located near Liscombe Park, two miles west of Leighton Buzzard[1].

Within the county boundary of Bedfordshire other highly classified establishments were set up, sometimes for the duration of the war and others for only a brief period. Howbury Hall, near Waterend, is probably better known as Station 40, a training establishment for SOE[2]. However, the Public Record Office (PRO) has a record of Howbury Hall being designated as an emergency Corps HQ in 1943[3]. On a much larger scale were the activities within the boundary of Luton Hoo. In October 1941, one particular house inside the grounds had an adjacent underground HQ[4], that housed the Eastern Command Signals Regiment formed from the previously four independent commands of Chatham, Felixstowe, Shoeburyness and Dover[5]. As with other major command and control facilities, Eastern Command also had an alternative site located at Tatmore Place just outside Hitchin[ibid.4].

One very important Command and Control centre in Bedfordshire, of which a good deal more is known, however, is 60 Signals Group Fighter Command, Royal Air Force (known as 60 Grp). The HQ was located at Plantation Road, Leighton Buzzard, where it remained for the duration of the war. This was the technical, administrative and co-ordinative heart of the RAF radar (RDF) and, in its time, it was by far the largest organisation of its kind anywhere…although similar (but much smaller) agencies served the needs of the naval and army RDF[6].

The 60 Group embryo was a group 17 civilian research staff from Bawdsey, who became the Base Maintenance Headquarters staff for all RDF stations. These and a further 50 or so other technicians from government communications departments (notably the BBC radio and television and the GPO telephones), moved to Leighton Buzzard in late 1939 and 60 Grp was formed within the Directorate of Signals ("Signals-4,RDF) Royal Air

Force on 23rd March, 1940[7].

60 Grp quickly assumed full control of Britain's electronic home defence system. Later, it also nurtured all of the overseas radar systems and finally became a leading player in the use of radio navigational aids (RNA). So important was 60 Grp that, at the time of its formation, its Air Officer Commanding (Air Commodore A.L. Gregory) reported directly to the Director-General of Signals, Air Vice Marshall Nutting, who, in turn, reported to AOC-in-C, Fighter Command, Air Chief Marshall Sir Hugh Dowding. Later commanders of 60 Grp were: from March 1942, Air Commodore R.S. Aitkin (later promoted to Air Vice Marshall), and from February 1944, Air Vice Marshall W.E. Theak. Finally, 60 Grp amalgamated with 26 Grp to form 90 (Signals) Group, on 25th April, 1946, under control of BAFO and Transport Command at RAF Watton[8].

Barton in the Clay airfield (the adjacent village did not change its name to Barton le Clay until 1956) was much busier than is generally realised. It opened in the mid 1930s as a business venture by Capt D.M.K. Marendaz, a pilot with the Royal Flying Corps during WW 1, to build racing cars and the Marendaz trainer aircraft. It initially consisted of around 30 acres of grassland with a workshop built by Braziers of Barton. But at the outbreak of WW II Capt Marendaz fell foul of the government of the day and was interned for the duration.

The airfield was then taken over by the Air Ministry who built a hangar and extended the airfield boundary to encompass around 100 acres ringed with Pillboxes. But there was no control tower, runway or even a grass strip landing area[9]. No. 24 Elementary Flying Training arrived at the nearby Luton airfield on 22nd July, 1940. Although based at Luton, their actual training was conducted at Barton and the aircraft returned to Luton at the end of each day. No. 24 left Luton in February 1942 to be replaced by No. 5 Ferry Pool Air Transport Auxiliary (ATA)[10]. Barton airfield was now used as an alternative landing site to Luton for ATA aircraft. However, flying training at Barton did not cease with the arrival of the ATA. During the summer of 1943 the ATA had great difficulty in finding pilots, so they created them…mainly from the Women's Auxiliary Air Force (WAAFs), non-flying RAF personnel and from the ATA's own ground staff. They all did their initial training at Barton and then moved to Thame, in Oxfordshire, for their Class 2 conversion course[11].

Barton was not without its share of incidents. Mr. Beechener recalls the airfield being bombed once, but not hit, during the early part of the war. An enemy aircraft flew in low from the east, dropped a stick of bombs and then circled to see what, if any, damage had occurred. The aircraft circled so low Mr. Beechener reports being able to see the colour of the pilot's flying helmet. However, bombers did not trouble them again for the remainder of the war. There are also reports of at least two accidents involving aircraft at the airfield. In December 1944 a P51D Mustang made a forced landing[12]... Mr Beechener recalls, 'I saw a Mustang and could hear its engine spluttering. It circled the airfield twice and landed safely. However, in coming to a stop, it tipped up on to its nose. A tall, gangly American climbed out of the cockpit unhurt and said "Dang! That's twice this month that's happened."' On another occasion in 1944, a Beaufighter from 51 Operational Training Unit was destroyed, but the fate of the crew is not recorded by this particular source[13]. Mr. Beechener further recalls that for most of the war, Merlin aircraft engines were tested day and night in the hangar, causing some disruption to everyone's sleep. A flying instructor, who was billeted with the Beecheners, was asked to take an aircraft up one night to ensure that blackout regulations for the airfield were satisfactory. Upon his return he reported that "The place was lit up like a Christmas tree." The engine testing stopped during the hours of darkness... "So from then on, everyone got a good night's sleep." This, incidentally, was the only night flight that Mr. Beechener can recall taking place. There have been several rumours that this airfield had been used for flights by SOE. However, on the basis of research done so far, there is nothing to support these notions. The airfield was closed at the end of the war and bought by H.C. Janes (Builders) and is now an Industrial Estate.

Note. The reader should be aware that all of these sites are now private property and there are few clues remaining as to their wartime use.

Notes and References.

1  Flint, P. 1996. Dowding and the HQs Fighter Command. London Airlife.

2  www.bbc.co.uk/threecounties/peoples_war/beds_secret_war.shtml

3  PRO. WO199/120

4  ibid. WO199/119

5  ibid. WO305/189

6  G.K. Grande, et.al., Eds. Canadians on Radar: Royal Canadian Air Force 1940
   – 1945. Chp XII by J.R Robinson, p4

7  Ibid. p6. Not only is Chp XII an excellent record of 60 Group and its activities,
   but the book as a whole is thoroughly recommended for those seeking a better
   understanding of the magnificent contribution made by the Royal Canadian Air
   Force to the war effort.

8  www.rafweb.org/Grp06.htm

9  Mr. J. Beechener lived and worked on his father's farm adjacent to the airfield for
   the duration of the war. Appreciation is due to this gentleman in no small measure
   for his help in recalling details about the airfield and its events that might otherwise
   be lost to time.

10  www.roll-of-honour.org/Regiments/CountyAirfields.html

11  www.airtransportaux.org/history.html

12  www.accident-report.com/uk/194412.html

13  http://freespace.virgin.net/pbratt.home.Bristol%20Beaufighter%0201F.htm

# The Meteorological Office

INTRODUCTION BY JEAN YATES

The new offices in Dunstable were not ready by September 1939, so the Met Office Central Forecasting (CFO) was initially moved to Birmingham from London and then to Dunstable in early 1940. The CFO at Dunstable was close to main lines of communication, 5 miles from the major RAF Communications centre at Leighton Buzzard and 12 miles from Bletchley Park.

The buildings (huts) housed a printing works for chart production and a NAAFI as well as the main operations area and were inside a high chain link fence with barbed wire on the top. There were two fences, an inner and outer with just one gate for access. The inner gate was guarded by Air Ministry Police. The receiving aerials for the Wireless Telegraphy (WT) room were a short distance away.

One unit was located in a Nissen hut camouflaged as a haystack right on top of the Downs, in Isle of Wight Lane. Another separate hut was involved in experimental radar. This was also camouflaged with hay. Twenty miles of chicken wire erected on the Downs at 400ft above sea level were part of this experiment.

When Brian Audric reported for duty on 1st April 1940 at Dunstable, he reported to Mr Hayes who was in charge of Administration. He was sent to find lodgings at the Priory Café where several other Met Office staff were living. They paid £1.50 a week for full board and lodging and earned £120 per year. His job was in the new and secret department at the Met Office named IDA. This unit was created to decode firstly Russian weather reports and later reports from all over Europe. The information arrived via the Wireless Telegraphy (WT) section. This new secret unit was formed to take the pressure off the cryptographers at Bletchley Park (BP).

Weather information from all over Europe had been freely available and exchanged before the war. Various countries now encoded their reports and

BP successfully decoded it before sending it to Dunstable, who then passed it on to the RAF. The Dunstable IDA unit took over the routine decoding. The work increased and so did the staff and Hilary Lowry now joined as one of the unit's supervisors. Hilary married one of the senior forecasters, Robert Ratcliffe, and her story is later in this chapter.

Forecasters who were civilians were accepted by the RAF as an essential part of their operational organisation. All staff wore civilian clothes until 1943 when forecasters and assistants were put into RAF uniform. Most services that the Met Office provided were to meet the needs of the RAF.

The Met Office had many outstations that reported to Dunstable from a number of countries. In the UK there were 500 outstations at the time of D-Day and most were reporting every hour. These were at airfields, coastal points, etc. Forecasters were stationed at night fighter airfields as the war progressed and briefed pilots face to face.

Pilots needed information about wind, clouds and fog. Bomber Command requirements were an area free from icing in the clouds for climbing and for descent when coming back. Cumulonimbus – the cloud responsible for turbulence – was to be avoided. Accurate wind forecasting was needed for precise bombing and for aircraft to keep together. Up to a thousand bombers could be on a raid and stragglers were more vulnerable to being shot down. Avoidance of well defended areas could also be achieved with accurate wind forecasting.

The Special Operations Executive (SOE) flights from Tempsford relied on information from BP and the secret IDA unit at Dunstable. The airfield operated on moonlit nights, delivering and picking up agents from occupied countries. It also dropped thousands of containers packed with radios and other essential supplies to resistance groups all over Europe. These flights were often made at very low altitude and accuracy was paramount.

From 1942 PAMPA (Photo-recce And Met Photography Aircraft) were used to help the forecasters by surveying weather conditions. In late 1943 it was the Pathfinders who went out first. They flew Mosquito aircraft that were faster than the bombers and they were asked to take wind measurements. This information was reported by the crews to Bomber Command and then relayed to Dunstable. Forecasters then updated their information, revised their charts and were able to give the bomber pilots accurate information just ten minutes before they reached their target.

Forecasters could work 20–24 hours on duty. They were secretly told at 0800hrs the bombing targets planned for the next 24 hours. Once the raids started they kept in contact with the planes until the last one had landed, constantly planning winds and rewriting their charts.

The headquarters of Bomber Command was at Naphill, just north of High Wycombe. Daily conferences were held over the scrambler telephones and from 1942 Dunstable contributed to these discussions up-to-date information from decrypted data from BP and the IDA unit.

The work for the forecasters became more interesting when they took over the decoding from BP. They were then responsible for supplying weather information for most of Europe. The Germans used to change their codes about every five days and it took our code breakers about two days to break them. Dunstable relied on BP to provide them with the new key sheets and this was aided by two events during the war when they acquired a German enciphering code and later the key. There were various codes: Russian, Vichy French, Italian, Hungarian, Romanian and Bulgarian – who used the same, and of course, German.

Everything decoded was sent to Station X (BP) by Service Motor Cycle Dispatch Riders. They made four regular runs a day, the first at 0800 hrs and the last at 2200 hrs, returning to Dunstable with any new information.

The Met Office used one-time-pads (see Beds Secret War chapter) and Brian Audric was asked to pick up a new batch one day when he was in London. They were considered too secret to be entrusted to the service dispatch riders. He brought them back to Dunstable on his bicycle!

The Upper Air Unit (UAU) at Dunstable was run by Sverre Petterssen with a staff of one Pole, several Norwegians and Robert Ratcliffe. The unit played a major role. Methods developed by this unit during the war became standard procedures for upper wind forecasting for about 30 years.

Robert Ratcliffe stated in a paper presented to the Royal Meteorological Society in 1986 "that the Enigma codes included weather reports which we had already decoded from another code, so by that means the Enigma code messages were eventually broken mainly because of the fact that we had an entry through the meteorological codes." They had been decoding the meteorological codes for some time and then discovered in about 1942 that the German submarine main reports in the Enigma code contained these same weather reports.

Working with the CFO the UAU produced the D-Day (Overlord) forecast for General Eisenhower. It was agreed that Eisenhower's Chief Meteorological Officer should be British, with the USAAF providing the deputy, and Dr Stagg was selected for the job. Colonel Yates was his deputy. Overlord conferences were conducted on scrambler telephones and involved the RAF and Navy Commanders in Chief, the Admiralty, USAAF, Dunstable and SHAEF (Supreme HQ Allied Expeditionary Force) – where Stagg and Yates were placed at Teddington and then as the day drew nearer at Portsmouth.

On 3rd June with the invasion planned for the 5th, both Dunstable and the Admiralty thought that wind and cloud would make the mission impossible. Eisenhower was advised and the plans were deferred for 24 hours.

The weather on the 5th June was disastrous, with force 5–6 winds on the beaches and low cloud cover. This would have prevented the aerial attacks and the parachute and glider landings. CKM Douglas, a senior forecaster, still had his reservations about the 6th, but it was agreed that conditions would be tolerable. Conditions were not ideal on the 6th but the decision to go ahead proved to be right, as later in the month the weather was stormy and destroyed a Mulberry harbour.

Nothing has ever been found to say that the enemy knew anything of the work of the IDA. The secrets stayed in Dunstable.

Sources: The Royal Meteorological Society Papers
1 Meteorological Services Leading to D-Day by R J Ogden
2 The Met Office Dunstable and the IDA Unit in World War II by Brian Audric
3 Meteorology and World War II transcripts of meeting papers 1986 and 1988, Bomber Command Upper Air Unit by R A S Ratcliffe

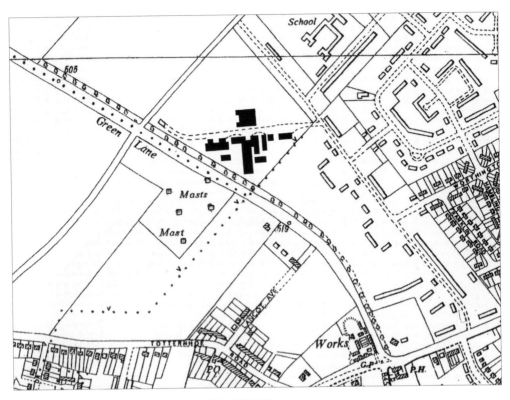

1950s PLAN of the Met Office at Dunstable *(HMOD)*

THE RADIO CABIN *(HMOD)*

*above* DUNSTABLE MET OFFICE *(HMOD)*    *top right* AERIAL MAST *(HMOD)*

MET OFFICE STAFF in wartime *(HMOD)*

COMMUNICATIONS ROOM in wartime *(HMOD)*

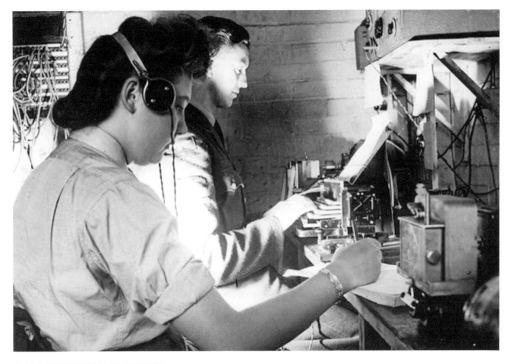

COMMUNICATIONS *(HMOD)*

DAILY BRIEFING *(HMOD)*

PLOTTING A SURFACE CHART *(HMOD)*

## Hilary Ratcliffe (née Lowry) – the Strawberry Blonde

The Air Ministry wrote to all the universities in 1941 asking maths graduates to apply. I went with 3 others from Queen's in August and out of 100 interviewed I was one of the 7 chosen. Four went to Bletchley Park and the other three including myself went to Dunstable. Firstly, we were sent to Gloucester for four weeks where we learnt a bit of basic meteorology and were security cleared.

At Dunstable we were billeted in High Street North but it was pretty grim. Luckily Dr Watson was a distant relative of mine and his wife took my friend Maud and myself under her wing. We stayed in Priory House for a short time until she could find us a proper billet. Miss L at the Priory was very kind but could not put us up for a long time; also the ghost of Catherine of Aragon was supposed to be there, so we were glad to move. We lived with a Miss W in West Street for over a year but she discovered that men would pay more and we had to move again. We went to Benning Avenue where we remained for over 2 years.

I cycled to work and passed men putting up camouflage netting, which covered all the buildings and the tennis court at the Met Office. They used to sing the Strawberry Blonde when I rode underneath! At the Met Office itself there was the NAAFI, the wireless room, communications, forecast room, the upper air unit and the IDA unit – a codename for a secret unit. There were also admin officers who all lived and worked in wooden huts; we had a grass tennis court as well. Mr Douglas, a brilliant forecaster but forgetful, once left his baby son on the Downs as he was so busy looking at the clouds. Luckily he remembered where he had left him.

A conference was held at noon every day linked up to Bomber Command, the senior forecaster, the aviation forecaster and the upper air unit. Station X (Bletchley Park) broke the codes and we actually did the decoding. A dispatch rider from Bletchley Park took the codes and the DDX code (German meteorological land observations) and DAN Sheets (the port and sea observations) to and fro twice a day.

I did shift work which was 8.00 am – 3.00 pm, 3.00 pm – 10.00 pm and 10.00 pm – 8.00 am; we worked a 54 hr week. I got paid £19 per month and paid income tax but got post war credits, which I got back in 1960. Going to the dentist cost £3 15 shillings (£3.75), a new coat was £7 plus 8 coupons, a dress was five and a half guineas, (£5.77) and shoes were 33

REUNION AT BLETCHLEY PARK in 1997. From left: Lady Maud Alexander (née Collard), Jean Parker (née Buxton), Mr E. Knighting – Head of IDA Unit, Brian Audric, Hilary Ratcliffe (née Lowry), Molly Neil (née Jarman). *(HR)*

shillings (£1.65), and I actually had a pair of wooden soles with hinges.

We used to walk over to Whipsnade and have tea at the Chequers Inn, which gave us a boiled egg for tea. We went to the Union cinema, played tennis and hockey at Cross's grounds and went to the swimming pool after night duty and slept and swam in the summer.

My wedding: I rang my mother on 24th January 1945, got a train to London to get my permit, then by train to Stranraer, boat to Laugharne, train to Belfast and arrived on Wednesday 31st. I got married on 1st February 1945. All my relatives gathered round and produced a wedding cake etc.

Robert Ratcliffe, (a senior forecaster at Dunstable Met Office), whom I married on 1st February, was linked up by phone to Bomber Command. I never knew if he was going to be free to take me out at night or not. The pilots sent back winds and visibility reports to the Upper Air Forecaster to carry out the forecast for the next stage. He was involved in the D-Day forecast, which was actually done at Dunstable and was sent on to Group Captain Stagg to present to General Eisenhower.

I spent VE day alone on duty – with no work to do, while my husband was on a ship outside Bombay on his way to Ceylon.

We returned to Dunstable in 1947 until 1951 and lived in Markyate, as my husband was posted to the Upper Air Unit. The Met Office closed at Dunstable in 1960 and moved to Bracknell.

### *Florence Bliss* - a Draughtswoman

I was at school in 1939 and living in Devon. We did occasionally get air raid warnings because we were close to Plymouth and Exeter. We were made to line up and go across the field to a deep ditch; that was our air raid shelter. I remember the trains full of soldiers going through the station. We lived in the middle near Totnes and could hear and almost see when Plymouth was burning.

I had kept in touch with my science teacher from school who had wanted me to become a teacher. She'd heard of this job in the Meteorological Office, which meant an interview in Bristol. I went along and got the job.

My first contact with the Met office was at Stonehouse in Gloucester where part of it had been evacuated. Stonehouse had previously been a boys' private boarding school. I was only there for about 9 months before moving to Dunstable. I believe the whole of Stonehouse moved because of security and the positions needed for the masts for the radio operators, because information came in via the radio to Dunstable. The Met Office in Dunstable consisted of a collection of huts, all of them under camouflage nets. People knew it was there but you didn't talk about it. You were made very conscious of security. When I met my husband, he was allowed to come as far as the camouflage nets if he met me after late duty, but he couldn't come in.

We had to go into digs; I lived in Borough Road with a nice family. Before I was involved in work in the actual office I attended a course in London for about 3 months in 1942. I went to London on the train every day to what remained of the Met Office. We were trained in meteorological observations, heights of clouds, how to read thermometers and rain gauges.

The draughtswomen prepared the observations of the weather over England. There weren't many reports from the Atlantic. We relied on about 8 weather ships in that area; there were no satellites in those days.

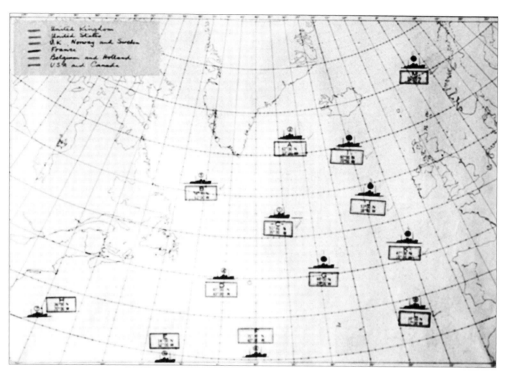

OCEAN WEATHER STATIONS in 1949 *(HMOD)*

The weather reports came in from wireless operators in Europe. There must have been people broadcasting weather reports but we didn't know who the reports came from.

It was all in code and my first job was to de-code it. I then went into the surface section where we prepared the big charts of weather across the world, as far as we knew it, and then I went into the upper air section before I went into the forecasting side.

The codes had to be broken – decoded, they were in sets of numbers, about eight numbers in a group. You didn't know where they came from, you accepted what you were given and worked on it. The reports were garbled sometimes. You had, when you were plotting the chart, to read from a list of 8 figure numbers telling you various things, 8 was high cloud, 16 was 61; we worked in centigrade then. We had charts and tables to help. The humidity was another number. Because you were plotting a chart, you knew the pattern, so when you were decoding, if you hit a garbled patch you were able to slide numbers along until you could perhaps place it and decode it.

I moved to plotting – a short spell on surface plotting and then I went into the upper air section and we plotted the radio sondes. That's a balloon with an apparatus hanging from it, that was sent 30,000ft up into the air to take the temperature, windspeed and humidity. Changes in the weather happen in the upper air before they're too obvious on the surface. Both sections worked together. I found the upper air work interesting and was there for a long time.

Plotting was done using two pens, a red one and a black one joined together, because you needed to change between the colours. We were using 'dip pens' that you dipped into inkwells then. The desks were lengthwise down through the middle of the huts and the desk tops were angled

We were civilians in civilian clothes but on the long range forecasting section there were about 10 WAAFs. There were always some people in uniform around. We worked from 8am–2pm, 2pm–10pm, 10pm–8am in the morning and there were at least 10 of us on at a time, plus the forecasters. Including the admin and drawing office, there must have been up to 200 people working there.

A lot of the RAF chaps worked as wireless operators but there were some civilians. The WAAFs left after the war. A friend of mine, Jessie, lived locally and was married to a radio operator; I think he was a civilian. Mr H was in charge of administration. He kept the place together and looked after digs. Eventually I had to move from Borough Road because the young boy of the family, with whom I was staying, needed a room of his own as he got older. Mr H gave me a couple of addresses but that was in 1948 or 49 and people were a little tired of having people living in, so I got a room on my own. Mr C owned a furniture shop in Dunstable and I went there for a while.

The Chief Forecaster when I joined was Mr Douglas, an elderly gentleman. He left and then Dr R S took over. Mr B was head of the office; he was in charge of communications, administration, the drawing office side and the daily weather reports, which went out to everyone.

You didn't need to know too much, in fact the less you knew, the better. I was a scientific assistant, not a forecaster. We were not encouraged to go into the radio section. There was a hut in the field and I believe there was some kind of experimental radar in there. We mingled mostly in the canteen – you didn't walk around. There wasn't much spare time to gossip.

At Christmas if I was on duty I sang carols.

Once, when I was on night shift I overheard a conversation. I think one of the radio operators was giving a weather report directly to a bomber pilot on an air raid, but you didn't ask, and I can't be sure, but the noises in the background made me think that at the time.

After the war in February 1949 there was an article in the Dunstable Borough Gazette called Young Wives Weather-Wise on Radio Watch – "four young weather-wise wives are helping to reveal the secrets of Britain's weather. They are scientific assistants in a special department at the Meteorological Office Station at Dunstable, where attempts are being made to lengthen the period and increase the accuracy of forecasts. They decode and record reports of local conditions in various parts of the world including ships at sea. The young women Mrs Evelyn Darnell, Mrs Jessie Bates, Mrs Eileen Purdon and Mrs Florence Bliss were drafted to the station during the war but have since married and settled down in the district."

The Met Office ADMIN STAFF *(FB)*

## John Grange - Secret Listening

In 1941 "McVittie and his meteorological organisation at Dunstable and Bletchley Park continued to rely on decrypts of enciphered Russian met reports." [1]

"Early in 1941 moves to bring the whole meteorological business under one head – the Y Service – began. The process dragged on and on until, after much wrangling, the Dunstable intercept station came under Y on 20 November. Dr. McVittie's Met-Sub Station at Bletchley Park was incorporated in GC and CS's Air Section and, in December, the Dunstable intercept station, reinforced by RAF personnel (including WAAFs), all of whom had to be trained, came under the control of Cheadle. Yet it was not until March 1942 that improvements were completed when an enlarged cabin was built at Dunstable to house between forty and fifty receivers. The majority of these were used successfully against enemy traffic and the remainder monitored Allied messages, including some from Russia." [2]

Sources: 1 & 2 Macksey, K. (2004) The Searchers: Radio Intercept in Two World Wars. Cassell, London. (pages 106 & 107)

## George Haltiner - the American View

First a brief review of how I 'landed' in Dunstable in 1945. I was a graduate student in mathematics at the University of Wisconsin when the Japanese bombed Pearl Harbour in December 1941. Three months later I was an Ensign in the US Navy at the University of Chicago converted to a meteorologist under the leadership of C. C. Roseby, a renowned leader in the field. In December 1941 I was ordered to Pearl Harbour at the US Navy Weather Central, which provided weather analysis and forecasts for the US Fleet in the Pacific, engaged in war with Japan. In July 1944 I was ordered to a joint Navy, US Government Weather Bureau in Washington DC. As military operations in Europe involved aircraft at increasingly higher altitudes, the weather services needed to provide weather forecasts, wind, clouds, etc. Toward this end, a group of meteorologists, British and foreign, at the Weather Centre in Dunstable directed their efforts.

Dr S Petterssen, who had escaped from Norway before the Nazis took over, was a leader in revising the method of analysis and prediction of winds, etc. The senior Navy weather forecasters decided to send two officers to Dunstable to learn these new methods, one of whom was myself.

I received a room in a small hotel the first night that was so cold that I put on every piece of clothing I had, including my coat and shivered most of the night. Fortunately, the next day I was given a third floor room above the restaurant (Priory Café), where many of the Weather Centre people gathered for lunch, which was more comfortable for a young man who weathered the winter storm of Minnesota as a ski jumper!

After I completed my temporary assignment I wrote a booklet on what I had learned. It was published by the Navy in Washington and distributed to the Navy Weather Centres.

### Joyce Samuels – a Tele-printer Operator

Joyce Norman, as she was then, worked at the Met Office located in Green Lane, Dunstable, during the years 1942–1946 as a tele-printer operator. There were about 40 tele-printers in operation. These were manned in 3 shifts 8am–2pm, 2pm–10pm and 10pm–8am. They were split over about 4 huts. There were no regular days off, you were just told when you could take a break. As was the case at Bletchley Park, there was no communication between personnel in one hut to another hut.

Incoming coded information was received hourly. This was analysed by the forecasting staff and a full bulletin issued every hour, again in code, to all designated recipient units throughout the UK and also Mr Salter in Dublin. The latter proved to be coincidental in Joyce's later life, as when she married and together with her husband bought a house in Regent Street, Leighton Buzzard, the owner turned out to be none other than the Mr Salter who had been stationed in Dublin during the war. You only knew the person working next to you. A lot of the people were drafted in from London, lodged in Dunstable and visited home on infrequent days off. A local man, from Totternhoe, was a maintenance engineer at the site. The man in charge of the Met station at this time was a Mr Bilham.

### A.W. Morgan – The Met Office and Bombs in a Field

When we went up to Dunstable Downs to play or to look for mortar bomb cases, we passed a gate to a long field that was approximately where the entrance to Drovers Way is now situated. There were animals in the field but beyond the far hedge was what appeared to be a small hill with a hut on the top. We knew that this was really some sort of camouflage but did not know exactly what was there. It was not possible to go very far along Green Lane as there was a barrier made from wooden logs covered by what we called barbed wire entanglements. Sometimes there would be soldiers behind the barriers. When my father was home on leave, we often went to see relatives in Totternhoe. As a family group, we walked across the field to Brewers Hill Road, along past Clark's Farm to the Green Lane and then down the lane to the village. Once again, there was another barrier preventing access to Green Lane between Brewers Hill Road and the Downs. High hedges prevented us seeing what was in the field under the camouflage, and from the Downs the spinney of trees restricted the view.

However, from Totternhoe Road, a number of aerial masts could be seen in the field between that road and Green Lane. To us, at the time, it was something of a mystery but after the war the camouflage was removed, the huts and buildings of the Met Office could be seen and the 'hut' turned out to be a chimney and / or a tall narrow water tower.

One night my mother and I were both woken by a series of loud explosions followed by the sound of falling debris. My mother came into my room and looked out of the rear window, fully expecting to see that the houses in Victoria Street had disappeared. We learned afterwards that some bombs had fallen near the top of Lancot Hill. A day or two later we went to see the damage. A bomb had fallen in a paddock situated between a bungalow and a house. The roofs of both were damaged and the bungalow was covered with tarpaulins. Across the road were three or four further craters in a line nearing the aerial masts. With hindsight, it is clear that the Met Office was the intended target.

In the late 1970s, the B.B.C. broadcast a series called 'The Secret War' in which Professor R. V. Jones described the way in which the Germans used radio beams to find their targets and how these were countered. He also published a book, 'Most Secret War', in which he explains how the Germans used some of our navigation aids, using 'rebuilt captured equipment' from bombers shot down over Germany and they also developed and improved their earlier beams. I now believe that the 'raid' on the Met Office was probably a single bomber using the more accurate beam system that they had developed for use during late 1943 and early 1944. Professor Jones tells how the R.A.F. needed their most accurate system to be calibrated and corrected for differences between the British Ordnance Survey and the Continental equivalent and how the members of the resistance in Belgium reported back to the U.K. the results of a bombing raid on a radar command post. Did the Germans miss the Met Office because they had insufficient means of calibrating their system?

### Derek Bonfield – Cut the Hay

When the Met station opened in Dunstable, there was a RAF chap named Sgt S who hailed from Essex and had been a butcher in civilian life. He cycled by one day, saw all these rabbits and asked if he could come and shoot them. He used a .22 rifle and was a good shot. It was through him that we were allowed to harvest the hay around the Met Station. We had the hay in exchange for cutting it and keeping the place tidy for them. My father was there one day with the tractor and mower. He liked to do a tidy job and was getting close to the mast; he accidentally cut through one of the wires and the thing came whistling down, but they soon had it up again.

The perimeter hedge used to run down where Drovers Way is now, and I was up there mowing a piece we hadn't previously cut before, so father said keep tight to the hedge. While doing so the tractor plunged into a hole where they had put some phosphorus grenades but forgotten about them; fortunately they didn't go off!

It was all very hush hush, what was going on at the Met Station; we knew and referred to it as a Met Station but the actual running of it, we didn't know anything about.

### Roy Turner – Played Cricket

Although we weren't bombed in Dunstable, we had plenty to do with the war – like the Met Station. We thought the main one was at Dagnall but that was the relay station where messages were sent around the world. I knew quite a few people at the Met Station through sport. I used to watch and sometimes do the scoring for the cricket matches. The Met Station played their home games at Waterlow's. Most of the people based at the Met Station were civilians although there were a number of Air Force people. They made the Station look like a hill with all different coloured cloths, but we didn't really know what was going on. (This was camouflage, which was changed to reflect the seasons).

# Allies Together

**JEAN YATES**

This chapter relies mainly on the research and translation work of two people, Neil Rees and Barbara Fryc. I would like to express my thanks for their hard work and their valuable contribution to our project.

## THE CZECHOSLOVAK RADIO STATION AT HOCKLIFFE
### Introduction by Neil Rees

During the Second World War a Czechoslovak military radio station functioned from a farm in the parish of Hockliffe, near Dunstable. At the time it was secret and today there is practically nothing left of the site, and there are very few people left who know anything about it. People can be forgiven for not knowing that it was ever there, but it played an important role in supplying intelligence information to the Allies and in maintaining contact with the Czechoslovak resistance.

### Political Background

The background to this station goes back to 1938 when the British Prime Minister came back from a conference at Munich with an agreement from Adolf Hitler, that in return for being given the borderlands of Czechoslovakia, he said he had made his last territorial claim in Europe, and he would respect the independence of Czechoslovakia. The Czechoslovak President, Dr Bene , was not invited to the conference and resigned after being forced to acquiesce to the loss of territory.

### Czechoslovakia at war

Six months later Hitler disregarded his promises; he supported a fascist regime in Slovakia, and invaded the Czech provinces of Bohemia and Moravia. On the eve of invasion, in March 1939, the Czechoslovak intelligence services were whisked from Prague and settled in West Dulwich, where they set up a military radio station to establish contact with the home resistance. Although Britain did not enter the Second World War until 1939, for the Czechoslovaks the war had already begun, and President Bene set up a government in exile in London.

## London Blitz

As the Third Reich spread across the map of continental Europe, Hitler's bombs rained on London with the Blitz of 1940. Even London became an unsafe location for the Czechoslovak exiles; they sought safe sites in the surrounding counties.

## Exiled to Bucks and Beds

President Bene of Czechoslovakia moved to the sanctuary of The Abbey, at Aston Abbotts, Buckinghamshire; his diplomatic staff moved to the Old Manor House in Wingrave, Buckinghamshire; and some of his military intelligence staff moved to Addington House, Addington, near Winslow, Buckinghamshire; although all of them maintained their offices in London, where the Czechoslovak Government-in-Exile was based. On 20th May 1940 the Czechoslovak military radio station moved from Dulwich to Dukes Hill, Woldingham, Surrey. Whilst there it handled the radio communications for Czechoslovak clandestine missions, including the operation to assassinate the hated German governor Reinhard Heydrich.

## Local Connections

On 23rd September 1942 the radio station transferred to College Farm, Hockliffe, Bedfordshire, which was farmed by Mimi Tompkins. The station was built by the Special Operations Executive (SOE) who were based locally at Woburn Abbey, Bedfordshire. The equipment was supplied by the Special Communications Unit (SCU) at Whaddon Hall, Whaddon, Buckinghamshire. It was located in the north Bucks and Beds area which was dotted with secret facilities such as Bletchley Park. The station was called in Czech *vojenská radiové ústředna* (military radio centre) known by its initial letters as the VRÚ.

Nearby at Potsgrove and Milton Bryan in Bedfordshire, were black propaganda studios which broadcast Czech and Slovak programmes to Czechoslovakia operated by Czechoslovak refugees living at Aspley Guise, Beds.

## The Military Radio Station

The station used 12 aerials for transmitting, 12 aerials for receiving and had 2 miles of barbed wire to keep out the farm animals. The transmissions kept in contact with the Czech resistance, wireless operators on SOE parachute missions, and with Czechoslovak Embassies in unoccupied countries such as Sweden and Switzerland. The site was just off the main cable routes from Fenny Stratford to London and information was sent by G.P.O teleprinters connecting the site with locations in London: the 64 Baker Street headquarters of the Special Operations Executive (SOE); the Broadway headquarters of the Secret Intelligent Services (SIS); and the 11 Porchester Gate, Bayswater headquarters of the Czechoslovak military intelligence services. The teleprinters were maintained once a week by G.P.O telecommunications engineer, Mr Roy Tink.

## Personnel

The radio station was manned entirely by Czechoslovaks who lived in Nissen huts on site. The men were mainly recruited from the Signals Unit of the Free Czechoslovak Army, based in the Leamington Spa area of Warwickshire. Sometimes other men were appointed who had injuries that made them unfit for active service. The station was under the control of the Czechoslovak military intelligence services under their head Colonel Franti ek Moravec, with rare visits from representatives of the British secret services. Most of the men were radio operators, under a commander, but there were also a technician and his assistant, and a cook. The men also had a pet dog, a kitten and a pet crow called Káča.

## Training Centres

Some of the men had received radio operations training in the Signals Unit of the Czechoslovak Army, and others received it locally at Special Training Schools (STSs) run by the SOE. Chicheley Hall (STS 46), Chicheley, near Newport Pagnell trained Czechoslovaks from 1942 to 1943 and Thame Park (STS 52), Thame, Oxon trained people in wireless operations. Howbury Hall (STS 40), Bedford, trained parachutists for ground to aircraft wireless contact.

The station operated in full capacity until 1945, when most of the men flew home to Czechoslovakia in Dakota planes, landing at Plzen (Pilsen), which was part of Czechoslovakia liberated by the US Army. They left behind a commander, 2 men and a cook, who ran the station until 1946, when they went home on a repatriation train, leaving one man in charge. The station ceased shortly afterwards.

## Social Life

Some of the Czechoslovaks at Hockliffe Radio Station would drink at The Bell in Hockliffe, or at the Saracen's Head in Dunstable, and then go dancing at Dunstable Town Hall. Some of the men made friends in Hockliffe, and some of them had tea at weekends with the policeman and his wife, Mr and Mrs Perkins. They also made trips to local places such as Ivinghoe Beacon and Whipsnade Zoo. Some had local girl-friends and at least two of them, Franti ek Pospí il and Miroslav Novák, married local girls and settled locally.

## Today

The Nissen huts and buildings remained at Hockliffe until the 1970s, but today there is nothing left at the site except some concrete bases and some cables, which were ploughed up by the farmer.

## Personal Stories

The information for this chapter is based upon interviews with people who worked at the station, or in some cases their immediate families. They generously gave me information from their memories. I would like to thank the following people, without whom this story would not have been known: George Bearfield (grandson of Jaroslav Bublík), Jiří Louda, Tony Shackleton & Sonia Novák (daughter of Miroslav Novák), Roy Tink, and Miroslav Umlauf. I would also like to thank people from the Dunstable and Hockliffe area who have given me local information.

# SHORT BIOGRAPHIES IN ALPHABETICAL ORDER

***Jaroslav Bublík*** was transferred to the radio station at Hockliffe, having previously worked at Woldingham in Surrey since 1942. He worked at Hockliffe until December 1944 when he was trained by the SOE for a parachute mission. He returned to Prague in 1945 and worked as a radio operator at the Czechoslovak Embassy in Berlin, and escaped communism in 1948 coming to London where he worked for the Post Office. He retired to Lincolnshire in 1975, where he died in 2000.

***Jiří Louda*** was a soldier in the Czechoslovak Army. He was posted to the VRÚ in January 1943, due to a knee injury incurred during commando training in Scotland. He knew good English and made friends with the people at The Bell in Hockliffe. He went back to Czechoslovakia by plane in 1945 and was later imprisoned without trial by the communists, and on release worked as a university librarian. He now (2006) lives in the Czech Republic.

CZECHOSLOVAK RADIO OPERATORS at Hockliffe Radio station in 1944, showing the transmission hut in the background *(JB)*

CZECHOSLOVAKS at Hockliffe Radio Station, showing aerials in the background. Date on the back of the photo is 18th November 1943. *(JT)*

CZECH RADIO OPERATORS *(JB)*

**Miroslav Novák** was in the Signals Unit of the Free Czechoslovak Army and he was posted to the VRÚ in Hockliffe from 1942 until 1945. He married a Dunstable girl, and after the war they settled in Czechoslovakia. In 1946 they moved to Bern, Switzerland, where he worked for the Czechoslovak Embassy. During communism he was recalled to Prague and was given a job as a welder. The family, which then had 2 daughters, emigrated and settled back to Dunstable in 1964, where he died in 2005.

**Roy Tink** was a telecommunications engineer who worked for the G.P.O. Engineering Department at Bletchley Park and on outstation radio installations. He used to service the teleprinters at Hockliffe once a week from 1942 until 1945, and was the only Englishman to regularly visit the site. Whilst there he became friendly with some of the Czechs, and sometimes ate with them at their kitchen. He now (2006) continues to lives in Buckinghamshire.

**Miroslav Umlauf** was a soldier in the Czechoslovak Army. He was appointed to work at the VRÚ from 1945 to 1946. He operated the teleprinter and lived on site in a Nissen hut but visited his English wife in Northamptonshire at weekends. They returned to Czechoslovakia by train in 1946, but escaped communism in 1948, settling back in England, and then later emigrated to Ontario, Canada, where they now (2006) live.

Further Reading:
For the background on local wireless communications read *The Secret Wireless War – The Story of MI6 Communications 1939–1945* by Geoffrey Pidgeon
For the background on local Czechoslovak operations read *The Czech Connection – The Czechoslovak Government in Exile in London and Buckinghamshire* by Neil Rees

THE TWO NISSEN HUTS at Hockliffe used as accommodation by the Czechoslovaks. Photo taken in 1964 *(SN)*

RADIO EQUIPMENT built by Simandl at Hockliffe *(MJ)*

# THE AMERICANS
## Introduction by Jean Yates

Many people have told us that Dunstable was full of Americans, but it has been impossible to track down exactly where they were stationed. We know a number were at Cheddington and came into Dunstable for their R&R.

Chicksands was home to many more, and there were lorries sent from there to Luton on Saturday evenings, to pick up young women and take them to the dances. To warrant a permanent presence of Snowdrops, as the American Military Police were called (because of their white helmets), there must have been considerable numbers of American servicemen in the town at that time.

## *Maisie Bates* - Paying Wages

I know that there were Americans staying in Dunstable because I can remember paying them their wages before the bank opened. They came into the back through the side door beside my counter. To our amusement they had two soldiers standing outside with loaded guns; an old lady walked passed them, stopped and looked at them and said, "Is that loaded, mister?" He replied, "Mother, you try me!"

## *P Underwood* - B17s

The Americans arrived in Dunstable. They were so generous, I loved them and being an aviation nut, they let me go on to their airfields and took me for flights. Not like the RAF when I couldn't get past the guard. They had an airfield quite near at Mentmore.

A friend of mine went there regularly and flew with them in their B17s, and we used to see, as their numbers increased, the B17s flying round here in big formations. We'd see them go off in the daytime and at night we'd see the RAF. Most of the B17s we saw round here came from Bassingbourn; I think it was the 93rd Bomb Group. They had a big triangle with an A on the tail.

I remember an incident in Dunstable with a GI and probably a lady of the night in the narrow passageway between Middle Row and the High Street. There was a great shrieking, shouting and swearing of this American and this lady. I often walk down that passage and think about it. The Americans were great. Whether you were over-fed or over-paid, if

MODERN LAUNDERETTE – wartime home of the 'Snowdrops'– the American Military Police Unit *(JY)*

you make the supreme sacrifice it's just the same. They brought their music – Glenn Miller; I still listen to him. For me there is still a special relationship with the Americans.

### *Patricia Morgan* – **Toilet Paper or Sweets**

We did like the American convoys coming through. If you put your ear to the ground as you walked down Priory Road, you could hear them coming from a long way off, and if you walked slowly with a bit of luck they were coming through before you got to Ashton school. You could sit on the high kerb on the church side of the road and wave and the Americans would throw sweeties.

By '43 or '44 there were an awful lot of troop movements. The Americans were billeted in Dunstable. The lady next door took in coloured Americans because not everyone would. She had 2 billeted on her and they were very nice fellows. I'd never seen a black man before; I was totally fascinated, Robert and Lloyd they were called. We were always told that if the Americans asked us if we needed anything, we were always to say toilet paper, not sweets. They did give us toilet paper and sweets. They were stationed at the back of Moore's, through the arch in what became the Index Publishers. There weren't that many of them but they were very nice.

### *Philip Buckle* - in Convoy

The Americans had a military police presence in Dunstable. I won't say headquarters but it was in one of the shops, near Fred Moore's (a small department store). I can remember the military policemen on their Harley Davidson motorbikes coming up High Street North, stopping, and getting off in their white helmets and truncheons.

We had a lot of American convoys (always with their headlights on, which in those days was very unusual) coming through Dunstable, generally with the coloured members of the forces driving them.

### *Valerie Cousins* - Cheering Lorries

I also remember watching lots of American lorries driving through the town from Luton. They had coloured soldiers, whom we had never seen before, and we children used to cheer them along and were given chewing gum. A real treat!

## POLISH ALLIES AND THE ROAD THAT LED TO DUNSTABLE
### Introduction by Barbara Fryc

It is amazing the route some people take to get to Dunstable. The Polish Community found a home in the Dunstable area via Siberia, Kazakhstan, Iran (Persia), Iraq, Palestine, India, Egypt, Italy, South Africa, Kenya, Scotland, Germany, France, Holland, Belgium, Spain and of course Poland. What map were they following? The one marked 'Freedom'.

They started their journey when Germany invaded Poland in September 1939. Polish Armed Forces and civilians escaped to France and England. Those left and captured were shipped off to Concentration and Labour camps, civilians and soldiers. When Russia joined the German side, thousands were shipped off to Siberia and Kazakhstan and other remote areas as forced labour or internment. Life was very harsh; thousands and thousands, amongst them whole families, died of starvation, infestation, disease or were worked to death or shot.

When Russia joined the Allies side in 1942, the situation changed. The interned Polish ex – forces were released by Russia and made their way to Iran (then Persia). Families and dependants were sent to friendly, safe countries for the duration of the war.

The Polish Free Army were mobilised under the command of General Anders, trained by the British and fought with great courage, honour, valour and sacrifice in Europe and Africa for the freedom of Europe but unfortunately as history recalls not freedom for Poland. The cruellest betrayal of all, by the very Allies with whom they fought side by side – Poland was given to Russia to rule at the end of the War! [Yalta]

History has noted the part the Poles played in the struggle for freedom and the price they paid. The Poles were the fourth largest national group in the Allied armies after the Russians, Americans and British. Polish pilots were the second largest group in the RAF.

Six million Poles had been killed by the end of the war – that's about 16% of their people.

After the war Field Marshal Viscount Alanbrooke, Chief of the Imperial General Staff, would declare that, 'Without the 2nd Polish Corps, the series of offensives carried out in Italy from Monte Cassino onwards would hardly have been possible.' Sir Arthur Harris (Bomber Command Chief) also declared 'The debt owed to the brave men and women of the Polish Resistance is beyond price'. A comment referring to the part the Poles played in providing intelligence and a sample of the V-2 rocket, which led to the Peenemunde site, where they were being manufactured, being destroyed by the RAF.

Polish airmen fought and died in the Battle of Britain, Polish ships took part in convoys, guarding the British coast and in the D-Day invasion. 'So much owed to so few'.

Polish forces had been stationed at the RAF station near Bedford and some Polish code breakers were involved in the Enigma Code deciphering, which was based at Bletchley Park, but the Polish contingent were not housed at Bletchley. It was the Polish Intelligence Section that gave the Allies [the British & French] the first captured Enigma machines and code at the start of the war.

Victory in Europe came – Peace at last – but what about the Poles? No Free Poland for them!

What were they to do? Going back to Poland would mean death for many and an uncertain future. They would carry on the struggle for freedom for Poland – a struggle that would last another 45 years before Poland would cast the shackles of Russian Communism.

Thousands of Polish soldiers, airmen and sailors, men and women found themselves in a dilemma. Where would they go? Some of the forces continued in the Army of occupation in countries freed and in Germany. The rest were demobbed in 1946. Countries like America, Canada, Australia, South Africa and Britain were offering refugees, ex-soldiers and their families, stateless people from Europe a place to settle. People went where they could, where they would be accepted and transport was provided.

For those considering Britain, there were a few reservations, not least the fear that the British would also send them all back into the hands of Russia. However, all the Polish Armed Forces were given a letter from the British Organisations Committee for the Welcome of Polish Soldiers – issued in 1946 in London – this was still in the possession of Wojciech Winnik, still living in Dunstable in 2005. This letter was meant to reassure the men and women who had fought with the Allies, that the British would offer them a place to live and work and to bring up their families in peace and security and recognised their contribution in the fight for an end to the war.

Resettlement camps were set up all over Britain, which had previously been used by the Armed Forces of the Allies armies. On arrival in Southampton, the Polish forces were distributed to various camps to await demobilisation. There was little accommodation available in the towns, villages and cities in Britain that had been damaged during the war to deal with such large numbers of people. As a temporary measure, these ex-military camps seemed the best solution. Even in parts of England, some English families ended up in such camps because housing was so short. Post war house building could not keep up with demand.

These resettlement camps or 'Hostels' as they were called in some places, became self-contained communities. Little Polands in Britain. I remember my years in such a camp vividly. As I close my eyes I can still visualise the camp, Doddington Park, near Wydenbury, Cheshire. The barracks which

BARBARA FRYC (left) with her sister Teresa in Polish costumes made by their mother, in Doddington Park Resettlement Camp *(BF)*

became our home – no bathroom, no toilet, no running indoor water. Water came from a standpipe, positioned in between several barracks outdoors. You would go with a bucket or a pan to fill up with water. Some years during winter the taps were frozen, so you had to go further to one of the wash houses dotted around the camp. These wash houses had large sinks and boilers, mangles and wooden tables and draining boards. You could do your large washing, sheets, blankets and heavy clothes. There were some shower houses as well around the camp but only a few of the showers still worked.

Washing of clothes was done using a washboard in a metal wash-tub. Bath time involved heating up buckets of water on the stove in the kitchen [coal and wood for fuel was used]. Mother would bath two of us at a time in the tin bath-tub, and the same bathwater was used by everyone, with hot water added as it got colder.

For toilet facilities you used a chamber pot kept under the bed, which was emptied into a slop bucket that had a lid. This then would be emptied every day into a cesspit at the end of the garden. There were some toilets in the camp, in the areas which were used as a school, nursery school, theatre and what had been the recreational areas for the army – the billiard halls and community mess areas. The living quarters did not have such luxuries. The odd ex-senior officer barrack might have a sink with one tap.

You can see from the picture of me and my elder sister, the type of barracks we lived in. The barracks were partitioned inside to accommodate families. So one large barrack was divided into two with enough space for living and sleeping space with a kitchen. They were heated by one or two iron stoves in the centre or at two ends of the barracks and the cooking range in the kitchen. It was quite cold in the winter time. Electric power for lights and radio.

Around each of the barracks, some land was fenced off to form a garden where people grew vegetables to supplement their diet. They grew traditional vegetables and fruit associated with the Polish diet – potatoes, cabbage, onions, beetroot, garlic, tomatoes, cucumbers, peas, beans, horseradish, strawberries, raspberries and blueberries. We also had chickens and rabbits, which were reared for their eggs and for meat. There was a shop in the camp, a Post Office, a hospital clinic run by our own Polish doctors and nurses, a welfare office, an accommodation office for the camp and a church with our Polish priest. Some businesses were run by Polish people; a garage to repair not only the few cars and lorries in the camp but to service and repair local farm machinery and anything mechanical in the camp. People were found work with local farmers and in the towns near to the camp.

We had very little contact with the English people. We were taught the Polish language, history and geography at the Polish school in the camp, we spoke Polish at home with our parents and siblings, with our neighbours and all in the camp. We celebrated Polish festivals, religious feast days, Polish national holidays, kept Polish traditions and the Polish culture. The photograph of my sister and me in national costume shows a very basic design and decoration – money was short and to have produced a fully decorated costume would have been expensive. Our life-style was very much on the Polish way of life as in pre-war Poland. The people in the camps held the hope that we would be able to return to Poland and therefore it was important to teach the children the language and not lose our Polish identity.

How long could Russia hold on to power in Poland? We had a government in exile which was continuing the fight for a Free Poland. Surely the British would realise their error of their decision with America to give in to Russia and help gain Poland's Freedom. It was to be a very long 45 years.

My family lived in the camp for 12 years before they were finally allocated a council house in an English town, Crewe, in which we grew up, went to English school and went on to make a life for ourselves. It wasn't until my first visit to Poland in 1979 when I saw the conditions in which Polish people lived in the villages, that I realised why the people living in the resettlement camps in Britain put up with such basic amenities and sparse conditions for so many years.

This was very much the case for the Polish community in Dunstable/Luton too. Most of the community members came from a resettlement camp/hostel near Tring at Marsworth.

Mr Jan Sadowski was in the first group of six soldiers who were sent to Marsworth Camp to guard it, as it was being converted to accommodate the demobbed Polish soldiers and their families and civilians from transit camps from Europe and other parts of Britain. He remembers well how friendly and kind the people were, bringing them food and tea. The parish priest in the camp was Father Frankowski. Many of the ex-soldiers had to wait some years after the war before their families who had been in safe countries while they fought the war, were repatriated and reunited with them in these camps. Mr Wojciech Winnik didn't see his wife and child again until 1948.

To prepare the men and their families to integrate, English classes were held to teach everyone English, and training was given to teach men a trade which would help them find work in the towns. The Polish Organisation SPK (The Polish Ex-Combatants Association) was the driving force in setting up and supporting the training and education of ex soldiers and helping them to settle in. They provided tools for men with a trade to set up in business and find work. Everything from an accordion for a musician, Mr Jerzy Jeron, who was the parish organist for over 50 years, to carpentry tools. At first they would travel to work and live in camps in Dunstable and Luton, which were the nearest towns for work. Later from 1953 onwards, they would find lodging rooms or with a family, then eventually buy or rent a house of their own for their families. The base for the parish then moved from Marsworth to Dunstable/Luton. Father Wlodzimierz Cienski was the first parish priest in the new Polish parish in Luton/Dunstable.

There was a very strong bond of national identity, language, culture, religion and community, which was nurtured during the war and the years of life in the camp. This bond was maintained once the camp finally closed in the early sixties. The Polish community was scattered about the town, living close to other Polish families where possible. The first people moved into the town as early as 1948 and early fifties. A Polish church was established, from an old Baptist church in Victoria Street, bought and converted by the Polish people. Volunteers worked to build on a community centre at the back of the church, where it still stands today. The Polish R.C. Church – our Lady of Czestochowa in Victoria Street, Dunstable, was opened and blessed in 1968 by Bishop Rubin, the Polish Bishop responsible for the Polish emigrants in G.B. Previously St. Joseph's R.C church in Gardenia Avenue, Luton, and St. Mary's R.C Church in Dunstable were used to celebrate Mass, and local halls were used for social occasions until our own parish centre was built.

The Polish Saturday School was held here to teach Polish to the next generation of Poles. As the population in the community grew, local English school premises were used on Saturdays to meet the demand for the numbers who attended.

Today with new generations of Poles coming to the area as economic migrants from Poland, now part of the European Union, the numbers in the community have swelled to unforeseen numbers. Where the post-war community integrated into the English community was declining, there has now been a significant upturn.

The Polish community in Dunstable/Luton – so referred to because the parish is served by one Polish parish priest, at present Father Czeslaw Osika – has the church at its heart. The parish covers Dunstable, Luton, Leighton Buzzard, St.Albans & Milton Keynes. The Parish Committee organise

We proudly celebrated the 50th ANNIVERSARY OF THE POLISH PARISH in Dunstable in 2003. The concert celebrated this occasion – here representatives of all the parish organisations with their banners, children in national costumes and the Polish dance troupe 'Wawel' join in the finale song. *(MB)*

activities and everyday running of matters associated with a community with the guidance of the parish priest.

We look forward to life as members of the Polish community within Dunstable/Luton and with the multi-cultural community at large. Many people have been pleasantly surprised to find out that a large and active Polish community has existed here so long. We are proud and happy to have found a place where we are part of the English community and still maintain our links with our culture and heritage.

## Phyllis Kaye and Pauline Richards (her daughter)

### – Happily Married

It was while I was at home in Aston Clinton one weekend that I met Jozef. It was at the local village 'hop' that he asked me if I would like to dance, clicking his heels and bowing. Jozef was from Poland where his family owned a large farm. He was in the Polish army when the Germans invaded Poland. He was taken prisoner and sent to a concentration camp in Romania. He escaped from there when he was allowed to go to the local market to buy chickens and vegetables for the camp. He caught a train at the station and had a narrow escape when he was asked for his papers. As he could speak perfect German he pretended he was a German soldier who had been separated from his unit and asked how he could get to the German embassy, get help and rejoin his unit. The ruse worked and when he left the train he went instead to the British embassy and eventually reached England, via Palestine. In 1942 he reached this country and joined the RAF. Here he was sent to RAF Halton, to train in bomb disposal and one Saturday evening went to the dance in the nearby village of Aston Clinton, where we met.

Jozef and I were married in 1945. In 1947 Jozef left the RAF and worked for a time for my father, who was a builder. But farming was what Jozef really knew and later my family bought Shepherd's Farm for us. It was in a poor state by this time but Jozef built up a successful arable and livestock farm. There was electricity but water still had to be drawn from a well.

After the war Churchill announced that all Poles who had come to England in the war were welcome to stay. Eventually Jozef became a naturalized British citizen and later changed his surname to Kaye, which he thought would make life easier for our young children when they went to school. Jozef became Chairman for the local Polish community and we led the negotiations to buy the church in Victoria Street, Dunstable, for them. Three of Jozef's sisters were nuns and his brother became a priest.

We had 3 children, 8 grandchildren and 9 great-grandchildren. After the war we visited Poland but it was very risky, as Jozef could have been called up by the Polish authorities. Security was very strict and there were armed guards at the borders. (It was still part of the Soviet Communist bloc.) It would not have been safe to stay there. What became of the family's farm we do not know.

## Zdzislaw Maszadro - Buchenwald

When he was 16 years old in August 1939, he joined the First Aid Service and the Fire Defence Service. On September 17th 1939 he escaped from the invading Soviet Army, after Poland had been invaded by Germany, and became a refugee in Romania before going to France.

He attended secondary school in Paris between November 1939 and May 1940 when he matriculated. In May 1940 he joined the Polish army in exile, the 3rd Artillery Regiment in Coetiguidan, Bretagne, (Brittany) France. On 16th June 1940, France fell and the Polish army was demobilised at Carpiagne Centre near Marseille. In November 1940 (in Vichy France), Zdzislaw went to sixth form college to continue his studies at Villard de Lans near Grenoble. Whilst there he joined other demobbed Polish men and Frenchmen in the Resistance, helping escaped Allied Prisoners of War from Germany to get to Spain and England.

In September 1943 he attended the University of Strasbourg, the Clermont Ferrand Medical School, again in Vichy France. On the 25th November, he was arrested and deported along with all the university medical students and professors to Buchenwald Concentration Camp in Germany.

"Buchenwald was set up in 1937 when the first inmates were Germans," he says. "When Germany finally took over Vichy France, everyone from the university was sent there as forced labour. One of the lasting memories of the camp where 60,000 people died, mainly from starvation and exhaustion from working in the quarries, was the methodical manner in which the remains (ashes) of the cremated victims were placed in cardboard containers, stacked on shelves with their names on and then sent home to relatives where an address was known."

On 11th April 1945 he was liberated by the Allied Forces from Buchenwald and rejoined the Polish Army in Exile attached to the Allied Forces. He was shipped to Scotland to join them. In September 1948, after being demobbed, Zdzislaw went on to medical school in Galway to complete his medical training. After qualifying as a doctor he took up various medical posts in hospitals in France, Ireland and Great Britain.

Zdzislaw's family lived in France after the war and his father practised there as a doctor. When Zdzislaw graduated as a medical cadet in Scotland his father presided at the ceremony and congratulated him on

ZDZISLAW MASZADRO *(BF)*

his achievement. His father was the Commanding Officer of the Medical Corps at the time.

In July 1962 Zdzislaw became a G.P. in South Wales. In 1964 he moved to the Luton/Dunstable area and served as a G.P until his retirement in 1993. He has worked for the S.P.K – the Polish equivalent of the British Legion – and has been a guiding light of the Anglo-Polish Association. He was decorated by the French Government with the Croix des Combattants Volontaires given to members of the French Resistance and Voluntary Forces.

### Jan Sadowski – War Veteran

I was born in Poland. At the outbreak of war in 1939 I was wounded during fighting in Ciecanowie. After recovery I ended up being interned. I joined the Polish Free Army and took part in fighting at Tobruk, Gaza and Bardii, and in the Italian campaign at Monte Cassino, Ossimo, Ancora and Bolognia.

After the war ended I came over in 1946 with the rest of the 2nd Corps of the Polish Army to England to the camp at Brandon. After demobilisation I was allocated to the resettlement camp at Marsworth near Tring. Here after training for work I found employment with my wife at Vauxhall and bought a house in Dunstable.

*Jan has been an active member of the Polish Ex-Combatants Association in the Luton/ Dunstable Branch and in the local Polish community.*

### Kazmier Tule (née Szikona) – a Nurse

Kazmier was born in 1932 in Brzessor Bogiem, Poland, near the Russian border. At the outbreak of war there were 11 members in her family. She was only 9 years old when she and her family were taken away and transported to Kazakhstan and the family were separated. Kazmier's older sister had been arrested and put in prison in 1940 because she was in the Polish Army. She too was later transported to Russia and on her release, when Russia joined the Allies, she rejoined the Polish Army under General Anders and went on to Palestine where she became a member of the Nursing Corps.

At the end of the war this sister became a Nursing Officer at the 4th Polish Hospital in Penley, Wales. A brother also ended up in Palestine with the Polish Army 2nd Corps and went on to fight.

The most vivid memory of Kazmier's family life is the harsh conditions under which they had to survive. The lack of food was the worst. Her father and one brother died of starvation. Her life was only saved when she was dying, by an aunt from whom her mother begged bread. The daily ration was 30dg of bread for an adult and 20dg for a child. Sometimes they would not get any rations for three days on and off.

The people; whole families and villages were transported by the Russians for labour. In the area where she was held, vast fields of crops were grown to feed the Russians. The Polish were not allowed to take food from the fields and penalties were harsh. No special accommodation had been provided, so families had to build their own shelters. The houses they built were called 'Lepjanki', made out of straw and mud mixed and then stuck together to form a shelter. One window only, no glass, one door, one room with a hole in the roof for smoke to escape from the fire, used for cooking and to keep warm. Fuel consisted of dried reeds collected from a nearby river and dried dung collected from the animals in the fields. In winter, when snow covered the shelters, all that was visible were the swirls of smoke from mounds of snow. The temperature was as low as −30 degrees.

She remembers too the infestation by lice and mites because of the poor sanitation and lack of hygiene facilities. Over a third of the people who were transported to Russia did not survive. Most died from hunger, emancipation and disease from harsh and inhumane conditions.

It was only at the end of the war when the family were released, after searching through the list of survivors who had joined the Free Polish Army, that they found that the rest of the family had survived.

They joined the thousands of refugees looking for a safe place to live and finally ended up in England with the resettlement programme. They found her brothers and sister in 1946 in Iscoyd Park, Whitchurch, then they moved to Marsworth near Tring, and finally settled in Dunstable.

"I lived through too much horror and endured much sorrow to dwell on," she says. "Some people would find it hard to believe today; I try not to think about it. You had to live, look forward to life, there was a better world that a lot of people fought and lost their lives for."

### Ludomir Cabut - Seeing Action

I was born in Poland in 1925. The road to Dunstable began on 10th February 1940 when, after the fall of Poland, I was deported with my whole family to Siberia. In September 1941 we were released and allowed to travel south. After 12 weeks of train journey through Siberia, the Ural Mountains and Uzbekhistan we were put to work on cotton fields.

In February 1942 I joined the Polish Army being mobilised again. In September 1942 we were evacuated to Persia (Iran) and next we were moved to Khanaquin in Iraq. In April 1943 we were transferred to the Polish Army in Scotland through South Africa, arriving in Scotland in September 1943. Here I joined the 1st Polish Armoured Division, Signal Unit. I trained as a telegraphist in Catterick Camp returning to Galashiels. On 31st July 1944 I landed in Normandy.

I was then in action through France, Belgium, Holland and Germany until the end of the war. I stayed with the Army of Occupation in Germany until 1946 when we returned to Witley Camp in England. I was demobbed in May 1948 from the Army and ended up in Marsworth Camp, Tring, in 1950. In November 1961 I moved to Dunstable and was employed by the Empire Rubber Company. After 34 years I retired in 1990.

### Mietek Szumski - from Siberia to Scotland

Mietek was born in Poland. In 1940 he was transported with his whole family to Siberia by the Russians.

In 1942 he was released, joined up with the newly mobilised Polish army with others and made his way to Iran and then Palestine. He then went to Scotland where he underwent training under the British and served in the 1st Tank Division.

### Stanislaw Czaczka - in a Settlement Camp

I was born in Poland in 1924 and transported to Russia – Kazakhstan in 1940. When Russia changed sides after the Germans invaded Russia, I was released with other men and joined the Polish Army, the 2nd Corps, which was being mobilised under General Anders. I altered my date of birth on my papers making me 18 years instead of 16 years so I could join. The whole corps went to Iran, Iraq, Palestine, Egypt and Italy. I fought in Italy at Monte Cassino.

I came to England in 1946 on a ship from Napoli to Liverpool. After arrival in England I was sent on to camps where the Polish army were stationed, then on being demobbed I went to a resettlement camp where Polish dependants, families and ex-soldiers were housed before integration into the English communities from Marsworth Camp near Tring to Dunstable.

### *Stanislaw Morgownik* - **Badly Injured**

Stanislaw was born in 1917. At the outbreak of war as Germany invaded Poland in 1939, Stanislaw was badly injured. He was shot in the side of the head. His ear was badly damaged and at one time was gangrenous; what was left of his ear was sewn together. He was taken to a hospital in Warsaw, but because of his injuries they weren't too keen to take him and he was transported to Prussia, where the skill of the doctors saved his life.

In February 1940 he was transported to Russia along with the rest of his family. In 1941 when Germany invaded Russia and Russia joined the Allies, Polish soldiers who had been interned in Siberia and Kazakhstan, were then released by the Russians and mobilised to fight and return to Poland.

The re-mobilised army went on to Iran (Persia) to train with the British Army and Allies. He remembers how in April 1942 they sat all day without food until midnight before something was organised. Then it was a whole week before accommodation and facilities were organised for the soldiers and families.

From Iran he went on to Palestine in April 1942, and then on to Tobruk. He fought at Monte Cassino on 10th–12th May. There was a big barrage of artillery, the storming of a monastery by the Polish Brigade and, with an already damaged ear, he is now severely deaf with a constant ringing in his ears.

At the end of the fighting some of the men returned to Poland and the rest of the 2nd Corps came to England. "I ended up in Brendtree Camp and after being discharged from the Army, found agricultural work near Letchworth. I then moved to the Marsworth Camp near Tring and then on to Dunstable."

### *Taduesz Boron* - **Platoon Commander**

Taduesz was born on the 6th April 1913 in Poland. When the war broke out in 1939 I was working as a border guard. Towards the end of September 1939 together with other border workers, I crossed the border into Latvia and was interned. From here the group were taken by the Russians to Kozielska, where we stayed until the Germans began the war with Russia. Twenty four hours before the war between Germany and Russia started, we were put into wagons and shipped off to Northern Russia to a camp. From there we were moved to Tocho-Busuch-Koybyszew where the 2nd Corps of the Polish Army was being assembled and mobilised by General Anders. I was put into the 6th Division under the command of General Tokarzewski.

In 1942 I became the commander of the 2nd Platoon, 2nd Company Parachute Training School at Szachrizjabz, Uzbehistan, from here we travelled on to Syria, Persia (Iran). In 1943 I read in the daily army bulletin that they were looking for volunteers to join an elite group of the Underground Army who would be dropped behind enemy lines known as Cicho-Ciemni, or the men who dropped silently in the dark (paratroopers).

Together with other officers I volunteered for this assignment. We were personally dispatched by General Anders. We left for Great Britain, journeying through Egypt and Durban in South Africa, where we waited for several weeks for a ship in Cape Town. We travelled on the luxury liner Queen Mary which was being used as a troop ship to Rio de Janeiro, then on to New York where we stayed for one week.

When we left New York we travelled on the ship with the American soldiers. We landed in Greenock, Scotland, where we underwent training with the army, including parachute training at Ringway, driving at Falkirk and tank training on Sherman tanks. During this time, 1943–44, a group of officers were assigned to various units and I was sent to London where I worked with the Special Parachute Unit preparing to drop into Poland.

In 1944 I lived in Kensington and during a raid was injured when a bomb exploded in Ealing. I was never able to take part in the parachute drop into Poland. When I recovered I helped organise a new battalion in Scotland in 1945, made up of Polish soldiers who returned from the war to England.

I was demobilised in 1946 in Ross and Cromerty with the rank of

2nd Lieutenant and went on to study textiles at Nottingham University. I graduated in 1948 and got a job with Vita Tex in Slough. In 1962 I got a job with the Luton Knitting Company and moved here. I retired in 1978. I have been a member of the Luton/Dunstable Polish community since moving here in 1962 and am now 93 years old.

### *Wojciech Winnik* – **Trained by the Allies**

When the war broke out I was a farmer married to Anna (1938) and working on my family's land. In February 1940 my wife and I and the rest of our family were transported to Russia.

In April 1942 we were released and made our way with others to Persia (Iran). Here I was called up to join the Polish Free Army. The army went on to Palestine and Iraq to be trained by the Allies, mainly British and then took part in the fighting in Italy at Monte Cassino, Bolognia and Ancora.

The families and dependants of the soldiers and others released from internment by the Russians were sent on to East Africa, India, Lebanon and Palestine, wherever there were

WOJCIECH WINNIK
and family at Marsworth
Resettlement Camp *(BF)*

places offered by those countries. The British dispersed these people to safe places. At the end of the war I went to England in 1946 with the rest of the 2nd Corps, 3rd Division, Carpathian Rifle Brigade.

I was demobbed in 1947, found work and was then reunited with my wife Anna who had been in South Africa. We were housed with our firstborn in 1948 at a resettlement camp near Colchester. The families and dependants were brought over to join the soldiers returning from duty in Europe or ending their service in the Army.

I was awarded medals for fighting during the war and hold the Defence Medal with Silver Laurel Leaves with the Kings Commendation for brave conduct.

From here I moved to Marsworth Camp near Tring, where I found work and settled in Dunstable where I eventually bought a house. I am an active member of the Polish community today.

### Bill Woolley – Dunstable's Fire Officer

"We had a fire down Long Lane at Toddington. Turn left at the church and then right towards Tingrith. Down at the bottom there was a farm with Polish officers and tank tracks. When the big shots from the fire brigade came, we wondered, because it was only a hayrick fire.

Then it used to make you wonder how something that isolated could catch fire. There was another one on a farm at the bottom of Poynters Road. The same went on there.

If it hadn't been for the fire we wouldn't have known, but we didn't have to shout about it afterwards."

### Tony Woodhouse – a Telegraph Pole in the Middle of our Lawn!

Bennett's Brewery was situated in Chiltern Road and was always guarded by a soldier with a rifle. It was used as some sort of military headquarters. I think they may have been French or Czech as they wore these strange hats. My father was annoyed because in order to keep in touch with their counterparts in Europe, they stuck a huge great telegraph pole in the middle of our lawn! My mother said she knew when D-Day was about to take place, because a few days beforehand the whole place became a beehive of activity.

# Serving in the Forces

## INTRODUCTION BY JEAN YATES

Everyone involved in World War II served King and Country, either by defending the Realm or keeping the home fires burning. This chapter contains some fond memories but also many sad ones. We are honoured to have been allowed to gather and print these stories, some told for the first time in 60 years.

The two counties of Bedfordshire and Hertfordshire fielded five battalions in the Second World War. The Fifth Battalion was captured in Singapore in February 1942, having landed on Singapore Island just five days before its surrender to the Japanese. The 5th Bedfords made a series of withdrawals as the island's defences crumbled. Three dreadful years of captivity followed the surrender during which time about one third of the battalion died from overwork, sickness and starvation. The remnants of the battalion returned to England in 1945. Prisoners of war in the Far East were not allowed to keep diaries, and did so under threat of death if evidence was found.

## LT. GEOFFREY MOORE

### Experiences as a Far East Prisoner of War 1942–1945

*This is a typeset version of a four-page pencil record kept by Lt Moore.*

13.11.1941 – Left Gourock. Heavy weather N. Atlantic. Arrive Durban approx 20.12.41. Magnificent hospitality. Taken to P Maritzberg and Howick Falls, valley of 1000 hills. Left 24.12.41 after getting extra day due to anchor breaking away. Went ashore with Tony and had difficulty getting back in docks. Durban very attractive town. Fuelled at Maldives coral reefs. Air raid entering Singapore. Smell of Chinese quarters. Confusion and lack of information during campaign. 'All aircraft are hostile'. No concentration put down on Jap positions in Johor. Fires everywhere. No water. Hospitals crowded out. Civilians in bad way.

15.02.1942 – Tremendous disappointment on 15th. Singapore in bad state, bodies everywhere. On 16th stopped and searched by 2 Nips. Furious temper. Ordered to march to Changi. Took all men and food on trucks. Just as well as there were no rations. All VERY hungry. Had to draw well water. Baths once a week. Chinese shot. Started garden. Hospital supplies taken by Nips. Seldom saw Nips. Church services as normal. Concerts in due course, very good ones too. Saturday evening concerts at D block overlooking Straits and Fairy Point. Football, little cricket. Hunger appalling. Plain fried rice ball great treat. Black market flourished, immense profits made. Working parties sent into Singapore. Food better there. Chaps used to try to pinch stuff. Also used to flog anything they could lay their hands on. Petrol, tyres, etc. Incident of milk episode. Wonderful singing. Morale tremendous. 3 or 4 black sheep who signed. Amazing trek to and fro. 6.10.1942 – Ration parties in Changi Flyer.

26.10.1942 – Up country – 32 to truck. Terrible conditions. Hot in day, cold at night. Diarrhoea. 10 hard boiled eggs. Shocking state of Bampong camp. "Electric lights, running water!!" Lorry to Kanburi. Barge to Karyn. 50 to bays.     pomets. 8 bananas for 4 days. "All men push." Rain. Floods. Karyn built camp appalling. Rice and wee bit of pumpkin. Men up hill every day. Soon 100 sick out of 600.

Dec 1942 – Malaria very bad. Got malaria and jaundice in Dec. Blackouts. Cold intense at nights. Mist over river till 4. Wore all clothes but still shivered at nights. Huge fires good thing. Day temp in shade – 85, in sun 110. Nights 45. Nips very anti. Bashings up frequent. Mad Mongrel. Karyn Kid. Fit for Christmas day. Pig for 600 men. Peanut toffee gone bad. Up hill camp for week in Jan. Still very weak from malaria.

March 1943 – Fish caught in river. Eggs from Thais. Little else. Wood and water fatigues. Dysentery. Malaria rife. Work to dark. 5 sick men allowed for sanitation for 1000! No roof to cookhouse. Many of us in huts or own shacks. Food dreadful. Sick forced to work. Up at dark, get breakfast and haversack rations, parade for work, go out, home at 8, roll call, supper, wash if not too tired, bed. Diarrhoea very bad, but weaker, weaker.

17.5.1943 – Couldn't step over tree trunk. Nips very anti officers. May 7th – so ill was taken off work, lucky to be sent to Tarsoe with 50 others by truck. Karyn got worse and worse. 5 and 6 died daily. 60 officers died and about 350 men in 4 months. Often went to sleep while frying little whitebait for following lunch. 120 yards to latrine. Mud everywhere. Stream 6 inches by 3 foot for Nip C'house, our C'house and washing. Best day working with elephants. Drivers anti. Heat in day terrific. No shade. Nip promises never kept. Their treatment of sick appalling. Beatings up daily. Treat their own sick same way. No news. No letters. No food. No drugs. Morale very low – never a smile or joke. Except for F H force. Karyn worst camp on river. Hell Fire Corner. Saigon force came up – very fit. Jack's crowd very fit. Appalled at poor state of men but within 2 months both had lost 1/5 of men. Couldn't eat for 5 weeks. Food much better but attitude of Tarson officers very poor indeed. Rats, lice and bugs appalling. Sweeps on whether people would live. Malaria again and bronchitis. Moved into new hospital. Ulcers frightful, no dressings, seven died. Over 200 lost legs. Smell appalling. Fellows from up country absolute skeletons. Some with one sack. No bedding.

LT. GEOFFREY ERNEST MOORE R.A.S.C. (PK)

June 1943 – Dunlop improved cleanliness of camp. Letters in June. Had pellagra. Get small ulcers in hands. Bathing in river good. View along river very nice. Letters great event. Get a spot of news from time to time. Jerry H and other officers beaten to death at Kanburi for working wireless.

Dec 1943 – Heard good reports of Chungkai. Had good Christmas day 1943. Reasonable food, good pantomime. Communication and services very good. Casualties around hospital and camp. Lectures and talks very popular. In January Nips stopped all talks and entertainment. For some time past not allowed to sing The King or use flag for funerals.

March/April 1944 – Deaths still 2 or 3 a day. March and April slept in open – very nice too, good crowd and conversation. Food simply dreadful. April evacuated to Kilon Paton – new hospital camp. Good camp built by Thais. Food better. Quite comfortable. American Red Cross supplies came in. One parcel to 10! (This and some S African in 1942 was the only stuff apart from little Thai Red Cross that we received before August 15th 1945). Also got some drugs. Camp flooded in rains. Duck stocks reduced by 100 in a week. Canteen good. Food deteriorated. Steadily improved.

September 1944 – Took over Messing Officer in Sept 1944. Rations not good.

Made ourselves chairs and had my bed and so were quite comfortable. Night raids particularly one on Nong Pladuk clearly visible.

December 1944 – Very heavy raids heard on Bangkok. Bob P good chap – took 2 services, conducted choir, carols, etc. Felt very queer Christmas Eve. Went round carolling. Got pleurisy. All right after few weeks. Newspaper news from time to time. Racketeers over fence. Big round up. Bunds and fences built.

April 1945 – Constant uncertainty of staying or going. Nip doctors inspections April 45. Moved to Kanburi, carrying John. Very small camp. Miserable Nip Commander. Dryer incident. Pump house incident. Confined to huts. No reading, laughing, talking, acting, etc – 10 days. Dumb Crambo great success. Stopped due to laughing. Work on fence and bund. Catching fish. Food quite good. Canteen reasonable. Wireless news service. Chaps that worked it deserve decorating.

July 1945 – Talk of move to new camp. Advance party left in July. Concerts allowed but no acting. Eric's 2 classical concerts very good.

August 1945 – Left Kanburi, 30 to a truck. Door closed. Heat terrible. Eventually allowed on top. Arrived in Bangkok on top of truck. Then barge journey, 2 nights rest and on again – 36 to a truck. Tremendous damage in Bangkok. On top again. Then unloaded train and started out on a 48 kilometre march after a    hour rest. Rained heavily. Had to help with sick people's kit, then with stretcher case. Then rained again. Kit weighed twice as much. Got in, in 22    hours.

15.8.1945 – Work in new camp very heavy. Worked 8.15 am till 7.30 pm. Some jobs walk 25 kilos carrying bamboo. Food good. Aug 16th Karyns started boozing and dropping hints. Drunken Nip said "War finished."

16.8.1945 – Thais said the same. Nothing official. On 17th announced officially. Thanksgiving service in evening, practically whole camp there. Later singing and National Anthems. First time we had been able to sing them for years. Nips issue Red Cross food, small amount and drugs enough to have saved 100s of lives 2 years before. Food had been in for over 2 years. Nips must have eaten rest. Accumulator taken from Nip truck to work wireless. Some Nips try to get good conduct chits. Pony race meeting. Sent officers to O.R's camps. O.Rs come to us. Red Cross clothing issued. Food very bad for few days till Lt. Col. C takes over. Food then very good – meat plentiful.

29.8.1945 –American comes in who has been in Siam 2 months on intelligence work. Promises to radio out for supplies this evening. One of our aircraft came over other day and acknowledged us but no supplies dropped. Letter from lady internees, Bangkok. Climbed 700ft hill behind camp. Nothing but paddy fields.

*The record ends here. The original, owned by Lt Geoffrey Moore's widow, Mrs Christine Moore, is now in the Imperial War Museum.*

## MR E SAMUEL – in Singapore, late January 1942

Singapore, size of Isle of Wight. Population 550,000, mainly Chinese with Tamils and Malayans. Over 1,000,000 after capitulation. Water from mainland, Johor Bahru, piped over causeway to reservoirs on NW of island. Humid hot damp climate, 90°. Europeans changed clothes three times a day. Regular tropical storms at 6.00pm. Fireflies on shrubs like Christmas in Oxford Street and beautiful sunsets. At docks we disembarked, civilians and the RAF embarked on US transport 'Wakefield'. Absolute chaos. We unloaded our guns and transport. Kit was stored at Teckhor village. We carried essentials in our haversacks, main possessions left at Teckhor.

Gun positions – first at Changi, NE of island on smallholding – cocoa palms, bananas, pigs, chickens etc. Built gun position under banana 'tree'. First salvo and only stem and main veins left – no camouflage so moved under tamarind tree. First salvo – millions of red ants (1") showered down – it felt like red hot needles. Then moved to perimeter of Singapore to a Chinese cemetery. Could not dig slit trenches, water table about 9" down, constructed shelter with sand bags. Here we experienced 5th column. Guards on guns dusk to dawn. In morning in front of each gun 3 palm fronds were placed as an arrowhead pointing at the gun. As the Japs bombed from about 500ft they could hardly miss.

February 15th – capitulation. Jap infantry had crossed the causeway and captured the reservoirs. Without water Singapore could not carry on. We blew up our guns, rammed shell down the muzzle and one in the breech and fired. We drained vehicles and then ran them until they seized up.

P.O.W. on Singapore 15.2.42 to 14.10.42. After being left alone for 3 days we were moved to Changi. Japs provided transport for cookhouse, anything else you needed you had to carry – no going back to Teckhor for kit bags. Lined up 6 abreast, about 60,000 men, Sikh (SE Asia Co- Prosperity Sphere) guards. We had to salute as we passed their guard positions. We arrived at Roberts Hospital Changi – officers in barracks, we slept in the open. We guarded ourselves. Foraging parties – one group found by Japs, as half guard was sent to Changi prison – interrogated by Jap office and let off.

Only had clothes we were wearing plus some extra in our haversacks. Sanitation a must. We had augers to drill holes 1ft in diameter, 15ft deep with a standing plank each side. Soap and toothpaste soon used up. Food atrocious – ballast rice, weevils, mice droppings cooked in kwalis like a 5ft wok.

Sloppy ground rice porridge. Douvres, (hors d'oeuvres) rice dumpling with a mix of vegetables fried in coconut oil. Little roughage, constipation (20–30 days) followed by diarrhoea. For frying we had coconut oil or ghee, gula malacca (palm syrup), katcheneju black eyed peas and dried vegetables. Rice 12–16oz per day, less for sick people and those who couldn't work. Work parties clearing bomb damage in Singapore.

Sent to new camp River Valley Road on outskirts of Singapore. Huts had been used for cattle, built of bamboo and attap. We had bamboo to build platforms to sleep on. Work parties still clearing up in the city. Then, building Go Downs on dockside – used by Japs for storing equipment also as barracks. We took supplies of lice and bed bugs to give them some of their own medicine.

We could still barter with locals. LW and myself bought an unmarked tin for 1 tical. Back at camp we found it to be 1 kilo of Marmite, a great treat and possibly a life-saver. I also bought a tin of Zambuck which I know saved me from many ulcers. I also kept myself reasonably civilised as I could, shaving with my Rolls razor which was self-strapping – no soap though.

Another development at meal times was the 'leggy' queue and graded rice supplies. 20oz heavy work, 16oz light work, 12oz sick. Guards would inspect sick to see if they were fit for work. Because of poor diet diseases increased. I had dengue fever – loss of appetite, sickness, aching in joints. Prickly heat rash – irritating red patches set off by sweating. Tropical storms used as shower-baths eased itching. Malaria – 8–10 days sweating, shakes, nausea, limited Asprin. Scabies – scabby ulcers mainly on hands with swelling. Dysentery – bad diarrhoea. Scrotal dermatitis – weeping wet sores, had to wear a sarong – only treatment local raw spirit. Excruciating. Some ran to standpipe to cool off and get relief. Disappeared as quickly as it came. We received bulk supplies of Red Cross in cook house – decent food for about a fortnight.

14.10.42 – Marched to Singapore railway station for journey north to promised better camps, better climate, better food and better conditions!

Bad start 30–34 in an enclosed metal truck with solid sliding door with kit. Couldn't all sit down at once. Freezing at night, cooked during day. 3 stops per day for water, rice and toilets in jungle.

17.10.42 – Ban Pong Camp, a paddy field with huts. Bed platform 3 inches above water. Latrines overflowing, a carpet of maggots. Tarso after 5 days marching. First day flat paddy fields, then park-like countryside, then foothills and jungle, rising all the time. We had to help the weak and sick, some were left by the trackside. The Japs said they would pick them up later! Most people without boots. We made flip flops from balsa wood – soft and easy to work, with old tyre for strip or kitbag canvas. Useless when wet or sweating – feet slip off. Tarso was a clearing 200 yards from steep river bank. River Kwai in spate would rise and fall 25 – 30ft, no huts – building first job.

Bamboo a most useful commodity but lethal spikes caused terrible cuts and ulcers. Formed A frames lashed together with rattan and strips of bark from tree – pliable while wet. Rafters as spacers, thin bamboo lashed to these, then covered with attap tiles – sliver of bamboo, palm fronds bent over – skewered with another sliver of bamboo. These were laid overlapping like tiles and would keep out most of the rain. Also used for sides of the hut to protect our sleeping platform. Cook houses had mud banks into which we installed kwalis – 5ft wide woks with a fire hole underneath. Latrines were slit trenches with either bamboo laid across to squat on, or bamboo perches to sit on. These became heaving pits of maggots and eventually we had to make covers to put on when not in use. Big blue-bottle flies by the millions in every camp. You had to fan your food all the time you were eating.

Next to bamboo the most useful items were 4 gallon tins, used for any liquid, initially kerosene or fat (ghee), gula mallaca (palm syrup) – we used them for carrying water from the river to the cook house using a bamboo yoke. You developed a waddle to compensate for the spring in the yoke.

Barges pulled by pom poms brought supplies up river. Mainly rice or dried vegetables with canteen supplies for the Japs. 100kg rice sacks. The supplier Boon Pong was pro-British. He supplied batteries for illicit radios. He took post-dated IOUs for payment after the war.

From Tarso we were sent south to Wampo camp where the railway work became harder and harder. A granite like ridge butted up to the river. Working in pairs with a 14lb sledge hammer and a 4ft chisel cross bar we had to drill a 1m deep hole per person – wire scoop made to get powdered rock out. In the evenings the engineers would blast the rock out. Next day one party clearing rock, other party still drilling. P.O.W. camp over the river opposite rock face – when blasting took place, showered with rock. Another group were cutting teak logs which were hauled to the river and used to build viaduct by the rock ledge.    day rest each ten days. Camp repairs – boiling blankets in 40 gallon oil drums to get rid of lice, singeing bed slats to get rid of bugs and swimming. Sometimes a Jap engineer would blast the river which stunned fish which we could collect for extra food.

Returned to Tarso – building earth embankment, bamboo proforma anything from 6 to 30 ft high. Groups of three. One digging with a chunkle, 2 with stretcher – a rice sack and 2 bamboo poles. 1 cubic metre per man per day. The higher the bank, the deeper the hole, the harder the work. When it rained the holes filled up, the banks became slippery. The Japs still wanted their quota. Engineers pegged out areas to be dug 2m deep. When unobserved site roughed up, 6 inches back, pegs moved 6 inches nearer the face. Work got behind hand – forced to do speedo – work through the night, 1 on, 2 off.

Shorts and shirts now in tatters, shirt sleeves torn off to make a strip about 9inches wide. String tied to 2 corners – tied round waist strip, hanging down back – pulled between legs and looped over string at the front – a Jap Happy or G string. Monsoon weather, the sergeant major in charge embankment led singing – "They're pulling down the Rose and Crown (all) Boo. They're building up a new one (all) Hoorah etc". I was sergeant in charge of drinking water. Fell into latrine slit trench. Tried to tell Korean guard and ask to go to river to wash. Then overslept – water not ready for work party – put on charge by R.S.M. and brought up before the Captain.

Entertainment – usually too tired. Permission for concert on    day rest. Gunner W, an ex ballet dancer – marvellous morale booster, complete with chorus line dancing, mosquito net tu-tus and coconut shells. We finished with the National Anthem, all stood to attention including guards. Japs decided they could do as well – we all had to attend – orations, singing – one Korean guard played a mouth organ and finished with 'a popular

English tune', the National Anthem. When we were out on a work party we always listened for pig squealing – Japs ration. Collected entrails, took to river to clean, cooked in 4 gallon tin in evening – chitterlings.

Tonchan Camp – about 3km north. More hammer and tap and embankment building. Got job as dynamite assistant. Japs seemed to favour big men. Day off – when men finished prepared charges. 1m of fuse split end casing, not spilling powder, other end into detonator. When each hole had a detonator and fuse, got a burning ember and dashed around lighting each fuse and then ran to shelter – job finished – much better than clearing rock or hammer and tap. One day Jap engineer didn't arrive and 'Gunso', Jap Sgt, told Korean to take over duty. Instead of giving each hole 1m fuse, he cut fuses to depth of hole. He then wanted to light fuses, short ones as well as 1m ones – not me.

This was a terrible camp, diarrhoea and cholera. Native labourer camp upstream from us thought to be source of cholera. No medicine, patients isolated, given tins of salt water to drink. Hygiene essential. Cremation then communal graves. Nips terrified and isolated their camp, rice sacks soaked in disinfectant at entrance and wore face masks – but no let up on work. Weakness due to straining with no motion to pass, stomach cramps – everything had to be boiled and sterilised. Worst day 26 new cases, 13 deaths. In total there were in our camp 107 cases and 97 deaths.

Moved to Kanu Camp – thank goodness. More embankment building and hammer and tap. We now know that the railway was to run from Ban Pong – near Bangkok to Moulmein in Burma. We worked from south northwards, H and F force worked from north southwards. 415km due to meet at 3 Pagoda Pass. There were 60,000 Brits, Aussies and Dutch working of which 22,000 approximately died. There were also about 200,000 native labourers with over 100,000 deaths. We worked 10 days then day rest and were paid 25 cents per period. The Japs printed their own money and in the bigger camps allowed Thai canteens to be set up.

Moved again to Kingsyo – a very big camp but still embankment work. Very senior Jap officer arrived, unhappy with progress of line – Camp Officer publicly punished in front of all guards – slapped by private from office. Diesel lorries which could also be adapted to run on rails first used and eventually log burning steam engines.

Bad bout of malaria and beriberi. Sent down to hospital camp at Tamuan,

5,000 patients. Marvellous medics, innovations, surgical instruments, amputees limbs, cycle wheel centrifuge to separate blood, distillers for pure water, use of native remedies, some Red Cross. Self administered camp. Work parties still required by Japs – water carriers from river to cook houses and hospital and collecting wood.

Jap officer set up brick yard. Mud from river bank and elephant manure with chopped up bamboo and rice straw puddle in a pit, pressed into formers and cut with a wire, sun dried then fired in a kiln and sold to local Thais. I got a job in Nip canteen, cooked rice doughnuts for them and made Jap Xmas cake – steamed gooey rice pounded with a wooden mallet into a rubbery sheet, cut up and sprinkled with gula Malacca syrup.

Met brother for first time in dysentery ward, 6 stone. We vowed to stay together. A list of all able bodied men was drawn up for transportation to Japan. Convinced officer of need to look after him – got taken off list. Boats left Bangkok in appalling conditions, crammed in layers. Attacked by U.S.A. subs and most sunk. Gunner G from Bletchley and S from Watford picked up by subs and taken to U.S.A. and home. Gunner C visited my mum and dad.

Sent to Tamakan to build wooden bridge – USA bombed the concrete one. The bridge over the River Kwai. Australians cut teak logs and dragged to river. We erected bridge with Nip engineers. Bamboo 'A' frames, ropes and pulley. Ichi ni asiko pile driving logs pinned with 18 inch iron dogs (staples). Got job in Nip cook house, learned how to skin chickens.

Bomb on beach, area cleared – Asta Asta bomb (delayed action), 2 days off work. Party detailed to dig out – only a base plate! Americans still bombing in B27s. Returned to Tamuan. News very sparse and unbelievable – rumours rife.

Sent to Pratchai on Indo China border. No officers. Built a new camp surrounded by 'bund', 15ft wide and 15ft deep trench. Machine gun pit in each corner. I helped in office allocating parties for Nip engineers building slit trenches – petrol and ammunition stores and gun positions in hillside. Rumour rife, many Jap infantry in area. One day work parties returned, had only worked half day. Next day work parties returned at mid-day. That evening at 'Tenco', roll call, Jap officer with the Korean guards took numbers, saluted and informed us that the war was over, marched out of camp and left us on our own.

Lady Mountbatten visited. Col Lilley took over the camp. Red Cross food, clothes. Visited Bangkok to collect any mail. Trucked to airport and on a Dakota to Rangoon and a medical inspection. Home or recuperation in Australia. Len took SS Ormonde to Southampton via Ceylon (Colombo) and Suez. Here we received our first proper winter kit. On board help yourself to food ad lib and no duties. Home at last!

### *Derek Gilbert* - PoW of the Japanese

I was a member of the Territorial Army from 1938 to 1945 and before the war we used to meet in the TA Drill Hall in Dunstable. From October 1939 to January 1940 I was stationed at Lowestoft and from there I was posted to Hawick in Scotland with the 148th Field Regiment of the Royal Artillery. I then went to a camp on Lord Derby's estate at Knowsley and from there to Monmouth where we helped out on a local farm. Whilst there, we were visited by King George VI, and to my surprise he was wearing make-up. (Perhaps to hide how ill he looked?)

In 1940 we embarked on HMS Andes (?). It was her maiden voyage and sailed to Halifax, Nova Scotia. There we embarked on the liner Wakefield and proceeded to Cape Town where we stayed for 3 weeks, then on to India, spending some time at Poona. While there we played hockey and were issued with equipment for the desert. We then sailed to Singapore (January 1942), being bombed and machine-gunned on the way, but we had no support. It was on my 21st birthday that we disembarked and moved up to a pineapple grove with the Ghurkha Rifles. Four of our 25-pounder guns were lost in Singapore harbour when the boat they were on was bombed and sank.

We were in action for three weeks. Then the Japs cut the water supply and Singapore surrendered. We were lined up at the side of the road and watched as the Japanese marched in. We were marched up to Roberts Barracks at Changi and after two weeks I was put in a working party to clean up Singapore. There were dead bodies everywhere; the stench was awful. Our first job was to put 12 bodies at a time from a lorry into plastic sacks. The Japanese trucks were full of Chinese boys who had been made to march down towards the sea and then machine-gunned. 7,000 were massacred.

At Singapore station we were put into steel trucks – 36 men in each truck, standing room only. We travelled for 5 days with only one stop every 24 hours and given only boiled rice and water. Two of the men got dysentery and one died. We had one day of rest at Bangpong then had a 125-mile route march through the jungle during the monsoon. Those who fell sick were dragged into the jungle and shot.

At camp Wampo we started work on the railway, working for 16–17 hours a day. We had almost no food. My brother only lasted for 10 months in those conditions and died of beriberi. We ate snakes and baboons and rats, grilled on sticks of bamboo like kebabs. I tied a lizard to my bed to eat the bugs but eventually I ate the lizard too. In a year the railway was completed but we spent another 18 months in the camp maintaining the railway, before we were moved to Ubon in North Thailand. Here we built a runway for the Japanese Air Force, before being made to dig an enormous pit. If the Japanese had been attacked we would have been shot and buried there. The atom bomb saved my life and millions of others.

At the end of the war the Canadian Air Force landed on the runway and took us to Rangoon, 36 men on each plane. I weighed only 5 stone, 3 pounds. I had weighed over 14 stone at the beginning of the war. It was November 1945 when we sailed back to England.

When I worked on the Burma railway, one of the guards was a Korean Sergeant-Major we called 'Tiger'. In 1943 I had to go into the camp hospital; each morning one man from the hospital would be picked to go to work. One morning, although I was suffering from dysentery, I was picked. That day, because I did not ask the guard's permission to go to the toilet, I was punished and made to hold a sleeper above my head. My knees began to give way and the guard stuck his bayonet into my knee, leaving me with a permanent injury. I dropped the sleeper, which caught the guard's foot. He knocked me to the ground and beat and kicked me as I lay there. But I always thought I would survive.

For many years after, I was very bitter against the Japanese and for 48 years I never spoke about my experiences as a PoW. Then the MoD sent me to see a psychiatrist at the L & D Hospital, who told me that I needed to talk about what had happened to me during those years. I began to talk and after that my nightmares disappeared.

Some years ago my son was working in Tokyo and invited me to visit him; I would not go, I still hated the Japanese people. But five years ago in 2000, a Japanese lady visited our Association at Woburn Sands and persuaded two of our members to go with other Far East ex-PoWs on a reconciliation trip to Japan. During the visit I met two former prison guards. One of my former guards had been sentenced to life imprisonment but had been released after 11 years. He went down on his knees and asked for forgiveness with tears streaming down his cheeks. For a time after that I corresponded with a Japanese Officer. I have now completely forgiven the Japanese for what they did to us, but I cannot forget.

On my visit to Japan, I talked to schoolchildren about what it was like to be a PoW and the teachers encouraged me to tell the children exactly what happened. At the end the children were all in tears.

## *Gerald Wheatley* – with the Gurkhas

Initially I was to serve in The Reconnaissance Corps and after primary training at Bovington, Dorset was posted to the Recce Corps at Catterick in Yorkshire. Here the training was very thorough and required a certain amount of technical ability. The latter was not by any means my major attribute and it was suggested that I should apply for an infantry commission. This I did and to my surprise, after various physical and mental tests, was accepted.

In 1944 I was posted to India as an Officer Cadet. The course at Bangalore took six months and included all the usual subjects plus training in jungle warfare and a compulsory component was instruction in Urdu, which was the language of the Indian Army. The first Gurkhas I met came aboard our ship at Alexandria on our way to India. They were such a cheerful bunch of lads that I decided if ever I had the opportunity, I would feel privileged to serve with them.

At O.T.S. Bangalore (Officer Training School) subject to good reports, we were able to state a preference for the regiments in which we wished to serve. I was very fortunate for I requested 'The Royal Sussex Regiment attached to The Gurkha Rifles' and in July 1945 to my great delight, I was commissioned in The Royal Sussex Regiment (my county regiment) and attached to The First Gurkha Rifles.

Whilst at O.T.S., the end of the war in Europe was announced in May 1945. The surrender of the Japanese came a few months later in August, while I was attending the Gurkha Jungle Training School at Hardwar near Dehra Dun. It was here that I was instructed in the use of Gurkhali language.

Because hostilities had ceased I expected to be sent home to the UK. After all I had volunteered for 'hostilities only'. This term, however, was liberally interpreted to include all areas of unrest in the Far East. So I found myself posted to the 1st Battalion of King George V's Own Gurkha Rifles, which together with the rest of the 20th Indian Division was expected to disarm the repatriated 70,000 Japanese troops who had formed the army of occupation in French Indo-China. They outnumbered us 3 to 1. But our Commander, General Gracey, would not repatriate any Japanese who did not assist him in his other task of returning Indo-China to French colonial rule. The situation was complicated by the fact that, apart from the large fully armed Japanese army, the local population did not wish to return to French rule. So they formed insurgent roaming bands to oppose any attempt to support the French. We were caught in the middle for what was really the start of the Vietnamese War and were ambushed on many occasions. However, our Gurkhas were marvellous and all our convoys up-country got through.

In October 1947 I was a spectator at the surrender of the Yamaguchi Battalion of the Japanese Army to my Indian Army Gurkha regiment. Soon after this, I was ordered to attend a course at the Tactical Training Centre in Clement Town, near Dehra Dun in India. As I received late notice of the course I was allowed to fly from Saigon to Calcutta. The aircraft was an old Dakota fitted with a few bucket seats. It was fascinating to fly right across Thailand and the Burmese jungles, which had been so hostile to our troops only a few months previously. My Gurkha orderly, who had never flown before, was also taken with the view. He said that it was just like a map.

Whilst I was at Clement town the First Gurkhas were also posted back to India and at the end of the course I was sent to the Regimental home at Dharmasala in the Himalayas.

At the Regimental Centre I carried out various jobs such as interviewing our Gurkhas who had been captured at Singapore about conditions in Japanese PoW camps. Some of their stories were appalling. I also served as Unit Education Officer. This was a job that I enjoyed.

But by July 1947, my release order was imminent and I was ready to return home. By the time it did come through in August 1949, India had

Pencil sketch of LIEUTENANT GERALD WHEATLEY in the uniform of The First Gurkha Rifles
(GW)

split into Muslim Pakistan and Hindu India. The border between the two new states had been decided fairly arbitrarily; both sides were disappointed by the final demarcation and both sides retaliated by butchering their neighbours.

The worst task I had in India was to cross the border near Lahore on several occasions as a courier from the Regiment. So bad was the carnage that all trains were stopped and I decided that since I could not get out I might as well stay and help where I could.

I was put in charge of Lower Dharmasala, a small township with a platoon of Gurkhas to keep the peace. We managed to do this but we were unable to prevent an attempt to burn down a Muslim hotel in the middle of the night. We did put out the fire and were able to save the lives of the occupants who would otherwise have suffocated from smoke in their sleep. We received no help from the locals because they were of a different religion.

In September 1947, at long last, my release number was announced and I reported to Deolali transit camp near Karachi in Pakistan.

We sailed for home on 12th October 1947 on the SS Franconia, a lovely gracious ship. We docked in Liverpool on 31st October 1947 and after demobilisation at York I was able to return home to Leagrave.

That Christmas at home made it all worthwhile and it was only recently that I discovered that I was on the Reserve List until 1959!

## *Felix King* – the Desert Rats

I received my call up papers on my nineteenth birthday but my mother hid them away until the following day. I did my training at Beverley in Yorkshire and joined the Durham Light Infantry.

We sailed out to North Africa from West Scotland, joining a large convoy and making our way to North America. We stayed there for about two days but we did not step on land. Many other ships joined the convoy and we sailed back over the Atlantic around South Africa. We stopped for two weeks in Durban for a very nice break. We then sailed on and landed close to Cairo, joining the forces at El Alamein.

The German forces had been forced to move back and our army were moving forward. We were called 'The Desert Rats'. I was asked by a captain what my job had been before the war. I told him that I had just finished a five-year apprenticeship in carpentry and joinery. "You're just the person we need," he said. Most of the time I was used as a backup and timber repairer. Our forces fought along the north coast of Africa until the Germans were defeated. We then sailed across the Mediterranean to land on the south east of Sicily. We forced our way northward until the opposing forces gave up.

Our next move was back to England through the Mediterranean and the Atlantic. We stayed for a while in the Plymouth region, before joining forces in Europe, some on D-Day.

We continued right through the northern districts of Europe, and after a great struggle for everyone, we finished in Trieste. We were sent there as a precaution. We were then transferred to the Oxfordshire and Buckinghamshire Regiment. After a short time we returned to England where a number of us stayed in Saffron Walden in Essex. After about five years I returned to my home in Tilsworth.

### Albert Morgan – my Father's time in the UK and the Far East

My father was Sergeant Major of D Company and after initial training around this area, he moved away from Dunstable. The Company were moved from the 5th Battalion to form the nucleus of the newly formed 6th Battalion Beds and Herts under the command of Major Alistair Miller.

My father went with two of his half-brothers, one of whom was the commanding officer's batman, and the other a squadron/platoon runner. They were moved to guard the radar station at Bawdsley, Woodbridge. They were then moved to Alnmouth in Northumberland to guard RAF Bulmer on the cliffs. My mother laughed – she had a postcard from my father saying, 'I can't tell you where we've been sent to'. But it was post marked Almouth! A day or two later Lord Haw Haw announced on the German radio that the 6th Battalion had been moved to Alnmouth. So much for security. He used to come home whenever possible, about every 6–8 weeks for a weekend or a few days, but it all depended on what was going on. The army came first.

My father received new W.O. II insignia and later was made acting R.S.M. of a new battalion of the Royal Fusiliers. I believe he was involved in the formation of three new battalions of Royal Fusiliers before he went to an Officer Cadet Training Unit. He was commissioned into the Pioneer

Corps and after working in the Liverpool/Manchester area controlling troop movements, he was promoted and became adjutant of an Italian PoW camp at Bryngwyn, near Hereford. He made lifelong friends during this period including his C.O., Major Bramfell and the camp Medical Officer, Dr. Fillipazo, with whom he corresponded at Christmastide until their deaths in the 1970s.

In 1943, my sister, who was in the A.T.S., got married to a serviceman from Sandy, where, incidentally, she still lives. My father 'gave her away' wearing his uniform. By scrounging various bits and pieces my mother was able to make a wedding cake with the thinnest of coatings of icing. The family helped out with items of rationed goods for sandwiches, etc. at the reception.

In 1944, he was posted to India and was stationed at Jalna, in Hyderabad, with a unit of the Indian Pioneer Corps. On completing their training, and that included his learning some Urdu, the unit moved to Burma and followed the frontline advance. Their job was to repair and maintain the lines of communication and help the supply of materials to the troops in the front line. Whilst in India and Burma, he sent me butterflies that had been caught and preserved by his Indian servant. I kept them for some years but eventually they disintegrated.

Just before VE Day as they approached Rangoon, he was told he was being replaced and sent back to the U.K. for demobilisation. He arrived back in June 1945. My mother and I went to Luton Station to meet him off the train from Glasgow, where he had landed, having sailed back on a troopship called the Chittral. He was wearing a 'Bush Hat' with the side turned up similar to the Australians. This hat was covered with red, white and blue bunting for the VJ Day celebrations.

---

*opposite* SEPTEMBER 1939 "D" (Dunstable) Company, The 5th Battalion, The Bedfordshire and Hertfordshire Regiment of the Territorial Army, step out smartly after having refreshed themselves at The Bell, Edlesborough, during their initial training in the first few weeks of the war.

The senior N.C.O. leading on their left is C.S.M. Albert Morgan. The name of the Officer at his side is not known.

These soldiers were shortly to become the nucleus of the new 6th Battalion and were later to be engaged in guarding 'Radar' establishments at Bawdsey Manor, near Woodbridge, Suffolk and Boulmer near Alnmouth, Northumberland. *(AWM)*

### Mrs Joyce Smithson - Discharged

My brother was 19 and became a valet to an officer in the Beds and Herts Regiment of the army. On one occasion he ran up the stairs and started gasping for breath. The officer asked him if he was always breathless after exercise. He said yes, so although he had passed a previous medical he was discharged from the army, which upset him immensely; he was very depressed about that. My mother was naturally pleased but there was a lot of nasty talk from some of the other mothers; they were very unkind. My brother then got a job in the Dunstable Gas Showrooms in High Street North, opposite Grove House.

### Tony Lock - Training Bomber Crews

When the war came I joined the Home Guard first and then the ATC, as I longed to be in the Air Force. Until I was called up I worked at Lloyds bank. I had some good friends in those days; we went dancing to Fred Janes and his band at the town hall every Saturday night. I spent most of the war in the RAF out in what was then South Rhodesia, training bomber crews. After various moves I finished up in Cornwall where Margaret and I still live and attend church regularly.

### Robert Hawkes - D-Day

Early in 1943 I left school with my School Certificate but with absolutely no idea of a career and with the prospect of 'call-up' when I reached 18. I decided to take temporary work at Luton Library and it was there that I met up again with my old childhood friend, Paul. He had volunteered for a young soldiers' regiment and was on leave from Bovington Camp, Dorset. He was enjoying life in the Royal Armoured Corps and I resolved to join him. Naturally my parents were very concerned but accepted that call-up was inevitable and that, by volunteering, one could enter the Service of one's choice. So I cycled to St Albans and signed on and by August 1943 I was reporting to the 58th Training Regiment, R.A.C.

At Bovington there was general primary training followed by a few months intensive course on all aspects of armoured vehicles including driving, maintenance, gunnery, wireless telegraphy and the tactics of tank warfare. I found this difficult and discovered I had little mechanical aptitude. What was I doing in the Armoured Corps? Nevertheless I 'passed out' and was drafted to the 5th Royal Enniskillen Dragoon Guards, then in Northumberland. The year was 1944, when the Allies were expected to invade Europe.

There was great excitement in camp when D-Day was announced over the radio. Then 'Skins' were mobilised and ready to move south, only to be disappointed when orders came to move to Kirkcudbright, Scotland, for tank gunnery practice. July came and the Normandy invasion force was still fighting hard to reach Caen and move inland. At last we were ordered to move to Bury St Edmunds where we received a book on 'France and the French', 200 French francs and we made our wills. From Bury we went by train south via North London where we witnessed the aftermath of a V2 rocket on houses near the railway. Rescuers were frantically digging in the rubble and shouted, "Give the bastards hell," as we passed slowly by.

In full marching order, but without our tanks, we marched on to an LSI (Landing Ship Infantry) in Portsmouth harbour. In convoy we eventually passed out at dusk into the Channel to the accompaniment of the woop, woop, woop of destroyers and the loud intercom instructions between ships, across the water.

The French coast came into view at dawn and with it the amazing sight of hundreds of ships including the Warspite, which was firing broadsides inland. We went ashore on motorised rafts and marched in file up the beach between white guide tapes. It was my first time abroad and I was fascinated by the scene, excited and apprehensive.

The regiment became part of the 7th Armoured Division, a replacement for a regiment which had suffered heavy casualties. We collected our Cromwell tanks and I was made co-driver/hull machine gunner in a crew of five. The city of Caen fell at last and then it became a race for the Seine.

My brief contribution to victory came to an end on August 26th, when, as leading tank we encountered stiff opposition at the entrance to a village. Our tank was hit twice by armour piercing shells, one of which ignited around 150 gallons of petrol. In the resulting conflagration sadly two crew members were killed. I escaped through my hatchway, helped by two colleagues who had dismounted from their vehicles and by returning fire, forced back enemy infantry. They were subsequently awarded the Military Cross.

This part of my war ended in the British General Hospital in Bayeux. While in there I received the distressing news that my friend Paul had been killed in action whilst serving with the 13th/18th Hussars. I still keep in touch with one of my brave rescuers and on the 58th anniversary of the battle I had the honour, as sole survivor of our crew, to unveil a roadside memorial plaque to those who died, provided by members of the French community.

My abiding memory of Normandy will always be the lush closed-in character of the Normandy bocage and the pervasive smell of dead cattle.

### Roy Oakley - Building Bridges

Leaving Dunstable Grammar School in 1939, I spent two years at university and a spell of engineering on air-raid shelters and other wartime activities before joining the Royal Engineers. I took part in the 'invasion' of Europe mostly building bridges and repairing roads, but with no news-worthy incidents (my platoon distinguished itself building a bridge across the Rhine under fire, but I was on home leave at the time. The officer who stood in for me was given an MC – I was not envious!)

I crossed over to France on D+6, and in one of those curious coincidences, walking up the gangway of the LSI which ferried us over, I saw to my surprise two of my school friends, Cyril (a naval sub Lieutenant) and John (a Lieutenant in the Marines). They gave me a warm welcome and I travelled across the Channel in one of their cabins, in a great deal more comfort than I expected!

### Douglas Darby - a Surveyor and Saxophonist

I was engaged as a surveyor in a professional office in London but naturally enough at the beginning of the war, they gave me notice and I left in the middle of October. I then had one or two temporary jobs, partly with a friend of mine, who was working with the Great Western Railway, and we had quite a few good times planning extensions to wartime factories. One was in the sugar beet factory in Whittington, where we spent 3 or 4 days carrying out a survey for an extra rail line. Then I thought I'd better look around and see what the army had to offer and found that a local organisation working with the county council were forming a surveyors and engineers unit to go over to France. When I had a word with them, they said that they had enough people but that they would keep me in mind. They were sent out forward of our lines and within a week of them arriving in France, were all captured and spent the whole of the war in prisoner of war camps.

We then waited for my call up papers; being a surveyor I had ordinary, preliminary training in an artillery unit at Brighton (a general call-up station). After the formal training certain of us were given an exam but it was so simple I just filled in the forms without thinking really. They wanted to sort out the people that could cope with written work or map making. That resulted in me being posted to the First Survey Regiment, Royal Artillery, at the time stationed in Scotland. We had quite a journey and as soon as we got there we were met at the station by a large van. As I stepped towards the tailboard somebody called out, "Is Darby here?" I said, "Yes!" "Right, I'm the sergeant that runs the unit band and we've heard that you're not bad on the saxophone. Oh good, I see you've brought it with you. Right, 8 o'clock tonight, canteen, first rehearsal!" That began a very, very interesting and informative development because right through until I was demobbed six years later, I was given all sorts of privileges. I worked in the adjutant's office and whenever there was any work to be done I was called, but mainly we formed a little band and were in great demand. We were stationed in Yorkshire for quite some time, training after Dunkirk; there were various ATS units, land army people and canteen staff and every Thursday night, it was open night and the band played on!

We were then transferred to another unit and I'm not going to say it was arranged but, on the morning when the whole of the first unit was taken down to the station, I asked the sergeant major, "I've got enough kit to carry, what do I do with my saxophone?" He said, "Keep quiet, Darby. If you tell anybody else, you're on a charge, but you're not coming with us. There's plenty of work for you to do here and we've got you posted to somewhere, where they'll want you." From there we went to another unit, which had just been formed because they knew there would be artillery work wanted in England. Well, that suited me down to the ground. Then we were sent down to Salisbury Plain for a time for further training on detailed work and then the whole unit moved down to the south coast, stationed either at Canterbury or Hastings. We didn't know it, of course, but we were in preparation for D-Day, although it became quite obvious from the build up of troops and so on.

I think it's true to say that we had no real equipment, as we know today. All we had were ordinary microphones, but we set up a network, more or less across the whole of South East England, which was to pick up any noises from the other side. I suppose somebody knew that it was going to be the terror weapon, the V1s, the buzz bombs, and our network picked up the sound. We could plot it as it came in because of course, once it set off, it was always in a straight line and by reversing that we could tell roughly where it had come from. By this time our unit was nearly 1,100 strong with all sorts of meteorologists, RAF liaison, Royal Engineers and so on keeping complete control of that area of South East England. If on the news bulletins you heard our bombers were out again over Pas de Calais, that was as a result of some of our work.

I remember the first one coming in, or one of the first ones; I was off duty actually and while I was walking back from the local forces canteen I heard a very strange sound. There was a warden on the other side of the road saying, "What sort of a plane is that?" I said, "I don't know, it isn't a plane, and it's not like any of the German engines that I know." He replied, "I think you'd better get back to your unit, don't you?" That was one of the earliest V1 plottings that we located.

Germans, of course, are as clever as we are, or they were then. When they found out what was happening, they made moveable launching pads. So, whatever our bombers did, they missed them because the V1 launchers had moved away. Off duty, we used to sit up on the cliffs and watch the Americans, who had a technique of flying alongside the V1s and by flipping their wings, flip them over. That was all very well, but only for a few weeks, as once they tipped one over and it landed on a school some few miles inland and all the pupils were killed. They then cancelled that way of doing it and we were very much engaged in positioning rockets right along the front of Hastings. Our survey people carried out proper positioning of 8, 16 and 24 rocket launchers, which were quite effective. Still some of them got through to London, but many were caught up on the balloon barrage.

On one particular short leave I went to London to see my aunt but spent the whole of one night underneath the shelter in the front room. It was quite a reasonable visit but we didn't do much, except sit there and listen to see if anything came a little bit too near! I also cycled quite a bit and one incident

I do remember was putting the bike on the early morning train to get home (when on leave) and then cycling across London to St Pancras station. I got there quite easily as I knew most of the streets, having worked there before the war, but as I got to the bottom of Tottenham Court Road, a policeman and several wardens were standing right across the street. "Where are you going? You can't go there," they said. An unexploded mine had not landed but was caught up in the overhead wires and they were evacuating the area. I got on my bike again and cycled over to St Pancras via a different route and went home for a good 24 hours leave.

As the fighting moved northwards it was decided that it wouldn't be a bad idea to take our whole unit over to Belgium. We went in over Mulberry Harbour; it was very rocky and we had a very seesaw journey from the boat until we got the trucks on to the land. The place was absolutely just as you could imagine, completely churned up everywhere, but fortunately it was dry. When we got up the slopes further on, what was up the top? A Salvation Army van! "Want a cup of tea?" I've always remembered the Salvation Army after that! We moved along to somewhere near Brussels and set our unit up there. We had shifts of 8 hours on and 8 hours off then 16 hours off so you could carry out your other chores. Things died down as we got further and further up into the country. One particular day I borrowed the unit bike and decided to take a look at Brussels, as I had not been there before. About half way there I was stopped by the military police and had a bit of a job explaining why I was there! They told me to go back to my unit and stay there. By the time I got back, I realised they had broken through the French line in the Battle of the Bulge and for the next 3 or 4 days we were confined to barracks. There was so much noise with all the troop tanks, vehicles, etc that came thundering through from all units, American as well. Of course we now know they stopped the Bulge breaking through into our territory.

We then had no time for the band but we did have some very good friends, including 2 or 3 musicians in the unit. We were also befriended by a professional architect, a gentleman: the man who had designed the chapel for the former Queen of Belgium. We had a musical evening on VE day after I borrowed a saxophone that had been tucked away in an attic to prevent it being taken by German troops. We had a very good concert that night and then it was a question of waiting to be demobbed.

I was then posted to a unit right on the Danish border with the job of looking after 3 SS men who were being held in the barracks prison. There, I approached the senior officer and suggested keeping up morale by having some music. "Well," he told me, "You've got yourself a job, organise a band." I had previously written back home on official paper and asked for my own saxophone to be sent over. Father crated it up in his factory in Luton and within a week it was delivered to me with no damage at all. We then looked around for other musicians and with no difficulty at all we found a pianist, a bass player, guitarist, trumpet player and started off by playing a lot of the popular tunes without any music. One day a chap came up to me and said,"I play the trombone, do you think I could come along?" I said, "You are!" He came along and said, " I don't know what my band master would say, I've never played this kind of music before, I'm in the Salvation Army." But of course with the training he had received, within 2 to 3 weeks he was able to perform solos. We found a permanent place where we held weekly dances, which lasted for about 6 or 7 months. Some of the older residents asked us to play in their village hall and so we often went out to different places to play. I had a really happy time there. I had duties to do during the day, rehearsals if necessary, or what we called blanket drill, asleep in the afternoon as we would be playing late that night!

We then moved back through Germany and into France on our way home. At one staging camp they knew I was amongst the people in that particular unit and I was asked to play in the interval for a band that were entertaining people in the local village hall. For about half an hour I played solo; it was quite an experience. I was finally demobbed in Northampton and caught the train back home to Luton.

### Reg Geary – the Fitter

I went for a medical and was told I'd got heart problems and would not be able to fly, so they suggested that, as they badly needed engineers, l could train to become one. Engineering was, and still is, a hobby of mine and I took a piece of my work along with me to show the officer in charge. After looking at my work he said he'd put me down as a flight mechanic. Then he said, "We'll give you promotion straightaway, you can be a fitter." I said, "What's the difference between a flight mechanic and a fitter?" Well, he said, "It's a shilling a day more and you'll get promoted quicker!" So from there I was kitted out and received my injections. I'd told my wife I would see her later that day but I was sent straight up to Morecambe for very intensive drill training. From there I was sent to Cannock Chase in Staffordshire for ten month's technical training and passed with flying colours.

In early December 1940 I got a fortnight's leave. Towards the end of the second week a policeman came to see me with a message to report to Thorney Island. I'd never heard of it! Luckily when I got off the train I met a couple of chaps that I'd been with while training in Staffordshire.

It was very noisy because there were 49 guns on Hayling Island, helping to defend

REG GEARY (RG)

the south coast. At first I was afraid that the camp could at any time be bombed, but we only had one daylight raid. On my first night, a group of chaps that had been stationed there for some time were sitting round a table calmly playing cards with all this gunfire going on. I was sitting on my bed in the corner when one of them said, "Don't worry; someone will let us know if there's going to be a raid. This happens every night." I was surprised just how quickly I got used to it all.

We were sent to various places. At one camp in 1941 we met several young ladies that flew bomber aircraft, smashing looking girls in beautiful uniforms. One of them called me up into the cockpit of a Blenheim. "Corporal," she said. "I haven't flown a Blenheim for some time; will you run over the controls for me?" I told her that I'd be only too pleased! I met her after the war. She was one of only a few girls that could fly four-engine bombers.

Shortly afterwards we started to look after Hudsons, originally designed as a passenger aircraft. We were posted to Ireland in 1942, working on long range Liberator aircraft. Occasionally I'd be posted to Iceland where on two or three occasions I was in charge of the ground crew for three aircraft and was mentioned in dispatches. I thoroughly enjoyed my time there.

## P Underwood – the Bombing Campaign

My brother (a photographer) went to France with the R.A.F. at Dunkirk and he came out from St Nazaire with a convoy in which one of the troopships was sunk with a great loss of life. Luckily he wasn't on that particular ship and was taken to Liverpool. Everything was chaotic in England at the time and a lot of troops were sent home. When he arrived home he was absolutely shattered and slept for several days. Mum said he was home on leave for a month.

In 1942 my brother was killed. Prior to that our bombing campaign was beginning to get under way and early in '42 we had that first 1,000 bomber raid on Cologne. My cousin Jack was a pilot in a Lancaster on that raid and was shot down and killed. He'd been shot down before and survived, but this time he and his crew died. That hit the family. Casualties were coming in all the time, some you knew, some you didn't. Cliff, a friend of my brother, he was a favourite of the family – I remember the last time I saw him and he said, "Cheerio, you won't see me again," and the next thing we heard, he was dead.

## Ulric Craig Carpenter – the Tail Gunner

At the age of 12, I moved with my parents and four siblings from Canada to Britain in the spring of 1938. My father was an 'Old Boy' (former pupil of Dunstable Grammar School) and I was enrolled as a boarder in the same school commencing the Fall term of 1938. I was a very proud member of 'Brown House' and I produced a fair number of points in all of the sports and cadet company endeavours.

1939 saw the outbreak of the Second World War. We had all seen the graphic pictures in such magazines as The London Illustrated News, of the German bombers striking at cities in Spain. I remember sitting in the 'air raid shelters' behind the main school building and wondering when we might make the Illustrated News. Soon we saw the names of 'Old Boys' appearing on the school honour roll, some were known recent graduates. I had six brothers and sisters in the Canadian Forces and by September 1940 my brother Jack, a Hurricane pilot in the Battle of Britain, was killed in action. I could hardly wait to join-up.

In the summer of 1943 I travelled to London, a letter from my father to the Canadian High Commissioner in my hand, and was sworn in as a

ULRIC CRAIG CARPENTER *(UCC)*

member of the Royal Canadian Air Force. I was instructed that I would be notified when and where to report for duty.

I received my posting notice – report to the RAF Air-Crew Receiving Centre in London at 0800 hrs the following Monday morning. I also received my first taste of 'military discipline'. The night train from Holyhead to London was held up due to the tracks being bombed. We had to detrain and take a bus to complete the trip. I arrived at 1030 hrs at the RAF Air-Crew Receiving Centre in Regent's Park for the three-week selection process and was promptly charged for being late for duty! At the end of the course a group of teenagers were selected for transfer to Canada for pilot training. Not wishing to return to Canada for fear of missing the entire war, I requested other aircrew training being conducted in England. My posting notice was for Air Gunner training. Off to war I went. However, before leaving London I managed to make a two-day trip to Dunstable Grammar School to attend a dance at the Priory. I was very proud of my new RCAF uniform. It was great seeing and talking with members of the Cadet Corps and the many boarders with whom I shared happy memories.

I was transferred to Bridgnorth for Ground Training, then on to Dal Cross for Aircrew Training. So much training in so short a time. At RAF Station Dal Cross, in the heart of Scotland, I found myself the only Canadian (Colonial) in a mixed bag of Czechoslovakians, French North Africans and Polish, along with a large contingent of young British airmen. I was assigned as an air gunner trainee with a crew of French North Africans with a Czechoslovakian pilot (who incidentally won the Iron Cross when flying for the Germans against Spain). I was the tail gunner and the only one that spoke English.

When my tour was up at RAF Dal Cross I had received my wings and the rank of Sergeant. I had requested a transfer to a Canadian Air Force squadron and was subsequently posted to RAF Wellesbourne. The first day on site I was picked as tail gunner in an all-Canadian crew; and a first rate crew we became. We flew day and night becoming ready for Operations very quickly. However, the Lancaster as the bomber of choice had now superseded the Wellington aircraft. We, as a crew, were posted to RAF Topcliffe to join number 6 Group Bomber Command.

Flying this huge four-engine bomber was a delight. Our 'corkscrew' to evade German fighters did a first rate evasion manoeuvre. Our first cross-channel dodge run did not end as smoothly as expected, as we landed in a farmer's field wheels-up and out of fuel. Various scrapes and bumps had us off flying for sometime. I ended up as the Fire Chief for the Base, the town of Thirsk and RAF Dalton. We came together again as a crew at the end of the war to empty the 'Bomb Dumps'. This day and night flying saw us dropping bombs in the North Sea until the dumps were empty.

I returned to Canada, obtained my release and returned to college to finish off my education specialising in Public Relations, subsequently returning to the RCAF Air Defence Command during the 'Cold War'. I was transferred from the air force to Public Service and ended my career on the staff of the Prime Minister of Canada, The Right Honourable Pierre Elliot Trudeau.

### Yvonne Wooster - Wireless Training in Blackpool

I wasn't in a reserved occupation and I didn't want to work on the buses or in a factory so I joined the WRAF to become a wireless operator. After completing our square bashing in Wilmslow in Cheshire, which was torture really, I was sent to Honeybourne in Worcestershire which consisted of a huge training aerodrome. About 1,000 pilots were in training there from all over the world – New Zealand, Australia, Poland and Canada. We were just used as skivvies really while we waited for our training. We had a woman flight officer and a WRAF flight officer who were real battleaxes and if they didn't put us on lavatory duty they found some other horrible job for us. One day we had to take the dining tables out of the huge mess hall, turn them upside down and remove all the chewing gum stuck to them. It was a very hot summer and sometimes we went to the local farms and picked fruit to earn a bit of extra money. In July some of us were sent to Blackpool to do our wireless operator training. I went with 6 other girls and was billeted with a lovely family.

We then stayed in a boarding house where there were 14 of us and only one bathroom. Even then, we were not allowed to use the bath! We had to wash using just the hand basin. There were 3 of us in one bedroom and 2 of us slept in a double bed. There was very little light in our room, so we bought a lamp from Woolworth's and left it in one of our bedroom cupboards, but while we were working the old boy came in and pinched it. The owners also used to pinch our rations and we were given really awful food. When on washing up duty we found our rations hidden away in the cupboard. We were very unhappy there. Once or twice a week we used to march with a band from central Blackpool where we were based, to the Derby Baths in north Blackpool with our towels under our arms. I remember all the holiday makers used to line the streets when we did that! A few days before Christmas we moved to Wiltshire and missed all our Christmas mail that year. This upset some of the girls, as many felt very homesick. I was jolly lucky because I was courting Bob and, while we were stationed in Blackpool, he was also sent there on a course for a few weeks. He took me out to the pictures and the theatre and stopped me feeling too miserable. He had some relatives in Bath and they asked me to stay for Christmas. I hitched a lift in a lorry to see him then.

When I was qualified I was sent to Chatham in Kent to the Fleet Air Arm headquarters which was built underground. Just before D-Day the two girls that I worked with and myself were sent to Maidstone in Kent. We had to take messages from the Fleet Air Arm reconnaissance planes. We were there for about 3 or 4 months and during that time we saw the first VE bombers (the buzz bombs) coming over. They made the most peculiar noise that we had ever heard, a bit frightening really. I then went back to Chatham until I was demobbed.

### Aubrey Jones - out in India

Having sat and passed a competitive exam in May, on Tuesday 5th September 1939, on the third day of the Second World War, I reported to RAF Halton in Bucks. After medicals and uniform issue, I started life as an aircraft apprentice in the skilled trade of airframe fitter. This was a three-year course, combined with a mixed programme of marching, drill, school and practical training. Pay was 1 shilling per day, receiving 6 shillings a fortnight, the balance paid when going on Christmas or summer leave. In April 1941 we were told that a shortage of skilled labour meant our apprenticeships were being terminated. The marks for continuous assessment of practical work were averaged, weighted and our final school exam added, giving me 57%, Aircraftman Second Class. Pay – 1 shilling and three pence a day.

23rd March 1941, posted to 32 Maintenance Unit, St Athan, South Wales. Week 1 – cleaning lorries, I complained. Weeks 2 and 3 – nominally in charge of six young ladies (WAAF) – embarrassing. They knew what they were doing. Mid June – detached to 13MU, Henlow, Beds, sorting out boxes of odds and ends into matching nuts, bolts, etc. It was very hot, 12-hour days, 7 days a week; I became run-down, developing boils, whitlows. After 3 weeks I returned to St Athan, unfit for work and detailed as an Engineering Officer's runner. Early August 1941, volunteered for Overseas Service. Sent to Personnel Dispatch Centre, West Kirby on the Wirral. Embarkation leave, given draft number and kitted out in khaki drill. Inoculated. Waited.

Early October 1941 – caught the slow train to Glasgow Docks, then boarded the SS Almanzora for a night passage to the north of Ireland and then on to Freetown in West Africa for fuel and water supplies. Explosions were heard and rumours of German U boats circulated. They were then detected and depth-charged. We then arrived in Durban in South Africa a month after leaving the UK.

Seaman's Mission, Durban – walked along a brightly lit sea front on a balmy spring evening in the southern hemisphere and ate bacon, egg, liver, kidneys, steak and tomato for 6 pence. Next day we caught the train for a three-day journey to Cape Town and on to Pollsmoor Rest Camp for 'Fitness and Acclimatisation'. The former consisted of PE, drill – marching three miles to Muizenberg for sea and sunbathing.

7th December 1941 – after a two-day train journey, we set up a tented camp on the Veldt, a couple of miles outside Port Alfred, Eastern Cape, about half way between East London and Port Elizabeth. The Japanese attacked Pearl Harbour the same day. Mornings were spent transferring equipment from railhead to field. A concrete apron, hangers, storerooms, cookhouse and dormitory blocks start being built. However, our Christmas dinner, and a proper one at that, was served miraculously from a field kitchen. There were no officers on site; they would traditionally serve Christmas dinner.

In February 1942, aircraft arrived. These were Airspeed Oxford wooden twin-engined carrying a pilot, a gunnery instructor and two trainee gunners. Each gunner carried his self-assembled belt of ammunition, each bullet tipped in blue or red dye, to be fired from a Vickers machine gun situated in the turret. The other aircraft were Northropp (USA built), containing a pilot and drogue operator. A drogue (cloth tube) is released and towed above the Indian Ocean; the gunners then fire at the drogue and their hits are recorded. The drogue is then repaired with stick-on patches. I was allocated to B Flight Hanger to carry out overhauls, servicing, modifications and repairs to the Oxfords. There was an unwritten rule that the fitters flew on air test completion of a job. A Warrant Officer pilot, a German Jew, South African Air Force veteran, invited me to take over on one occasion. Accepting, I piloted on a compass course, eighty odd miles to Port Elizabeth. On March 1st 1942 I took an exam, passing as an Aircraftsman, first class. In May I was nineteen and in mid July, I passed another exam with 80%, to become Leading Aircraftsman.

The River Kowie, where the 1820 settlers had landed, was silted over but there was a blue lagoon we could use for a swim as long as we avoided the sharks! The area was predominantly used for fruit farming – oranges, pineapples and peaches. The East Bank of the River Kowie sported an Anglican Church, a cinema and a chemist. West Bank had more shops and houses together with a Methodist Church and residential hotel, the latter becoming the Officers' Mess. Almost all the civilian population were of English descent and we were well looked-after.

All good things must end and I left in August 1943 to join RAF India Command, subsequently South East Asia Command (SEAC). Had short stops in transit camps in Bombay and Calcutta before reporting to No 1 Reserve Aircraft Pool at Asansol, near Burnpur Steelworks, Bihar Province, looking after Wellington bombers. No actual work to be done except when a squadron needed a replacement aircraft. In October 1943 I was promoted to Corporal on 2s 6d a day. The following month we flew the unit to Bishnapur in the Bengal jungle. The Vickers Wellington was a twin-engined medium bomber; the structure designed by Barnes Wallis (he of the dam-busting bomb) and was made of strong, slightly flexible, fabric covered lattice-work. On board with my full kit and tool-box, I watched fascinated as the long, narrow wings moved gracefully up and down.

Life in the jungle was not pleasant. Hot, humid, isolated and boring, living in bamboo and mud/dung 'bashas'. The only normal contact with life outside was the radio kept in the cookhouse, switched on in the evening for the news. The cook received a Christmas card from his wife, apologising for being pregnant by an American soldier. One of our group died of heat exhaustion, so with only 20 of us, tempers became frayed.

Not a happy time. We had transferred to Bristol Beaufighters; powerful, twin-engined fighter-bombers. Rather illicitly, I would ask the pilot if he would be retuning the same day, if so, could I go with him? Standing on the hatch behind the pilot, with my hands gripping the back of his seat, take-off along the runway between the trees was quite exhilarating! In the early months of 1944 I developed jungle ulcers, which wouldn't heal, then dengue fever. I was sent into sick bay before being sent to the Hill Camp at Chakrata. From the railhead at Dehra Dun, I sat next to the driver. Reaching our destination at about 2 am, he advised me to sit on a bench facing east. I wrapped up against the cold and waited. The sky started to appear behind the blackness, then a dazzling flash as the hidden sun's rays hit the snow covered crest of Nanda Devi, a hundred miles away.

The carriage of an Indian troop train was some 18 ft long with a doorway (but without a door) in each corner, a wooden bench along each side and two benches, back to back along the centre-line. At the front end there was a transverse bench for food preparation and at the other end, an un-partitioned hole in the floor. The ration truck supplied tins of corned (bully) beef, condensed milk together with sacks containing hard-tack biscuits, tea, sugar and a metal bucket. At meal times the train would stop, a handful of tea put in the bucket and one of the lads would take it to the engine. Placed on the ground in the right place, the engine driver would open a valve and steam would condense in the bucket, producing a welcoming brew of 'char'. On the second day of leaving Dahra Dun, I coaxed the ration corporal into giving me a jar of pickled onions for a party. It was my 21st birthday and I had a party on the train eating the onions, corned beef and biscuits!

On VE day I was in Secunderabad on a Junior NCO's course. Another Welsh corporal and I spent the evening in town. Returning to camp, a combination of alcohol and euphoria led to us hurling a potted plant through the guardroom window. Fleeing into the dark, we returned to our hut, laughing hysterically until the clump of boots from the Service Police caused instant sobriety. We quickly jumped into bed, pulled up the sheets and put the mosquito nets down – they didn't notice us.

Again, I spent another birthday on a train. I was being posted from Secunderabad to 362 Maintenance Unit, but this unit could not be located, so approximately four weeks were spent on trains or in transit camps until, as a temporary measure, I was attached to 1344 (Hurricane) Flight at RAF Sambre, near Goa. At altitude it was comparatively cool, so my stay from 17th June was a most welcome break. To my delight, in the middle of July I was listed for repatriation but fate (or the RAF) had its revenge. My previous unit had moved for Bengal to Agartala in the Tripura Estate, near the Assam border, and wanted me back.

I travelled from one side of India to the other via train, paddle steamer, then train again. The reason for my recall? They were holding a tin of 50 Senior Service cigarettes, sent by my parents for my May birthday! En route again but at a stop in the Calcutta transit camp, they lost my movement order. Several of us were in the same position but after some days we took the initiative. We identified the time and date of a train going to Bombay, bluffed our way past the ticket collector at Howrah station, mingled with legitimate travellers for rations and made it to the Bombay transit camp. There a friendly Australian Flight Sergeant put us in a dormitory, put our names in a hat, told us to stay put then proceeded to cut red tape. Several lucky souls were called for a flight back to the UK on returning aircraft. Mine was the offer of sole occupancy of a twin officer's cabin on the SS Orontes. As we edged our way out of Bombay Harbour, all the guns in port went off and I dived for cover. It was August 15th and the Japanese had capitulated. The war was over.

In November 1946, I met Ena. We were married in March 1947 at St Margaret's Methodist Church in Luton on the first day of my embarkation leave, prior to a posting to Japan. But that's another story.

### *Bernard Stevens* - in a Mobile Repair Unit

I was called up after 12 months deferment in the autumn of 1941 and had to report to Penarth in Cornwall, although we did our basic training in Blackpool. I remember doing PT in the middle of the road, in side streets. It was in quite a nice residential area; on one occasion we had to change out of our trousers into our shorts in the street, which I don't think the residents appreciated very much! We were there for about 6 weeks and moved to a unit in Chigwell where we were posted to the Second Tactical Air Force. (Before we went to Chigwell we went to Eastbourne and stayed in the Grand Hotel for about a month while training. We got leave that Christmas; the following Christmas was spent in Eindhoven. We stayed in a monastery there; the monks came to the church dressed in their brown robes, I think they probably lived in private houses while we stayed in their monastery!) We were in the equipment section while we were there (the barrage balloon storage place); there was a big field where ambulances were made ready for the African effort. We used to receive instructions to get so many ambulances ready for collection the next morning and paint all the shipping instructions on the doors for when they reached the docks. Although we used to have to cover these instructions up with brown paper before they left Chigwell so that no one knew where they were going.

I was then moved to Croydon Aerodrome where we were supplied the material for converting caravans for shipping to Africa; one of these caravans was for Montgomery – it had lots of furniture in it. That was the main job of the unit; it kept us very busy and was a nice job; preparing caravans for the African invasion. Then from Croydon we started getting ready for going overseas and after a trip down to the New Forest we finished up at RAF Faversham. We went from Gosport, we should have gone about D 13 – our job being a mobile motor repair unit. The idea was that we followed up the advanced airfields; we carried quite a lot of spares for cars, lorries and motorbikes. If any of the vehicles broke down they would be collected by our unit and, if they could be repaired in 24 hours, we would do the job and return them. We had a unit of about 70 people and travelled in convoy (in Normandy); sometimes we would be in a place for about 2–3 days and other times we would be there for about a week or so, it just all depended how the advanced airfields were progressing.

Before we went over on one of the tank aircraft, we were given one or two tryouts, driving through water, coming off ramps, things like that. We went down to Shoreham and went into a boating pool to practice for this; we drove though water and up ramps into the loading craft and backed out again and then we had to wait until it got dark and do the same thing again with torches. It was quite a good day out!

We loaded up at Fareham, then set off towards night-time and, when we got into the Channel near Arromanches, we anchored for the night. It was a bit rough because we had to go and anchor all the vehicles down. A lot of the war ships were shelling over the top of us on to the beaches but anyhow, by the time daybreak came it all quietened down again and we were able to drive off up Arromanches beach into a field. We took off all the sealing that had been on the exhaust pipes and did not see any trouble. We then set off into the countryside and stayed for about a fortnight; the conditions were fairly hard in a way, we ate tinned bacon, had only one slice of bread a day, otherwise you had these very dry thick biscuits. We lived in the vans and had our own beds; each van had a row of metal lockers for storage and our own generator to supply electricity. We were fairly near Bayeux at that time, then as we drove up through the Falaise Gap we saw our first sight of real bombing; we saw nothing but heaps of rubble. As the airfield moved forward, so we went up and then of course we got into Belgium and then into Holland. We finished in Celle where they signed the treaty. Our unit did not get attacked; there was a certain amount of aircraft about at the time but we were lucky, being a comparatively small unit, and covered all the vehicles in camouflage when we stopped anywhere. We were then posted back to Morecambe, England. I got put on to a billeting unit, checking up on different places where they put troops to stay; it was an interesting time. Some of our unit got posted to India from there but I got posted back to Henlow. I was there for about 12 months until the end of the war came and I was demobbed.

### C L Hughes – Volunteered for RAF Aircrew

1941 – Called up and posted for initial training to Torquay. After weeks of sunshine and exercise and frantic rushing around, we had become extremely smart and a credit to our uniforms. We all had a somewhat haunted look, however, due to the reported presence in Torquay of Air Commander B (I swear he was 7' tall), Head of RAF Training Command. Anyone who failed to spot his car and did not salute was destined for some dreadful punishment. We finally met him in an air-raid shelter in the cliffs where we had to wear our issued flying kit. Unfortunately this was old assorted stock and we looked a poor bunch.

At the passing out parade we had to join with other units in the area and march 6 abreast behind an army band whose music was slow and, when marching, was even slower. Whereas we only marched at light infantry pace; normally not a great success.

Then a rushed posting came through and we travelled by train to the Manchester area at night, in the rain. A military police sergeant with a torch took us to a field of tents and, after allocating 8 men to a tent, left us in total darkness to sort our kit and ourselves out. We slept in our wet uniforms and next morning all the glamour had gone and we looked like PoWs.

We spent two weeks on a troopship off Glasgow, which sailed and immediately broke down so we were given leave until another ship was found. This next ship was filled with 750 of us, hundreds of Scottish troops bound for Singapore and merchant navy seamen going to the USA to collect liberty ships. There were eight troopships altogether in convoy with eleven assorted escorts. We had a calm and peaceful voyage until a warship appeared, identified by many as German but it was in fact the Prince of Wales. Years later I found out that this was Mr Churchill returning from a conference with Roosevelt. Apparently he wanted to see a convoy and ours was chosen.

Nearing Canada we woke up to find ourselves alone until a Canadian warship arrived to escort us to Halifax. While travelling by train to Toronto, at every stop the local ladies set a stall to give us apples and chocolate. For a short time we lived in the Toronto Exhibition buildings with hundreds of beds and washing facilities for the first time since Torquay.

Since our draft was to train in America, we had to disguise ourselves in civilian suits to avoid breaking neutrality. But what a disguise; 750 airmen in double-breasted grey suits, either dark grey, nearly black, pale grey, nearly white or medium grey chalk stripe. Shirts, black ties and normal RAF shoes. On camp in Georgia, we wore coveralls and nothing else.

We now had US Army officers to control us and civilian instructors to teach us to fly. My group had a German instructor who appeared to hate us immediately. My exam results were good, so I was moved from the barracks into a bungalow by myself. However, my flying was not as good and after a report by our German, I was checked by the Chief Instructor, and then by a US army officer, who said that sadly I should return to Canada for the winter.

Canada – Prince Edward Island in the Gulf of St Lawrence. The pilots based here on Avro Ansons were members of the London Transport flying club at Broxbourne, Herts before the war. The Anson was an outdated aircraft, which had an opening at the top so you could stick your head out to take sextant shots and a hole underneath in order that you could see a target to bomb. Another even worse feature was the undercarriage, which you had to raise or lower with a handle underneath the pilot; something like 60 turns, I think, was necessary.

Navigation was truly annoying as, whatever course you gave the pilot, he would then tell you what he thought he would fly instead, especially at night when all towns were fully lit up. In the end we worked our flight plan after we had landed and the experience was useless. In any case, these pilots refused to let us move about in the aircraft after they had trimmed it. However, we graduated even if our standards were poor and of little practical use.

May 1942. We sailed for home on the Empress of Scotland, originally Empress of Japan but hurriedly renamed. There were thousands of French Canadian troops on board and we had to line the staircases, as they tended to kick the panelling if they didn't like the food!

More training, this time in the North of Scotland on Wellingtons. The first time I climbed into one, I found the smell awful. The smell was dope, (used to tighten the canvas covering), the Elsan toilet, which never seemed to be emptied, and of course the smell of oil and petrol. Apart from this it was a good aircraft and we came to appreciate it, although at 20,000 feet it was bitterly cold. With a geodetic body covered in canvas, it was never designed for the comfort of the fliers. At this time crews were formed. A pilot and navigator together would choose a bomb-aimer, wireless operator and a rear gunner from those thought suitable.

November 1942 – New Canadian squadron forming near Darlington. Due to the heavy losses of new crews on operation, this consisted of 50% Canadian airmen with the rest of the crew originating from the RAF, RAAF (Royal Australian Air Force) and New Zealand crews. Called the Lion squadron, we were adopted by the MGM Film Company and given some special privileges such as free entry to MGM cinemas anywhere in the world. Our gradual reputation as a 'safe' crew meant that many new pilots did their first 'op' with us.

When some 'boffin' at HQ thought it would be a good idea for 3 aircraft from our squadron to bomb Kiel in daylight, we realised this was a death or glory chance of suicide. The idea was for the aircraft to cross the North Sea in cloud, drop down over Kiel, bomb the German fleet, pop back into the cloud and fly home. The CO chose himself, a Flight Commander and our crew to carry this out. As we staggered out from briefing, a message came though to alter it to one aircraft. The CO said he would go but would take me as navigator, to the horror of the rest of my crew. Luckily someone on high came to their senses and it was finally cancelled.

In the end, we were one of the few crews who completed a 30-operation tour and were then dispersed as instructors. Some months afterwards, my pilot and I were decorated by the King with the DFC at Holyrood Palace. After courses at Staff Navigation College and then at RAF College Cranwell, I finished the war as a Chief Instructor with the rank of Flight Lieutenant. Aircraft flown in the 5 years were Ansons, Wellingtons and Halifaxes.

## *J Reason* – Volunteers

Those early months, stretching from September through to the following summer, became known as the phoney war. In the course of that time, my father was called up for the army. He snorted about that, because twenty-two years earlier back in 1917, he had fudged his age and joined the force that ultimately became known as the RAF. He sat behind the pilot, out in the open air from the waist up, while he wrestled with the Lewis machine gun mounted in front of him.

In 1940, therefore, he decided that if he was going to be called up, he would volunteer for the RAF, which he did. He got out his car, a newish Vauxhall, drove up to the Air Ministry in Kingsway, London, and volunteered. Volunteers were allowed to wear a badge on their uniform signifying that they were not pressed men! It set them apart. He was stationed in Lincolnshire which, being as flat as it was, and being as near to the continent of Europe as it was, had so many airfields on it of one sort or another that it was probably the biggest air base in Europe.

## *Jim Allison* – the Old Dunstablian who never became an Admiral!

I was 14 years old and in my third year at Dunstable Grammar School when war broke out. My immediate thought, "I shall never be called up. The war will end before I am seventeen." How wrong I was!

Progressing through school, I managed the school certificate with five credits, moved up into sixth form and was taught by the headmaster. He, mathematics and I were in different worlds and I left school in November

1940 to accept articles with a charted accountant, at a salary of five shillings per week.

In 1943, my intermediate examination was becoming due. I had decided that of the three forces, the navy was the safest and, in a foolhardy moment, volunteered for the Fleet Air Arm. I attended an interview in London confronted with the largest table I had ever seen covered with wooden models of ships and aeroplanes, which I was asked to identify but failed miserably. The officer present then remarked that if I was that keen to join the Fleet Air Arm I would have belonged to a cadet corps. I replied that my time had been taken up for the last two years studying accountancy.

He then suggested that I apply to join the R.A.F and an appointment was made to visit Petit France in London where I was sat in a cockpit and told to press a button when a light flashed. I managed and was told that I would be accepted. However, I turned this down and decided to await call up and join the Navy; what I did not know at the time was that my Principal had requested a delay in this to enable me to take my examination, which I did. On the 14th of September 1943 I joined the navy.

My first 'ship' was Highgate College where I sat an easy examination gaining a 90% mark, played a few games of rugby and marched up and down Highgate Hill, even visiting the grave of Karl Marx, buried in Highgate cemetery in 1883. The captain at the college also played rugby and at my interview before leaving informed me that I would be registered under the 'Y' scheme, which meant that I would spend a short time at sea and then be transferred to an 'Officers Training Establishment'.

The next 'ship' was Butlins Holiday Camp at Skegness, where I spent two bitterly cold months, October to December 1943, being kitted out in the fore and aft uniform as supply assistant, (a Jack Dusty)...pay 28d a day, having received my first promotion, being for three months a supply assistant probationer.

At Skegness we spent the days marching slowly, quickly, up the square, down the square and 'round' the square. The meal times were complete chaos. Hot trolleys were wheeled in to the dining room where everyone fought and scrambled to get a plate of food. This lasted until 13th December, when I was posted to Chatham in Kent, being a fully fledged supply assistant and took my place in the Blanket Store dishing out blankets and at the clothing store, dishing out clothes. This lasted until 20th February

1944 when I was posted to HMS Goodall.

The frigate was built in Canada, a welded ship, no rivets, not even a golden one. This we picked up in Boston, U.S.A, the home of the tea party and sailed to our base at Gladstone Dock, Liverpool. The Goodall's first trip was to act as one of the escorts to merchant ships sailing to and from America, with the duty to safeguard these ships from German U boat torpedo attacks.

My baptism of fire took place on this trip. It was after a few days in the Atlantic, when in the middle of the night there was a terrific boom and a flash of light as a ship, I presumed a tanker, was torpedoed and blown to pieces. We also lost one of the merchant ships on this trip.

These duties continued, escorting merchant ships across the Atlantic until they were out of range of the U boats and picking up the ships coming from America bringing food and stores to England. The Atlantic Ocean was at times extremely rough with waves coming over the bridge and the small frigate rose out of the water and then came down with a tremendous crash. We slept in metal bunks and at night would have to wedge our feet against the chains by which they were lowered or raised, hang on with our hands and hope that the weather would improve by the morning, but it seldom did.

We often took a northerly route through the ice packs, cracking the ice as we went, which was more sedate and spectacular. This accompanied a call to St. Johns, Newfoundland, a pleasant break with its wooden houses and beautiful girls.

My duties during action stations were to wind the depth charges up to the level of the guard rail, where they were primed by the electrician to explode at the required depth, push them overboard and trust that the captain piped sufficient speed to the engine room to get the ship out of the way before the explosion.

Did we sink a submarine, if that is the correct term? We certainly blew up schools of fish which added to our rations, however on one occasion a load of debris came to the surface, but no other sign!

Our sister ship, HMS Bullen (if my memory is correct), certainly did, and unloaded a number of German sailors when we returned to Gladstone dock. This was however revenged, as on our next escort duty the Bullen was torpedoed. We lowered our lifeboat, manned by courageous sailors who picked up a number of survivors and tied the boat to the stern of one of the escort ships. The captain of this ship, fearing a torpedo was approaching his vessel, ordered full speed and turned the ship in a sharp circle shooting the lifeboat like a stone from a catapult, and unfortunately the occupants were drowned. This was the Goodalls' first casualties of the war and we had the sad duty of auctioning the deceased sailors' clothes and effects and sending the money to their next of kin.

In between the Atlantic convoys we escorted Americans in a troop ship, which we picked up at Scapa Flow to Iceland and sailed in very rough seas, so bad in fact that one of our crew had to be restrained by being tied up to prevent him throwing himself overboard. In Reykjavik, I met a fellow Jack Dusty and was able to swap a ration of butter for a pair of American silk stockings. Further trips were to and from Gibraltar.

D-Day arrived and we were in Portsmouth harbour and had the duty of escorting a battleship, I believe the HMS Nelson. However, this ship signalled we were not required and HMS Goodall returned to Portsmouth.

My transfer from HMS Goodall finally arrived, however I had to leave the ship in Gladstone Dock and catch a ferry to Ireland to serve for three days on a banana boat.

Finally reaching HMS Pembroke i.e. Chatham, the first sailors I met were the survivors from HMS Goodall that had been torpedoed on a Russian convoy. Many of my shipmates had perished and others were in hospital in Russia. Good fortune had smiled on me. I had by this time been promoted to a leading supply assistant and attended the 'Y Scheme Office', with my officer training in mind, only to be told that they had received no papers on me from HMS Goodall. The torpedo had hit the boat mid-ships and the captain had been blown over the stern, obviously dead according to the sick bay Tiffy, who had survived. Whether the captain had ever intended to forward my papers, I shall never know.

The first visit to the bridge occurred after we had been in convoy for a few days and when all the bread had gone mouldy. I had told my tanky (assistant) to dispose of the loaves and he apparently threw them over the stern one by one. Called to the bridge, there appeared to be a mile of loaves bobbing in the ocean in a perfect straight line. The Captain told me these would be seen by U boats whose crew would then know that there was a convoy in the vicinity. My thoughts were that the periscopes would see the merchant ships before a loaf of bread... but I did not say so.

The second visit arose as follows. The chef cooked breakfast for each mess. However, in the Stokers' Mess where I resided, the greedy morning watch would collect the mess tray and eat the lot so that when the night watch were relieved, they had no breakfast. I was told in no uncertain terms by the captain that he would not tolerate his sailors not being properly fed.

The third visit was again caused by the stokers. Enough potatoes would be ordered for our three weeks at sea. However, these mysteriously disappeared after one week. The stokers on night duty had raided the potato cages and spent the night watch eating baked potatoes! A similar reprimand as before.

The fourth and final visit; I protested complete innocence. The officers' chef had put sugar in the soup by mistake and salt in the dessert. I pleaded 'not guilty'.

The final recurrence arose as follows. One of the ships in the convoy had been torpedoed, presumably in the stern as the fo'csle and large parts of the ship were pointing skywards out of the water. We were sent back to complete the sinking of the vessel, so as not to endanger the remaining convoy. The gunnery officer decided to treat this as a practice exercise. We had two large guns, A gun on the upper deck and immediately below, B gun on the lower deck. I was given a stopwatch to time the firing of the B gun, and the exercise commenced. However, when A gun was fired with a terrific bang, the shell passed over my head. I jumped out of my skin, causing me to stop the watch and consequently ruined the exercise. The gunnery officer was not amused!

My stay in Chatham lasted from 14th April 1945 to 30th June 1945, again working in the stores as a leading supply assistant. On 1st July 1945, I joined a minesweeper 'Laertes', a smaller ship than previously and spent a few weeks in Antwerp whilst the ship undertook a refit. We swept minefields around the coast of England and Ireland and then on Gibraltar and Malta. From there we went to Alexandria and Port Said where the young boys had sisters that we were invited to meet. However, we received black boot polish on our white uniforms when we refused their invitation.

On through the Suez Canal, a dip in the bitter lakes, next port of call Aden, where we played a game of football against the local garrison and lost badly. I played left half, the captain of our team said that I should have been 'left out'. Moving on through the Indian Ocean our next port of call was Ceylon, now renamed Sri Lanka.

We had been at sea a considerable time and were entitled to dress the ship with white ribbon, so many yards for each month. This was duly attached to the mast and the captain decided that we would arrive in Colombo in style. The Japanese war had ended, we therefore had to get over the sides and repaint the ship, 'the sailor's way… if it moves, salute it, if it doesn't, paint it'. That night the stoker on watch fell asleep and the piston or big end, or whatever a ship may have, blew up. This meant that we were ignominiously towed into Colombo Harbour rather than arriving in style as envisaged. I did not know what happened to the stoker.

From Colombo to Trincolomee, which has, we were told, the deepest harbour in the world. Here in the market place I cracked my head on the beam of a market stall, whereupon the owner of the stall informed me that he had a nice big girl in the back room just for me. I declined with the genuine excuse of a headache.

The next and final port of call was to Singapore, our Far East base, where we swept mines around Sumatra and Borneo, spending a day at the races. We had one trip up country in Malaya where we visited a Buddhist temple and, after dodging a few snakes, were led to a bar in the middle of nowhere, where hooch was served in half coconut shells.

We are now into late 1946 and commenced our homeward journey via Bombay and Karachi, where our lunch was slaughtered on the quayside. I do not remember whether we mineswept in that area.

Minesweeping for me was a sinecure. All the hatches were battened down, meaning I was unable to reach the stores; we could only sweep in shallow water, as the mines are held down by a weight on the bed of the sea, and we did not minesweep in rough weather. Paradise compared to the Atlantic. One of my jobs was to shoot holes in the mines as they surfaced. I had training and target shooting but I was never given a rifle during a sweep. They were commandeered by the officers. The danger arose when two mines collided on the wire holding the cutter – a rather large explosion was caused.

We finally arrived back in Harwich in October 1946 where the ship was decommissioned. The mosquito netting was missing, apparently it made very good net curtains! I was not guilty!

On 16th October 1946 I arrived back in Chatham and was released on 27th December 1946. I was not allowed home for Christmas but saw the New Year in a baggy brown pin striped demob suit, still a leading supply assistant with the Atlantic Star and other medals, whose character during three years sea service was very good, so said the Commanding Officer of HMS Pembroke.

A Jack Dusty who met admirable people but never became an Admiral.

## *Peter Croft* - **Mineswseeping**

I left the Home Guard in March 1943 to join the Royal Navy, doing ten weeks intensive training at HMS Ganges, the Navy's training establishment in Harwich, as an ordinary seaman, before being sent to my depot in Chatham, ready for sea duty. We were trained in navigation, gunnery and they made sure everyone could swim. If anyone couldn't swim they were thrown in the water, until they could! They had a very large mast there (about 75 feet high) and before the training session finished everyone had to climb up onto the first 'elbow' of the mast and go down the other side. Some people including myself went right up to the button at the top and putting the lightning conductor between our knees you could stand up and see all around the harbour at Harwich and out to sea. Life was a lottery there with the regulating officer's power to draft you to any branch of the service. I was put on to minesweepers, so off to Canada we went.

We were issued with a rail travel warrant to Liverpool and embarked on the Louis Pasteur. This huge liner was taken from the French and used as a troop ship crossing the Atlantic on solo runs, relying on its speed and zigzag course to out-fox the U-boats. On board were RAF personnel going across to be trained as pilots and aircrews, and prisoners of war from Rommel's Africa Corps still in their desert uniforms, caged in on the third deck. Naval personnel then became 'prisoners of war, sten gun party', guarding them on their daily hour of exercise on the upper deck.

We docked at Halifax, Nova Scotia, disembarked and made our way by rail to the Toronto ship yards to commission a brand new Algerine Class Fleet Minesweeper, built in Toronto under the American 'lease and lend' programme, called HMS Gozo, pennant no: J287. After sea trials and working in Bermuda, we proceeded to Newfoundland and on the 19th December we sailed as an escort ship for convoy HX271 across the Atlantic to Londonderry. HMS Gozo became part of the 6th Minesweeping Flotilla seeing service as convoy escorts across the Atlantic and North Sea before its main task of minesweeping ready for the Normandy landings.

On the 5th June 1944 the 6th Flotilla, with others, sailed out of the Solent in the late evening to sweep and clear Channel no 5 ready for the British landing on Gold Beach on the 6th. The 6th Flotilla did much minesweeping in the English Channel and the North Sea area to clear the minefields to open up the ports of Antwerp and Rotterdam ready for the army to liberate them. We had our area to sweep and each flotilla had its own method of sweeping. Most of the sweeps were for contact mines, but during the Normandy landings there were also a lot of magnetic mines dropped by aircraft at night. A different sweep was needed to clear them; we used an electrical pulse in the water to set these off. It was a battle of wits really because once the naval people had conquered the problem of one type of mine, another one would be produced which would require a new method of finding and destroying. In the very shallow waters of Normandy they had what was called an oyster mine. In fact the water was so shallow most of the minesweepers couldn't even get in there. They solved this by going back to Portsmouth and taking on board a big tube, like a drain pipe, and a couple of boxes of hand grenades. They then proceeded to push the hand grenades through the tube so that they dropped into the water, exploded and set off the oyster mines.

There was a friendly fire incident off Normandy after the D-Day landings. The ports of Le Havre and Cherbourg were still occupied by the Germans and our flotilla (the 6th) and the 5th Flotilla were sweeping in that area. There was a mix up in communications with the naval people and the air-force. They thought the flotilla that was sweeping the area in front of Le Havre were German ships escaping and they sent the air-force in. Many ships of the 5th Flotilla were hit in this incident. We actually went to the rescue of these ships, taking people on board. I always remember that I spent the whole of the first dog watch, the time between 4 and 6, doing nothing else but stitching up dead bodies in hammocks for burial next morning. However, at reunions I still speak to some of the survivors that I pulled out of the water that day.

On the 8th April 1945, the 6th Flotilla sailed from Falmouth to join the East Indies Fleet based at Colombo, Ceylon. On the 2nd July the flotilla sailed from Tricomolee to carry out Operation Collie, a minesweeping air and surface bombardment of the Car Nicobar islands, in preparation for the landings on the Malaysian mainland. In the event this did not take place, thanks to the dropping of the A bombs.

3rd September 1945 – led by the 6th Flotilla sweeping ahead, the cruiser HMS Cleopatra carrying Admiral Power, Commander in Chief, British Pacific Fleet, and other ships entered the anchorage of Singapore. Thus the 6th Minesweeping Flotilla became the very first ships of the Royal Navy to enter the harbour of Singapore since the disastrous evacuation in 1942.

As we came into harbour a lot of small boats came out, with people cheering and trying to sell us pineapples and other fruit. One of the most sought after things in Singapore was a bar of soap; it was like gold dust to them. But we could tell that they had been ill treated by the Japanese, because many people had limbs missing. They had been using Japanese currency but that was abandoned overnight, so the only way you could buy anything was by barter. We took soap and chocolate and bartered in the shops for goods in return.

We evacuated some of the ex-PoWs, most of whom were Australian. We had no room on board our ship to take them to sea, but while we were alongside the jetty we took some on board and gave them food and comfort. They were in such a bad state medically there wasn't a lot we could do for them. It wasn't until the hospital ships started to arrive that they could be treated. All the Japanese soldiers were rounded up and put to work clearing the streets and given other menial jobs.

My ship was still out in Singapore when we were transported on a tank landing ship to England and eventually I wound up in Chatham. There were so many people waiting to be demobbed that they put me on an old World War I Monitor. It had been used at D-Day for bombardment but had lain in the dock at Chatham. I had a nice little number! I was the Master of Arms, Mess Mate. I was there for some weeks and saw our ship HMS Gozo arrive back from the Far East before being demobbed. They gave us a very basic medical, a suit of clothes and away you went back to Civvy Street.

## CAPTAIN HERBERT MORDEN, M.N. – The Hat among the Caps

Captain Morden was apprenticed as a trainee merchant seaman in 1915 when he was 14  years old. He completed his apprenticeship shortly after the end of W.W.I and obtained his Certificate of Competency as the 'Master' of a steam ship in 1927. He travelled the world as he rose through the ranks as an officer in the Merchant Navy. He was promoted to 'Master' in 1940.

At about this time he considered that it would be preferable if his wife and young daughter moved away from London. Consequently they came to Dunstable where they initially stayed with relatives in Borough Road. A few months later the family took up residence at 11, Great Northern Road.

CAPTAIN HERBERT MORDEN *(AWM)*

In the spring of 1942 he was in command of the SS Pontypridd sailing from the Mediterranean Sea to the U.K. in a convoy. A German U-boat, U 94, commanded by Ober-Leutnant Otto Ites, spotted the convoy and proceeded to attack with torpedoes. SS Pontypridd was hit and began to sink. The crew abandoned ship and Captain Morden was taken aboard the U-boat as a prisoner of war.

As U 94 returned to its base on the west coast of France, it was detected by a British frigate and was attacked with depth charges but, fortunately for Captain Morden, it was not seriously damaged.

When the U 94 arrived at its base, the commander and crew were given the usual welcome for U-boats returning from a successful mission. Captain Morden was allowed to go up on to the conning tower of the U-boat and, unbeknown to him, was photographed among the officers of the crew.

Captain Morden was moved to a prisoner of war camp in Germany where he was interviewed. On the 11th July 1942 this interview was broadcast by the Germans, and his wife received letters from total strangers to let her know he was safe and well. Mrs. Morden had been advised that

The end of the SS PONTYPRIDD, photographed by U 94 *(AWM)*

**Ein Hut zwiſchen den Mützen auf dem U=Boot=Turm.**

Der Kapitän eines verſenkten engliſchen Frachters, der von dem U=Boot an Bord genommen wurde, erlebt den Empfang, der dem Kommandanten, Ritterkreuzträger Oberleutnant zur See Ites und seinen Männern bei der Rückkehr von erfolgreicher Feindfahrt bereitet wird.

Il capitano di una nave da carico inglese viene preso a bordo dal sommergibile tedesco che l'ha affondata. Il comandante è il tenente di vascello Ites, decorato della Ritterkreuz. PK-Aufn.: Kriegsberichter Vater (Sch.)

The caption of this photograph from a German newspaper reads:

A HAT AMONG THE CAPS ON THE U-BOAT TOWER

The captain of a sunken English freighter, who was taken on board by the U-boat, experiences the welcome given to the commander, Knights Cross holder, Ober-Leutnant zur See Ites and his crew on their return from a successful mission against the enemy (the gist is also given in Italian). *(Supplied by AWM)* the SS Pontypridd had been sunk and that her husband was not among the survivors. These letters were the first intimations she had to the effect that her husband was safe and well.

She obtained work in Dunstable as a schoolteacher at Doretta Lodge School in Great Northern Road. In due course they were able to correspond as were his mother, who also lived in Dunstable, along with other members of the family.

In one letter he states that he had received twelve parcels during the first two years of his captivity and, although such things as socks etc. did get through, tobacco does not. He states, "The tobacco isn't turning up. I think a lot is stolen at home, probably doesn't even start off, from what we can gather."

Captain Morden was released from captivity soon after the war and returned to Dunstable and moved to Ilford in 1948. Otto Ites also survived the war and he and Captain Morden corresponded, and he sent the newspaper cutting as well as the photograph taken from the U94. U94 was one of the smaller 'sea going' submarines used by the Germans. The first of the class was U 45. These U-boats were 213 ft long, their displacement was 517 tons and they carried a crew of 35. According to an inscription on the reverse of the photograph of the sinking of SS Pontypridd, that was the fifteenth sortie by U94 since it was commissioned in 1940.

### *Jack Carver* - a Cook's Tour

At the beginning of 1942 I joined the Royal Navy and chose to train for the electrical branch. As I had good results in School Certificate in physics and maths I had a flying start. Part of my training took place at Roedean Girls School at Brighton. I shared a girls' room with two other chaps. By the door was a bell button with a notice that read 'Press this if you need a mistress in the night'. No luck!

On completion of training I was shipped out to North Africa where I began what my more cynical friends and family describe as a Cook's tour at the government's expense. In Tunisia I was involved with getting LSTs (Landing Ship Tanks), ready for the invasion of Sicily. Then I was drafted to Malta where I joined, for the rest of the war, a new fleet destroyer, HMS Termagant, which did not do ordinary convoy work but escorted the big ships, especially aircraft carriers. Eventually HMS Termagant took part in operation Anvil, the South of France landings. Our greatest danger was from US Mitchell bombers!

On the successful conclusion of that operation we fully expected to come home. Instead, the ship was ordered to join the Pacific fleet attached to the huge American Pacific fleet. Soon after Japan had surrendered we sailed up Tokyo Bay – wonderful view of Fujiyama to Yokohama. I had shore leave and caught a train to Tokyo where I did a short interview for the US Forces Network.

The Cook's tour I mentioned earlier refers to shore leave in Gibraltar, Malta, Bizerta and Ferryville (Tunisia), Algiers, Alexandria and Port Said (Egypt), Aden, Colombo and Tricomalee (Ceylon), Freemantle, Perth and Sydney (Australia), The Admiralty Islands, Guam, The Philippines, Shanghai and Hong Kong.

We experienced several typhoons in the Pacific Ocean, which demonstrated that British riveted ships were superior to American welded ships in exceptionally rough weather.

## *Colin Bourne* – in the Wavy Navy

After I left school I went to work in Reigate, Surrey, at a publishing business called World Books, one of the earliest book clubs. This was an interlude between leaving school, my eighteenth birthday and being called up. When enquired what I wanted to do, I asked to join the air force. I went along to a medical and to my surprise they turned me down because during my later school years I'd had attacks of migraine. They did not think it would be a good idea if I were to have a migraine if I happened to be flying or doing armoury work, and I quite understood. This left me in a quandary because I could see the army looming up very quickly indeed and I didn't particularly want to join, with all due respects, so I argued for the navy and was accepted. So in the spring of 1943, I was called up to start a naval career.

We went first to a receiving camp, I think the name was HMS Gloucester in Bristol, where we were kitted out; the first steps to getting into one of the services during the war. That was a very rude awakening because on the very first day there were about 12 of us at the dinner table in the mess. The food was brought to the table – meat, potatoes and peas – and action started immediately. Most of the people round the table didn't wait; they just got hold of the meat with their hands and helped themselves, which left me completely bewildered. I had never seen this happen before! I remember absolutely my first night as a naval rating, so the next night I made sure I was nearer the meat dish than anyone else!

I think we only stayed there a fortnight; it was a case of signing on, making sure you had all your kit, do some square bashing and things of that nature. We moved on to another shore establishment called HMS Glendower on the Welsh coast. It was there that we started our training. Again we did a lot of square bashing, assault courses and on Saturday mornings we would be taken for a run over the dunes and have to go out into the cold Welsh sea. We got ashore generally on Saturday afternoons and evening. It was an interesting place, most people settled into it, learning, etc. If we didn't want to stretch our legs for a bit we just picked up a piece of paper and walked around the camp trying to look very official, as if we were delivering important information to someone elsewhere on the camp!

During that time we were taken out in one of the large ships for about 3 or 4 days off the coast of Scotland, for some 'sea experience'. Somewhere along the line at Glendower, the powers that be sorted us out in their own minds and decided that there were several of us likely to make officer material and I was put on this list. I look back on Glendower with interest as I met many good people.

Starting on my officer-training career, we were sent to HMS King Alfred in Hove. We attended lots of courses and lectures and every now and then we had to give a talk ourselves. We did a lot of practical work, man-management, etc. I was very fortunate as my digs were based about a mile from my sister and her husband who were living in Brighton at that time. We also attended Lancing College, which had a magnificent school chapel. When we had passed various examinations at King Alfred we attended a two to three week finishing course at Greenwich College. We came out with success; I was in the Effingham Division, if I remember rightly. I came out as a newly pledged midshipman, 'snotties' as they were called. On my lapel jacket was a little maroon strip of cloth with a little gold piece on the maroon. So here I was, a newly pledged officer in the RNVR, Royal Navy Volunteer Reserves, the wavy navy!

Home on leave, it wasn't very long before I received my sailing orders to report to HMCS Lunenburg in Londonderry, the C being Canadian (a

Canadian corvette). I went aboard and followed instructions issued to all young officers that go aboard a new ship for the first time, to salute and say 'Come aboard, Sir'.

I was very pleased to be on one of these ships. The corvettes have quite a bit of history attached to them. In 1938 when war seemed very close, the navy had very few escort vessels, so the powers that be approached one of the shipping construction firms and asked them to put forward a plan for a vessel to carry out anti-submarine and convoy work. They came up with this particular corvette; it started out with a tonnage of about 750 and a ship's staff of about 48 officers and crew. As the immediate years progressed (1939/40/1), it was so important to build as many of these corvettes as possible. As they improved them, the tonnage went up to 940 with a crew of 80; they were built in England, Canada and India.

We were an escort vessel, carrying out convoy duty. The Flower Class corvettes were referred to as uncomfortable in their extreme! It was also known that if you could stand a Flower Class corvette you could probably stand anything! That was right because when we did get started and I went out on the first sortie, I think I was seasick for about a day and a half but was all right after that. The corvettes proved their worth over and over again as they had very creditable results in sinking U-boats in the North Atlantic and Arctic convoys. They had a sharper turn than a U-boat and a very good radius of action. They were called Flower Class corvettes because each corvette was given a name of a flower. During the First World War, ships of a similar vintage were called the Herbaceous Class. The particular firm that was approached to produce a plan for a corvette was also involved in building warships in the First World War, so it was decided by the Royal Naval establishment to call them after flowers. We had Hyacinth, Starwort, Snowberry, Meadowsweet and so on; all sorts of flowers. The Canadian ships were not called flowers, quite often they called them after towns in Canada, hence the Lunenburg, which is in Nova Scotia.

So I joined this ship; I never knew why I had been posted to this particular ship, they dotted the officers around. There was a radar officer there, a petty officer; he and I were the only English officers on board. The crew were super and very enjoyable to work with. I know that there was more informality on board this ship than there would have been on one of the major RN ships.

From the point of view of weaponry, they had a gun fore and aft, mainly on the port side and pom poms (anti-aircraft guns). They had a thing on the starboard side called a hedgehog that shot missiles over the side, which wasn't entirely successful because sometimes they didn't go off. But all the ships had depth charges; they had a set of two depth charges at the back, so if they were attacking a submarine using radar, they could drop them over the side and detonate them at a particular time.

Being a midshipman and being a very young, raw junior officer, I wasn't allowed to take any watches myself; my job was a sea-going officer, looking after the ship's office and so forth. Of course I did my share of watchman-ship but I wasn't allowed to do one myself, quite understandably and rightly, otherwise there may have been total disaster. So first of all, I shared the midnight watch with a Canadian who was about 6 or 7 years older than I was; his name Tom and we became very good friends and kept in touch throughout our lives until he died about 2 years ago. I had the privilege of being asked to be godfather to his fourth and younger son, which I did with pleasure. I mention this because it shows how ties can be held together when you meet someone in circumstances of war service. I remember Tom with great happiness and I recall that there was a particular song called, 'I Wish I had a Paper Doll to Call My Own', which he sang endlessly during watches. Another thing I remember about these watches was that 2 hours into a 4-hour watch, one of the ratings would bring up 2 mugs of piping hot Ki, which was literally thick black chocolate with hot water poured on to it.

We went out with convoys, sailing down the River Foyle to meet them before taking them over to America, then we'd meet another convoy coming out of North America and take them back to Ireland. We would be at sea for about 2 – 3 weeks, have a few days in port before taking another convoy out again. We didn't, on that particular ship, tie up with any submarines. We saw one or two flashers overhead, a plane came down and a merchant ship caught fire one night. I remember very vividly the phrase that I think of a lot, while getting caught up on motorways, that was, 'the speed of the convoy is the speed of the slowest ship'. But we were very fortunate, we did the job and I found it very interesting to do this kind of escort work.

After about 5 or 6 months we had orders to sail down to Weymouth in England. We came into Weymouth Bay to join a whole group of ships all over the place; of course this was leading up to D-Day. With sealed orders no one knew what was happening; no shore leave apart from the Captain and the number one (First Lieutenant). To stop the boredom setting in we gave games to the crew to keep them occupied and played endless games of Monopoly ourselves on the bridge. Eventually orders came and we escorted ships, Mulberry Harbours and equipment over to France. In this small way I was involved in the D-Day landings.

Very shortly after this, while we were back in harbour, I had an order to report to a submarine base in Blythe, Northumberland. This came as a terrible shock. I had long, long, forgotten that for some extraordinary reason that I cannot remember, I'd thought that it would be good to serve in submarines. This had been registered somewhere in naval offices, though it was now the last thing I wanted to do, but there was no getting out of it!

Blythe on the Northumberland coast was a bit cold, a bit dark and wasn't the sort of place that you particularly wanted to be in during the war. Although I wasn't very happy about it, I went along and did this submarine course. After taking the examinations I found myself hovering between the people who had passed and those that had failed by about one point. An officer in charge came up to me and said, "You've worked hard at this but I don't think submarines are your forte, do you?" I replied by saying that I entirely agreed with him. He responded by saying "I hope it's done you some good, but we don't think you should carry on with submarines, what would you like to do?" Now it was very rare that any officer asked you this question; my instant reply was that I wanted to go back to serving on the Flower Class corvettes. "Fine, go home on leave." So I went home and very shortly I received sailing orders to Gibraltar.

I joined HMS Jonquil, a very happy ship with lots of different nationalities on board. We had people from Rhodesia, South Africa and Norway, a very happy crowd. This was followed six months later by joining HMS Bellwort, also a Flower Class corvette. There I met another officer who had been to a school that played a good class of hockey (as I had in Dunstable), and we decided to form a hockey team to keep the crew entertained. We bought some black and yellow shirts, got hold of some hockey sticks, gave lessons and off we went to play a match against another ship. I put a football goalkeeper into the hockey goal and started. The team did really well but when the first ball spun towards the goal, the keeper picked it up and kicked it out into the air like a football! The referee blew his whistle and looked on in horror; I tore over from my inside left position and explained the situation. We went on to blend ourselves into a nice little team, played about 15 or 16 matches and only lost one match and that was by default.

Of course going out to Gibraltar, getting away from the weather, blackouts and so forth in England was absolutely marvellous. There were street lights everywhere, the cathedral to visit, theatre, lots of different things to do.

We were tied up in the harbour, and at the end of the war from time to time we would go out on a few patrols. During one of these we picked up some U-boat survivors from the mouth of the Tagus off Lisbon. Towards the end of the war I was transferred home again and that was the end of my Flower Class corvette saga, which I so much enjoyed one way or another.

I received orders to get myself up to Arran in Scotland to join a Landing Ship (Tank), LST3015, totally different. By this time the European war was over but it was still continuing in the Far East. This ship was entirely different to the Flower Class corvette; a long ship with all the tanks ahead of you, the bridge at the end. A different set of people but again a very happy ship. We went out to India from our base and sailed through the Med, the Suez Canal and up through the Indian Ocean, reporting to the naval authorities in Bombay. Before arriving at our destination I was on watch in the afternoon (on my own, by which time I was a Sub-Lieutenant). We were going across the Indian Ocean and I saw, out of the corner of my eye, a flash in the water on the port side, and I thought, torpedoes. I rang the bell for action stations, yelled full speed ahead to the rating down below and of course everything happened all at once, as it does when everyone is half asleep in the middle of the afternoon. The Captain came running up, "What's the matter?" By this time I realised that my flash of light wasn't a torpedo, it was in fact a pair of dolphins. I said, "I'm sorry sir, I thought the dolphins were torpedoes!" "That's all right, you did the right thing, don't worry." Everyone was told over the loudspeaker system to go back to whatever they were doing and actions were closed off. Of course I got it in the neck for that over the next 2 or 3 days!

While in India we operated from Bombay down to Trincomalee, (Sri Lanka), Colombo and up to Madras. VJ was now over and independence was taking place and we had to get rid of a lot of things, don't ask me why; for some political reason we just took things out to sea and dumped them. I remember dumping half an aircraft and lots of casement windows, it was unreal! We also did a bit of service going down to Trincomalee.

From there I was demobbed and I was asked to take a message down to Colombo by train before going home on the cruiser HMS Diamead. We sailed back through the Red Sea where I got a lot of sticky heat and through the Suez Canal to home. So that was the end of naval life.

All the corvettes, some 300 or so, are no longer with us at all, except for one. There is one Flower Class corvette still in existence in Sackville, Canada, called HMS Sackville. They kept it as a reminder of the Canadian corvette and as a reminder of Flower Class corvettes everywhere. It was only through the Flower Class Corvette Association, of which I am a member, that we heard about this. I wrote to my friend Tom saying that I understood that there is a lone but looked-after corvette in Sackville. He wrote back confirming this and sent me a parcel containing a tankard with the outline of a Flower Class corvette and HMS Sackville written on it. That was the last letter that I had from Tom because he died shortly afterwards.

### *John Rushton* - **to the Middle East**

At eighteen I was called up and went to the drill hall in Northampton for a medical. All of us had to stand there naked in a large room being passed from doctor to doctor. I then had to report to HMS Collingwood in Fareham on May 8th 1942. I did my wireless telegraphy training there. We also had to take part in other exercises; I was in the spigot mortar crew. We had to practise firing these things that were very difficult to handle. We also had to peel spuds, sweep up, whitewash kerbstones, fuse bombs and fire rifles. When I passed out I was posted to HMS Mercury, which was the signals school near Petersfield. I was then drafted to Portsmouth, Victory Barracks, and from there we went to Iceland and joined another ship, HMS Blenheim on the west coast of Iceland. After about six months we came back to the UK for a re-fit. It was during this time that I managed to get leave and married Jean – I knew I was going away for a long time.

When the ship was ready, we joined a large convoy and sailed to Gibraltar and from there to Alexandria. I was then based in the Middle East until the war ended and eventually came home in January 1946.

### *John Gaskin* – D-Day Landings

I was nineteen when I joined the Royal Navy.

“D-Day – I was a Sub Lieutenant in the Royal Navy in charge of 3 landing craft, including a converted Thames barge when we were put on Omaha beach. The crossing wasn't good, the steering broke down half way and we had to bring over another craft to help repair it. It was so rough my gunner was swept overboard. There were 30 people on my landing craft.

The landings were a bit of a shambles. When I got on to the beach I thought where am I supposed to go? The Germans were everywhere in machine gun emplacements. We were under fire all the time. My second in command and his assistant went ashore, unfortunately trod on a mine and were killed. We were on the beach for about a week. There were whole flotillas of landing craft.

The saddest part was seeing those guys you were trained with, your good friends just… We could see everything. It was torture watching the boys cut down from the top of the cliffs and not being able to do a thing to help them.

All the survivors were taken to a Red Cross camp where they gave us a mug of hot water and a tea bag – I'd never seen a tea bag before.

Many Royal Navy seamen were seconded to US units. When I was seconded to the US Navy, I was pretty unhappy about it but after a short time with the Americans I felt like an honorary Yank. They were all brave men.

When they brought us back to the hospital unit in England they told me that I would be going to Japan. I didn't like that idea and fortunately for me they changed their minds. I then commanded minesweepers in Singapore. We sent down depth charges to clear areas of any mines. After serving in Singapore I was promoted to Lieutenant Commander.”

### *John Evered* – on the Landing Ships

“In May of 1944, as a recently commissioned Lieutenant of the Royal Marines, I joined the Assault Landing Ship SS Empire Halberd, the crew being from the Merchant Navy. Our job was to man the 19 landing craft slung aboard. The ship was one of a flotilla of 7 Weapon Class Landing Ships lying in the Solent off Cowes. On board I found one of the fellow officers was a chap who had been in the same form as me at school (Dunstable

Grammar School). A few weeks later, a couple of days before D-Day, we loaded troops. One of the officers, a Lieutenant, had been 2 years ahead of us at school. We landed him on D Day with the other troops. Many years later I saw him at a parents' evening at St Albans Grammar School.

Although our Flotilla of 7 landing ships made several trips over to the French coast in the following weeks, we were fortunate not to lose a man. Some 6 weeks later the 7 ships were sent to Glasgow for overhaul before going to the Far East via America. On the way to Glasgow, off Land's End, the SS Empire Halberd took a hit from a mine under the stern, damaging the rudder. After an inspection by a diver at Falmouth, we made our way slowly to Glasgow. There, after embarkation leave, I transferred to another assault landing ship, the HMS Empire Spearhead. All the landing ships were now crewed by the Royal Navy, instead of the Merchant Navy as previously. Also all the Naval Officers were replaced by Royal Marines to man the landing craft.

I proceeded with the flotilla to New York, where we picked up US troops to Charleston to avoid a hurricane and through the Panama Canal to New Guinea. After dropping the US troops in New Guinea we spent the next twelve months doing practice landings with Australian troops on the coast of Queensland, in dry dock in Brisbane, (after going aground in Cairns) and a night landing of US troops on the West Coast of Mindinoa in the Philippines. As our heavy armoured plated landing craft proved not to be powerful enough to deal with the heavy swells of the Pacific Ocean, we spent the rest of our time ferrying troops and supplies between Sydney, Townsville to New Guinea, the Admiralty Islands and the Philippines. Just before VE Day a decision was made that we should return to England for refit in preparation for going to Japan. However, shortly after arriving in England in July 1945, VJ Day was announced and the war was over.

### Mary Corrie (née Cheshire) – Brother at D-Day

My eldest brother, Colin, was already in the Territorials before he joined the Beds and Herts Regiment. He was called up but the company that he worked for, Gryson Young, said they had more important work for him to do because he was an engineer. The army released him after about 11 months to do this war work.

Colin joined the Royal Navy and was on the landing craft at the D-Day landings. That was just before he was 21. We didn't know until we received a card from him telling us that he was well. He came home for embarkation leave and then he went on a course in Scotland. I think he went backwards and forwards to France quite a lot on his landing craft. He used to tell us that on D-Day, 18 landing craft went out and only 4 came back; he was on one of the four. He made a joke of it but said he was shaking for days afterwards.

### John Russell - a Traumatic Day

I was in the 15th M.S.F (Mine Sweeper Flotilla), which was a 'Bangor' class fleet minesweeper unit. We sailed from Dover without navigation lights heading for France. Our flotilla consisted of HMS Fraserburgh (which was our flotilla leader) and HMS Ardrossan, HMS Bootle, HMS Lyme Regis, HMS Worthing, HMS Fort York, HMS Dunbar and HMS Llandudno.

We were to sweep Channel Number 10 to Sword Beach. We were at the eastern end of all ten channels, which was the closest to the German naval base in Le Havre. So thinking we might be attacked whilst sweeping, we were allocated two destroyers, HMS Scourge and HMS Serapis for protection. We had a further problem. Owing to our minesweeping motor launches not being able to carry out sweeping ahead of us because of the bad weather, we were on our own in un-swept waters. Luckily no mines were encountered going in, but we were all worn out since we'd had no sleep for about twenty-four hours, and were issued with pills to keep us awake! Our gun crews fell asleep by their guns!

I will always remember the noise of the guns behind us. They were being fired over our heads to try and silence the German batteries. We could see the gun houses on shore, but they did not open fire on us as they would have given themselves away to the big warships.

I will always remember it was one hell of a day!

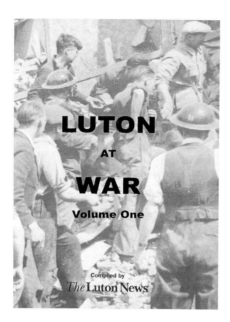

## LUTON AT WAR
### Volume One & Volume Two

Initially published by the Luton News in 1947, the story of how the people of Luton withstood the dark years of war between 1939 and 1945.

Luton and its population have changed so dramatically in the years since the war that now only a few will recall how the town stood up to the trauma of those war years.

Because of strict war-time censorship much of what occurred during those years was not mentioned in The Luton News. Once the war was over however, The Luton News set about the mammoth task of presenting a complete and vivid picture of war-time life. It tells of the long anxious nights, the joy and the sorrow that made even the most terrifying moments bearable thanks to the tremendous way in which the people joined to help each other.

Written and compiled by the staff of The Luton News at the time, it contains the most comprehensive and fascinating pictorial record. As well as being a moving personal account it is also a unique historical document.

This large format paperback is published in two parts.

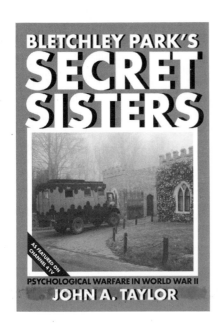

## BLETCHLEY PARK'S SECRET SISTERS
### *Psychological Warfare in World War II*

### John A. Taylor

Bletchley Park will be forever associated with the secret intelligence activities of World War Two. Yet in addition to the incredible achievements of the code breakers, only a few miles away several other secret organisations were also achieving clandestine success, with operations that were conducted from centres scattered around the local area. This region had been chosen by the Government because it was remote from the London Blitz yet still maintained good road and rail communications with the Capital.

In a highly subversive campaign, propaganda played an early and effective role, selecting recruits from amongst the refugees fleeing Nazi oppression. Gathered in large, local houses, there they would write and rehearse propaganda scripts for radio broadcasts to enemy territory. At a secret studio, these broadcasts were then recorded onto discs and taken by the Secret Service to radio transmitting stations hidden in the local countryside.

Under the control of the Communications Section of the Secret Intelligence Service, another radio station transmitted decoded information from Bletchley Park to Allied military commanders overseas. Further radio stations maintained contact with secret agents, sent on missions deep inside Occupied Europe. In hidden workshops, advanced radio equipment was designed and manufactured, and in various country houses specialised training schools were set up.

Later in the war, not far from Woburn Abbey an ultra modern recording and broadcast studio was built which, when linked to the most powerful radio transmitter in Europe, began sophisticated operations that would completely deceive the Germans. In just one example, actual German radio stations were taken over and, by mimicking the original announcers, all manner of false instructions could then be put out to confuse the German listeners.

This book tells the little known story of all these other secret activities, the fascinating story of Bletchley Park's 'Secret Sisters'.